LET MF
How tc

Recent
ningtor
of whic
lish Sha
Hamle
Richarc
Cade. l
and *Th*
2004 h
practiti

He h
ippo, E
O'Case
fer, Gr
Mamet
TV, Jud

He h
A Mids
hov an
liam: T

There, Crocodile?: Inventing Anton Chekhov. He continues to tour his solo shows on Shakespeare and Chekhov throughout the world.

'What can Michael Pennington not do? In the last few months he has toured Britain as Ibsen's John Gabriel Borkman, directed *A Midsummer Night's Dream*, brilliantly assumed the throne in Alan Bennett's *Madness of George III* – and brought out another book.' *Independent*

MICHAEL PENNINGTON

Let Me Play the Lion Too

How to Be an Actor

FABER & FABER

First published in 2015
by Faber & Faber Limited
Bloomsbury House
74–77 Great Russell Street
London WC1B 3DA

Typeset by Faber & Faber Limited
Printed and bound by CPI Group (UK) Ltd, Croydon, CR0 4YY

A CIP record for this book
is available from the British Library

ISBN 978–0–571–23106–5

10 9 8 7 6 5 4 3 2 1

Let me play the lion too: I will roar, that I will do any man's heart good to hear me: I will roar, that I will make the duke say 'Let him roar again, let him roar again'.

A Midsummer Night's Dream, Act 1, Scene 2

As an actor, on one level you're show trash, on another an artist.

WILLEM DAFOE

Contents

Preface: Robert De Niro

My agent rang me a few years ago after receiving a call from a New York casting director. There was a movie being planned (it ended up as *The Good Shepherd*) directed by Robert De Niro, starring himself and Leonardo DiCaprio. They would immediately express me the script, and Mr De Niro would be simply delighted (I don't exaggerate here) if I felt able to meet with him to discuss the project. Should we say twelve noon on Saturday at a certain venue in north London?

Even the fact that it was near my home seemed a good omen.

I got the script. The part was not long. Actually what it involved was emerging from the House of Commons in a pinstripe suit and being bundled into a taxi by the two stars, driven a couple of blocks while they leaned on me over some matter or other in that way that they're so good at, and then pitched me out of the cab. There were two lines, or rather half-lines, of remonstration from me: 'What the . . .' at the moment of bundling, and 'This is outrag—' at being propelled out of the cab. However Mr De Niro was obviously taking every detail of his project seriously, so who was I to argue. He clearly had something in mind, something I could help him with.

There was another, much better, role for an Englishman in the film, involving politics, possible gayness, despair and suicide. The terms of my forthcoming meeting with De Niro certainly suggested a man-to-man candour and a respectful exchange of ideas: perhaps I could use the opportunity to pitch for the better

1

part. Even if this didn't work, it would still be very pleasurable to play the man of two half-lines and to spend a day with him and DiCaprio, being inimitably leaned on.

I was in a restaurant on the Friday night with a friend, expatiating enthusiastically on the open-ended possibilities of all this. Would there be cocktails after the meeting with Bobby? Lunch even? The rendezvous being near Finsbury Park, I even wondered if Arsenal were playing at home: Saturday afternoons can hang heavy when you're travelling, and I wondered if he liked the game . . . My mobile rang. It was my agent, with a minor change of plan: could the time be not twelve noon tomorrow, but 10.50 a.m.?

I confess this was a setback. 10.50 didn't have the same ring to it. We might not have time to muse on all the possibilities I had in mind, and I tried not to acknowledge that it sounded like a ten-minute slot. I concluded instead that this was De Niro's variant on the fifty-minute hour – the appointment which ends ten minutes early so that the director/therapist can recover from one enriching encounter before moving on to his next. The problem was that the interview was to start at that point, not finish at it. I crunched the maths. Perhaps he worked forty-minute sessions, then the ten-minute pause. That would work.

I turned up the next morning in an agony of expectation quite inappropriate to someone of my age and experience. I waited; and waited. There were a couple of other hopefuls there as well, showing no sign of nerves: it was as if they cared less about meeting Robert De Niro than some old hack of a rep director. They even looked at their watches from time to time and chatted to me about the cricket in Australia. I think during one of these listless exchanges I may have caught sight of a figure in a baseball cap slipping out of a side door and into the interview room. How else to account for the fact that when I finally got into it Bobby was there – unless he'd been there all night, or his magical powers extended to levitating through the floor on cue.

In I went, busily talking to the casting director as I did so, so as not to have my eyes out on stalks. In my own time I broke off, as it were, to speak to him, almost as an afterthought. A bit shorter than I'd imagined (they always are), he was charming, seemed to have come off the golf course, and encouraged me gently into the hot seat.

I had already seen that this wasn't going to be so much a screen test as a reaction-shot test – 'What the . . .', 'This is out-rag—' – and then a lot of listening to whoever was going to read in the intervening lines. What struck me now was that I was about to do this in front of someone who perhaps does reaction shots better than anyone in the world. De Niro has the sublime screen actor's gift of projecting silent thought simply by thinking it, a complex state of mind just by having it. No faces pulled, as there tend to be with some of his closest competitors, no signals, just the thing itself, unmediated thought. In *New York, New York*, I think it is, there's a sequence when he takes a phone call in a bar, in vision but out of the range of hearing. We never learn what it's about, as it's never explained; I suspect a scene had been cut but this sequence left in because it's such a classy small collector's piece of acting. You sense the contours of the argument he's having, and the discontented compromise he's reached as he finally hangs up. It goes on and on, and could go on indefinitely. How you do this kind of riveting thing in the circumstances of a film set, with forty preoccupied bodies far closer to you than they should be, and all that equipment, I've never quite gathered – but then, some people are puzzled that you can sustain a three-hour matinee performance in the theatre and then do it all over again in the evening.

This, in any case, is one hell of an actor. And now he's slumped, director-fashion, on one side of the camera, while the casting director sits with her script on the other. And I'm about to start.

In case you don't know, most casting directors don't read well: in fact I sometimes wonder if they shouldn't take a course. On this occasion she had, self-evidently, a lot of reading to do. I had to turn her mentally into Bobby and Leo as she blundered from one end to the other of the intervening lines, weaving arabesques of meaninglessness out of them. As she did, my listening face began to lock into a rictus. Determined not to mug, I'd resolved to do less than nothing with it, and was being rewarded by a jutting chin and a mouth hardening into a set, mean line. Unfortunately I was also doing less than nothing with my mind. Even so, on 'Cut', Bobby leapt up enthusiastically and came bounding over. He knelt beside me and lightly placed his hand on my knee. For a moment I wondered what he was going to do next. Then I realised how classy he was being: his expectation as an actor is that when the director talks to him it's private, not to be overheard. This must be how Marty S does it, I thought. He started, sounding remarkably like his Pupkin in *The King of Comedy*, but more modest, far more, almost apologetic. 'What can you do?' (or 'doo') he said, making that small gesture of the hands towards the script, as if in a discreet vote of no confidence in the material. But did I think the feeling of the scene should be a little more . . . open?

I absolutely thought so. Absolutely. I agreed. How right he was. Oh yes. More . . . open.

Again.

After Take Two the huddle again, I think without the hand on the knee this time. Did I think (always did *I* think, never mind about him) the feeling of it should be a little more . . . closed?

I did a gesture of kicking myself, the one when you dip your head and make a sort of circular punch with your fist. Of course. How could I not have seen? More . . . closed.

Again.

Now, one feature of being Robert De Niro is that you do as many takes as it takes. Dozens, if need be. And in an infinity of set-ups, not just the close-up and the midshot, but half a dozen angles of close-up, a shot for every degree of variance and every metre of distance. Unless they're equally stellar, whoever he's acting with doesn't get that, because De Niro's where the money is: that's the reality. Of course the film's story has to be told properly, but it's amazing how little an unimportant character has to be seen. Think of it – the star speaks, the other actor's line begins but you don't cut to him/her till the middle of it, and then you rapidly cut back to the star's reaction even before the line is finished. Add up the footage, and quite important characters have barely been onscreen at all. That's how it works, and that's fine. Then the star may have an influence in the editing room, maybe even be an executive producer. Marilyn Monroe, condemned by so many as brainless, used to have an unerring instinct for which was her best take – 'Number 7,' she'd say, to the amusement of all, who then found in the rushes the next day that she was absolutely right.

And now, purring in my ear deferentially, Robert De Niro was treating me like Robert De Niro. Would I like to go again?

We did eleven takes. He offered me a twelfth. I said no, I didn't think I had any more to give him. We all laughed, as if we were working together already. 'What can you do?' he said again, with that same gesture towards the script, clapped me on the shoulder and declared his pleasure in having met. He was entirely charming and professional throughout. But we never had the cocktail. And of course I wasn't chosen. Nor were any of the string of extremely established leading men in films – you'd be surprised whose names I saw on a list on the way out – who had all thought it worth their while to meet with Robert De Niro on a Saturday morning, and go 'What the . . .'

Michael Gambon got the good part.

~

There is, of course, a reason I'm telling you this story: it's by way of introducing myself. At the time of the meeting with De Niro I was placed professionally pretty much as I am now. That is: I've worked closely with John Gielgud, Paul Scofield, Judi Dench, Meryl Streep, and George Lucas; Douglas Fairbanks liked my Hamlet, and I was briefly granted the freedom of the city of Assisi on the strength of my work, though they've taken it back now. I've premiered new plays by twenty-odd major playwrights and done most of the big Shakespeares. In fact I'm such a Shakespearian that I get birthday cards on 23 April, and today Amazon recommended my own book on Shakespeare to me. Indeed, when I bought and sent a copy to a friend in the US I likewise got a query from Amazon: So michael pennington, how did this item meet your expectations? A few weeks ago a woman called across the Underground lift descending at Holloway Road station that she'd very much enjoyed my Duke in *Measure for Measure* (a role in which I was, physically, deeply disguised) at the RSC thirty-five-odd years ago. I've been around such a good while that a recent Old Vic programme announced that I'd first appeared at that theatre in 1898.

I won't labour the point, but I've done pretty much what I hoped to in my youthful dreams, though relatively few films. Perhaps because of the latter fact, I've never sweated in the hot tub of celebrity – rather, I've been appeased by warm lapping waters of general approval, as if there were a little invisible crowd gathered closely around me, all murmuring appreciatively into the air. Half-smiles in the half-light of some restaurants have suggested that people appreciate my being around and would be sorry if I weren't.

At the same time the routine humiliations and setbacks of an actor's life, the ones which make you feel you might as well go back and start all over again, have buffeted me like everyone else. I've been nominated and not won, not nominated when I probably deserved to be, been the bridesmaid not the bride. I have no letters after my name, and not because I've refused them. I'm quite used to people I know fairly well cutting me dead at parties – or worse, looking vaguely discomforted at my approach – and being lionised by others I don't know at all, some of whom want me to help get their play put on. I get quite tired of being told what parts I should be doing, as if I could wave a wand and do them. When I'm not working I am overwhelmed by watching good actors on the stage – I can't imagine how they do it. Harold Pinter has looked on me with admiration; David Hare, it seems to me, rather more doubtfully. I know just about every mendacity, broken promise and abandoned hope that a life in show business brings: all the codes are familiar, and I'm quite proud of having drained both the bitter and sweet glass to the dregs.

And I've also had a hell of a time, the best of times. I'm still working at an age when quite a few colleagues are, if not retiring exactly, reluctant to commit to the rigours of a stage play, let alone a national tour. I've been mistaken for the theatre critic of the *Guardian*, whose name slightly resembles mine. My real name is shared by Johnny Vegas, but for one reason or another he changed it; however, ours has stuck to him, so I sometimes see reviews headed 'Michael Pennington – larger than life again'. Indeed, Johnny recently told the *Guardian* that he wanted to change the situation whereby he was always cheered as Johnny Vegas, but that Michael Pennington had never had a round of applause in his life. I'm proud of the connection.

Most actors make fun of themselves: it's a defence against never being sure whether they've done well or not. On the other hand they may react sharply if you make fun of them in return. The humiliations of the profession are our comic *lingua franca*: you try not to let this laughing mask slip, but some people, rather embarrassingly, do. I know, though I didn't know him, that Dirk Bogarde died thinking he was a failure; what a joke, but he did. Laurence Olivier, congratulated by a member of the public on having 'arrived', said 'An Actor Never Arrives'. Yes, Laurence Olivier, whose *amour-propre* was as famous as he was, enormous and jealous. Who am I to argue with such great self-denigrators?

I'm saying all this because I'm not easily impressed – except that I often am, very; and I learn from the De Niro meeting that one can be both an old lag and a kid. I have a feeling that this is a good thing, especially if I'm to write a book like this and propose myself as your guide.

Books about the acting life, like books about acting itself, wobble uncertainly between the daftly self-important and the ingratiatingly self-mocking, as if we were either earnest vicars or Uriah Heeps in cap and bells. This one is aimed – of course – at performers, especially those starting out, who may be more interested in the highs and the falls from grace of someone who's been at it for half a century than from any number of tablets patriarchally handed down the mountain. It is emphatically not coming from on high. My generation has an abominable Oedipal tendency to patronise: ah well, old love, you kids today can't do the verse/only care about celebrity/aren't curious about the past etc., etc. I am more impressed than I can say by the vast majority of the young actors I meet and work with, and this book is for them.

I also hope, of course, that I can illuminate the life – this deadly serious, sometimes hilarious, often misunderstood but infinitely enriching life – for any older performer or general reader who is halfway interested. Other voices will be heard from time to time, since who better to explain what it's like to graduate in 2014 (rather than 1964) than the graduates themselves? Who better to correct me if I make the wrong assumption about an actor two generations younger than I am who has to battle either with disability or ethnic isolation?

So, dear reader of every kind, let's start. And if at any point in the following you wonder, like Travis Bickle in *Taxi Driver*, who I think I'm talkin' to, I'm talkin' to you.

Introduction: The Way In

The 1960s: Michael Pennington – The 1980s: Jatinder Verma and David K. S. Tse – The 2000s: Annie Hemingway, Gwilym Lee and Gavin Fowler

On 28 July 1961 I found myself peering through two glass portholes – an enlargement of the round gig-lamp glasses on my nose – set into the double doors of St George the Martyr's Hall on Borough High Street in south London, wondering whether my grand determination to become an actor had all been a mistake. I'd left boarding school in Wiltshire early that morning to start rehearsals – a week late, but that had all been agreed since I only had a small part – for Michael Croft's 1961 National Youth Theatre season in the West End. Two plays had been chosen for his repertoire that I would come to know well over the next fifty years: *Richard II* and *Henry IV Part Two* (oddly enough not the sequential *Part One*, but then *Part Two* does have more good cameo roles for a big company). Off the train, I'd paused at home long enough to greet my mother and – which seemed as important – to change into my jeans and winklepicker shoes. I think I also wanted to reassure her – for far from the last time – that I'd be all right in the world I was about, albeit as an amateur, to enter. She'd had seven worrying years since I'd become stage-struck, in which her support had never wavered, except for one moment when she sadly confided in her sister that I still hadn't got over my 'mania for the stage'. For the subsequent half-century (she died exactly halfway through it, more or less content with the way things had turned out), the reproachful mantra I've repeated whenever I've felt professionally sorry for myself or worn out has been, I Told My Mother I Could Do It.

Not long before looking through these porthole windows I had, aged sixteen, played Prospero in a school production of *The Tempest*. The school had acquired for the occasion the magic cloak recently worn by John Gielgud in Peter Brook's production at Stratford. By now it was a threadbare thing, much hired out since he'd doffed it; however, the exceptionally cunning director of the play – a teacher of German with some of the instincts of an impresario – told me not to worry, it would look terrific under the lights. Convinced, I held my head high; but the cloak worked like a carpet sweeper, its extrusions of wire and jagged gauze efficiently hoovering up whatever was lying about the stage – nails, fluff, wood shavings. Since the theatre requires the willing suspension of disbelief, I stalked through the production, lamb dressed pretty much as mutton, but believing that the mantle of Gielgud had descended on me in more senses than one.

Now, taking in what I could see of the Youth Theatre rehearsal from the other side of the swing doors, I felt this power-investing garment slipping off my shoulders to reveal the pitiful nakedness of my ambition. The startlingly encyclopaedic knowledge of Shakespeare I'd accumulated during my ill-spent teenage years at London's Old Vic Theatre (I'd even seen two separate productions of *Titus Andronicus*) would have qualified me to win the £64,000 prize on ITV's *Double Your Money*, had I entered rather than staying at home fuming at the inadequate contestant on the box: suddenly it seemed so much idle fancy. What I was hearing and seeing was a great commotion of young men – no women at all – who looked like giants and sounded like the roaring sea. In full throttle were Robin Ellis, John Shrapnel, Ian McShane, Hywel Bennett, David Weston, Richard Hampton, Simon Ward and Martin Jarvis, their unnervingly well-trained young voices braying at each other in what turned out to be the gage-flinging opening scene of *Richard II*.

Could I go through with this? Should I push the door open, knowing that silence would probably fall as the giants stopped, swung round and looked at me (I who had felt like a giant at school) through thirty sets of unforgiving grown-up eyes; or do I go home to Mother, defeated before I begin? Yes, that would be, by a small margin, worse. You know the answer, but when, a few moments later and after an excruciating introduction by Michael Croft ('Ah, here's our public-school boy'), Robin Ellis showed me gently where to stand as the loyal Earl of Salisbury and I took up an appropriate anti-Bolingbroke posture, we not only started a friendship for life, but, dear reader, demonstrated a truth: be nice to the newcomer and he'll never forget you.

It would be hard to overstate the daring and resolve of Michael Croft's young company. Set up five years earlier at the end of his teaching career at Alleyn's School (founded by Shakespeare's great rival, Edward Alleyn), it had already presented *Henry V*, *Hamlet*, *Troilus and Cressida* and *Julius Caesar*, done a season at the Queen's Theatre in the West End as well as at the Lyric Hammersmith, played the Edinburgh Festival, Dartington Hall, Toynbee Hall and the Arts Theatre in Cambridge. It had an impressive overseas portfolio as well – a visit to Paris and tours of Italy and Holland. Croft's original idea had been altruistic – not to recruit from university or drama school, or in any way prepare actors for professional careers: he used to say he'd take a young man with character and general flair even if he couldn't act at all.

By now, 1961, the Youth Theatre's founding principles of involving disadvantaged kids in Shakespeare more for their own benefit than for the finesse of the results had been slightly diluted by the need of those who had gone on to drama school to have a final showcase to secure their first job: hence the clamour and sophistication, not to mention the prototypical leather jackets. The age range was fifteen to twenty-one, with exceptions for young men doing National Service. There were grammar-school and secondary-modern kids, and, very rarely indeed, one or two from public schools.

So three weeks after leaving mine, I was on the stage of the Apollo Theatre in the West End – alone, in a green velvet gown as I recall, and, as I like to think, a gently tightening follow-spot. It's a little-known fact that the Earl of Salisbury in *Richard II* has a soliloquy. It follows a brief scene with a Welsh Captain who reports to him that his regiment of soldiers loyal to King Richard has deserted, and he has no choice but to go as well. The noble Earl's soliloquy that follows may not be of the order of 'O what a rogue and peasant slave am I', but it has its moments. Here, in its entirety, it is:

> Ah, Richard, with the eyes of heavy mind
> I see thy glory like a shooting star
> Fall to the base earth from the firmament.
> Thy sun sets weeping in the lowly west,
> Witnessing storms to come, woe and unrest:
> Thy friends are fled to wait upon thy foes,
> And crossly to thy good all fortune goes.

And exit, sadly. I hope, I'm sure vainly, that I wasn't too slow. Anyway, a West End Wendy before my time, I was on my way.

～

Once in a while in the Youth Theatre someone farted on stage and everyone laughed. So naturally I laughed too. The Duke of York was awesomely drunk one night, and, little puritan that I was, I didn't know quite what to think. Still, things were going well. I was to be off to Cambridge in September but first there was a quick trip to Berlin with a few performances of the revived modern-dress *Julius Caesar* which Croft had premiered the previous year. I played a wheelchair-bound Caius Ligarius, hoisting himself to his feet in his enthusiasm to join the revolutionary cause, and then quick-changed into Cinna the Poet, murdered for his bad verses by a quartet of Teddy boys who looked very much like the newly emerging Beatles.

It was a remarkable trip for a couple of reasons. We were the official British entrants at the Berlin International Festival, even though we weren't professionals. We were playing at the historic Hebbel Theatre in the Kreuzberg district and staying at the Stuttgarter Hof (not nearly as grand as it is now) on Anhalter Strasse. What made this particular was the fact that the Anti-Fascist Protection Rampart (the Berlin Wall to you and me) had gone up six weeks earlier and both the theatre and the hotel were less than ten minutes' walk away. We were warned to stay in the hotel, so of course I crossed into the East without delay with three or four pals, armed with some kind of barely official authorisation, to visit the legendary Berliner Ensemble (we saw a dress rehearsal of *Arturo Ui* with Ekkehard Schall) – doing my bit for East–West relations by making the terrifying border guards laugh at my passport photo. I was lucky: soon after I left Berlin, a US diplomat, also on a cultural mission – he had tickets for the State Opera – was denied entry to the Eastern sector. As a result of that, US diplomats going into the East took to being accompanied by American Jeeps. To emphasise the point, US tanks then rolled up to just short of Checkpoint Charlie and sat there, gunning their engines; the Russians rolled up an equal number on the other side, and for a moment it looked as if World War Three might break out. Meanwhile Kennedy quietly negotiated with Khrushchev, and one by one the tanks rolled away again. My attempt at conciliation by means of comedy had clearly paved the way for peace.

~

My time with Michael Croft had been the first part of an unofficial two-stage training, in life as much as acting, to be completed by the time I was twenty-one. I bounced into its second phase with the same abruptness as into the first: I got home from Berlin on the Friday and went up to Cambridge on the Monday, determined to miss no opportunity to continue training myself as an actor, albeit without teachers. The theatre we handful of undergraduate devotees were to make at Cambridge, unlike at drama school, cost us nothing except academic approval: it was extra-mural and well against the official tide, though that tide was unpredictable, and taught us a certain resourcefulness. For one thing we invented an infinity of dramatic societies with essentially the same personnel to avoid the rule that any society could only do one production a term. Even so, my contemporary John Shrapnel had to borrow the name of the famous wicker chair, Lloyd Loom, as a pseudonym in order to play Willy Loman in *Death of a Salesman* without his tutor finding out; we presented Lloyd to the local press as a distinguished visitor from the Actors' Studio in New York. Meanwhile Kingsley Amis, as his tutor, was keeping a close-ish eye on Richard Eyre as Happy in the same production; I, on the other hand, playing Biff, was untroubled by my relaxed (with the emphasis on lax) overseers.

In the overheated atmosphere of undergraduate theatre, standing for a particular something was a point of honour: sidestepping the doctrines of both Stanislavsky and Brecht, I introduced to our community such esoteric stuff as the Laban Carpenter theory of movement taught by Yat Malmgren and John Blatchley at Central School (and later at the Drama Centre) – an exotic feather in my cap that I'd stolen from a girlfriend at the school. Vacations were spent on the road – squatting in semi-derelict houses to play Ibsen, Cocteau and Beckett at the Edinburgh Festival Fringe, battling with the Lord Chamberlain to premiere Henry Miller's only play, and appearing as Malcolm in a touring production of *Macbeth* directed by Trevor Nunn, the last show to be seen at the Empire Theatre in Newcastle before it was demolished in 1963. The Empire had been a music hall for most of its life; as was the way then, a pianist was on permanent call to play interval music, and opted for 'Loch Lomond' as we were doing a Scottish play. All this self-conscious blooding by means of touring and fit-up was unusual then either for university or drama-school students; now it has an echo, for example, at the Bristol Old Vic School, who send their second-years out on split-week tours all over the country in a van, achieving much the same thing – a taste of the grim realities, the fatigue and the mutual dependency.

Having to fight for what we wanted certainly sharpened our intent. Most undergraduate actors got poor but adequate degrees and few have become theorists. I appeared in some thirty productions in my three years, unguided by any professional hand but gaining a precocious knowledge of the ups and downs of live performance: the drying, the unpredicted laughs, the nightly highs and lows. No new university term seemed ready to start unless I had two productions scheduled within it: I felt as if I was in rep and probably referred to being 'out of work' if they weren't in place. And by the end I had a job to go to, graduating on a Friday and starting on the Monday (again) at the very bottom of the Royal Shakespeare Company's pack of supernumeraries – a far bigger crowd than it is now.

One of the performances that had knocked my socks off as a twelve-year-old was John Neville's 1955 Richard II at the Old Vic. Then, as it happened, the Youth Theatre's *Richard II* had been my first appearance before a paying public; now, my first as a professional was in the RSC's production of the same play, and it aggravated my burning desire to play the central part one day – which I'm glad to say I did, in 1988, before graduating to John of Gaunt in the RSC production of twenty-five years later. In 1964 I had no words, just held the orb for David Warner to give away to Eric Porter's Bolingbroke in his Deposition Scene; and, just as I couldn't factor the fart and the giggling in the Youth Theatre into my ideals, I was horrified at the RSC when somebody corpsed or pulled a face behind the audience's back. However, from time to time I used to hear my old Salisbury soliloquy and felt arrogantly encouraged: I thought the present incumbent did it too quickly, which probably tells you more about my performance than his.

Joining the RSC like this was an unorthodox angle of entry into a career. As you're probably tired of hearing, there was still a flourishing network of regional reps at that time in which to learn your trade – or some tricks of the trade: and my contemporaries were duly fanning out to Salisbury, Manchester, Edinburgh and Birmingham. There they played Shakespeare as well as Ann Jellicoe, Agatha Christie and Oscar Wilde, while I mutely held my spear at Stratford, chalking up my forty weeks as a provisional member of Equity before officially joining its closed shop. Perhaps it wasn't ideal, but I learned things from watching Ian Holm, Paul Scofield and Peggy Ashcroft that I've remembered all my life. All big semi-permanent companies such as the RSC will use beginners in their ranks; the advantage then – and increasingly again now – was that there was a debt of management conscience involved. Not only did we walk-ons have an opportunity to do voice and movement classes and to show our understudy work to all the directors, but there was an autumn season of closed studio projects, also attended by all the directors, in which to strut our stuff – I remember working on *The Persians* with the legendary Michel Saint-Denis and on Plato's Dialogues and John Donne's love poetry. These were all good opportunities to audition after the event, and led to my being asked back to do a second season with well-judged junior casting, good but nothing too onerous.

~

In our profession there are circularities within circularities, unlikely congruences, examples set and then contradicted; for all that the tribe is diverse and scattered, there are rarely as many as six degrees of separation between any two of us. In 1971, **Jatinder Verma** was to have less of a good time at the Youth Theatre than I had had ten years earlier: he lasted one day. Born in Tanzania of Indian parents and brought up in Kenya, Jatinder had arrived in England three years before, when he was fourteen: he was part of the first wave of Asian immigrants to be given British citizenship (this, by the way, being one of only three laws in Parliamentary history to be passed within one week). He was just in time for Enoch Powell's 'rivers of blood' speech in April; he took in the death of Martin Luther King the same month, the Paris *évènements* the next, Bobby Kennedy's death the next after that, and the Czech uprising in August. The baptism was energising, but the racism he increasingly encountered in London shockingly unexpected; and I can see that he would have swiftly decided that the Youth Theatre's air of precocious professionalism was a little bit irrelevant to him. So he quit and formed his own company in Tooting and put on *The Sacrifice* by Rabindranath Tagore, the Calcutta-born poet and artist who'd been the first non-European to win the Nobel Prize in Literature. The play deals vividly with the cruelty of inherited superstitions: a traditional father's religious bigotry causes his son to kill himself when his beloved's pet goat is chosen for ritual sacrifice.

Then, in 1976, seventeen-year-old Gurdip Singh Chaggar was murdered in Southall, London, by racist thugs. The National Front leader, John Kingsley Read, declared, 'One down, one million to go,' but was acquitted of inciting racial hatred, the judge observing that 'In this England of ours, we are allowed to have our own view still, thank goodness.' An era of Paki-bashing followed as surely as darkest night follows day. For Jatinder, now graduating from York University, this was enough: almost as abruptly as he'd quit the Youth Theatre, he launched Tara Arts – at twenty-one, the same age, as it happens, that I was sitting down to learn my treasured first few lines of Shakespeare at Stratford.

~

In the year that I did so, 1964 – the Year of the Dragon – **David K. S. Tse** was born in Hong Kong. He and his family moved to England when he was six and settled in Leominster; when he was old enough he worked with them in their Chinese takeaway.

David's passionate eloquence and courtesy now seem to me simultaneously Chinese and English. His mother spoke no English and his father only a little, but having arrived here so young, David became more familiar with the new language than with Chinese, which he found increasingly difficult to use for want of practice with his own generation. As a result he lacked the vocabulary to communicate deeply with his parents – unlike his older siblings whose Chinese was more secure.

On the other hand he won a scholarship to boarding school, and became a Christian, largely as a defence against racial bullying by the other pupils. As a good Confucian child as well, wanting to please his hard-worked parents, he got nine A grades at O-level (which of course aggravated the bullying). He didn't tell them about the racism in case they worried – and in fact it was only a continuation of what he'd experienced in the takeaway at the weekends. But also at boarding school, he found – as I did – a father figure in his English teacher, 'a salt-of-the-earth Christian gentleman', who introduced him to Shakespeare and cast him in school plays. Simultaneously, his knowledge of East Asian culture was rapidly growing: clearly, his need to understand and be affirmed by that side of himself was running in tandem with a developing instinct for a life in the British theatre.

At this point his story pleasantly converges with mine: he moved to the Perse School for Boys in Cambridge – the city of my birth as it happens (my mother had attended the Perse School for Girls). David's 'tiger mother' was bitterly opposed to his idea of going to drama school – surely a waste of the money they'd spent on him; and he deferred to the extent of taking a law degree at Southampton University. This is exactly what my father would have preferred for me; I did oblige him by going to university, but read English. David's law grades tailed off progressively as the theatre took over, but he learned much about life and developed a taste for political campaigning. At twenty-one, his parents' typical immigrant ambitions for him in accountancy, medicine or the law finally thrown off, he began to train as an actor at Rose Bruford College. As we shall see later, he has not only succeeded as a director and writer as well, but, like Jatinder, has represented something more in his dedication to the interests of Asian actors here. Both men, whether they intended it or not, have been driven by something other than simply shaping a career for themselves.

~

Over to the west and nearly a generation later, **Annie Hemingway** is playing Prospero at the all-girls Royal High School in Bath, the city where she's grown up. The production is set in space; and rather than John Gielgud's tatty magic cloak she's wearing a silver babygro topped off with mad hair as she summons up the 'elves of hills, brooks, standing lakes and groves' – who are on roller skates. It is a serious, and, she says, seriously loud, performance of which a highlight is a stentorian 'and deeper than did ever plummet sound, I'll drown my book'.

She's fourteen, and this is the second stage of a theatrical *coup de foudre* – as touching and unexpected as such a thing can be – after her performance as Electra on a summer-school course:

the same age, in fact, at which I first got a part at school, the English Chaplain in *Saint Joan*, and barnstormed him to within an inch of his life. After Prospero, she'll do Celia in *As You Like It* with Bath Young People's Theatre, finding it to be as good a part as Rosalind. Her die pretty much cast, she then starts looking into drama schools, particularly RADA, who in due course, together with two others, offer her a place. She chooses RADA not so much because of the quality of the teaching, of which she can't yet be sure, but because it is, after all, RADA: you can feel history in its corridors and see quotes from famous alumni on the walls. She is impressed, but she also feels ready.

Annie is a courageous, funny and inventive actress, an eccentric who perhaps doesn't believe how attractive she is. While she was pondering RADA, **Gwilym Lee** was leaving school in Birmingham and, instead of thinking about drama school or even the Youth Theatre, was preparing to come down west to Cardiff University. He had been supported in his decision to go on to higher education by his parents, who were both doctors and to whom he was very close. He'd been quite academic as a teenager and, unlike me, still saw acting as a hobby; but he'd loved being in his school drama group and playing in *Animal Ark* on TV when he was fourteen; even more perhaps being let out of school to play the young Prince of Wales in *Richard III* for the RSC for its entire run in Stratford and on a UK tour.

His choice of a relatively academic course at university – rather than Drama or Theatre Studies – seems almost perverse for someone interested in an acting career; but it rings a bell with me, as does much of Gwilym's trajectory thus far. When I went up to Cambridge, drama courses hadn't been thought of, so English was the canniest choice given the ambitions I had in mind: it was obviously a related subject but also a soft ticket. Gwilym, with more choice but also no doubt more honourable intentions, was starting from the same point, moving towards a 2:1 in English (same as me). He also found time to play, as I had, Biff in *Death of a Salesman*. He is in many ways a classical leading man of a type you don't often see nowadays – you might call my first Richard II, John Neville, the prototype: he is open-faced, six-foot plus, very engaging, with beautifully defined features – and a Celt, guaranteeing the fires within.

At RADA Annie, like Gwilym (who went to the Guildhall School after university) learned fencing, period dance and how to do a good technical laugh at the age when I was planning budgets for the Marlowe Society. What they didn't get, as I did, was experience in front of an audience every month or two, since it was only in the third year that students were unleashed in a public show. On the other hand, by that time Annie in particular was used to working with visiting professional directors and getting the hang of the differences between them – the bullies and the teasers and the gentle ones, and the depressing ones who are determined not so much to help the students as to use them as guinea pigs to explore a play they hope one day to direct with professionals.

I met her in 2011 on a production of Eduardo de Filippo's *The Syndicate* (*Il Sindaco del Rione Sanità*). One day she was briefly and publicly lambasted by the rightly irritated director, who was being driven crazy by her gossiping (she says now she was discussing her character) in the corner of the rehearsal room while Ian McKellen, Oliver Cotton and I were running a scene. Her handling of the public humiliation was exemplary – an apology to the company but no grovelling, and on with the work. At her stage I would have taken days or maybe weeks to recover; but she understood the directorial outburst in a way that I wouldn't have known how. This psychological alertness was, I would say, one of the major advantages of her training.

As it happens **Gavin Fowler**, her co-gossiper (and he believes that gossiping, neither more nor less, was what they were doing), was also carpeted. It was bad luck: we've all been caught out at some time or another chatting in the corner of a rehearsal room. He is the most dedicated and gifted of young actors, partly Maltese, a performer to the tips of his toes and his fingers' ends, whose greatest fear is falseness. His effect on *The Syndicate* was to make McKellen, Cotton and myself into a clutch of granddads, cooing over him as if we'd invented him, with the absolute approval that two generations' distance (grandparents) rather than one (parents) might allow. This was partly because of his talent, partly because his ninety-six-year-old great-grandmother Guinevere Cross had worked with Ivor Novello, and partly because he seemed careless of every consideration except acting; he lived at that time in a shed at the bottom of Angela Pleasance's garden and generally looked as if he'd just got out of bed.

He especially endeared himself to me on *The Syndicate* by having the same response to de Filippo's world as I had had when I'd first done a play of his (*Filumena*) a few years earlier: on securing the part Gavin had straight away gone to Naples and traipsed around its mean streets for a week, getting to know every alleyway mentioned in the play. The local names are profusely sprinkled through it like a celebration, the purely musical thing Shakespeare sometimes does with dukedoms or myths: de Filippo normally wrote only about a small network of neighbourhoods as well known to his audience as to him and his characters. Now Gavin, like me, knew them too, and we had esoteric discussions. We also understood that the Neapolitans' shift out of standard Italian into their own dialect was, if it meant anything at all, a defensive mechanism to assert themselves as a great family and remain incomprehensible to northerners. It has nothing whatever to do with class, as English productions of this writer, anxious to reinterpret the play in British terms, tend to assume. We both also grasped that one of the very worst things that could happen to a Neapolitan, as bad for the moment as being betrayed by his wife, was the lack of breakfast coffee in the house – a scene of such awesome consequences that in *Filumena* it is set up rather as Shakespeare prepares for the Ghost in *Hamlet*:

> LUCIA: Donna Rosalia hasn't made fresh coffee.
> ALFREDO: Couldn't you?
> LUCIA: Me, make coffee?
> ALFREDO: Can't you make coffee? . . . I've got to have coffee. I tell you what we'll do. Take half of Don Domenico's coffee out of his cup, give it to me, and fill up his coffee with water.
> LUCIA (*with a shudder*): But what if he finds out?

The Syndicate was Gavin's second job: on his first he'd been criticised by the other actors and director for being – wait for it – too serious. But like Annie's, his perception of directors was ahead of his years, and he was as dignified under pressure as she was. At his age, apart from the Marlowe Society budgets, I'd known only the extreme intellectual claustrophobia of Cambridge, in which the blind had generally been led by at best the partially sighted. I by no means had the wisdom to assess a director's professional idiosyncrasies.

~

Annie Hemingway has still predominantly done theatre and regrets having been persuaded by her then agent to turn down Duckling in *Our Country's Good* at the Watermill in Newbury for TV work that never materialised. After *The Syndicate* Gavin Fowler was with the RSC in no time. Gwilym Lee was immediately cast after leaving Guildhall as the Messenger and understudy for Ralph Fiennes as Oedipus at the National Theatre, and has since played many of the same younger parts as I did – Edgar in *King Lear*, Leonidik in *The Promise* and Laertes in *Hamlet* (also at twenty-six, also on Broadway). My own half-century's

25

work is certainly more noticeable for theatre than film – though a brief (and in my view very poor) week on *Star Wars* has given me a spurious something and some strange encounters at stage doors as I limp out after playing some classic and am met by George Lucas fans.

It's obvious that all six of us, Jatinder and David included, have in common an instinctive preference for the theatre; and I should say that the four other actors are of the same standard as I was at that age, though they're not all getting as much work as I did. Nowadays, when senior figures in the industry are quoted as saying that young actors don't have the interest in or talent for the theatre that we had, they should, most emphatically, zip up, or show more class. I once took part in a day-long seminar at the National Theatre on the subject of the survival of the classics; it was chaired by Trevor Nunn, Peter Hall and Adrian Noble. It was all fairly predictable: a number of middle-aged performers like me – but I must say not including me – got up and murmured in a melancholy way about a great lost tradition, the history of the Shakespearian ensemble and so on, and how it had all gone to pot. This sentimental threnody was too much for the understudies of the current NT *Antony and Cleopatra*, and a number of them got to their feet as furiously as if they were at Prime Minister's Questions. They were overcome, they said, to see these three great directors, let alone the famous actors, all in the same room; they wanted nothing more than to be part of that community, but the constriction of the industry in the Thatcher years had led to their getting fewer and fewer opportunities to do the classics – and in any case, were the big companies really doing their part in nurturing young classical talent as they traditionally had done? It was extremely heartening, and an invitation to the elders not to waffle.

The fact is that the same proportion of talent and willingness is flowing into the profession as it ever did. Likewise all that's certain in any career is that nothing is certain: however, things usually steady themselves in the end, assuming you're some good, whatever shape the first few years take. It's nowadays faintly absurd to sit down and plan a career along the old lines – the theatre debut, then the TV and film, then a triumphant return to the theatre: most people, unless they have an exceptional following wind, are simply glad to get a job and then another one. But the chances of stage experience for today's graduates do shrink further if they fall into the hands of a certain kind of agent, with disproportionate power and not enough scruple, who may have grabbed at them after their final show at drama school. He or she may have advised them to look askance at the theatre and to wait for a *Casualty*, an *EastEnders* or a *Coronation Street*, as constituting their real 'break'. A couple of years ago I was involved in the casting of Ibsen's *The Master Builder* in a major revival: it was important to find the right young actress to play Hilde Wangel opposite me. We saw many within their first couple of years out of school but, casting being what it is, we went in a great looping circle before ending up, mercifully, with the experienced actress we should have had in the first place. Meanwhile the agents of the young graduates we enquired about with a view to playing what may be, apart from Juliet, the best part in the classical repertoire for a young actress, withheld their interest, as their client was 'planning to do television'. Sometimes the planned offer was not yet in place, so they were turning down something for nothing. I ran into several of these young performers later: they hadn't got any TV work after all and regretted the choice. Or they'd got one TV job but not a second.

What's dispiriting about such tales is that young clients may well be in awe of and feel dependent on the agent, and are therefore persuaded to make entirely mercenary decisions if the opportunity comes up. Such agents are like the bad guardians of orphans in Charles Dickens' stories. Experience in the theatre is a reliable qualification for good screen acting, not the other way round: and I know of very few young actors who go through training with the express intention of ignoring the theatre altogether. They all see it at the least as a means to an end, and some as much more than that.

There are exceptions of course, and as always, they prove the rule. Daniel Radcliffe was picked up by film at an early age, and has recently, with the authority of that, made a determined move into the theatre. His success in *Equus* and *The Cripple of Inishmaan* has been met by a certain snobbish surprise among critics that he should have turned out to be good. Why shouldn't he be good? Is it a small thing to play Harry Potter well? Or *My Boy Jack*? The point is that he was always a good actor, whatever he was doing, and his career path is not in itself a model for anything except the intelligent use of fame. Even an actor as stellar as David Tennant was, on the occasion of his casting as Hamlet by the RSC, assumed by an ignorant elder to be just 'that man from television' because of *Doctor Who* – despite an earlier CV which included the RSC, Royal Exchange, Donmar and the National Theatre.

However, things being as they are for most graduates, what is the Holy Grail these agents are holding out for? For my generation it would have meant feature films, or maybe a multitude of good, cheaply shot – or even live – original plays on TV. For you, dear reader, it's a Soap or a series, almost never a single play. In any event, you need to be prepared. Some drama schools teach screen technique, and some don't: Arts Educational spend fifty per cent of their students' time in this way, the more traditional schools much less. But one class a week is not enough to get you ready for this new industry. Some colleges go no further than a TV Cold Reading Class in which you're handed the script and required to learn it and get through it – in a hurry, as if shooting a Soap. And a Soap may indeed be your first job, fallen upon like gold by your agent, who will tell you that *Holby City* is for you what a classy rep would once have been for me. So let's start there.

PART ONE – The Screen

1 Television Now

Trust Me, I'm a Doctor – The Continuing Drama of the Soaps –
The Guest's Tale – The Regular's Tale – The Director's Tale

The consultant surgeon looked at his notes and then, doubtfully, at me. Having just recovered from a bad asthma attack, I was wired up to an electrocardiogram and had a nebuliser over my mouth and nose. Then he looked over to the junior doctor on the other side of the bed – a handsome devil, with not so many scars in the service. Rather surprisingly in front of the patient, the consultant declared my atrial peptide rather low, seeming to expect the handsome devil to agree; but all he got was a quizzical glance. I looked from one to the other from my helpless position and momentarily wondered if there was some long-standing disharmony between them, and what that might mean for my survival.

The consultant turned to the attending nurse, who expressed the view that the peptide was about average. Then, not having got the confirmation he wanted from two people he regarded as juniors, he snapped his clipboard and stormed out of the ward. God, I thought, the tension for overworked doctors in these teaching hospitals. What is happening to the NHS?

However I wasn't in a hospital, I was at Elstree. In front of me was a camera, a sound operator, and the usual array of faces, as many as twenty, typical of a busy television studio. The disagreeing nurse was in fact the only medical professional there – she was the adviser hired to check the script and be on the set all day to authenticate the procedures. The junior doctor and the surgeon were actors and the latter was really questioning the medical accuracy of the script; the junior doctor didn't want to get out of line, and the surgeon was then being put straight by the one person present who should know what a peptide reading might be. He was upset. After three years as a regular on the show, he had, in his own eyes, become an expert himself; the way he looked across the bed over his spectacles was, by now, to the manner born. He also assumed that the actor playing his junior would share his self-confidence and likewise defy the nurse: hence his disappointment that the younger man felt he wasn't qualified to question her professional judgement. I was reminded that Richard Chamberlain, having starred for years as the glamorous Dr Kildare on television in the 1960s, went on to do a commercial for a drug company. In it he declared that since he'd played a doctor on TV, we should trust him and buy the product. Such are the penalties and profits of the Continuing Drama – the Soap Opera to you and me.

All this was happening when I was doing a guest spot as a patient in *Holby City*. And such a job may prove an important one for you. *Holby* produces fifty one-hour programmes a year – a staggering turnover: in fact, the one thing the actors around me had in common with the doctors they were portraying was overwork. And as for the consultant's self-delusion, perhaps it's not surprising: when you arrive at Elstree Studios, even for a day or two, you think you've come to a hospital, so studded is it with authentic-looking NHS signs directing you to Reception, A&E, Outpatients and Theatres – after a year or so, you might well need a reality check.

The whole annual operation, pardon the pun, is only possible by having two separate units working at once, each doing two one-hour episodes in four five-day weeks. You see the arithmetic. It boils down, for each unit, to six minutes of completed and edited film each day: a feature film, on the other hand, might achieve three minutes. As a result, the lighting tends to be a bit flat and generalised, but the lightweight video cameras can move from one set-up to the next very fast and be shooting again a matter of minutes after completing the previous one. This is instead of the couple of hours that a feature film, with its higher standards of cinematography, might need to turn itself around.

The fellow playing the tactful junior doctor later told me that he'd been out of work for six years since leaving drama school and had been reduced to making a DVD of himself tap-dancing (the one part of his training he'd enjoyed): he'd made ninety copies and circulated them. As an unexpected result he's now a *Holby City* regular, on, I should guess, £100,000 a year, though I doubt if he tap-dances very much; so it's certainly a lucky break for the agent. And he's a good actor. He can speak well, he processes thought, his lines come from a lifelike centre. So why wasn't he working all that earlier time? It's the unanswerable question that sits crouched in every actor's thalamus. If the answer were to come back, it would be another question: why should any one of us expect to get a job, ever?

Soap Operas have a noble history. They're so called because when they were launched, on American radio in the 1930s – *Young Doctor Malone, Just Plain Bill* – they were sponsored by detergent manufacturers. Here in Blighty in 1948, *Mrs Dale's Diary* embarked on a twenty-one-year career on the BBC Light Programme (now Radio 2) – one fifteen-minute episode in the afternoon, to be repeated the next morning, five thousand of them. Each episode was prefaced by Mrs Dale, the wife of a Middlesex GP, confiding to her diary that she was 'rather worried about Jim'. Two years later the series was joined by 'an everyday story of country folk', *The Archers*, which at its height was heard regularly by sixty per cent of British adults, and is of course still running, now billed as a 'contemporary drama in a rural setting'.

The emphasis of UK Soaps was from the start quite distinct from that of their US counterparts, and more educational: *Mrs*

Dale answered a need in the still-young NHS to get us to under-stand the lives of hard-working doctors, just as *The Archers* was originally backed by the Ministry of Agriculture as a way of bringing information to farmers to help increase productivity after the war. *Mrs Dale* is easy enough to mock, but it was origi-nally co-authored by Ted Willis, en route to *Dixon of Dock Green* and greater things beyond; and for its time it was surprisingly unafraid. At one point Mrs Dale caused a man's death by care-less driving, and a heart attack forced Dr Dale to retire from practice, so she had been right to be rather worried. One of her children got measles – twice, the writers having forgotten about the first time: listeners complained in their thousands. Another time Derek Nimmo played an artist who tried to hire a neigh-bour's Scandinavian maid as a nude model, and – astonishingly – a sympathetic gay character was introduced, long before the legalisation of homosexuality in 1967. The whiff of real scandal produced by the 1963 sacking of the actress Ellis Powell from the central role, to be replaced by Jessie Matthews, oxygenated Frank Marcus's play and film *The Killing of Sister George*, which featured an actress who loses her part in a long-running serial. (For a reassuring Soap Opera, *The Dales* – as it now was – had quite a touch of melodrama in its making: you could have writ-ten another play about the Jessie Matthews era because of the erratic behaviour of one of its stars, which precipitated a nerv-ous breakdown in a director baffled at being continually accused of conspiring to assassinate the Queen.)

By the 1950s, Soaps had crossed over to television, again with rather separate emphases in the US and Britain – put simply, consumerism was the preoccupation there and the life of the working class here. *Coronation Street* began on Granada TV in 1960, initially for just six episodes; fifty-four years later, it is one of the longest-running television programmes in the world.

If you think of the glossy escapism of *Dallas*, the history of

British Soaps is tough, proud and vigorous. *Brookside* has gone, but *Emmerdale* is a ripe forty-year-old, *EastEnders* is approaching thirty, with *Casualty*, the grand old man of medical emergency shows, a couple of years behind. Australian Soaps like *Neighbours* and *Home and Away* were so popular with young viewers that they provoked our very successful *Hollyoaks* (nearly twenty years old). These shows share some defining features but they differ in manner, audience and filming technique. As an actor, whether or not a stretch as a regular appeals to you as a way of making a living and an impression depends on your circumstances: a longish run is either something to be avoided at all costs or very welcome. You'll earn money (though the rates have flattened out a bit in the last ten years) and you might achieve something between fame and notoriety, high future employability or none at all. But above all don't despise them: you might, as I do, draw the line (so far) at daytime Soaps but be happy to do *Coronation Street* or *Holby City*. The Continuing Drama may not be Mecca but it's a remarkable fact of life and a short stretch on one of them can do no harm at all.

The Guest's Tale

For your *Corrie* audition you'll have to go to Manchester, probably paying your own fare, just as, if you live in Manchester, you have to pay to come to London to audition for *Holby*. Try not to feel the expense too keenly, even though you may have also spent money on clothes to look dead right and on childcare for the day. You've learned the 'sides' (pages) you're going to perform: older actors don't seem to be required to do that, perhaps as an acknowledgement that they remember less brutal days, but you've never known anything else, so you have to. You walk into the room feeling an interrogatory glare of light scanning your face, body and voice, even if the lights aren't on.

You've read the script and you didn't think much of it. Still, you've come to the audition, which you must do with the same enthusiasm as me meeting Robert De Niro. Apropos of which, who indeed do you think you're talkin' to? The figure sitting opposite you probably has an imaginary ideal for the character, but might be flexible: your confidence, the truthfulness of your reading and your ability to take notes may cause a little rethink – though since you don't know what was being imagined in the first place, that's beyond your control. If you do have an idea, try and demonstrate it in the reading rather than talking theoretically about it in advance.

As one of the themes of this book may be Understanding your Director, let me tell you what will play well and what will piss him or her off. The one thing you should at no point do, not even hint at doing, is hold the script at metaphorical arm's length. The very fact that a Soap is not high art is irrelevant: the people making it are proud of what they can achieve in what, as we shall see, are very difficult circumstances. If you're going to be dismissive, or say the character or plot doesn't seem logical, you might as well go home immediately – where your agent will shortly call and upbraid you, having heard from the casting director that your attitude was all wrong. Well, obviously – it's not a good idea to knock the script about when you're auditioning for a stage play either – but it does happen: I have a friend who's been directing *EastEnders* for a dozen years off and on, and he tells me the best reason for keeping an audition short is even the slightest whiff of patronage coming across the table at him. He also acknowledges this is a rather intemperate reaction, but I can see why. He may not think so much of the script either, but he's in the middle of the fourth or fifth, and toughest, week of an eight-week contract which culminates in shooting a four-episode block which will end up as one week's viewing. So he deserves your respect.

Ten minutes later, you're catching the train, trying not to run it all over again in your mind. This time, however, you get the part.

On the day, there may be a douse of cold water even before you arrive. Unlike for the most routine one-off TV productions nowadays, there will have been no car to pick you up from home; on most Soaps, unless you're called before the Tube starts running, you walk to work or catch the first train. (The exception to this depressing rule is *Emmerdale*, in Leeds, who give you transport to the studio and also help you find somewhere to stay in good time.)

Once arrived – this is based on a few weeks I once did on *The Bill*; the programme is long finished but the model will serve – you may have to evade the amateur photographers at the studio gate who, unbelievably, are there at 6.30 a.m. looking for some famous-ish face to snap; then go through Security, where thirty grams of useless plastic is clipped on to your lapel for identification: it will probably end up in your pocket, as a feeble gesture of individuality. On this first day, you'll need time to work out roughly where Wardrobe and Make-Up are, since there may be nobody about with the leisure to tell you. The corridors are alive with a general rush of people who know where they're going; many carry rapidly dissolving paper plates of baked beans, toast and eggs, their plastic forks snapping, and Radio 1 blasts out from behind forbiddingly closed doors. Feeling very much back in the recurring dream of your first day at school, you eventually find Make-Up, which looks less like a salon than a small hangar or very large Barber's Shop. Nobody says anything much.

A peremptory order comes over the PA system: 'Orange Unit leaving twenty-five minutes'. Are you Orange? Or Green, or Blue? You look at your script, which is in a universal Pink. You approach someone tentatively: 'It's my first day – which Unit am I on?' Somehow, they know. A girl who may or may not seem happy in her work will wash and cut your hair, thus taking a decision about the part that you might have thought was yours or the director's to take. This is more an initiation, like a young man getting a Pudding Basin cut on joining the army. You may spot one or two of the Regulars here, eating or shaving, and so see a chance to solve the acting problem you've been feeling for some weeks: your character's ABC. In the sequence of scripts, of which you only have some, what is your relationship with him? In Scene 93, are you guilty and hiding something, and does he realise you are? This is a question that literally has no answer: the episode that settles the matter, Number 96, may not yet be written, or cleared by the Story Editor, let alone released to the actors, even to you, the one person who really ought to know.

You approach your Regular to see if he can illuminate you; as he catches your eye, you see for the first time a typical glaze of panic. This is because most days he will be going to and fro between all three varicoloured units, shooting scenes from three different storylines, all out of sequence with themselves. He may not, offhand, even recognise the name of your character: apart from a general idea of who's on his side and who isn't, he may not have much clue where he is in which story. He's like an engine programmed to navigate by predetermined rules, but of course timings are fallible: when she was an actress, my agent Lesley Duff once played an emotional scene with a cardboard box since the other actor, a regular, had gone to another schedule. However, somebody had drawn his face on it to help her along.

The next question is how to get into costume, as there may be no sign of any dressing rooms of even the most general kind. The wardrobe department may be doubling as an office: you dress off a rail and leave your civilian clothes on someone's desk. Eventually the Costume Supervisor comes in; like most of the workforce, she is friendly enough but says that when you're changed she must throw you out and lock the door. Where are you to go? Into the foyer, of course, to the sofas in Reception, to watch the human traffic. You feel only marginally more at home than when you came in.

On *The Bill*, I guested as a paedophile judge – this was the year after the Soham murders, so there were many such storylines. I was warned that the gullibility of the public is such that, given the character, I would myself be attacked on buses after the show went out, but I haven't been yet. I remember odd events tumbling over each other: for my first shot I was put in charge of an expensive Jaguar automatic, which was a surprise as I'd been told the day before that I had to do a driving assessment before being allowed near the vehicles (this to protect them of course, not me) and that had only been booked for later in the week.

Whether your experience on any Soap of being a Guest, featured or not, is nice or not largely depends on how much film has to be shot in a day to keep up with a schedule which is mercilessly worked out in terms of economy, not art. Or rather, its impact on the human organisms around you: the more naked the priorities, the greater the pressure and the more provisional the smiles on every face. To the director and regular actors, the newcomer must seem almost like a dilettante.

Still, once started, you may get a pleasant surprise. In a way it's refreshing to work so fast – no final make-up checks, little sense of where the camera might be hiding, not much strict continuity. The one thing everyone will have warned you of is that you'll get no rehearsal and will need to be ready to shoot first time. Actually this is unusual: the day's turnover is fast not because of lack of rehearsal so much as because camera angles can be so rapidly changed. You may well rehearse a couple of times, and then do half a dozen takes, largely because lighting are unhappy – which is hilarious, since lighting is what sends most of these shows down into their boots, just as the quality of the actors and of the directors (sometimes old hands from the glory days of BBC drama, eking out in later life) sometimes raises them to respectability. Still, there's something Heath Robinson about it all: a take may be aborted because there's a light visible in the shot; this is followed by a discussion, and then a second take is likewise aborted because the light hasn't been moved since the first one. A regular playing a *Bill* copper gave me my cues from off camera while continuing his breakfast. He had clearly developed a point of view on the directors passing through: when asked if he could get from his place in the court to the prosecutor's desk more quickly he said yes, if he did a pole vault. This was a mildly aspiring version of the kind of Celebrity Behaviour you might meet on a show like *EastEnders*. These, after all, are people about whose personal lives fresh newspaper cuttings are pinned on the Green Room noticeboard every day, and about whose storyline on the show website spoilers are always in circulation.

As always, a slightly inhuman situation is often rendered OK by the people working in it. Your Regular, if he senses you have a theatre background, may strike up a helpful conversation between takes about Harold Pinter or Tennessee Williams, as if he were discharging a debt of honour. His implicit message is that he was once a stage actor, maybe RSC even, and would love to get back to it. Of course he's in the perfect position to do so, as even that august institution tends to look favourably on TV stars when casting their next Shakespeare. But somehow the years have gone by and he just hasn't. And the money – he raises his eyebrows apologetically. Well, at least he's talking to you.

I also found that the schedulers, those creators of robots, are not robotic at all. After my first day – within minutes, in fact, of shooting my first scene – I had a call from my agent with a very much better TV offer starting in a week's time and ending before I was to finish my stretch on *The Bill*: a direct clash. I cursed myself for having got into all this, for ignoring the actor's instinct when offered a job – sometimes deluded, but often surprisingly accurate – that something better might turn up. That first scene was now recorded, so I was committed. I went to the schedulers and begged them to crunch the dates and release me for the crucial period of the new job: the quite junior girl there did so and made both of them possible. I blessed her and still do: schedulers know there may be more attractive addresses than theirs, and just as most technicians have a statutory clause about work enhancement, they feel that actors implicitly do as well as long as it's physically possible.

Enough. It was easy to laugh at *The Bill* – real policemen certainly did – but as a public utility it served its turn, fulfilling an important function by introducing young audiences to vexatious subjects, without, at that early time before the evening watershed, exposing them to anything prurient. The subject might be delicate, but you wouldn't see anything bad: and there the issue was, aired, keeping parents alert and ready with their answers.

One moment in the programme's history provides a good example of the changing *zeitgeist* and may be typical of the Continuing Drama form – a decision in response to ratings which contained the seeds of its own destruction. Within three months in 2002 *The Bill*'s ratings slid from ten million to six, and its advertising revenue with it of course. When I was on it in 2003 the producer Paul Marquess had just come over from *Coronation Street* with a plan to adopt a serial format and add a romantic element to what had been simply a police series. Many characters were summarily burned in a dramatic fire, and the rest suddenly got a love interest. Being a copper was not enough: you had to have an exhausting sex life as well. The stage directions in the scripts that I worked on (which shouldn't really be in my possession still since a paranoid fear of press leaks dictated that you shredded them at the end of a day's work) drip with male wish-fulfilment:

43

she feels the glow of their night together . . . she's sick with love for a man she can't have . . . she is aching . . . Cathy's heart is broken . . . Cathy & Brandon are playful with regard last night's loving . . . Phil is aware that Cathy's 'had some'.

Hard behind the fantasy comes the moralising. The cops confront the dead junkie:

How can they do it to themselves . . . what a waste of a young life . . . gunned down needlessly in a drug war . . . not a pretty sight . . .

Then, forever impenetrably:

Jen gets nowhere with Keith so Eva plays hardball and gets a lead . . .

It was clear enough: the interesting matter of being a law-enforcement officer was making way for nightly sexual cliff-hangers. PC Kerry Young was given a sensational private life – she married a gay man, had a miscarriage and accused someone falsely of date-raping her, only to be raped in revenge by him. It was rather a questionable method of grappling with the ratings – a failure of nerve really – but more women began to watch: the figures were pretty soon back up to eight million and in 2005 they edged ahead of *Coronation Street* to eleven million. All the same, I wouldn't want cops like those to see my grandchildren across the road.

The Regular's Tale

Being a regular on a Soap may feel like working for a corporation. The hours can be 8 a.m. to 7 p.m., with an hour for lunch, then home to learn lines, at which you get prodigiously fast. The overnight break is supposed to be twelve hours, travel time not included, but sometimes you're asked to run over into it, and it's difficult to refuse. There may be an Equity deputy but it's doubtful they'd be listened to: after all Equity is not a closed shop and fairly toothless in this setting. Remember, other departments have less fun than you: Make-Up suffer more from broken breaks, as they have to be ahead of you in the morning and stay later at night; likewise the crew, who start work at 7 a.m.

Be prepared each day, as prepared as the director has to be. Don't change the script except by prior agreement: writers on TV can be strangely puritanical. You have to find your own character motivation, but once that's done you're your own master; if you're a regular you come to know your character better than the succession of writers do. Make bold choices in your playing, then writers will identify you and develop character-driven storylines for you. In other words, give them ideas.

Be nice. As time goes on and if you can, make friends with the schedulers, who are often helpful, as I found on *The Bill*. Be friendly on the set too – the directors go on to other things and will remember you. In fact, make yourself agreeable to everyone: bad reports always get back to producers and reputation is everything. If you're exhausted don't let on; the schedulers will rest you apparently for reasons of storyline, but in fact worried by personal frailty.

Put up with the Publicity Machine: you've bought into a celebrity culture by joining the cast. Theoretically you can control what goes out about you but Upstairs tends to insist: if you turn down the front cover of *Loaded*, you'll make no friends. Publicity can be addictive, and actors very competitive for it. It's important to have a publicity person in attendance at any interview, so there should be some control over the questions and over what could otherwise be horrible photo sessions. In any case there is a Book of Rules on *EastEnders* – what publicity you can and can't do. If you're asked to open a supermarket you'll need written permission: the perks from it are yours and don't benefit the producers.

The money on the Soaps is not what it was. Ten years ago on *The Bill* a regular could work for a couple of years at £1,750 a week plus paid holidays, which could usually be confirmed and therefore booked a comfortable three months ahead. Now, unless he or she is a real six-figure-a-year celebrity, £600 an episode is a good fee, though it doubles when, as in the case of *EastEnders* or *Coronation Street*, there's an omnibus edition at the weekend. (It's a little difficult to make a direct comparison between a weekly salary and an episode fee because of the multi-scheduling; but for these two figures to match, you would each week have to complete your own contribution to three episodes to make the £1,750 – which is unlikely: in itself a single episode could take two weeks to shoot.) If you're to be a regular without a particularly high profile, your agent will fight for a guaranteed number of episodes or money in lieu, hoping for fifty rather than twenty-five over six months: but if they overprice you, you won't be back next year.

On *Family Affairs* you get paid a weekly wage plus overtime. *Holby* pays its regulars on an annual basis, so if you're not in an episode you may be glad of the break and untroubled by it. However, on the others, you're paid by the episode, so if you're missed out of one or two *Brookside*s there is the fear of your character being laid off for a bit and some new one brought in who may become more interesting than yours; your livelihood will be affected, unless your agent has been smart – see above. Panic is built into this culture: as a guest you notice how nervous some of the regulars are about their future – they almost check the ceiling for microphones before confiding in you.

As for Life After Soap, you may feel elation when you leave the bubble, but also disorientation. The chronic dissatisfaction will have been shortage of time, and you may in the end decide to give up the regular money and head for the hills. If you want to leave before you're pushed, there may be a bit of low-key bullying to stay from the programmers, followed by amiable capitulation. Your working life may never be as consistently busy again (six days a week fifty weeks of the year) or as well paid, but the money you've earned will have given you the freedom to experiment a little.

Although one of the few things the public knows about the life of actors is that they can be typecast if they do too many Soaps, that's less and less true. If you've been a character for more than three years, say, there could be a problem; you may temporarily only go up for Essex girls and gangsters' molls in your bleach-blonde hair and permatan. There was a time when panto, voice-overs and commercials were considered professional death but much of the old snobbery is gone: they're obviously a benefit after you've done a Soap. And there's a healthy understanding in the industry these days that actors have to earn a living: everyone knows you can go from the National Theatre to *Coronation Street*, into a movie and then onto the Fringe.

My friend Stephen Boxer, a fine classical actor, can't speak too highly of spending two years on *Doctors*, the BBC's lunchtime soap made in Birmingham – though he points out that when he graduated from drama school in 1971 none of us would have been seen dead in a Soap. But in 2006, when he was doing Strindberg's most obscure play *The Great Highway* at the tiny Gate Theatre, he was called up – after a silence of ten weeks between the audition and the offer – to start in ten days' time as a regular on a year's contract, which was then extended to two. *Doctors* produces about twenty minutes material a day (nearly three times as much as *Holby*) for five days every week in order to generate three complete thirty-minute episodes on the screen. It currently goes out at 1.45 p.m. to an audience of two to three million, and is content with that fairly modest figure – compared to evening Soaps.

Shooting *Doctors* is like speeded-up feature filming: two cameras producing a master, some two-shots and singles, then moving on fast; you might, as ever, be filming scenes from three different storylines at different stages of the day. (Stephen is unable to confirm a rumour that a regular recently shot scenes from twelve episodes in one day.) A feature-film Director of Photography would have a fit at all this but it's perfectly acceptable on episodic TV. The only true pressure came towards the end of the week: Stephen says that if you see a scene covered entirely by one master shot, it was probably done at 5 p.m. on Friday, as the clock ticked down to the week's wrap.

The contrast appealed to him, as all professional contrasts have during his distinguished career. Everything else was predictable in the pleasantest way, especially for a man with two children: not only financially but in terms of guaranteed free weekends and predictable holidays (ten and two weeks a year), to be planned just as ordinary folk do. There were easements: *Doctors* pays the standard rail fare and they find accommodation in Birmingham (likely at Jury's Inn, as do *Corrie* and *Emmerdale*) though no overnight subsistence or expenses. You might get a meal allowance if you're a regular.

He found there were appeasements in the studio too: writers writing for you, less general pressure, being on BBC rather than on ITV – and on BBC daytime rather than on BBC evening slots. Once he went on a day trip to Spain to shoot a short sequence on the Costa Brava – so at least he was only on one storyline that day. The technicians were mostly local people of tremendous skill and warmth, proud to be generating the programme in their own city; some had joined the operation as office staff and ended up as script editors. There were football matches between cast and crew every Monday evening, also a relaxed attitude to hours: if you ran over five minutes no one complained as long as five minutes were saved some other time. It was as near to the community of theatre as you could get on television: continuity and lots of work to do, unlike the single TV drama where you might be waiting nine hours a day and working three. Promising young directors, some from documentary, passed through. He became such a quick study that he could learn seven or eight pages of dialogue at home while watching the European Cup through the other half of his bifocals; he took pride in turning in work of quality in such a context.

The remit of *Doctors* is to reassure: it addresses ordinary people's preoccupations, and the occasional melodramatic script is very jarring. Compared with the graphic *Bodies* on BBC3 in which the doctors sometimes shoot up heroin, or with Hugh Laurie's *House*, the show is thought a bit anodyne: but Stephen had passionate love scenes on a kitchen table, was kidnapped and beat up a boy who had made his daughter pregnant. Eventually, after two years, he came out of it, nevertheless feeling sensitive, like all regulars everywhere, about how his character would be disposed of. In his case he was sent to the US to live with his daughter. He is occasionally offered the chance to come back and do a few episodes; he does better therefore than a friend who, having spent several episodes in a wheelchair, recovered, leapt out of the chair and was immediately run over by a lorry. This reminded Stephen that it was generally worthwhile being cooperative with your employers.

The Director's Tale

Max and Tanya step out of their front door, continuing their conversation as they cross Albert Square to the Minute Mart. After a couple of exchanges they're interrupted by Jack emerging from the Minute Mart with six bags of shopping. He says he's glad to have run into them: he won't be able to meet them this evening after all. Right away Tim Mercier, the experienced *EastEnders* director preparing his shooting sequence, sees a problem: the writer, who may not be familiar with the show's permanent exterior, has forgotten to check how far the Minute Mart is from Max's front door. So he goes down to the set while it's not being used and like a madman walks through the scene as written to see how far the dialogue will take Max and Tanya on their journey to the Mart. The answer is barely halfway, not far enough for Jack to see them at a distance and speak or even hail them. So how is he to avoid fifteen seconds of Max and Tanya walking with nothing to say till they get close to the Minute Mart?

First Solution: begin the action by picking up Max's and Tanya's conversation halfway to the shop. The shorter journey will deliver them near enough to the door of the Minute Mart as Jack emerges. Good: this can simply be done on the day of shooting, no change of script so no need to involve the writer. But what if the previous scene (half a page long so about fifteen seconds in length, to be shot on a different day in the shooting schedule) features Max and Tanya walking from their kitchen to their front door and opening it mid-conversation? It's a time-jump: think again.

Second Solution: start on Jack with his shopping bags further along his journey home so he can collide with Max and Tanya right in the middle of Albert Square. Looks good; and again no need to involve the writer in changes. But what if a little earlier Jack was seen arriving in the Minute Mart and telling Patrick the shopkeeper that he has a great deal of shopping to do so hasn't time to chat? When he meets Max and Tanya thirty seconds or so later he won't have had time to do it all.

Third Solution: more drastic. Move the scene between Jack and the shopkeeper to earlier in the episode so that he's had time to make all his purchases and is now leaving the shop! This is structural, so it does have to be discussed with the writer. Moving scenes within an episode can be tricky as another character's 'journey' from place to place in a parallel story within it might depend on that Minute Mart scene staying where it is.

Another solution: Tim could suggest to the writer that more dialogue be added to the initial scene between Max and Tanya to cover their walk across the square. However, half a page of superfluous additional dialogue is a waste of 'storytelling real estate', and unlikely to be popular with anyone: it lengthens the episode, which has to be delivered on the button of between twenty-seven-and-a-half and twenty-eight-and-a-half minutes.

This is the fourth week of Tim's contract and shooting is still two weeks away. The first thing he inherited a month ago, like the Sinai tablets, was the schedule, devised many weeks before after careful analysis of time and motion. He may achieve a limited reordering of the sequence above, but still on any given day regular characters will be running laterally between three units and storylines, so it is an extremely vulnerable piece of time-keeping. So if, for any number of good reasons, another scene with another director takes longer to film than expected, one of them may arrive with him to shoot an exacting sequence from his script flustered and with only half the allotted time now available. *EastEnders* can't blame shortage of shooting time for any failure to deliver the best to a greedy public, who expect half an hour a day, four days a week, fifty-two weeks a year – a hundred and four hours a year down its maw, half as much again as *Doctors*, and twice as much as *Holby*.

The mechanics are familiar: Production Team A starts a nine-day shooting schedule for one week's story; the next Monday, Team B does the same; the Monday after that, Team B continues and Team C starts, while Team A gets ready to start a new story. All three are sharing the permanent *EastEnders* studio, its interiors and exteriors reassuringly familiar and unchanging. Since two crews can't work simultaneously on one set (nor can one actor be in two places at once) each crew stays in one for as long as possible, shooting all such scenes from all its scripts, rather than wasting time moving from place to place.

Tim's input into the shooting schedule when he arrived was inevitably minimal; he simply had to sit down and visualise his shots. He haggled a bit with his Production Manager (who was assigned to two other units at the same time, so wasn't entirely available to him) to secure special equipment – a camera crane, much loved of the old school of directors, and, for one day, a Steadicam, the marvellous strap-on development of the old handheld camera that seems almost independent of its operator. It was a struggle: reduced budgets mean less complex equipment, as well as pressure to reduce the number of working cameras. He wanted to shoot a scene in the snow but couldn't secure a snow machine; though if only the writer had specifically asked for it in the original draft script, it would by now have been on its way. For a couple of scenes he felt he needed more shooting time than the schedule allowed – one because it was emotionally taxing, and another a wedding involving a lot of people. He managed to manipulate the schedule to shoot them at the more leisurely beginning of the working day rather than at the very end, when the ticking of the clock is getting very loud indeed and he would have to depend on the traditional talent of most actors to pull something miraculously out of the bag with minimal rehearsal.

At the same time he met with his script editors to bring its first version (printed on pink paper) to its second (blue paper) preparatory to arriving at its final (white). As part of this, the Script Supervisor checked the implications for subsequent episodes of any script changes, so that the narrative information the characters had wouldn't be altered. There were necessary pow-wows with the more watchful regular actors. And there are certain house rules. Most episodes take place on a single story day, and a character never, as he might in a movie, leaves one scene and then, in a great jump of continuity, walks straight into a new and distant location in the following one. The impression of sufficient 'real' time passing to get from one place to another is, perhaps quaintly, a requirement of the form.

And it's now that Tim breaks off from these speculations to meet you, the hopeful actor, in from some distant city for your audition. Which is why I say again: don't arrive with criticisms – the script is already an interlocking thing on which much time has been spent. By the time you, hopefully, see Tim again, he'll have really earned his money, having sat down with some hundred and sixty scenes of the final script to prepare for the cameras in time for filming in Week Six. All his decisions continue to be made between rocks and hard places; a large cast and crew, and demanding executives. I once asked him, if you had an extra week, what would you spend it on? His eyes went dreamy but his answer was simple: to have the final shooting script at the end of Week Three rather than the beginning of Week Four, so that he had just one weekend's more leisure for detailed camera planning.

Imagine doing all this for the first time. When Tim joined *EastEnders*, he was given some pungent pragmatic advice by his producer: not to let 'the best be the enemy of the good'. He'd already prepared thoroughly: he'd trailed the director of the previous episodes to see how this organism (as opposed to those of other Soaps he knew) worked. He carefully introduced himself to the regulars, only to be advised by one of them: 'Don't tell me how to act, Tim.' He thinks this was not unreasonable of the actor (I disagree – he sounds a tosser to me); maybe Tim put one word out of place. At lunch on the first day, after shooting a party scene (always difficult to film – think about it) with a dozen more regulars, he sat in his car, feeling all talent and control draining from him; he almost turned the key in the ignition and drove away.

After lunch he butched up and realised what his power actually consisted of: though this is an engine you can't stop, you can drop the clutch, and everyone knows that to pause mysteriously for a moment's thought or a little more rehearsal is a director's prerogative. And every director knows a big secret: if you don't feel in control, bluff it out, and by the time you're found out, you'll probably have come up with the solution. He has at least to seem capable of answering any question from anyone without rumination: with three different 'script weeks' in their heads the regulars are bound to forget where they're coming from, going to, what's happened or not yet happened to them. The wardrobe and make-up team have to have all the answers too, or a major change will be missed, and an actor will embarrassingly arrive on set in the wrong clothes or sporting a bruise they haven't yet received.

As for helping you towards your best performance, shortage of time obviously threatens this desirable end: if as the actor you're struggling – or, in particular, not proving flexible enough – Tim may just get the camera off you or be brutal in the editing. As a guest you have one advantage. Your scenes will be scheduled tightly for as few days as possible in order to avoid paying you too much: the company, as the cheery saying goes, needs to 'shoot the shit' out of you and in the nicest way get you out of the door and off the payroll.

~

For all this Tim Mercier, like Stephen Boxer with *Doctors*, pays tribute to the brilliant *EastEnders* machine. Everyone is determined to deliver the story compellingly and not to let it sink to its lowest artistic denominator, where plot contradicts character and logic. Certainly more time for rehearsal would help the actors cross over from Just Speaking Their Lines to a real performance, and the director to plan a shooting sequence that's more than just 'Bat and Ball' – that is, two-shot / close-up / reverse close-up / back to the two-shot. But with luck and a following wind, actors find the truth and play it passionately once the cameras are rolling; and if this is a drama form close to industrial in its practicality, a good director can make you forget it for the moment. And – a rogue thought – it may be that in such fast-moving, high-volume television as this that doesn't pretend to be Ken Loach, pressure is not such a bad thing. There's no time for over-analysis of what may be a frail commodity, but there's high adrenalin and maximum instinct. Tim has had some of his proudest – and most electrifying – moments watching four cameras trained on a group of actors smoothly doing their stuff on a ten-minute scene as sure-footedly as on a stage. In fact you could argue that *EastEnders* is a natural, if slightly sanitised, successor to the glory days of *The Wednesday Play* in the 1970s – the same immediacy, the same topicality, the same empathy with a very large audience. So maybe it is Ken Loach after all.

2 Television Then

The Single Play – Green Shield Stamps and Craven A – Geoffrey

In the last few years the National Theatre, the Donmar and most recently the Royal Shakespeare Company have transmitted live performances of a number of their shows to cinemas all over the English-speaking world. Their project has been extraordinarily successful in attracting huge audiences to the theatre – or to something like the theatre. Some one million people have seen such productions as the NT *Phèdre* and *Othello*, the Donmar *Lear* and the RSC *Richard II* at the very moment they're being performed: their ups and downs, their mistakes, if any. While some 250 or 1,500 spectators have watched the actors in three dimensions, infinitely more have had the odd experience of looking at a screen on which, instead of the subtle lighting and big close-ups of movies, they have caught the energy of the performers and understood the stage production. Having implicitly participated in a Shakespeare or a Racine, they have ended their evening with the odd but harmless experience of watching in silence (it being a little embarrassing to applaud in a cinema) while the actors take frequently rapturous curtain calls on the screen.

This can be nothing but good: theatre is getting to places it has never managed fully to reach before, to more schools and to many people for whom theatre-going is not practicable; it's also to be hoped that it all leads to future good business for the live theatre, the only place where truly 3D performances can be seen. The method of its doing is both brand new and to some of us strangely nostalgic. Live screened drama has barely been seen on television since the 1950s and early 1960s, when *The Qua-*

termass Experiment, 1984 and the early *Z Cars* went out as they happened, with a few filmed inserts; now here is the same multi-camera technology, back in a more sophisticated form, featuring in particular a highly regarded specialist, the Vision Mixer – who apart from sporting events and rock concerts has been absent from television for years. The Vision Mixer (usually a she) is one of TV's hidden virtuosos and crucial to multi-camera TV, though that phrase has itself changed its meaning a little. When you hear it nowadays, it normally means several cameras shooting the same sequence of events from different angles, all filming all the time, so that the editor will have various versions of the entire action to cut between. But there are actors around still who remember the Vision Mixer from the days of pre-recorded and live drama, and they'll tell you all about it, given half a chance, as I'm about to. I think it will interest you.

I pass over the live transmissions of those days with something of a shudder: it's difficult to think of anything to recommend them from an actor's point of view. There are stories of cameras being caught in shot; terrible rumours of performers finishing and going home early, only to remember they had another scene to do towards the end; and worst of all, in a 1958 *Armchair Theatre* one actor (Gareth Jones) died early on in the transmission: his lines were rapidly reallocated, the camera script adapted on the move, the show went on and nobody knew the difference. It's been said that the seat-of-the-pants-ness of live performance conveyed itself to the audience and added to the general edginess and sense of occasion: viewers felt they were contributing to an unrepeatable event (not quite unrepeatable in fact, since the show would sometimes be performed a second time a few days later). Well, perhaps.

Here's how we did videotape-recorded drama in the 1960s and 1970s. For the BBC, an actor was contracted (and not much argument) and paid either a Category A fee (dramas up to thirty minutes), Category B (up to sixty), Category C (over sixty): the trick was to negotiate the basic unit of multiplication. Very occasionally you got a 'Special High' if you were suddenly starring, or, sadly, a 'Special Low' if it was a smaller part than you might have expected. Re-computing these numbers to find their equivalent is tricky, but my impression is that a week's work on television paid about twice what you could earn on the stage; what matters more perhaps is what proportion of the production's costs the actors' fees accounted for. When the RSC filmed their *Wars of the Roses* with the BBC in 1964, the production budget was £81,000 and the actors cost £42,000. As an all-purpose estimate that percentage will have shrunk by now from fifty per cent to fifteen per cent.

The commercial channels – ATV, Granada (especially), ABC, London Weekend, Yorkshire, Anglia (also especially) and Associated Rediffusion – paid a bit better with fewer rigid guidelines. You then rehearsed, as for a stage production, for two or three weeks, working up to the runthrough attended by the Producer, in some distant mouldering rehearsal room (until the BBC opened its dedicated rehearsal block in Acton). The company then moved into the studio for Camera Rehearsals, the equivalent of Technical Rehearsals in the theatre, and the single Big Night when everything was committed to magnetic tape, with some film sequences, usually the exteriors, cut in. (These were, illogically enough, filmed right at the beginning of the job, before the main rehearsals.) The recording session usually went forward in half a dozen or so longish sections, depending on the show's length, with short recording breaks to draw breath, change sets and costumes and so on. During the rehearsal period there had to be a great deal of what would now be called storyboarding: the director needed, well before going into the studio, to produce a shooting script which identified, line by line, phrase by phrase, which camera would be 'on' and using what lens, through the entire script. This in turn had to be absorbed by the department heads (and the Vision Mixer of course, who would crucially be hitting the buttons activating each camera on cue) and agreed as being practical, then transferred to camera cards attached to each camera for the operator's reference together with the obligation to get it right first time on the night.

Once in the studio, directors needed the actors to find their pre-planned marks carefully and to stay there, so that they could achieve a tightly composed shot as rehearsed with the utmost precision: it wasn't a moment to improvise, though one or two bold directors such as James Goddard (who directed the original *Blackstuff*, which led to the series *Boys from the Blackstuff*) sometimes did. A gun flung across the floor had to glide to exactly the right place so that the Vision Mixer could cut to it and the chosen camera hold the shot steady; an actor's move across the set, or even the placing of a coffee cup on a table, had to be done on a given line or even word. Although pernickety, it was also a little unpredictable, and so unlike cinema filming that rather than preparing yourself specifically for your big close-up, you assumed that everything you did would be covered in the best and most practical way. What you did learn to recognise was that little red tally light on the 'live' camera. There's a merry – though probably libellous – story of the great stage actor Donald Wolfit doing his first TV drama fairly late in life; realising that the red light meant he was 'on', he would attempt to turn his face to each lit camera in turn, but too slowly, so that most of the shots were of him gently rotating into view.

At one extreme, the cop series *No Hiding Place* – the *Bill* of the sixties – used to record fifty minutes of television in a studio hour. But for big drama productions of ninety minutes there would be a three-hour recording session, 7 p.m. to 10 p.m. Someone's big moment always suffered from being scheduled as the last event of the evening. Alan Clarke had worked out an interesting way of shooting the climactic speech I had in *Danton's Death*, but in the end, it being 9.55 p.m., he had to stick a single camera in front of me and hope that I didn't make a mistake. And you know, it was rather good: so maybe the apologists of nail-biting live TV have a point.

The plugs were ruthlessly pulled at 10 p.m.: overtime bills beyond then were massive and indeed permission to continue at all would have to be secured from ACTT, the TV Technicians' Union, and might or might not be granted. The virtuosity achieved by the cameramen under these conditions was remarkable: each electronic camera was a one-man operation, apart from technicians moving the cables around, and the operator had to flip the lens turret on the camera's front – you'll have seen them in pictures, four lenses mounted on a rotatable disc, 50mm, 90mm, 135mm and telephoto – to achieve everything from a midshot to a big close-up. (Nowadays it's done on a single zoom lens.) These lens adjustments sometimes had to be achieved during a split second in which the action was off that camera, so that both the previous and upcoming shots were cleanly achieved: looking at the programmes now, you can sometimes see a lens only just making it in time. The camera could tilt up and down or pan from side to side (up to a point) and achieve different heights on its column, but that was about it. Some people insist this made it all seem 'real' – yes, perhaps, in the way that sometimes seeing the overhead lights and even stage management in a theatre performance can be said to do the same thing.

Claude Whatham, a quiet revolutionary among directors, once directed me in a J. B. Priestley: he planned to shoot it straight through in one ninety-minute take, despite the fact that the play, Priestley-fashion, ricocheted from one timescale to another, one setting to another, from dream to reality. So all changes of set and costume had to be achieved within the action, just as they might be on the stage. He planned carefully and achieved something unprecedented along the way: a 360-degree pan by one camera, during which the set in one area was changed while the camera was off it – this involved scenery flats being moved silently into and out of place while the camera was slowly gyrating, so that a completely new set (and timescale) would greet it when it reached its original point of departure – new actors standing in a new drawing room in a different period. As for Claude's larger dream, the ninety-minute take, it was scuppered on the night by a single, human failing – a bad 'dry' during the last lap by one of the actors, which necessitated going back and doing a retake.

All this heart-stopping stuff was part of that most questionable of things, a 'Golden Age', the era when British TV woke up, between about 1960 and 1975; a time when the male directors all seemed to have names such as Claude, Herbie, Cedric, Basil and Gilchrist; when the women were respected, rather like Mrs Thatcher, according to the extent to which they took on the values of the male world – they often seemed to have double-barrelled names. The make-up girls on the other hand were very much girls, wearing blue gingham smocks like nurses, and some actors, falling in love with being constantly fussed and primped over, managed to marry them. Scenes in *Z Cars* (which chose to continue to go out live when it had the option of telerecording) were shot in the sawn-off half of a stationary car against a back-projection of the moving street. In the BBC's (recently sold off) Television Centre – a building designed as that most disorientating thing, a circle – you regularly got lost between Green, Red and Blue Assembly areas, as you later might between the colour-coded units on *The Bill*. There was quite a lot of lunchtime drinking on the premises: you hoped to get your next job by working the Club, where directors might be reminded of you by simply glimpsing you. (This wasn't confined to the BBC: a friend reckons she worked at LWT for five years all because of her diligent attention to this visibility.) In extreme cases you might get yourself paged to come to the phone – 'Michael Pennington, your agent is calling' – a practice eventually undermined when some wag had a call put out: 'Mr Andrew Pandy to go to Studio Five'. It was so difficult to get past Security and park your car at Television Centre that on one occasion, refused entry, Michael Bryant turned around, went home and waited by the phone to be called and raced back to do his recording by chauffeur. As I'm writing, the Jimmy Savile scandal has been breaking, so I mustn't get sentimental about the culture: but for the most part the buccaneering, gamey, faintly disreputable air of the BBC was harmless enough, and was soon much missed in the new John Birt world of consultancy, outsourcing and digitalisation (without which, it should be said, the government might have removed its Charter). Curiously enough this raffishness was more evident at Auntie BBC than on the commercial channels.

The writers meanwhile form a (rather masculine) Hall of Fame: Dennis Potter, Alun Owen, Alan Plater, John Hopkins, David Mercer, Jack Rosenthal. The single play, to be largely superseded in the 1980s by the series, ruled: batches of them would be tied together as 'anthology strands' whose generic titles roll off the tongue – *Theatre 625*, *The Wednesday Play*, *Play for Today*, *Play of the Month*, *Armchair Theatre*. All these titles, interestingly enough, declare a relationship with the theatre rather than with movies: even *Tinker Tailor Soldier Spy* (1979) leads out with the screen credit 'starring in order of appearance' – a format that originates in theatre programmes and which I've rarely seen in a film. And the end credits moved at a speed at which you could actually read them. The current barbarism whereby they might as well not be there because of the breakneck speed they're raced through on a quarter of the screen – following the famous comment by one BBC Controller that nobody cares who the actors are except their mothers – was yet to take its poisonous grip.

For good or ill, this era gives a perspective on the Tennies (is that what we're in?), and they on it. To look at what survives (an enormous amount doesn't: magnetic tape was ruthlessly wiped and reused) is to get an impression of quite low technical standards but an idealism and seriousness of intention that puts much contemporary TV drama to shame. For one thing you'll be startled by the crudeness of the lighting. The reason was simple and practical: twenty minutes or more was being shot at a time, all over the set. Unlike in a film, when each close-up, two- or wide-shot can be separately lit and make-up checked likewise, one state had to suffice for each lengthy sequence, so it all ended up pretty dull. You see wigs which are not only unconvincing in themselves but whose lace is no finer than theatre wigs of the time: that awkward little bit at the temples which puckers when the actor crinkles his face into a smile always lets him down. Beards likewise. When colour arrived, make-up tended to be on the orange side and eyebrows blue. In *Middlemarch* (1968) – one of the first examples – the skies behind us were turquoise and I had lips of a lascivious red which Mick Jagger might have envied. It improved of course, but studio TV never got over the inherent unsubtlety of its cinematography.

You'll see as well that the camera, frequently static and wide-angled in a way that would horrify those used to the jittery editing of *Holby City*, looks shyly at as many people as possible, like a modest intruder at a rather interesting party. No wonder: if it moved you could hear its cable gently swishing across the studio floor. Seeming reluctant to interfere, it preferred to let intimate conversations go on at the far end of an unmoving long shot while the foreground characters listened as intelligently as they could. If an actor fluffed he kept going: only a catastrophic dry (as in Claude Whatham's show) earned a retake. Surprisingly, what is not often visible (though it happened a lot) is a painting or mirror on the wall swinging open so that a camera could shoot through it onto the set. My pal Guy Slater tells me that during one scene in *Dolly Dialogues* (a title that wouldn't be allowed now) it was necessary to get a cable past his feet while he was leaning on the back of a chair making a speech to Felicity Kendal. This meant him releasing the chair he was leaning on in mid-sentence while maintaining his lean: the chair was then removed by a kneeling Floor Manager and the ungainly cable passed through the space, while Guy continued to lean on air until the chair was gently insinuated under his fingers again. All in the one shot. One of the writer's imperatives meanwhile was never to have a character ending one scene and opening the next. However he or she could be imagined *listening* to the new sequence's opening speech while racing across the studio floor (another Floor Manager clearing the path) from Set One to sit down in a chair on Set Two; the speaking actor in the second scene addressed the empty chair till he got there, just in time for the camera to cut to the panting newcomer for his reply.

There wasn't much editing in the post-production period: a single cut could take a good ten minutes to do. In fact you could hardly call it editing, more selective copying, since you didn't physically interfere with the original tapes. Imagine having two tape machines (VTR 1 and VTR 2) in front of you, and beneath it another (VTR 3); you stopped and restarted the first two with the utmost precision on the required cues to produce a master on the third that was thus already one generation down from the studio recording. Any second thought on such an edit involved putting the acceptable part of the new master on VTR 3 into the first machine with the new bit you wanted to tack on alongside it and copying the joint effort onto another tape beneath, thus going down another generation, by which time the quality was declining and it might be deemed unbroadcastable.

This 'three-machine editing' was felt to be a big advance on doing it all with a razor blade, but was still cumbersome enough to make 'pick-ups' and 'cut-aways' – the little inserts and reaction shots that are one of the staples of filming – severely frowned upon: everything ideally had to be achieved at the time of recording by the Vision Mixer. Sometimes a microphone or a cable got into shot. If it was glaringly obvious the whole scene might be shot again: if it was fleeting it might be allowed to pass. It was all part of the general dynamism.

So this was a Golden Age with a good bit of alloy: we muddled along. Nostalgia has its limits and though good actors are always good none of it was conducive to the best work: period drama tended to be stagey, slowly directed and spoken, with little of the lightness and accuracy of the best screen acting. It's as if we hadn't quite worked out how to perform for the best in this halfway house between the proscenium and the big screen; perhaps at some level we doubted whether there even was such a thing as integral TV drama. The exceptions proved the rule, of course. The surprise in the archives is to see the astonishing dexterity of Judi Dench in *Talking to a Stranger* (1966), or Anthony Hopkins in *War And Peace* (1972), already with the great screen actor's gift of thought: not just one thought, in fact, but a scudding movement of contradictory feelings from which a thought would emerge; never expressing one thing only, never thinking one thing twice, his mind always in motion, going here and there – and all in a single mute reaction shot.

From this and every point of view, the best work was done outside the studios, on film, with cinematic techniques – if you were hired for an 'all on film' drama you were generally onto something special. This is where the era emphatically justifies itself: film emancipated TV from both studio and live performance and also, finally, from the theatre. For many people the evening when British television drama started as a true public service was 16 November 1966, with the transmission of a single work of this kind – the devastating *Cathy Come Home*, from the dream team of director Ken Loach, writer Jeremy Sandford and producer Tony Garnett. Loach's realism, the sharpness of his editing, his mix of sound montage, dialogue and narration, his use of some non-actors and of 35mm stock on location mixed with grainier 16mm for the interiors were all techniques borrowed from documentary. (Union regulations of the time forced about ten minutes of *Cathy Come Home* to be telerecorded on tape and spliced into the film, but it hardly affects the issue.)

It is hard to imagine now the effect on the nation of such a single evening's television. This was a time when the unhoused in Birmingham ran to some forty thousand, many of whom would statistically have to wait a lifetime for a house because mortgages were most easily available to those who already had homes and wanted to improve them. Then twelve million people – more than for *Coronation Street* now, and adding up then to about a quarter of the population – watched Cathy's and Reg's helpless decline through the housing spiral, to caravan to hostel and in the end to separation from each other and their children. Debates in Parliament followed; the newly formed Shelter got a huge boost, and Crisis was founded the following year. It wasn't that TV hadn't touched such subjects before: just that nobody else in public life was discussing them and the intensity of the film woke them up.

Of course, it wasn't by accident that that many people were switching on: like all great moments, it had been prepared for. The audience had become used for a couple of years to the unmatched *Wednesday Play* strand which had given them Dennis Potter's *Nigel Barton* plays (politics), and Nell Dunn's *Up the Junction* (Ken Loach again), which included an abortion scene accompanied by voice-overed statistics; the debate it provoked would finally lead to the legalisation of abortion in 1967. Peter Watkins's *Culloden*, furiously reconstructing the stripping of the Highlands by the English and the disastrous ineptitude of 'Bonnie' Prince Charlie, was equally provocative in its use of documentary techniques; his *War Game*, which reported an imagined Soviet nuclear strike against Britain as if it was a news programme, was so powerful that the BBC took fright and refused to allow a screening for twenty years (although it got a cinema release in 1966). *The Wednesday Play* accounted for thirty-five dramas in 1965; it and its successor *Play for Today* averaged an audience of six million between 1967 and 1973. Both were under the aegis of a Canadian, the great Sydney Newman, whom those with longer memories also remember from *Doctor Who*, and, for ABC, *The Avengers* and *Armchair Theatre*, which he had produced since 1958 to his own very precise brief of abandoning adaptations of stage plays that dealt only with the upper classes. So television was becoming a vehicle for a generation for whom John Osborne's play *Look Back in Anger* (1956) had re-angled the theatre and *Saturday Night and Sunday Morning* (1960) and *This Sporting Life* (1963) the cinema. Ted Willis's *Hot Summer Night* (1959) dealt with mixed-race marriage for the first time on air; in the early 1960s plays by Clive Exton (the law) and Athol Fugard (apartheid) were suppressed. Ratings for *Armchair Theatre* were high, and not only because it followed *Sunday Night at the London Palladium*. Harold Pinter once estimated that his stage play *The Caretaker*, enjoying its first run at the time, would have to be performed nightly for thirty years to match his *A Night Out*'s TV audience of six million. This kind of work evokes its time, in David Hare's comment, 'more powerfully than Green Shield Stamps or Craven A'.

Rather as British Soaps have always shown a more serious impulse than the American ones, angry conscience to the point of cussedness continued to mark our best TV drama. There's a direct link between *The Wednesday Play* and the next eruption of the absolutely dispossessed against the absolutely unsympathising: Alan Bleasdale's *Boys from the Blackstuff* (1982), about

67

Liverpool tarmac layers, produced by David Rose and Michael Wearing. This being a series, the same characters kept cropping up, sometimes featured for an episode and sometimes in the middle distance: in many ways it was the ideal television model, the nearest the form gets to a novel. The men moonlight to work on a building that turns out to be for the Department of Employment, which would be funny except that the idealist Snowy Malone dies trying to flee the undercover social-security officers who come after them. Yosser Hughes, like Cathy in *Cathy Come Home*, fights the authorities' continued attempts to take his children (played by Alan Bleasdale's kids) away from him. In these films the children look through the bars of the staircase at their quarrelling parents in almost every episode, while the men glare at snotty employment clerks through the wires at the Labour Exchange like animals in a cage. The stories embedded themselves in the public's mind to the point that the characters seemed real; Yosser ('gi' us a job') became almost as familiar to the public as their own family. *Plus ça change*: after only a one-off appearance in *Cathy Come Home*, Carol White, who played Cathy, had been offered money by strangers for years because they assumed she was still broke.

TV drama has also had its classical side, with something of a radical instinct there as well. The BBC's *Play of the Month* in particular: Alan Clarke, a director who would seem to have been more at home with *Blackstuff* – he went on to make *Bob, Carol, Ted and Alice* – was, by a brainwave, invited to direct *Danton's Death*, taking his leading actors from the RSC. This was a stream that also included the great late Don Taylor, writer, director and producer, who, recklessly making it known that he considered Sydney Newman an uncultured populist with no theatrical knowledge, believed that the BBC should be the 'National Theatre of the Air'. Taylor (who had started his television career collaborating with the highly progressive David Mercer) insisted through the 1970s and 1980s that it should be possible to occupy three hours of peak time on BBC1 on three successive Sundays with a trilogy of Greek tragedies, or to put a classic like *The Crucible* into the same slot. When I did Oedipus for him, in a cast that also included John Gielgud, Claire Bloom, Cyril Cusack, Juliet Stevenson and John Shrapnel, he, like Clarke, was drawing his actors and much of his aspiration, unfashionably, from the theatre: and in fact he planned to do the whole play, as Claude Whatham had, in one continuous take, because he felt that would best simulate the rising tension of a stage production. Don's ambition was thus to achieve the precariousness of live transmission, even if that involved less than perfect compositions. (His plan was spoiled in the climactic blinding scene by a hammering from outside Studio One in Television Centre where we were working – a car park was being built and someone had left a door open. We came back the next day and did it all over again, as if it were a second night in a theatre – OK, but not quite as good.)

Programming like this is unthinkable now: a classic on TV is very rare, unless it's an RSC buy-in, or the recent *Hollow Crown* cycle of Shakespeare's Histories, which had the luxury casting values of cinema and which in any case could be seen as a proud part of the great Shakespeare/Britain/Olympics hoopla of 2012. It certainly couldn't be mistaken for Don Taylor. It's always refreshing to see the classics asking the TV audience for more of its time, if only because it reminds us of when we were in less of a hurry and more inclined to give good work its due. The 1972 *War and Peace* ran to fifteen hours in twenty episodes (all directed by one man, John Davies) on BBC1 on Thursday evenings; *Talking to a Stranger* brilliantly told the same story four times in four weeks at ninety to a hundred minutes' length each time. The 2007 *War and Peace* mini-series was a fifth of the length of the 1972 version; the 2003 *Forsyte Saga* remake half the length of the 1967 prototype. Such is the *zeitgeist*: the recent feature film *A Dangerous Method* was obliged to tell the story of Freud's and Jung's complex relationship (plus a bit of love interest) in a hundred minutes, but the six-part series in which David Suchet starred thirty years ago accounted for three hundred and fifty minutes of television spread over six weeks. In terms of satisfaction, the new haste could make the angels weep.

Television has spread far and wide since the 1960s: there's been classic TV, and TV classics. Dennis Potter's 1978 *Pennies from Heaven* was made into a feature film and then re-broadcast by the BBC; Mike Leigh's *Abigail's Party* has been many times revived in the theatre (where it originated); but you could hardly imagine Loach's or Watkins's pressingly topical work being blessed in the same way. It was absolutely of the moment, a quick response to current crisis; literally unrepeatable, what it stood for has worked itself into the marrow of the form.

The main point in our constituency is that television was a living for actors then as it rarely is now. Even without a big reputation, you could always do telly for a bit: there was a new play every night, to be taken apart in tea breaks all over the land the next morning. Nowadays a good part on TV is a champagne moment for most actors and a series a life-changer. As for the small parts, every evening now and across the nation, viewers are pointing briefly at the screen – at the Judge, the Housekeeper, or the Visiting Head of State – and asking, 'Oh, who's that, that actor – wasn't he once in . . . ?' Producers can get anyone to do almost anything; and the pressure top-down from actors who would normally do film but are now happy to undertake TV applies a downward weight which forces many 'jobbing' actors out of work.

We may not often achieve the high polish and intelligence of *The West Wing*, *Homeland* or *Borgen*, or the comic fizzle of *Frasier* or *Friends*, but they in any case satisfy a curiosity for the imagined unknown – top-of-the-line political intrigue, speculation about the behaviour of the CIA, or a slightly sanitised vision of middle-class life in Seattle and Manhattan. What we have nurtured is a classical strain, a mighty comedy strain, and also an insistent, cussed and very British streak of indignation running all the way from Watkins to Loach to Roy Minton to Sandford to Jimmy McGovern. I doubt if there's another TV service in the world with quite such a distinctive history, even if the digital proliferation has resulted, paradoxically, in there being many nights when you don't want to turn the set on at all. It's a pity you're coming into it at a time when the casting can be unimaginative and Reality TV is cheaper to make and more popular; when the aping of the historical upper classes or heritage bodice-rippers get the ratings; when the trailers offer a surfeit of more or less explicit sex every week on some pretext or other. But there's still a great deal to be proud of, and much for you to look forward to – not excluding the Soaps, but also some really first-rate projects that will continue to redefine the form.

As for my generation: having been around the block a few times and waiting for my own Second Coming, I am briefly on *Holby* again. I get out of bed, go to the studio and there go back to bed for the day. This time I'm playing a university professor who's overdosed on Viagra. I wonder who's in the next bed: maybe we can reminisce about the old days. Or, if we flag, about what happened to me a couple of weeks ago. I was entreated to a 'meeting' by a casting director who was working on a pilot for a TV series – the try-out episode, in other words, as a result of which an entire series will develop or the idea be quietly dropped. She claimed to be a passionate lifelong fan of mine, and though she herself felt that what she was proposing was 'beneath me' she would so appreciate my coming in to meet the director. The reason she was apologetic was that the character, the hero's father, didn't appear in the pilot, in which he would merely be glimpsed in a still photograph on the mantelpiece. But should the pilot go to a series, then he would of course be a leading character, and had to be established in this way. So, my agent said, Michael is to come and audition to be a photograph? Yes, yes, said the casting director, we all appreciate the absurdity and possible insult involved.

I went along, arguing to myself that it was on my way to where I was going for the evening, even though it wasn't really, and glad to meet a fan. I waited for nearly half an hour in a dreadful waiting room of broken dreams with some desperate fellows who looked as if it was their first interview for many months. I was thinking of cutting and running when my admiring casting director at last came running out, breathless with enthusiasm and apology, flung open her arms, beamed at me, and advanced on me with the greeting:

'Geoffrey!'

3 Film: Rehearsing

Who Does What – Your First Day on the Set

By the early 1980s, the videotaped multi-camera single play was a rare bird indeed. Taking its place on television were fewer, but much more expensive, filmed productions, still made with less money or available time than a feature film would have had but emulating its manners; and, since there were fewer of them overall, there was less work. As a very rough guide, a 1960s BBC studio drama might have cost £2,000 – maybe £30,000 now; by the end of the 1980s it might have cost £80,000 (about £200,000 now – but in both cases there were charges already covered by the BBC in-house, such as studios and equipment). Today, a standard hour of high-quality filmed costume drama comes in at around £800,000, while a show with a lot of computer effects is budgeted in excess of £1 million.

In feature films of course the budget soars – though rather more steeply than your fees will. And nowadays, while waiting for your movie break, you'll be glad to get a good part in that halfway house, a film for TV. In fact it'll feel much the same as being in a feature: whether the medium is film or digital, the method is now cinematic, with one or sometimes two or three cameras working at a time, shooting the same sequence from what seems like an infinity of different angles, each sequence perfected before moving on, one after the other. The eventual result will be perhaps three minutes of complete edited film per day. It's laborious and painstaking, something like constructing a giant gadget in which you're one of the joints. And, if you do

73

enough of it, completely obsessive: after seven months on *Midsomer Murders* Gwilym Lee declares that daily exposure to the camera is, in his well-chosen cricket analogy, like having time in the middle to work on your form.

However, let's imagine this is a feature and this is to be your first day (as in a sense you'll always feel it is). Let me try and see you through it.

First of all, will the car arrive?

Chauffeur-driven cars used to be the badge of stardom, and my generation still finds the idea of what I've heard described as Horizontal Ground Transportation for all quite surprising. In past times you definitely found your own way to work – certainly on television – and as Michael Bryant learned in the last chapter, if you chose to drive yourself, you more or less had to do a second audition for the beady-eyed gentlemen of Security to get into the studio car park.

In the Soaps too, as I said, you still find your own way. But as domestic TV increasingly imitates movie practice, the famous film car is with us too, purring like a mechanised tumbril outside your door at 6 a.m., complete with sat-nav and driver – sometimes an old rock 'n' roller, sometimes discretion itself, but, thankfully, not often keen to share his political views with you. And quite used to you stumbling blindly out in the dark to join him with half a cup of coffee. All this attention is not really a compliment to you: it's greatly in the film company's interests to shepherd you from door to set to door again, with expert drivers in radio contact with the base – far better, they would say, than trusting a bunch of actors to get there on time under their own steam. This may be a slander, but you do get a free ride out of it. Or a share of it: if there are other actors living in the same area being called at about the same time they'll be in the car with you.

Anyway it arrives. Or doesn't. The day I was to work with Meryl Streep for the first time, mine didn't turn up because the driver, having collected two others in the vicinity, forgot about me and headed straight off to the location in deepest Hertford-shire. When I could stand the suspense no more, I rang Tom, the **Second Assistant Director**: he magicked another car out of thin air. I was very late in terms of my call, but in acres of time still for shooting, as all calls are extremely conservatively timed. Tom was all apologies, saying it was the first transport glitch they'd had in the whole shoot; as they'd only been working for three days this wasn't quite as impressive as it sounded, but I appreci-ated him trying.

It's this Second AD you'll meet first: apart from your casting session or advance costume fittings, he's your first point of con-tact, and you'll get to know him well. He will have rung you up a day or two before you start, pleasantly breaking the ice by tell-ing you at what unearthly hour you're to be picked up and what scenes are to be done so that you can learn them. When he does, express no shock at the earliness of the call, even if he lets on that you're not even in the first scene of the day. Everyone has to be in the right place at the right time, and then some: a timekeeping delay hurts the film's schedule and budget and reflects badly on Tom. He will have spent much of the previous day pinning down these timings; his natural fear, after traffic jams, is that filming will get ahead of itself and you won't have arrived. As it's his job that's on the line, take the news in good grace.

Broadly speaking, you'll be working on one or another kind of location or in an equipped studio. As for the locations, you'll have noticed those cryptic little road signs with arrows ('WD', say, for *Waking the Dead*, or 'GE' for *Great Expectations*) on the far reaches of the commuter belt; you may find yourself in an Oxfordshire field as dawn peacefully breaks. Or you could be in a remote wing of a stately home. If it's a studio, you might be in some dispiriting retail park recently converted and now resembling a police station or a morgue, say. (The set for *Silent*

Witness, the BBC's long-running series on forensic pathologists, is so convincing that, arriving on it and seeing a warning that surgical scrub suits must be worn at all times, I looked around for one.) Or you might be in a proper, bespoke old-fashioned studio. Granada used to own a set for the House of Commons which they let out to anyone who needed it: a profitable enterprise, even though the set is lopped off at about a twelve-foot elevation and Computer-Generated Imagery generally has to supply its higher reaches. (Granada then sold it to the writer Paul Abbott, who passed it on to Wimbledon Studios; as I write they've tired of it and put it on eBay.)

Tom will greet you at the Unit Base, which may be right next to the location, or, if parking for so many vehicles is hard, at some distance from it. This is Tom's kingdom. Of the three Assistant Directors on most shoots, the Second is only rarely on the set and the First never off it. The Second works for much of the day not just on the next day's call but on two or three beyond: every stage of the schedule has to satisfy everyone in the Production Office. Meanwhile the First, in the thick of the action on set, will be radioing to tell him that shooting is falling behind or getting ahead, and what adjustments he therefore needs to make. Not so simple: this location may be lost at the end of today, so everything essential has to be completed or the Production Controller will have to negotiate another day there later on at some expense. The Second AD will also be aware of your contract – if you run over it by a day you'll need to be rehired (more money for you).

As it takes its meticulous shape – there will sometimes be an emergency meeting around teatime, when judging time and motion for the next two hours is critical in finalising tomorrow's schedule – the call-sheet becomes a thoroughgoing logistical document, listing not only who needs to be where and at what time but also their transport arrangements, the weather forecast, the addresses of the local hospitals and the traffic news – and, rather surprisingly, the precise time of dawn and sunset. It's distributed to cast and crew soon afterwards like the early copies of tomorrow's newspaper, and you'll find it a good read if you enjoy jigsaw puzzles. If the star of the movie is big enough to constitute a security or paparazzo risk, they will be a notable omission from the sheet, since their movements, the identity of their driver, the hotel they're picked up from and at what time, may well be secret: like extra-terrestrial beings, they seem to arrive fresh as a daisy and good-to-go in the morning (make-up in their trailers) and then vanish in a puff of smoke at its end. They certainly won't have their name on any trailer door. It's an odd effect: as you mill around in the working day you forget that there's a very famous person somewhere in the atmosphere, eating the same hamburger (unless they have a diet adviser – I've seen it on credits) but in a more paradisal setting.

Tom will have been there half an hour before the first arrival, which is very early, checking that the caravans are in a good state and the unit parking is OK. Your caravan will contrive to be musty but still very cold, with an air of having been hastily cleaned out for the new tenant and then left to refrigerate. Or, sometimes, inexplicably hot. It may have a CD player mounted vertically on the wall and a brown nylon flock couch, and other eccentricities. Tom may even organise some breakfast for you from the Catering Van (you've seen the titles of the firms – Abitofamouthful, Moveable Feasts; they don't all offer chicken vindaloo for lunch in midsummer, and the best are very good indeed). As you eat it, he'll try not to hustle you too obviously along to **Make-Up**, though he will soon after.

The first thing you may notice about the make-up trailer is that it wobbles every time anyone climbs the three or four steps up to or down from it, so you can imagine eyeliner brushes jabbing into corneas and hairspray going into the ear. It doesn't

77

seem to happen; it's as if the head of make-up and her assistants (mostly women, though the new prosthetic specialists often seem to be men) have mastered the art of precision surgery on shipboard in high seas.

This is likely to be a lovely initiation into the day. Filming is a caffeine addict's paradise – 'cappuccino' is synonymous with 'good morning' – so the coffee is on, the craic is good, and largely you get the warmest welcome, whoever you are. Some actor you may vaguely know will be huddled in the barber's chair next to you, so you can catch up on the gossip via the mirrors in front of you. A waggish colleague may be doing impersonations, and make-up will be in polite stitches. I don't know how they do it – they have to be there very early and always seem to have come, under their own steam, sadistically long distances from home: from Waltham Cross to Shepperton for example. On the other hand, your next port of call, the **Wardrobe** caravan, though manned by equally professional and friendly people, feels like a large, well, wardrobe, but then how could it not, with all those hanging rails and musty cloth? There's so much fibre in the air it can be hard to breathe.

The **Third Assistant Director** (call her Charlotte) you'll meet either during this first sequence of events or when you get to the set. Apart from providing general support, she'll have found and taken charge of the background artistes (extras), sometimes in large numbers at short notice, and she'll be guiding them through the day. I leave the subject of extras to Ricky Gervais, but it's enough to say that as they may be on standby all day but only needed for a short period, a kind of humiliation is synonymous with the job; they sometimes compensate in odd, self-boosting ways, and need to be handled right. They may befriend you as a 'featured' player and tell you an anecdote just as you're squaring up for your close-up; they may ignore you completely or bid you farewell with hugely exaggerated gestures of respect or comradeship.

There are other diplomatic skills needed by the Third, such as keeping curious members of the public out of shot. Charlotte is the one on location who prevails on the guy in the next garden not to use his lawnmower during – and only during – the take, hopefully without parting with money, and persuades irate motorists to wait a minute or go another way round. Her talent therefore is to be likeable, well informed and calm. All the same, there must be an ever-present fear of personal failure, similar to that of a Second getting the calls wrong. It will have been a Third who, in a very funny story Ewan McGregor tells, went so far as to follow him every time he left his caravan for a cup of coffee or for a pee, murmuring into her walkie-talkie: 'Travelling . . . travelling . . . Ewan drinking coffee . . . with milk . . . Ewan in toilet . . .' Be nice to Charlotte.

A Third may carry messages, but is not the same as a **Floor Runner**. This job is the most junior way into the business, one up from work experience, and not specialised at all; still, many film-crew careers have started here, as theatre ones have from the position of ASM. The role requires good humour, tolerance of long hours, a driving licence and not much else. On big-budget features separate Thirds may be assigned to Sound, Camera, Art or Editing departments as well, but it's in the Production Office, the hub of it all, its many chains of command radiating outwards, that most Runners start running.

~

You're made up and dressed and back in your trailer, ready to go but with nothing to do. It won't be the last time today that you'll feel displaced. You still haven't met anyone reassuringly central – the entire behemoth seems to be stirring into life somewhere that you aren't. You may also have noticed from the call – glanced at idly for lack of anything better to read – two entirely typical examples of Sod's Law (Filming): either you're in the first two scenes at its start and then not until the tenth scene at its end; or the very first scene, breaking your ice, is the one in which your mother has been murdered, and the last will be the one in which you casually look up from a desk and say, 'Good morning.'

As you sit and sit in your trailer you'll get sick of your book, turn to your lines and go over them more than is necessary. You might go for short walks – not too far – to give yourself the illusion of forward movement. Or if this is indeed your first time, you might, with call-sheet in hand, try to grasp the multitude of specialist departments serving the project. A startling number of actors old enough to know better still aren't aware of what some of them are and what they do.

Sooner or later Charlotte calls you to the set. You trudge along behind her, trying not to think of the scaffold, nervous but reassured that you're needed. Once arrived, take a look around. There are a lot of people in a small space, quite sure of what they're doing and having apparently known each other for years. Some of them look like gunslingers, their belts gorged with rolls of gaffer tape of all colours, watches and walkie-talkies: they may be in baseball caps. As when you're introduced at a party to far too many people to remember, you hope, after a day or two, to be able to address most of them by name and have some notion of what they do in this complex, intricate dance.

The remaining **Assistant Director**, the **First**, (Harry let's say), greets you, probably breaking off from an impressive huddle with the director, and clearly belonging at the very heart of things. He's the head of the pyramid – or rather the head of a pyramid within another pyramid; or you might call him a two-way valve between the director and the rest of the unit, able to open or narrow the flow at will. At the same time, it's him, rather than the director, to whom a Producer may turn when visiting the set, for an unbiased view on how things are going.

What he doesn't do, despite his title, is assist the director in directing in the way that, theoretically at least, his theatre equivalent might. However, he may describe the situation and mood of a scene to the extras or small-part players so that they know what to act if the director isn't one of those who likes to give them a generous initial briefing himself. He will also be quite a lot older and more assertive than his theatre counterpart. To you he will be respect itself: this is perhaps the one moment in the day when you will be referred to as 'the Artist'. He keeps you steady with one hand; with his other he metaphorically holds the director's, insulating him so that he's free to do the thinking.

Harry has been with the project nearly as long as the director. During pre-production, he was involved in the crucial process of breaking down the script into a provisional sequence of shots (the storyboard) and determining the most efficient order (unlikely to be chronological) of doing them; also how long each would probably take to complete. Then he drew up the overall schedule for the shoot, in as much detail as he could. He knows the distance from one location to another; he knows the budgetary constraints and he passed an outline on to Tom of the cast's availability. Once started, he has to be sure that the work keeps to time, making sure that everyone is ready to shoot when the director is: he drives the day forward with more or less urgency. He has, if he can, to keep everyone informed: it's very alarming for any department to feel they're not in the loop. He creates the discipline too: so many people in a small space, however professional, can get noisy. Shutting a unit up in a moment, he is like a more affable, invective-free sergeant major. You can tell a good First by how long it takes, after he calls for silence on the set, before the inevitable next wave of conversation begins to build up. Sometimes it's five minutes, sometimes one: this is the indefinable matter of personal authority. Another symptom: sometimes the First AD calls for a rehearsal for the actors, but then nothing happens while lighting and camera continue their

81

work; it should, of course, start straight away. Or it may be that in one of those inexplicable pauses – the passages of time when everyone is waiting but it's not clear what for – someone pipes up to remind the First that they're ready to go, a thing of course that he should have sensed for himself.

So this job – leader and team player, multi-tasker and crisis-fixer – is not for the retiring. There's a career approach to it – Harry may have been a Runner once – but it doesn't usually lead to another job: I've only known one First AD who became a director, though another might end up as a Producer. So he's already on top of one of the taller trees in the jungle. I don't need to tell you to respect him – you can hardly fail to, and you need him on your side: it's to him that you'll turn at the delicate moment just before a take in which you're to stare meaningfully off camera at a distant horizon, only to see an electrician standing there fiddling with a roll of gaffer tape. It's very distracting – in a big close-up, you really need to be seeing that view, and you've a right to help, whatever the size of your part. If it happens, don't shout at the distraction, but murmur to Harry and he'll fix the problem – 'Clear the eyeline, folks' – without making any department feel defensive or you that you've been unreasonable.

Time to rehearse.

Gathering around you now are the director, the First AD and the other actors: also the **Director of Photography** (once known as the Lighting Cameraman, and often now by the more painterly title, Cinematographer), the **Camera Operator**, the **Script Supervisor**, and, at a little distance, **Sound** and **Lighting**. As you start sketching out the sequence together, the lines you learned last night seem somehow not so secure. You're nervous – you may not even have met the director at the audition, simply been filmed by the casting director; you don't feel ready. Everything is unfamiliar – it's as if in a theatre job you arrived for your first rehearsal and the set had already been built around you.

Most directors know this, and will be relaxed and welcoming (it's a technique as well as a virtue). You may get to improvise your moves, at least up to a point. This point will be well short of what you might expect in a theatre: for one thing they're circumscribed by the physical objects around you, inevitably different from what you imagined last night. You may find a staircase just where you proposed to execute a little dance, or no table – a camera even – where you imagined a drink waiting for you. These unexpected realities determine everything – pitch, tone, attitude: you may be much closer to your colleague than you expected to be, or calling from the hallway, or lying on your back. If this is unnerving, spare a thought for the writer: so careful to craft the lines which you've laboured to get exactly down, and now they're cut, reorganised, newly improvised. Meanwhile the director is talking in two directions at once: to you, to put you at your ease, and to a technical team whose eye is on feasibility. They'll address each other rather than you, but it's not meant rudely: to you they will likely be very polite, especially if you show confidence and competence.

The First and the DOP know that the director wants, say, ten set-ups for the scene – a wide master shot, two-shots from this angle and that, various sizes of close-up, and others. As to the order in which they're done, the DOP will already be concerned with matching up the exposures from different angles and with what he imagines the overall effect will be, once the sequence, shot in a practically convenient order, goes to the editor to be turned into a smoothly flowing scene as originally written. (If you're in the open air, there's the possibility of changing weather playing havoc with continuity, and the question of how to make best use of the available daylight: rain machines and compensatory lighting can create almost any effect that's wanted, but the real thing is better.)

The DOP knows all the tricks. He knows the vocabulary for

your Favourite Frightening Moment as the predator climbs the stairs towards the unsuspecting victim in the bedroom; that shadow is as important as light; that a hand-held camera, with its very slight wobble, is very good for creating anxiety, and indeed can be used to represent the stalker himself: the woman turns to face the lens and screams, or the hero does so, with astonishing reflexes, and punches his way out. Behind this lies a lot of arcane lore (ignored by more adventurous directors). For instance, the theory goes that in a culture which reads books from left to right, a film director will do well to place the on-going normality on the left of the frame, and the element that's going to make the audience jump at the extreme right (it's something to do with ocular saccades). Likewise, in the theatre, there are old pros who recommend entering audience left if you're in control of the scene, but audience right if you're interrupting something. On the other hand Alfred Hitchcock used the convention that the screen's left side (*sinister* in Latin, the left being thought unlucky) is for evil or weak characters, and the right for those who are either good or temporarily dominant. All this, I should say, is interesting rather than important.

You stand in the midst of this thoughtful group as it murmurs the pros and cons: rehearsals seem to have less to do with your acting than with mechanical niceties you don't altogether grasp. It is, of course, all for your ultimate good. The Second AD now stands you down again, for what will once more be an unpredictable period of time: you could sit around near the set, or, probably better, go back to your caravan for what feels like most of the day, while camera, lighting and sound continue their deliberations and sort out the machinery. If there's the budget for it, a stand-in of roughly the same shape and height as you will take your place.

The director Michael Newell says that this first half-hour – the closest you get to a rehearsal in the theatrical sense of the word – is like gold dust for him. It's where he sees any lack of confidence in an actor whom he'll therefore have to handle with compliments, reassurance, a making light of difficult things. He sees who is properly prepared and who isn't. Unless you've been lucky and managed to speak to him on the phone, this will be your first assessment of him too, but you will (must) have done everything you could on your own: learning, preparing, privately rehearsing. For his part, if you're not completely new, he may have done some homework on you, talking to other directors who've worked with you. Now, one of his skills is to make you feel that not all the decisions have already been taken. There is a template in his mind of course – a sequence of events, a manner of shooting which Michael describes as the best plan he can think of until someone has a better idea; in particular what your emerging performance may suggest to him, whereupon he may change it. His skill will be to make you feel organised but not imprisoned. Michael, of course, is one of the best; you may not be so lucky.

Back in your trailer or just ligging around, this is going to be the hardest time, perhaps because you've had a little taste of the action. Although you still feel miles away from it and unable to contribute anything, your concentration needs to be there – at a low level, but still present, an engine gently turning: you may be called back with great suddenness at any time. Meanwhile, camera positions are settled, lenses of certain sizes chosen, the camera perhaps mounted on tracks. The electrical department calls up certain lights; this is where you might have enjoyed staying on the set to hear everyone's favourite Masonic glossary, since it may be a matter of a 200 Chimera or a Polly, a Blonde or a Wendy or a Dino, a Brute to be strawed or a Melvyn. Lighting is a huge subject, its finesses still zealously cherished by some Directors of Photography wary of the growing fashion for shooting on High Resolution tape, more compatible with

Freeview but liable to compromise the traditional craft. All you will notice meanwhile of the digital revolution will be that the studio is not so hot: big heavy lamps are often being replaced by 'Gekkoes' which provide a halo of LED lights around the camera lens, doing the job just as well but more temperately.

The DOP continues to paint the scene, as if he has a commission from the director and is instructing his pupils how to do the brushwork. Obviously enough, a good director will regard the DOP as pretty much an equal partner: his position is extremely hard earned, and he'll have done all the junior jobs in his field in his time. Now he's the one with letters like BSC after his name (British Society of Cinematographers – a guarantee of quality: they only elect two a year). His remit is executive too: he knows the internal politics of the project, any tensions between front office and director, and he shares the crucial responsibility of getting the job in on time; it's bad for his reputation if it overruns by an expensive day or two. Do pay attention to anything he says, do what he asks, and respect him: he's an artist, and he'll appreciate you too if you expect the best of yourself.

As it is, you mildly fret in your captivity, wondering, not for the last time, if being in a movie is a well-paid invitation to catch up with your reading.

~

However long this goes on and however becalmed you've felt, the knock on the door cheerily inviting you back to the set is always a shock: you were getting used to idleness. Juddering, you crash up through your gears, feeling more unprepared than ever. On the set you find the atmosphere transformed. What was casual and makeshift now has life: a well-lit room, hall or church, though invaded by robots and cables. Another surprise: the DOP has disappeared. Instead there's a fellow sitting behind the camera, his eye to the viewfinder: the DOP will more likely be watching a monitor somewhere else on the floor. You're looking at the Camera Operator, who does just that. He probably owes his job to the DOP, who knows he can make a camera move around as smoothly and calmly as a pilot taxiing a plane. Not that the Operator is a mechanic, like a **Grip**: since he's the one looking through the eyepiece at the composition, he's its master – he will fine-tune between takes, and perhaps make suggestions. He can be a great help to you, letting you know the size of the upcoming shot – head and shoulders, waist-high: things which affect the pitch of your performance; he'll tell you if you're doing something that can't be clearly seen in the frame, or whether you're leaning too far across the lens and obscuring its view of what lies beyond you. He will remind you that in front of a camera you invariably have to read a letter by holding it unnaturally high and close to your face, as if seriously myopic.

This is all on the supposition that you see the camera at all. Things have become so sophisticated that it may be operated by remote control from something like a siege engine in the corner of the studio: hanging above the action on the end of a protruding arm, it peers at the whole set like a great inquisitive dinosaur, casting its eye this way and that, swooping and swinging nosily about as if looking for water, bowing its head to drink and then straightening up. I was recently asked to be sure to move out of my position during one shot as the camera would otherwise knock me out of its way. This kind of device explains the lengthy shot you see of characters moving in a straight line towards the camera but in which you can't see any tracks behind them (think of the misty morning Regent's Park sequence in *The King's Speech* between Colin Firth and Geoffrey Rush). Where once much effort would have gone into concealing the tracks beyond the actors, now the action may be shot from mid-air, all the camera's mechanisms lying beyond the side of the frame.

You notice some more people. With the Operator are at least two **Camera Assistants**. The first, or **Focus Puller**, is a man or woman of keen eyesight, reflexes and spatial intuition: this is someone who senses changing distances between machines and humans as other people feel the temperature in a room. His (let's say) is one of the longest days: arriving on the set in time to ensure that all likely lenses will be ready when they're called for, he'll end the day cleaning and packing them up for the night. If there turns out to be a problem with the previous night's rushes, such as a scratch on the film, he'll also be finding the time to call the lab to establish the reason and whether the problem can be fixed in post-production.

Meanwhile the job is to attend religiously to the sharpness of every image. It draws little attention to itself, but it's critical, perhaps the most exposed on the set: an actor is rarely blamed for a mistake, but a Focus Puller's error broadcasts itself a mile high in the rushes. If a focus turns out to have been soft, the take is unusable, its reshoot expensive, and there's no doubt whose fault that is. One of the toughest parts of this tough job may indeed be 'pulling focus' – that is, changing the lens's setting as the actor moves closer or further away from the camera: this has to be done during the take itself and correspond to your movement, which with the best will in the world may not be exactly at the same speed or precision each time. Or perhaps the focus needs to switch from one thing to another within a single shot to redirect the audience's attention; if it's done right, they won't even notice. You've seen it often enough: a foreground character is in big close-up and beyond him another interrupts, so the focus flips to put the newcomer into relief and the closer character a little out of it. Sometimes this is done to startle the viewer, but more often it's discreet: the foreground actor turns his head, scratches his nose or performs some other momentary decoy that prevents the audience noticing the change. During the take the Focus Puller will need to compensate on the hoof for any unforeseen movement: if the lens is very long (far away), or short (close), or the aperture wide, a subject that moves even a few millimetres will need attention. If, at the end of a take, he feels he's made a mistake or let the focus soften, he will report to the Operator (who may also have noticed in his viewfinder): they may go and huddle round the video monitor to have a look, and ask for another take if another wasn't already planned. You will be pleased or not by this to the extent that you were pleased or not by your performance.

The Second Camera Assistant is the **Clapper Loader**, who marks on the floor the positions you're to pause at before moving on, so that your distance from the camera is predictable at each point. She (let's say) might use tape, or better, wooden blocks, or even better (to save your toes) soft sausage-shaped bags that your feet can feel without your having to look down to check. Having confirmed the distance between these positions and the camera's focal plane, she will pass them on to the Focus Puller to record as a series of marks on the barrel of the lens. She has other, less visible jobs. Hers is the closest physical relationship with the precious film stock: she loads the magazine (usually a thousand feet, about ten minutes' worth, but digital cameras can shoot infinitely longer) onto the camera, checks its usage so that it doesn't run out in the middle of a take (her nightmare) and maintains all the camera department's paperwork. She's the only person to handle the unused negative on its initial journey from manufacturer to camera and then, exposed, to the laboratory. She checks for light leaks, charges the batteries, keeps her clapperboard up to date, makes meticulous notes and liaises with the **Script Supervisor** as to which takes are to be printed. She could render an entire day's work useless if she did any of these things carelessly.

You rehearse again, more intently: you need to get used to all this and the camera crew need to practise and test their assumptions. They'll be checking for lens flares, getting rid of them by using a mattebox (the solid shades round the camera lens which in stage lighting would be called barn doors) or a flag (the same thing but free-standing). The Focus Puller, if he's working manually, continues tirelessly to measure the distance from where the film passes through the camera to your moving face and operates the focus wheel – he also perfects the marks he made on the barrel of the lens. You're unlikely to be asked to make any of this finicky stuff easier: it's a courtesy not to give the actor more than he has to think about already. Like many things in filming, there is a bargain of respect: your job is to be technically accurate while reserving the tiniest right to let inspiration take you. It's tricky: on film you're never going to feel as free as you (generally) are on the stage, but you may come to love the precision. It also intersects with status: if one of the great improvisers – Brando, Dean, Streep – does something spontaneous, no one's going to mind much, but lower in the hierarchy there isn't quite the same licence. To be blunt, it depends where the money is.

Once again you may wonder what's happening to your performance, and even whether it matters compared to all these huddles. But your experienced director will make you feel that you're simply continuing where you left off at the last rehearsal, that you're the whole point of the operation and never mind all the ironmongery. Once the camera crew is happy, he may rehearse for performance only, several times now, or he may prefer to 'shoot first time' – that is, go for a take imagining there may be better ones to come; it depends on the nature of the scene and his instincts about the actors. You never know, you might get it in one.

~

At this point I have to acknowledge that some of the above and what follows is, by degrees, slipping out of date. If you only film every year or two you'll notice new technology each time you come back. The Focus Puller now measures distances with a laser device, as estate agents measure rooms, and exports the distances electronically to the camera with another gadget. Some things, however, will never change: if the focus has to be altered during the shot, there's still no substitute for his eye, his judgement, his hand on the wheel.

Since the camera may itself be unmanned on its great mechanical arm, you may, not being able to see the Operator, have less and less of a symbiotic relationship with him – let alone with the director, who used very often to choose to be in the thick of it, as close to the static camera as he could get, in preference to looking at a distant and perhaps not very good-quality monitor. (Now, even if it's static, he might have to fight for that position with the unit photographer, who needs to get his shots as close to the camera's point of view as possible.) On the other hand, consider what the machine's achieving, turning through two or three axes, all programmed from up to fifty metres away: for instance, the shot that comes swooping down threateningly on a figure, circles him through 360 degrees in close-up and then swoops away again. Or the aerial establishing shot in a courtroom that covers everything in it before settling intently on the face of the prosecuting counsel. Perhaps it's like keyhole surgery – the operator is far away looking at a monitor, but not getting his hands bloody in the muscle and bone itself. You may also find two cameras side by side looking at you, apparently on identical angles: but one is on a close-up lens and the other on a wider, and the lighting is good for them both. Or so it's said: cameramen would always prefer not to be sharing in this way, but time is money, and this saves a lot of it. For you too, all this is less comforting somehow, but it's made an enormous technical difference.

What doesn't really change is the anthropology, the structure and the job descriptions. Above all, the peculiar excitement in the sound of the mythic clapperboard, which the Loader is now presenting, with the number of the shot and take, to the camera. She announces the same information aloud so it's sound-recorded, and a devout silence follows. The director Roger Michell eloquently described this recently as the moment when all the anxieties of pre-production (the period, David Mamet says, when all the mistakes are made) fall away. This, he says, is when the fifty cars parked on location in a field that looks like a hybrid between an illegal travellers' encampment, a rock festival and a car-boot sale, becomes a gathering for which he's responsible – though now that it's here, he's initially so nervous he'd prefer to be run over by a car. It's when a field alive with strangers, knobbly blokes shod like plough-horses, in orange jackets and multi-pocketed beige shorts, assumes a meaning; when the evil-looking toilets and the bacon rolls are forgotten; when the director's novice-like nerves evaporate, and the thousands of hours he's spent in rehearsal rooms, looking at scripts and screens, the wrangling and intellectualisations, all come hurtling to his rescue and he is finally in his element. For you as well, after your first couple of hours' work, a cluster of different specialities has turned into one engine, facing in the same direction and pulling confidently away, hoping for the very best. It's what you signed up for.

4 Film: Shooting

Your Story in Eight Set-Ups – Steadicam – The Wrap

Let's see. You're playing a young woman who's moved to Paris
and become a successful fashion designer. You have a younger
brother, by contrast a bookish fellow, a librarian and archivist,
whom you've left back in London living with your widowed
mother. At first you went back to see them regularly, but as time
goes by you're beginning to lose contact: there's just so much
to do when you run your own business, and truth to tell your
relationship with your brother has always been fraught with differences of temperament. Now he's called to say your mother is
developing dementia and, apart from the long-term handling
of this, it's really important you drop everything for at least a
weekend and come and see her while she can still appreciate it.
Alarmed, you agree. It takes a bit of arranging: you had American clients coming in and so on.

We first see you just off the Eurostar and stuck in a cab in
a London traffic jam. You pay off the cab and run the last few
hundred yards to the house and up the stairs to your mother's
flat; your brother lets you in and after only a little small talk
you start a solemn discussion. Your Ma is asleep and the doctor has just been. You sit awkwardly across the table from each
other: you argue a bit, calm down and your grievances subside.
At a certain point, the door opens and your mother, dressed to
the nines, comes in, thrilled to see you. What a surprise! Your
brother drops the pretence and pulls a bottle of champagne out
of the fridge. It was a hoax; it's your brother's birthday (you'd

93

forgotten) and though you have mixed feelings about how he's got you there, it's fairly clear your mother hasn't known about any of it. As we leave you to your evening you're opening the second bottle and planning dinner.

Well, I've read worse.

There's quite a swirl of emotions involved here, their temperature changing; there's an outside scene leading to an inside; a backstory and relationships, especially with your brother, to be clear about; and of course it's got to end up believable, even though it's been shot disconnectedly. Today, on your first day, we shoot the interiors only: the first sequence – the traffic jam and the taxi – will happen somewhere else at another time.

Set-Up 1

The first thing to be done is the master shot, an establishing view of the first part of the scene: the camera at some distance across the room from the door, a table and chairs in the foreground of the shot, set on a straight line between the camera and the door. Your brother enters the side of the frame from between the table and the door, approaches and opens it, lets you in. You're out of breath and worried; you embrace, and gently he leads you to the table, sits you down and explains about your mother's condition. Then, sitting across the table, left and right of the frame, you run all the dialogue up to the point your mother comes in, when the camera will cut. It's a fixed shot without movement – all the action is held within one frame, though there may be some focus adjustment as you approach the table, depending on the lens chosen. Technically it all needs to be achieved as simply as possible.

After a brief rehearsal, you're thought to be ready to shoot. The atmosphere is surprisingly relaxed. The lighting state is OK for every stage of your physical progress. Final Checks are lightly called for by the First AD – they're wardrobe's and make-up's last chance to see that you're looking all right. This will become more crucial when you get to the closer shots, but still it needs doing. Most wardrobe and make-up artists have an admirable gift for not being hurried at this most important moment: everyone else is waiting and they may only step out of view when the First AD is at the point of getting assertive. Naturally: there are many specialists on a film set, all perfectionists, and they all have reputations to protect.

After Final Checks here's the standard countdown, which may vary a bit but you need to be familiar with it, if only to know when you're to start acting. This – with apologies to those of you who know it all – is the routine:

> FIRST AD: Quiet on the set. [*Or sometimes 'Lock it down' – a warning to the Third AD to ensure nothing interrupts the take, especially if you're in a not altogether controllable location.*]
> FIRST AD: Turn over. [*This signals both the camera and sound departments to start rolling. The sound department rolls first – film shouldn't be wasted – and a second or two later confirms it.*]
> SOUND: Rolling. [*Or 'Speed'.*]
> CAMERA OPERATOR OR FOCUS PULLER: Roll camera.

A moment or two to get it to the right speed, then:

> CAMERA OPERATOR OR FOCUS PULLER: Mark it.

This is to the Clapper Loader who will show the clapperboard (the slate) to the camera, and announce the scene and take number so that these details are on the recording. Then she snaps the clapper down to make the point of synchronisation for audio and picture. The slate is taken out of shot, the camera refocused or slightly re-angled if necessary for the opening framing, and if so:

CAMERA OPERATOR: Set.

FIRST AD: Action. [*Sometimes 'Action' comes from the direc-tor; and sometimes it's preceded by 'Background Action' if extras must already be moving as the main action starts.*]

And at the end:

DIRECTOR: Cut. [*That's unless the Operator has called it first, abandoning a take he already knows is unusable.*]

FIRST AD [*having checked the director's opinion of the take*]: Going again. [*Or, if everyone's happy*]: Check the gate.

If it's the latter, it cues the Focus Puller to confirm that the camera has not malfunctioned, and that there's no foreign body in the aperture where the film is exposed. With luck (and it's usually so):

FOCUS PULLER: Gate's clear!

FIRST AD: Moving on.

General relief, and immediate activity towards the next set-up.

There are variations, depending on this and that: if, unusually, the shot is mute, obviously the sound calls and the clapping of the slate are cut. Or, if the set-up is congested and there's no room for the slate, it may be done at the end of the take, upside down, rather than at the beginning.

Essentially that's it. Remember not to start until 'Action' – it's a surprisingly easy mistake to make.

Shit. It didn't seem much good to you: you felt, after all that waiting, tight and unconfident. Surely they'll do it again. But with a Master they may not: one take will be enough, a second only done as insurance (the 'Lloyds shot') in case there's something physically wrong with the film. The director reassures you: it doesn't matter, the thing to understand about the Master is that it's only for cover, the lowest common denominator;

the initial part of it will probably be used to set the scene, and then possibly a couple of moments during the conversation to remind the viewer of the geography or in case the editor needs to avoid an ugly juxtaposition of closer shots. So think of it as a late rehearsal. In fact, this time there's going to be another take, but it's nothing to do with your work: the lighting as you approach the table needs a little finessing.

Take 2: That's better for them, and you feel more confident of the process: you've broken the ice.

The gate is checked. It's clear. Moving on.

You may still be dissatisfied; but from another perspective, completing the Master is a great moment. Everyone has come together to collaborate, almost in a theatrical way, as they never will again. The actors feel at home, the director remembers the shot as a template for the rest of the day, and may even adjust his subsequent plan in the light of it. You're on the move.

Set-Up 2

The same sequence, shot from the same angle, but on a tighter lens, so you're both a little more prominent. The important element of this may be when you approach and sit at the table: the initial parts of the shot surely won't be used, but it's very useful for the Editor to have this one as an alternative to using too many close shots later.

Take 1: OK, good in fact. You're getting the hang of this: if it's like building an elaborate piece of furniture piece by piece, that's a load-carrying part in place.

The camera team wants another take, for luck.

Take 2: OK. You slightly preferred the first – but you may not be the best judge.

Gate clear. Moving on.

Set-Up 3

A change of angle to make a tight two-shot at the start of the scene, the camera aimed over your shoulder (you're camera left), quite closely at your brother: he looks at you, embraces you, looks at you again, and then moves to the table, the camera panning with him as he begins to break the worst part of his news to you, sitting as he finishes. Your face won't be seen in this, but the back of your head will initially be on the edge of the frame. It's called a dirty two-shot, i.e. it has a main point in focus while the supporting presence is much less distinct. As the camera is quite close on your brother's face, the lighting has to be designed specifically for that, and for the first time you properly notice the **Lighting** team: the **Gaffer**, his **Best Boy** and the **Sparks**.

A Gaffer is not a roll of sticky tape or something you might call your grandfather, but a term of respect for a man who's been in charge of workers since the nineteenth century. On a film set he is very important indeed: he is the Chief Electrician, and he consults with the Director of Photography, who will take advice from him. In fact their relationship is intimate: DOPs will always try to use their usual Gaffer, sometimes trusting him to create lighting states which he will then simply refine. The Gaffer knows exactly the right colour gel to put on a light to achieve an effect indoors, and outdoors he can transform midday into a beautiful sunset. The lights flickering on an actor's face from passing traffic or a subway train are no problem to him. His Sparks, or Lighting Technicians, haul the lamps around and connect them, making sure it doesn't all go bang. To achieve the Gaffer's tricks, they come with an armoury of diffusers to modulate the light, and plywood stencils called gobos to suggest the dappled light coming through trees perhaps. Once they've established your key light – which is what it says, the main one illuminating you from the front or one side – they may use those large incongruous-looking sheets of polystyrene ('poly') reflectors to bounce some light back onto your face from the opposite side; or, conversely, black fabric flags ('solids') to reduce the light on the non-key side and increase contrast – a very typical cinematic effect. For the time being it's your brother's face they're looking at. His key light might be an imagined window where the camera originally was, opposite the door, and, depending on the time of day, some might need to be bounced onto his right, 'door', side.

The Gaffer's assistant is the **Best Boy**, or **Assistant Chief Lighting Technician** – much more important than he sounds and certainly not a boy. Like the Gaffer his title is historic: long before film, in the English apprentice system, the 'Best Boy' was the Master's oldest and most responsible pupil. Now Best Boys hire and schedule the crew, order equipment and return it; they're safety experts, they load trucks, they rig locations and sound stages, coordinate second camera units if they're needed. Like the Sparks they know how to Straw a Brute (a nine-kilowatt stack of lamps), Snoot a Pup (attach a cone to a one-kilowatt lamp to narrow its focus), handle a Blonde (a two-kilowatt tungsten lamp), as well as a Kitten, a Wendy and a Honker-Bonker, and how to Break the Neck of a Redhead (sometimes blue, an open-faced lamp of 800 watts which you 'break' by bending it to adjust its focus). I once asked a Gaffer what his requisitioning order to his Best Boy and Sparks for a certain day's filming might be, and here it is:

> From the 55 with 50 foot .2 run to a 4x4x11 to a 100 foot .1 to a 4x45 50 foot 45 – 6x16, 2 x 50 foot 16 to a 2.5 with 216 & CTO as well from the 4x4x11 use a .1 – 63, 100 foot 63 to 63 DIST – 200 foot 32 to a 3 x 16, 30 foot 16 – 16A Y to 2x44 with 75w 5500 with 251 + quarter CTB + 2 x 300 + 2650 both with Snoots and 251.

So there.

The only thing to advise you of about this shot that you're hardly in is the need to keep your standards up. The camera comes off you early, but you really must do your colleague the favour of engaging with him properly on this take as if you were in close-up yourself. At the same time, for obvious technical reasons, you mustn't waggle your head around too much.

Rehearse: it goes OK.

Take 1: Acting fine, but the camera's pan wasn't smooth – not an Operator error exactly, but he feels he could do it better and less distractingly. As time goes by, you may feel that there's always another take for sound, camera or lighting, but rarely for you; if so, it's because there's less margin for error on the technical side, whose mistakes glare more than yours do.

Take 2: Loss of perfection is like a virus. This time your brother sat down too quickly, ducking out of shot, and the camera couldn't hold him in the frame.

Take 3: OK. Do another for luck.

Take 4: OK. Gate clear. Moving on.

Set-Up 4

This is a disconcerting jump in time for you: it's to be a close-up of him again, over your shoulder as you're both seated at the table a little later. In real time you haven't even approached the table yet, but here you are, sitting at it. Don't worry.

The dialogue, though, is moving logically forward: his further explanation of your mother's state; you complaining that he should have told you about it sooner; he protesting that your mother had said in a moment of lucidity that you weren't to be bothered; your anger at that idea, including some guilt that you've given the impression of being too taken up with business to attend to your mother; the sneaking self-knowledge that that could be true. The temperature continues to rise until your brother sees something behind you and shifts his eyeline to it.

We find out later that this is your mother coming in.

Once again, you have the back of your head to the camera but must still inhabit these feelings. Some people would advise you to hold some of your acting back till the shot is on you; but I don't know how you do that while being fair to the other actor. When the camera comes round to you, you're going to want the same from him.

This is the heart of the scene, its acting centre: in every version of it, to state the obvious, remember you're talking to someone only three or four feet away from you, not a large audience of spectators. But on the other hand, don't underproject. Microphones are so powerful now that they can almost record your thoughts: as a result actors sometimes work so quietly that you can't hear your cue at all. I once played a scene with the late great Tom Bell. You couldn't hear him across the desk as we rehearsed; but he knew the instrument inside out and was wonderful on screen. However, he was an exception. If you speak even more quietly on camera than you would in real life, unless you're as vibrant as Tom was, everything flattens and neutralises: you become incomprehensible because you're not articulating at all. Cinema may not be a very linguistic medium, but we do have to hear and be interested, and you're still trying to contact the character you're speaking to. Reach out. I've been to big films and not been able to hear the words at all.

Take 1 is good; but now you hear from the **Sound** department. You're overlapping your dialogue, cutting in a little on your brother's lines (as you might in an argument in life). This, they say, will make a problem for the Editor: the shots of both you and your brother need to be clean and separate and their sound balanced. This is entirely technical, and very unlike the theatre: you just have to do it. You feel bad – you didn't know this and you've spoiled the take even though you were barely in it.

I've heard Sound described as the least assertive people on the set – the quietest, in fact. If so, it may be because they feel they have the least leverage on events: this being a visual medium, theirs is sometimes an underrated department. Their basic decision on each take is practical: whether they will get the best results by bugging the set with hidden microphones, or by using a pole boom or a radio microphone – that magical new device that is dangerously liable to pick up static from, for instance, a silk blouse. They'll usually choose a pole if it's practical, and you will marvel at the steady, upper-arm strength of its operator. The dull task of balancing the vocal volume of two actors who may be working at different levels falls to them; and the job is forever undermined by the acknowledged fact that it can all be post-synchronised if necessary anyway. Certainly there are those who say this overlapping business that spoiled our Set-Up 4, Take 1, is all nonsense – one-person-at-a-time doesn't reflect the way we talk in life, and with all our filming technology, any overlaps can be manipulated later. It's perhaps become a point of professional honour for some Sound Departments to resist this argument.

Take 2: Remembering not to cut in, remembering to keep the temperature up. Unexpectedly the close-up on your brother is allowed to run on a bit (it's always up to the director when to 'cut', and he may like how it's going) to cover his reaction to whatever appears behind you.

OK. Moving on.

Set-Up 5
Essentially the same, but with the camera closer on your brother – a 'clean' single with nothing of you in the shot at all. The mean little person inside you wonders briefly if you're ever going to be on the screen.

In case you're thinking this, let me explain: in terms of time and motion, which more or less governs the working day, it's much easier to keep the camera on one side of the room and light and shoot everything that's to be done from there for the whole length of the scene, and then to turn around and do everything necessary from the other side. It's possible the director will break this rule for the actors' sake, but, since time is money, more likely not. This is especially true if there are to be camera tracks, which take a little while to lay – once down they won't want to take time pulling them up again. The advantage for you is that by the time the camera's on you, you'll have had a lot of practice with the lines and should be feeling at home and relaxed – perhaps more so than your brother, who will have more or less finished by then and may be kicking himself for not having been quite at his best when it was called for.

In any case, you calculate it's your turn now. No, it's time for lunch. You'll be the first shot afterwards. See you in an hour and a bit.

Lunch

A film unit at lunchtime can resemble a well-to-do gypsy village. If you're on location, your choice is whether to eat in the communal bus for company – with technicians, extras and other actors – or, in grand solitude, in your caravan. (If the latter and you're really lucky with your Second AD, he might even offer to bring your meal to you.) Otherwise, while deciding, you stand on a wobbly platform set against the side of the catering van looking up at a man in a chef's hat – like Oliver Twist asking for more, and you've had nothing yet. The guys are invariably charming as well as astonishingly talented; but the physical relationship is supplicatory.

Much as you want comforting, don't overeat – back at work and first up, you won't be so alert if you're busy digesting a beef stew, and then you'll reproach yourself for the rest of the day. Leave plenty of time, maybe half an hour, before you're called back to the set: have a coffee then and start thinking again. That's unless you're one of those very self-confident individuals who just slip in and out of their performance in a second; but there won't be many of them reading this book.

Set-Up 6

With luck you'll now be moving in chronological order through the scene concentrating on you, parallel with what was done for your brother – I don't see why you wouldn't. The difference is that whereas his move to the table was done on a pan (the camera swivelling from a fixed position), yours as you listen to him is to be a tracking shot. This isn't only for variety: if you and the camera are moving along together it might suggest the mounting tension of someone listening to bad news rather than the more perfunctory pan that emphasises only that he wants to get away from you. A slightly extended lunch hour has been a good opportunity to lay down the tracks, like a narrow gauge railway, on which the camera will roll, perfectly smooth and level, on its wheeled 'dolly': you can imagine the spirit-level accuracy that calls for.

Now, this is quite tricky at first. In partnership with the camera operator, you move slowly along, listening carefully to your brother, reacting appropriately, popping in a word; you accelerate as you reach the table, and, at some especially shocking part of his story, you stop. It's quite an elaborate procedure for a simple shot, but effective: it's as if you and the operator were holding hands. In order to get to know each other, you'll have to rehearse more often than with some set-ups, being sure not to vary your speed or distance, accelerating at the same moment and same velocity each time, otherwise the composition will be broken: there must be no surprises for the camera. As you labour with this, remember it might be worse: it could be one of those shots with two people walking forward and the camera tracking alongside, trying to hold both in the same frame, so that their angles to the lens and to each other are near enough constant. And when that's done they have to turn round and do it all again on the opposite angle. Worse yet, that shot is crucially affected by any large discrepancy in height between the two actors, as they both have to be held in frame; in which case the shorter of them might be walking along a little raised wooden walkway, just as, if the sequence were stationary, he might be on a 'pancake' – the kind of box Alan Ladd famously used to stand on.

With luck, there may have been a few moments before lunch to plan and practise this sequence without the tracks; you'll be readier to shoot when you come back and they're down. Or there might be a break now to lay them. You step out; the Second AD, transferring his favours to you after his morning's attendance on your brother, might offer you a(nother) coffee.

As the tracks are laid you watch the **Grips**: so called because in the early days of the movies when cameras were cranked by hand, they were the burly men hanging on to the tripod legs to keep the shot steady. What they were and still are is butch. These are the guys you saw first, the ones with the belts, the wrenches and the clamps. The Grips move the camera around, onto and off its tracks, up and down the stairs and into confined spaces. The **Key Grip** is the equivalent of the Gaffer in Lighting and he too has a Best Boy to book his crew and equipment. As though it were mother's milk, they all understand the odd mixture of bulk and delicacy that constitutes cameras, tripods, dollies, jibs and cranes. They can rig picture cars for the shot through the windscreen of the moving vehicle, mounting camera and lights all around its bonnet. If the camera is mounted on a crane for a high shot, a minimum of two Grips collaborates closely with the specialist Crane Operator, for safety's sake. In many ways the buck stops with them: people will be climbing on to and walking around their heavy equipment, and the Key Grip could be held responsible for injuries. The DOP and Operator utterly depend on this department; and their jargon tends to be the most impenetrable on the set.

As for you, with a shot like this, part of your collaboration with the operator is to be sure to Hit Your Marks. Or rather, Hit the Groucho, the taped cross or obstacle on the floor that the Focus Puller has provided as your ideal position to stop. This is tricky, but again, it could be worse: you could be running to the table and skidding to a halt on that exact mark – right foot here, left there, weight slightly on the left – before doing your line. Our example is relatively simple; still, if you over- or under-shoot, you'll go out of frame or out of focus. It can be a pain, even offending some of your instincts, but there's no escaping it in filming, and it comes to be a pleasure. Prepare carefully: rehearse starting your journey on the same foot each time and remember how many steps it's likely to take to reach the mark. Practise until it's a muscle memory. They'll all love you if you pull it off, they really will, and you may even get that most precious of gestures on a film set, more precious even than a slap on the back from the director – a discreet thumbs-up from the Operator.

Of course all this technical stuff coincides with what feels like the first real acting you've had to do – your character is getting a piece of news and responding to it. No, not responding to, but absorbing it: there's a big difference. This is part of your life's work, the permanent review of your experience and observation. What actor would think of doing what Romania's dictator Nicolae Ceauşescu did when he was summarily sentenced to immediate execution: while his wife broke down operatically, he just irritably flung his hat down on the table in front of him as if he'd suddenly remembered some trivial, forgotten thing. Your life will involve building a library of such odd human reactions for use in your work. Unfortunately, the fiction business sometimes asks for fictional reactions: to keep the story going you play shorthand Surprise, Shock or Pleasure to show the audience as quickly as you can what you're feeling. But in fact you're building a false repertoire, a whole array of acting alibis. When did you ever look at the telephone in your hand in surprise when the other party has hung up on you? Never, but I've often seen it done in a film or play. When did you last put your hand over your mouth (rather than your ears) when you heard bad news? Not as recently as you've seen it done on the screen. This kind of acting is a little like answering a dumb question in an interview: you tell the truth, but in a stupid way.

An American actress I once worked with – she played Dr Jane Watson to my Sherlock Holmes, if you can believe that – used to talk of the acting requirements in the general run of episodic television, of which she'd done a lot. (She might as well have been speaking of any kind of filming where there's overt pressure to get it done, rather than the pleasant illusion that there's plenty of time in hand even if there's not.) She said that just as the job of the director was to tell the story and capture attitudes, fast, that of the actor was often a matter of making Appropriate Faces quickly. The event happens, the kid falls off the roof, and the camera looks at those involved to pick up their reactions. That's the language and it's not, after a while, much to do with life. In fact it plays to an actor's least advisable instinct: that if the camera is looking at you, you ought to give it something. And since the eventual cutting may be neurotic and panicky, if the shot comes to rest on you at all, you'd better have something ready.

This sort of bad screen shorthand is sometimes almost inevitable. But though filming can feel like designing a vast jigsaw puzzle, mechanical and hermetic, your audience – huge, unknown, and in any case living in the far distance, the other side of all the post-production – will expect an absolute naturalness. Fortunately, you're not alone in the elaborate construction of the spontaneous effect: there's the cunning of the lighting, the cinematography, even the music to be added; the angle of your face, the unprepared flick of an eye. All this can help you out a lot, allowing you to do a bit less yourself than you thought you had to. We all know that the best screen acting is when the actor, so to speak, does nothing – no face is pulled and there's precious little change in the eyes. But we still see that he or she is thinking, and as in the case I quoted of De Niro in *New York, New York*, by some alchemy we seem to know what the thought is. This is what the actors you admire do all the time – as you so often say of them, they don't appear to act at all, they just are.

So, for the time being, just take the impact of your brother's news and don't demonstrate; and don't worry – if you're not doing enough the director will soon tell you. You try a take, but with a shot like this, everyone has to be sure. The team (and you if invited) may huddle around a video monitor (what did they used to do without them?). They think it's OK – but they need one for safety.

And then another. Three takes. You're becoming an expert; and maybe you even stop worrying about which you yourself thought was the best.

Gate clear. On.

Set-Up 7

Continuing where you left off, you're to sit down into the chair and do the dialogue you did with your brother this morning – another 'dirty two'. The decision will have been to start this new shot with you sitting down rather than finishing the previous one with it. If it had been part of the tracking shot it would have been more difficult to execute – a downward tilt at the end of a track – and would in any case look odd, because your brother wouldn't be in the shot and it would be as if the camera were between you and him. Instead the director assumes that at the end of the previous shot the Editor will cut back to your brother and then to this new shot of you sitting.

Take 1: Felt good to you, but they want another, straight away, while the concentration holds.

Take 2: OK, but you're approached by a figure, carrying a very big file with many pencils in its little silver clamps, and a stopwatch. The Continuity Person has always been one of the few figures in filming that the outside world – by which I probably mean newspaper cartoonists – thought it could recognise. There would be the Producer chewing on a big cigar, the Director wearing a peaked poker cap and yelling at everyone, and the anxious Continuity Girl by his side with the file and the watch, perhaps in love with him.

I make her female only because it's traditional, like the genders I've used through this chapter; that won't last much longer, but the movie tradition that some roles are male and others female still, just about, holds. The physically arduous jobs like Grips remain a male province, and there was a time when being a First AD was thought to involve so much macho shouting that it was man's work; nowadays about one in three of them are women. Also, there are quite a few Continuity Boys beginning to come through, and some Best Girls. If, meanwhile, Continuity remains woman's work, it may be because the typing and paperwork and multi-tasking doesn't feel as sexy to a young man as carting equipment around or operating a big camera.

In any case the Continuity Person's title has now been corrected to still the more neutral **Script Supervisor**. This elevation is right enough, but it slightly disguises the nub of the job, which is to be in charge of an entire genre – Continuity Editing – which is extremely demanding and specialised. Film continuity is absolutely vital, but its human operative is unlikely to make many friends. Although each department (including you) is responsible for its own logic, anyone can make a mistake, and the Script Supervisor is the expert who is ready, embarrassingly, to point it out. If this were an eating scene, she's the one who'd be telling you that in the last take of this bit there were peas on your fork, not carrots. Or that you scratched your left eyebrow on a certain word in the master shot, and so will need to do it in the same place on the equivalent close-up; otherwise the editor may be faced with cutting from a master in which you raised your hand to your face for the scratch to a close-up in which your hand is securely by your side, then back to the master where your hand is coming down from your scratched eyebrow. Given the firmness with which the Script Supervisor needs to assert this, it's ironic that in the end it may not matter: the Editor may not want to do it in that order anyway. On the other hand if he does, he will be much put out by the scratch business (might even, in his heart of hearts, blame you for it).

As for the director, he may not want to be reminded that the road was wet when he did the previous shot yesterday and now it's dry. What must be really hard for a Script Supervisor is to raise an objection to a popular take on the basis that it won't cut together, only to be greeted with a dismissive wave as if they were a fly, this having been the best take for performance. At such moments the Supervisor must feel no one's on their side: and indeed there are directors so senior or so revolutionary that they abandon the rules, confident that the public will be having such a good time they won't notice: certainly you didn't preach continuity to Jean-Luc Godard or Stanley Kubrick.

You might say therefore that a necessary quality for a Script Supervisor is discretion, the ability to take a calculated risk. The job aims, after all, for an impossible perfection. No actor wants to be held down to a gesture that he probably found instinctively on the first take and doesn't necessarily want to repeat for the rest of the day's shooting, any more than he would want to repeat it in a subsequent performance on the stage. There are Script

Supervisors who are over-zealous to be sure, as if the action of correction were to be relished for its own sake; but there are also more talented ones who give the actors their head a bit and guess that enough editing alternatives will present themselves to harmonise everything in the end. So it's an oddly existential job, both fragile and assertive, its very best efforts not always welcome but always, necessarily, heard.

The Script Supervisor also holds the bible of the film. When it comes to editing, weeks after the shoot and with all memories fading, this is the person who's noted down in a great book every detail of every shot, including the ones that were abandoned for technical or line-fluffing reasons; and, for each of them, the size of the lens and everything else. Whatever the director or Editor needs to refer to, it's there if it happened. Then, if not before, the Script Supervisor is appreciated.

And now here she comes, to point out that last time you held your shoulder bag differently. Try not to think, Christ, Cate Blanchett wouldn't put up with this: she's only doing her job. If (and I don't know) the Cate Blanchetts just do what they feel on the take and leave it to the editor to deal with, then it's their privilege; in their case there may well be a seemingly infinite number of set-ups and therefore variety of editing choices. For the time being, you should try and do what you're told. It's in your interests: what a shame if your close-up at the point the tears start flowing is unusable because you had your right hand up at your mouth and not your left as you did in the wider shot. One way or another, you'll do yourself a favour by becoming a minor expert on your own continuity, and then you'll probably be left alone.

Take 3: Good, but you didn't like it. You obeyed Continuity but it cost you your concentration – no, your sense of who your character really is. You want to do a fourth: and there are many actors who would support you. I don't though, not really, because I'm no longer certain that the actor knows best about his own work. What I would say is, don't ask for it: it amounts to a criticism of the director's judgement. He knows his business, and he may have got what he needs, whatever you think. Once in a while I've asked for one more take 'for me', only to find it was significantly worse.

Gate clear. On.

Set-Up 8

This is quite a moment: your first ever close-up. You're to look down a lens that's like a great glass eye trained – curiously? thoughtfully? intrusively? – on your face. This, you know, is where the real test is and it's certainly what you've been waiting for. As make-up and costume fuss over you, it's as if you were about to have an operation. It's time to stop gossiping with any colleagues who may just have done their stuff and, relatively off-duty, are in need of a chat, and to concentrate hard, hoping to stay this side of tension. In a moment, after all, you're going to have to stop your jaw locking and your eyes staring madly while you try to think your character's special private thought with twenty pairs of eyes staring at you in a dispassionate way and several hundredweight of machinery crowding you into a corner.

Use every moment to stay loose and prepare: a technical delay is an opportunity to run the lines, even if your brother is chewing a doughnut. Don't go off the boil, or suddenly they'll be ready to shoot when you're not. You may only get one rehearsal – or, if the scene has been covered quite extensively, not even that – so don't be caught out.

Much is made of the difference between shooting a big wide shot and a close-up, and how you must adjust your scale for each. Well, yes and no. You can't fling your arms about and gaze from extreme side to side in a close-up, that's true; but there's also a fallacy about 'going small'. You've still got to be in the moment and feeling the feelings. Again, the director will advise if you get it wrong.

At the same time, try not to overplan: with luck, you've practised so much that when the moment comes, the ideas may, paradoxically, strike you afresh. The camera loves the unguarded moment and rears away from calculation. This, by the way, is one of the reasons that you may not be the best judge of a take: the one you thought was an improvement on its predecessor may have been the one you coated with a slight sheen of skilfulness.

A close-up may also involve Eyelines and (from your colleague) Lines Off. The eyeline you take to convince the audience that you're looking at your brother is not the natural one with which you looked at him in the wide shot; with the camera this close the angle will be more acute, just to the side of the lens (very occasionally, into it), because that's how the perspective works. To give an eyeline from offscreen, I once sat next to a camera and leaned sideways to place my head on the little platform right underneath it, as if I'd been decapitated and it were being presented on a plate to the wicked king.

However, your colleague may not even be there this time – there may be no room for him, much as you hope to see him peering at you through a little gap between the camera and the **Boom Operator**. He may have been stood down, or be changing for another scene, and you have to imagine him. It may be just as well: you could be better off looking at a little white mark in the mattebox than be straining to glimpse him through a forest of equipment and people. The more difficult stars don't always do you the courtesy of supplying Lines Off, but most do: it's a point of some etiquette. It's obviously very unhelpful to find yourself acting opposite the Script Supervisor – as unhelpful as when you went for the job and the casting director blundered through the lines off and you had to pretend she was your exciting boyfriend. Even if he's there, the actor giving you these cues won't exactly be on his mettle – the camera's not on him and his voice is unlikely to be used in the edited version – but you've a right to expect the same concentration as you gave him.

If it's just a matter of looking silently at something off camera, do pay close attention to whatever little landmark the DOP or operator asks you to look at. As you get ready to shoot, practise looking up at that spot, or across to that spot, whichever it is, until it becomes second nature. Don't be vague, or leave it to chance, or on the take you may be distracted by the absurdity of looking at a tea urn rather than a human being.

Take 1: You've been doing the lines all morning; now, amazingly, you suddenly forget them and grind to a halt. Cut. Nobody minds except you – and you mind a lot. But it happens, and it's not like the theatre – you don't have to make amends to the audience, we just throw away the take. Go again.

Take 2: This time your brother, doing his lines off, dries. It shouldn't matter but it's hard for you to deal with. You might muddle through as if he'd said the right thing, or the shot might be abandoned. You're pissed off with him for not concentrating. He says sorry, and you have to go again, even though the shot is on you. With slightly less good grace, the director agrees.

Take 3: Aeroplane, church bells, some other unidentifiable sound from outside the set, sent by a malevolent deity. Naturally, and insistently, Sound wants another.

Take 4: By now the frustrations have upped your game in some mysterious way. You hit it plumb. It's a defining moment: everyone is happy, you know it was your best take, and you hold your breath. The Focus Puller (even nowadays) takes a little torch and a magnifying glass, opens the lens hood and peers into the lens. He's looking for the legendary Hair in the Gate. This is one thing nobody has found a non-human way to prevent; nobody can control hair, dust, or, more commonly, celluloid that's stripped a little as it passed over its sprockets and caused little filaments to fly across the lens. Once magnified, they are hideous and utterly taboo.

A hair in the gate is rare, but as you wait to see whether your best and surely unrepeatable work is ruined (there are at least a dozen others feeling the same) you feel alone, reflecting whether you're naturally lucky or unlucky, whether your glass in life is generally half full or half empty. Hours seem to pass. Then the Focus Puller straightens up, looks at the operator, and speaks: 'Gate's clear.'

~

That's probably enough. Much of the imagined scene is still to do but essentially that's the way things go forward. During the rest of the day there could be a shot down from the ceiling, recordings of wild tracks (sound without vision), or the camera might move across the set to the other, 'door' side – raising the old question, often selectively ignored these days, of 'crossing the line' (theoretically the camera always has to stay the same side of two actors when they play a scene together). The thirty-degree rule, whereby you must change the angle by that amount when you do a new shot on the same character in the same position, may be ignored too, as it cheerfully is from time to time, notably by Steven Spielberg in *Lincoln*. Then it's a Wrap (which actually stands for Wind Reel And Print). You may yourself be about to run into a second day's work: if not, the First AD, in a moment of gallantry (but forgetting you still have the exterior to do), will announce publicly to the crew that you're done, and everyone applauds you in farewell. And there's your day: maybe three edited minutes in the can.

You go home and try not to fret. You watch a movie. Look at your favourites and figure how they do it. Look at Streep. Or Jennifer Lawrence in *Winter's Bone*. Or Marion Cotillard in almost anything. Or look at Ray Winstone's control of the eyeline, the economy and compacted power of his acting, as if it were being reduced for the medium rather than worked up for it. Have a look lately at Damian Lewis and Claire Danes in *Homeland* playing a fifteen-minute scene entirely in two dirty twos. Figure out whether it was perhaps done on a single two-camera set-up looking both ways – that is, shooting simultaneously, one camera on each face, as such a scene was between Robert De Niro and Al Pacino in Michael Mann's *Heat* – or with two separate set-ups in the conventional way; and why they were dirty twos rather than close-ups. At the same time try not to be a bore, interrupting your partner's attention with 'Christ, that's a bad cut . . . I'd have used a 60 millimetre and snooted the pup.' But yes, watch movies in the evenings instead of worrying about your own day's work. You're beginning the great neurosis of filming, writ even larger now you're home – I Could Have Done Better. Why Didn't I Think of That at the Time Instead of Now? Will They Use the Take I Thought the Best? Well, them's the breaks: cricketers only return to the crease in their dreams. Just leave it and try to go to bed sober if you're working the next day. Don't worry about it. In fact, never worry at all. It shows.

~

I've had less to say about film acting than I expected: many of the normal rules apply. Martin Scorsese says there are only four notes to give to an actor – louder, softer, slower and faster – just as some crusty old rep director in the theatre might once have said Be Louder and Funnier. But Michael Newell has a revealing thing to say about the difference between stage and screen acting, and it links up with the distinction between British and American actors. In the theatre the actor is a storyteller: he's in charge. In a movie he is anything but: the storytelling is in other hands, and his job is to provide the director with brilliantly executed bubbles of intense feeling and states of mind, like so many bulbs of strong garlic in a stew. A pair of spectacles to be used in a part, such as Gary Oldman's in *Tinker Tailor Soldier Spy*, can take an age to choose – it may be seen larger than life two hundred times in a film, so it really matters. American actors are paramount at this kind of detail because they genetically understand the medium and may not have been distracted by the theatre. However Michael also says that European actors, being theatre-based, provide something which for him is inestimable: a technical discipline which allows them invariably to hit their marks and find their keylight and all the rest of it, together with a proper discipline in handling the text and playing it well. The fashion whereby star actors sometimes don't bother to learn their lines but have them fed through a bug in their ear, he says, could only have started in America.

In other ways, good film acting both is, and isn't, much different from its stage equivalent: it isn't insofar as the basic alchemy is the same, but it is since of course the camera picks up any lie, histrionic hint or undigested thought in nothing flat. Like the Esperanto of technical terms, the received wisdom on screen acting is entertaining but not always useful. On the one hand the director Michael Cacoyannis used, valuably, to tell me: Always Come Up Into the Shot – train your eyes below the camera and raise them into the lens, don't bring them down from above: it's always better. Unscrupulous old lags will tell you of various tricks that ensure the editor can't cut away from you before you've finished speaking. No doubt, but that is X-rated information, and very ignoble. The best you can do, every time, is to try to create the right circumstances for yourself. It seems to me that to be at ease on the set, it helps to understand what's going on, and then act as truthfully as you can and don't worry about anything else.

A hint on temperament: in a way the theatre requires adrenalin, the movies the opposite. You usually need nervous energy

117

to get onstage and start working at a fairly high voltage if you're to offer something worth paying money to see. Oddly enough, filming is rather the opposite: apart from very emotional scenes which will always require your all, nervous energy generally baffles the camera, so it's often more a matter of calming down than psyching yourself up. Be neutral, and let the lines take you where they want. You may do something you hadn't planned, and all the better. Or you may do virtually nothing at all: after all, a face in close-up is as often hiding its feelings as showing them.

What, after all, does film acting aspire to? Absolute verisimilitude. Think of the best screen performances you know. In my case, Marlon Brando picking those bits of straw off the wire of his pigeon coop as he begins to fall for Eva Marie Saint in *On the Waterfront*. Why do I still remember it, even better than the famous scene in the taxi cab? Meryl Streep making *Sophie's Choice*, when you believed the actress was collapsing in front of you – as indeed she was. Your mental list will be different, but mine tend to be moments that seem offhand, found on the spot, their depth lightly carried. Shadow moves, displacement activities, small gestures that reveal everything. Paul Scofield in *Radio Days*. Montgomery Clift, over and over. Marilyn Monroe in *Some Like It Hot*. Jack Lemmon in *The Apartment*, probably the best example of his gift for speeding up real life, all its highs and lows, so that it becomes funny without short-changing its realism, its emotional truth.

Perhaps logically, there are directors who prefer, or occasionally say they prefer, or at one stage or another do prefer, to work with non-actors, at least some of the time. Ken Loach of course. Miloš Forman's *A Blonde in Love*, one of the loveliest and most pungent comedies of the last half-century, was shot almost exclusively with friends, relations and likely types he met on the bus. He believed that non-actors, who would be terrified of a live audience, weren't at all shy in front of a camera, because to them it was just an inanimate Thing. Professionals, he says, love an audience reacting to them but are scared by the impassivity of the camera. Well, maybe. But he said this soon before he went to Hollywood and worked on *One Flew Over the Cuckoo's Nest* with Jack Nicholson, who doesn't seem particularly nervous of the camera. I still think – and I would, wouldn't I – that professionals tend to be the best people for the job; but there's no doubt that getting rid of everything extraneous, stripping it down to a simple thought so there seems to be no professional skill, will obsess you all your life if you work in films. Dustin Hoffman says he likes about a minute or two of most performances he's ever given; Al Pacino once tried to recall and re-shoot a film after it had been released. We may not approve of non-professionals getting the job, but most of us will admit that the untrained sometimes have the edge when they're gifted. Especially children: look at *Shadowlands*, at the scene when the little boy plays side by side with Anthony Hopkins. On the other hand kids have to be handled right, and in particular not over-rehearsed: they're unlikely to be able to do endless takes to the same standard. Adults too: though some of us get better and better with each take, some get it right the first time and then go gradually downhill.

In any case, as you sit glumly at home looking at the masters of the art, you do have another chance. Remember the taxi sequence and your run along the street to the front door that hasn't been shot today? It's probably been scheduled for four weeks later, in a different city. Because of the agitation and movement in the action, it might well be done with the miraculous Steadicam – the relatively recent beast that used to be called a hand-held camera – which is a bit of a misnomer as, at forty kilos or so, it takes not so much hands but brute strength to pick up, let alone cart about. For a moving shot a director used to have to use either a dolly (the mechanism that did the tracking shot above as you approached the table), or perhaps a crane with an arm reaching through the air, or a hand-held. However, track-laying is finicky and time-consuming; a crane is elaborate and expensive; and no operator could avoid shaking, if only minutely, the hand-held, which is nowadays kept for news reporting and other events that you can't rehearse.

The Steadicam is a marvel in three parts. It starts at one end as a complicated harness worn by the operator (who is usually a specialist hired by the day, perhaps bringing his own equipment), which is then attached to an arm constructed on a spring-and-pulley system to keep the movement at one end more or less independent of the movement at the other. On its other end is an armature with the camera mounted at one extremity and a counterbalance opposite it. The counterbalance carries a battery pack and a monitor (rather than a viewfinder, which the camera's motion relative to the operator makes impossible). The combined weight of counterbalance and camera makes for a mass not easily disturbed by small body movements: so the operator gets his smooth shot even when moving quickly over an uneven surface. If it's adjusted right, he can even take his hands off the Steadicam entirely: he can twist and turn inside the harness and it'll still stay steady. Or he can rest his hand on the camera handle and guide it. When a focus adjustment is needed during the shot, it's done by a wireless remote operated by his assistant. So this astonishing piece of ironmongery can do almost anything – look at the uninterrupted five-and-a-half-minute Dunkirk sequence in *Atonement*.

~

You'll never understand all the lacunae of filming, all the technicalities, every last job description; on the other hand you may be thrilled by this magnificent medium, one of the greatest of the last two centuries. To state the obvious, in the theatre the audience can look at the lights and the proscenium while the actors do what they do exactly at the moment it's seen; it's odd to think that behind every tense, brilliant scene in a movie was the same huddle of microphones, cameras, men with gaffer tape, shouting, settling down, going again, studio bells for silence, shifting of reflectors, jokes off the set and even on, good and bad humour.

You may sometimes find filming mechanical and laborious and lacking the sense of community you generally find in the theatre. It takes an age to do and so much happens after you've gone. Actors come and go, disappearing after their last shot: you don't know when they've left and you didn't say goodbye. Hence the slightly forced habit at the start of the day of a hail-fellow-well-met greeting – 'And a very good morning to you, Mr Pennington, sir'; 'The moment has arrived, sir' (to go to the set) – which jollies everything along but isn't quite the same as collaboration.

Film is a different organism, but it's similar from the point of view of anthropology as well as efficiency: like a new human experiment, its character will always be a little different. If the Artistic Director in a theatre is hands-on, if the director of the particular project is accessible and reasonably calm, if stage management are friendly as well as efficient, and if you go in with a good heart, there will be goodwill everywhere, so by and large a good time. But any weakness in the chain of command makes it wobble dangerously. Likewise in a film, tension between departments, an unkind director, ADs who are not sufficiently briefed, all mean that inefficiency and unease spread quickly. It comes from the top of course, whatever that's seen to be.

There are people on a film set who, however hard-nosed they may be in the office, are largely diplomatic when it comes to you – an agreeable atmosphere on a set is obviously the ideal for you to do your best work. It doesn't always happen of course. If you open your mouth to say your first line and you've not met the director, or you suspect that he hasn't taken the trouble to learn your name, you're going to be nervous or upset. In the theatre all the ceremonies of a first day's rehearsals – cordial support for the designer, good cheer from the director after the readthrough, however well or badly it's gone – are specifically designed to encourage: the rest can wait till tomorrow. It's possible that friction sometimes produces good art; but in any medium that's collaborative, it's best to leave all its potential inside yourself where it belongs.

In any case, you don't have to decide now between these two giant beasts, and perhaps you'll never be in a position to do so. Try to love them both.

PART TWO – The Stage

5 Getting Hired

The Audition – The Wait – The Phone Call – An Interlude of Pleasure

What's the best way to make an actor complain? Give him a job.
ANCIENT PROVERB

When I used to go to chapel at school I always wanted to have a look behind the reredos to see how it was physically constructed and if there was anything as holy back there as the images on its front. Now I enjoy standing behind a canvas-and-pinewood frame that from the front looks like an Egyptian palace or a Renaissance portico, a restaurant kitchen or a library, judging the angle to stay just out of sight of the people who've bought tickets at the sides before taking a single step out into a pool of light and their view. Perhaps you too are the kind of person who likes peeping through curtains to see an assembling crowd. Perhaps like me you used to thrust a script into your visitors' hands when they arrived for Christmas lunch and insist on a rehearsal before any present-opening to prepare for the afternoon's performance of a self-penned play – in my case generally featuring myself sitting cross-legged in front of a teepee uttering grave and beautiful thoughts while my visitors handed me my props.

Perhaps you couldn't be stopped from doing handstands for Daddy when he came home from work; perhaps you're old enough to regret that with the passing of curtains you can no longer get the sudden smell of the painted scenery, released by the curtain's rising, billowing into the stalls. Perhaps you're someone who gets tired doing the washing-up but feels as fresh as a daisy after two three-hour shows and could probably do them all over again. Are you moved by the idea that you're inheriting fairly esoteric skills that have been practised for two thousand years, ever since a masked actor stepped out from the Chorus and spoke in his own individual right under the ancient Greek sky? Do you like the idea of an illusion beginning at exactly the same time each evening and continuing, usually without being interrupted, to exactly the same finishing moment too, one that seems to interest a thousand people at a time, all gathered in silence? Or the fact that this ritual, apparently of superhuman difficulty while you prepare it, becomes after a few weeks well within your stride? Or do you like sitting in a small underground dressing room eating a sandwich while someone on the stage says your character is the most beautiful woman in the history of the world? Would you rather cut your own head off than be on the Northern Line commute at 8 a.m. every weekday of your life?

Good. So you'd quite like to be in the movies, but really your heart belongs in the spit and sawdust. So let's talk about the theatre.

~

First, get the part. The process of auditioning in the theatre has become a byword for everything in our profession that is gruelling, painful, and, once in a while, dreamlike. The word itself, with its associated emotions, has passed into areas beyond show business. Laymen use it to describe any professional encounter where they must justify themselves to a not-necessarily-approving authority figure in order to secure a job; it's also the event cited by the same laymen when they tell you they could never be an actor. As they say it, the look in their eye combines admiration for your courageous life choice with contempt that you would expose yourself to such ritualised humiliation so readily, so often.

What they're most often imagining is not so much the intent lining-up of an actor for a particular part – the provisional shaping up to the character, the homework and research beforehand – but the dreaded General Audition. That particular trial, for which you choose your own pieces to display your range in the hope of impressing a management in a general way, is pretty much a thing of the past. This is mainly because the seasonal repertory companies who used to put together a troupe of versatile actors for nine months in a succession of shows have largely disappeared. An exception is the Royal Shakespeare Company – in this sense the epitome of a seasonal rep – who generally recruit for a sequence of interlocking productions and therefore have to assess you both for acting range and staying power. Your choices of piece for them, as for the old reps, might be one classical, one modern, which you'll have selected to demonstrate effortless shifts between poetic tragedy and knockabout comedy, between high style and street cred. In times past you might, on the day, have waited in a corridor or waiting room – the auditions would usually be running late, despite the curtness with which they were conducted – and once on the stage you might never see the director, only hear his voice briefly booming out of the dark auditorium; according to legend at least, it would sometimes interrupt you with a brutal cry of 'NEXT!' to dismiss you and bid forth the next in line. The current RSC wouldn't behave like that, and actually few managements ever did.

In one area the old roughness may survive, and you may have experienced it. Remember your drama-school audition, when you were charged a fee for the privilege, so you already felt like a briber rather than an applicant? You might have been put at ease for a moment before you started, or the opposite may have happened: it may all have been made as intimidating as possible, the interviewers ignoring you, not looking up from their pads, or even openly hostile, along the lines of What Makes You

Think You Should Take Our Time? This certainly had the benefit of testing a mettle that was about to be tested daily for the
rest of your life: they wanted to know if you could even begin to
cope and would go on coping. It was unpleasant but maybe sal-
utary; you weathered it and you got your place. You're unlikely,
once you have the elementary dignity of being a professional, to
encounter that kind of treatment again.

Still, since there's nothing like feeling like helpless beasts in a
bazaar to raise actors' hackles, at times like this they can get cross
about even the slightest slight. The sight of a demeaning queue
ahead of them is as incendiary for some people as seeing their
predecessor emerging from the therapist's waiting room as they
wait for their own precious one-to-one session. I once turned up
to audition for the legendary Tony Richardson, who was casting
Nicol Williamson's *Hamlet*, after a liberal liquid lunch, under-
taken no doubt to keep up my self-esteem: I found a long line of
hopefuls stretching through the wings and down the corridor. I
declared I was in a hurry, jumped the queue, and went on, and
was later told that I had secured the job because without taking
off my donkey jacket I immediately sat on the edge of the stage
to talk chummily to Richardson with my feet swinging in the
orchestra pit. It may be so; more probably it had to do with the
cunning calculation I'd made (I was auditioning for Horatio) to
do a piece of Laertes instead, as I reckoned that was my part.
A few lines into it Richardson interrupted with expressions of
joy and an immediate offer. I don't recommend the first half of
this story as an example: this was the 1960s, and such tearaway
behaviour – perhaps sadly, perhaps not – doesn't play so well
any more; but the dropping of a broad and evident hint about
what part you should be playing without actually asking for it
is worth remembering for occasional use. Anyway Richardson
was so pleased to have found, as he thought, a junior version of
the hellraiser that Williamson himself was that, as well as giving

me Laertes, he immediately screen-tested me for the lead in his film of *Ned Kelly*. Then he realised that he was dealing with just another averagely insecure young actor with no special existential flair, and promptly lost interest. Mick Jagger got the part, and I've somehow ended up with the reel of film of my test (no one else had any use for it) lodged in my attic like a reverse Dorian Gray, youthful enough but putting out a slightly chemical smell in its decay, a symbol of disappointment long past.

The *Hamlet* experience was a long way from a general audition – I was there to read for one part and managed to hijack another. And nowadays you generally know from your agent what you're going for, and will have prepared to do it as well as you can without knowing what the director is after. Or indeed whether he is really interested in you, rather than dutifully going through a list of suggestions made by the casting director, now sitting next to him and doing the honours, such as they are.

How intensively should I prepare?

Very. Whatever kind of audition it is, get to know the pieces you're going to do inside out, so that they hold no surprises when nerves, perhaps, assail you. You need to follow their ins and outs, their sounds and shapes and colours, so that you can do them as if you'd just thought of the words for the very first time. Behind the spontaneity the director, with any luck, will sense the good actor's impassioned intimacy with the text. So go through it regularly, develop your ideas, play it this way and that, both mutter and shout – but do least on the day itself, when the best plan may be lightly to brush it up, rather as most male actors do little more than check their trouser zips a moment before going onstage. Try to feel the ground through the soles of your feet: it's your security, saving you from becoming invisible. And breathe steadily: that's your fuel.

Should I dress for the part?

Perhaps, but only discreetly: suggest your suitability rather than insisting on it. It's probably wise not to wear torn jeans if the character's a toff, but equally not an uncomfortable suit that you'll feel funny in. And best not to follow the example of an actress who turned up to audition for *Cats* with a cat's tail and whiskers. On the other hand, maybe she got the part on the basis of being a good sport, so you never know. Most theatre (as opposed to television) directors are used to the idea of inner transformation and aren't deceived by a costume.

Try not to be too early and be sure not to be late – a major mistake. Seem enthusiastic but not needy. Before or after you do your piece there may be pleasantries, some chat about the play which you'll find difficult to concentrate on. The fact is that for all the horror stories about bad treatment at auditions, most are run in a courteous and considerate way: directors appreciate that everyone in the room already has a job except you. The strain is so obvious that decency generally prevails, and the accumulated fatigue of those running the event as the day wears on is as carefully concealed as it would be by a competent host at a party that's gone on too long.

Then you read.

How to get started?

Well, they'll tell you. If, unusually, it's a general audition and you've chosen the speech, don't waste too much energy explaining its place in the play, let alone your opinion about it. Once, doing some workshops on audition technique, I listened to a young actress telling me the whole story of *Waiting for Godot* (such as it is) as a preparation for doing her excerpt. As the clock is ticking, there's a real danger of irritation here. On another occasion a student placed an empty chair in the middle of the stage and asked me to imagine the listener in it; he then positioned himself significantly to the side and downstage of it. The interest, of course, became the chair, exclusively: my imagination played over its infinite possibilities, as if I were watching a long and particularly fascinating reaction shot in a movie.

These are obvious mistakes. Remember the stage is there for you, take it with all the assurance you can muster, and get going with a minimum of fuss.

And as it's happening?

Damn, it's not working. This is not the performance you gave in your bathroom, at the top of your game. You were at ease with the material then, relaxed and confident, flexible and full of the joy of performing. Achieving that state now is about as likely as it is on a first night, though it can happen: the gods of acting are capricious. More likely, you'll be doing what we all occasionally kick ourselves for, Listening to Yourself: there's a little whiff of self-consciousness, caution and loss of pace; most of all, no spontaneity. Good acting seems unguarded, especially in a solo piece: the whole point of most soliloquies is to get you from one emotional position to another by articulating your thoughts for the first time, right there and then; only very rarely is it the giving of prepared information. There is such a thing as a show-off speech prepared to intimidate the listener: Mick's riffs about bus routes and beer glasses in Pinter's *The Caretaker* is a favourite, but even then, the sense of it coming off freshly for the first time is as delightful for the audience as it is alarming for Davies the tramp.

So nerves are making everything come out a bit differently from your plan. And the room is smaller or larger than you expected, the human eyes looking at you disconcerting; there may be noise from the studio next door, somebody may come in in the middle. If so, incorporate it if you can – you'll get extra points for the improv. Certainly there's no point trying to pull your horse strictly back onto its track: it may be taking an equally good route over the hedges. Hold the reins lightly. Better to do what you've never done before than a muddled version of what you planned. If you started in C major and drift into E flat, so be it: if you've prepared well, you're more in control than you think. Acting is all about making a hundred fast decisions on the hoof; you're about to spend a lifetime carefully preparing and then dealing with the unexpected. Peter Brook once (rashly) said that the actor he admired was the one with the courage to change everything on the first night. In an audition, even more so.

Good luck can descend like manna, or bad like hail; some tiny thing can blow you off course, but you may also feel a following wind. The odds of course are that it will be a compromised affair, patchy and uncertain, and you'll fruitlessly go over and over it afterwards. The underlying need for the job is in obvious conflict with the generosity of performing. You've simultaneously got to be open, available and co-operative, and to psych yourself into not giving a damn for the outcome. It's a perfect microcosm for a profession that calls both for vulnerability and devil-may-care.

If the director doesn't like it, or even if he does, he'll get you to do it again. So:

What if he asks me to do it differently?
Do it. It's a code. He's trying to find out what you're like to work with, if you're flexible and can take direction – he may even have preferred the first version. This time, do it as differently as he wants and don't argue. And don't – please don't – apologise afterwards or say it wasn't as good as you can do. That's fishing, and doesn't impress. On the other hand, you may find yourself with a sympathetic director who'll encourage you to talk, and you may want to ask his or her opinion about your take on the speech (not your competence), and whether he'd recommend anything different. In any case, let him dictate the terms – even though, odd as it sounds, it's you who are helping him, to make a decision.

What's he looking for?

There are two sides to the transaction, and you might as well know what encourages or disheartens most directors. They want to see that you're interested in the project and ready to discuss it without the breathless hyperbole that conveys only desire for the job, any job. That you're concentrating. If you can sustain a conversation about the script it gives the director time to expatiate and put you straight, thus filling the time most pleasantly. There is one unavoidable risk here – if you warm to your task and say something particularly intelligent, you may not get the part but find your idea turning up, unlike yourself, in the final production: some directors aren't above picking your brains. On the other hand keeping your counsel can play as defensive sullenness. If you like the script say so, this side of gushing; if you don't, then pretend you do, well enough. Directors are the buyers in a meat market and we're so many working girls leaning in our doorways, offering utter co-operation. Directors aren't all fools and knaves either, though sometimes the strain of working through so many auditions at speed causes them to behave oddly: to enjoy a bewildering private joke with the casting director that excludes you, for instance. But if you had to meet twenty nervous people a day and – if only from politeness – deal with each as if they were the first, you too might need a moment of relief. And the wrong casting decision can be catastrophic – hence the need sometimes for repeated recalls, annoying for the actor, but understandable.

So most directors know what you're going through and in this respect they're probably a lot more understanding than the kind of people who give out jobs in industry, whose instinct for low-grade theatricals causes them to act out rituals of power to keep the interviewee humbled. I recently took part in the selection process for a post in a company on whose Board I sat; most of my colleagues were from the business world, and they all gave terrible performances, as fierce and unforgiving as Alan Sugar in *The Apprentice*. They especially liked it if the applicant was a woman whom they could circle and pounce on like so many barrack-room lawyers.

When your audition's over, don't drive yourself nuts. The French call this *pensées d'escalier* – when you think of your best ripostes after the event. You may deliver your finest performance, muttering to yourself, on the Tube home afterwards. But the redeeming fact is that you never know quite what's gone across: only the close-up camera is better at catching the flash of unmediated personality than the audition process. For all the hard work, you don't know what it is of yourself you've vouchsafed; some unguarded moment could be the very thing, after all, that gets you the job. Don't worry too much, and get on with your day.

Postscript

A series of subtle English nuances plays about the very word 'audition'. Strictly speaking, when you reach a certain eminence in the theatre, you don't audition any more – you go for 'interviews', 'meetings' and 'discussions'. Sometimes you're asked to meet a director about a project with the strong emphasis that you're to have a talk, and certainly not read. Sometimes the director may even ask to come and see you (high status for you). Sometimes it's a meeting for coffee in a neutral place (equal status), or a lunch (slightly higher status for you as it's surely going to be paid for). These are all ways of looking you in the eye and assessing whether working together is going to be OK; of finding out that you don't, regardless of your reputation, smell bad to them. Before the end of the interview the director will perhaps be telling you how much he/she hopes you'll do it; if on the other hand it ends inconclusively, it's likely that he/she is backing off and needs to get out of the room to think again. And you can help: Marlon Brando in his pomp offered to screen-test as Don Corleone in *The Godfather*; Meryl Streep begged on her knees for *Sophie's Choice*. It is a very elegant thing to offer to read if you sense the director is privately a little unsure – perhaps there's a difficult accent to conquer, or you don't look exactly like the part. It's extremely cool and shows flexibility.

It's possible to be offended by some aspects of all this ritual, but I take the view that there's not much point in being offended by anything, not any more. I know actors of my generation who have reacted angrily to the very idea of a meeting if it's not underpinned by a firm offer – they need to know that the part's on the table and they hold the cards – but I think that's out of date and silly. Also there's no point in going on about your Hamlet all those years ago when you're up for the Gravedigger this time. So a word of advice now to my own generation: let's adapt. The world is changing and it's less and less respectful. People rarely seem to answer letters. We need to be flexible, to maintain self-respect and avoid false pride – while being determined, in the words of e. e. cummings, that 'there is some shit I will not eat'. And try not to mourn the fact that we're beginning to call all these variants 'auditions' again, as the Americans have always done. It's just simpler.

~

It all begins with the happy phone call, like the sound of a door swinging open: 'They want you.' I hope of course that you're still on another job when it comes, so that for a moment you get the feeling of continuity that makes sense of an actor's life, even gives a whiff of entitlement: one job followed by another, just as it should be. But if you're not working and you've been muttering discontentedly to yourself (even in the street), arguing with imaginary foes and remonstrating with your agent, then of course it's a red-letter day.

135

It's also the beginning of a blessed entr'acte – the interlude of pleasure between being approved of and the doubtful, doubting business of rehearsing. You have dignity and happiness, you feel like a grown-up. A new song accompanies you as you go about your day and something inside you lightens up. This new imaginary person you've been cast as comes to mind at the oddest times of day and night; not urgently, not yet so that you stop dead in your tracks, but while you're thinking of or doing something else. It's the most genial form of haunting. All this is quite apart from the practical stuff: curiosity about the rest of the casting, the question of whether you might take a holiday before you start – the holiday you were never confident of planning when you were out of work. As you begin to contemplate the project, your practical and dreaming sides come together: are there books you should read, the character's habitat you should visit, do you need to learn to juggle, speak French or sing? In other words, Research, a fine and scholarly word: this is one of the rare moments in your career when you'll feel intellectually respectable.

Not all parts need research ahead of time, and you might be better off taking the holiday. I'm not sure, apart from getting familiar with the text, why you would research for Hamlet. What, visit Elsinore? I imagine Hedda Gabler is the same. Studying the history of earlier performances is probably not a brilliant thing to do: you'll either want to imitate or will be intimidated. You're already at work in any case, scanning yourself dawn to dusk for anything Hamlet- or Hedda-like in you, in the world around you, in the newspapers, in your relationship, in the street. In the case of Hamlet, better to go to the gym for a month or two in preparation for what is for most people a cruelly physical role. The wisdom about such parts is that they lie somewhere within you anyway; if you're well cast, their inner currents must resemble your own. Others – mortal revenge, maternal betrayal – may lie outside your experience: these are men and women from other worlds. Nowadays it's highly likely you're to play a real person, as imaginative fiction gives way to docudrama even in the theatre. I once did nine in a row: Anton Chekhov, George III, Sydney Cockerell, Robert Maxwell, Charles Dickens, Richard Strauss, Wilhelm Furtwängler, Bomber Harris and James Agate.

When I did Furtwängler (listening to his versions of Beethoven's Fifth, watching film of him and trying to look like an ostrich – standard stuff, really) it was the second time I'd played in Ronald Harwood's classic *Taking Sides*, a work that raises one of the richest and most examined questions in twentieth-century drama – What Would You Have Done? It is set in Berlin in 1947 at the moment when the Allies, most determinedly the Americans, embarked on their de-Nazification programme: Furtwängler was a controversial figure suspected of habitual collaboration with the Third Reich, and at least one of the Americans had it in for him. As it happens, I've now taken both sides in this argument: in the original production ten years previously I had played his interrogator, the composite and imaginary Major Steve Arnold.

The climate of the time is extremely specific. Patten's Third Army had just opened up Buchenwald and other death camps on their route through Europe, and the shock of what they'd found meant they weren't about to listen to a pack of liberals in Berlin defending Furtwängler's decision to stay in Germany through the war as Hitler's favourite conductor, on the grounds that art such as his was 'above politics'. Preparing to play Steve, I looked at rare colour footage of the camps, which certainly woke up a palate slightly dulled by the familiar black-and-white images. I combined a holiday in the US with a visit to the military historians at West Point. They were a fascinating bunch, not only for what they said about the period, but in themselves: they marched rather than walked and took no interest in the extraordinary bird life on the Hudson River on the declared basis that they were military men, not ornithologists. By the time I got back I felt I pretty much knew Major Arnold, his particular zeal, and what woke him screaming in the night.

The point of the story is that the play was being directed by Harold Pinter, and I made what in retrospect was an error by sharing some of my findings with him before rehearsals began. He was friendly and polite; and then, on the first day of rehearsal, he announced to the company that the one thing he didn't want to get into was a lot of irrelevant historical detail, let alone what the characters had for breakfast. It was a standard anti-Method position, entirely in character, and an elegant oblique rebuke to me. After all, the author of *The Birthday Party* is celebrated for having replied most succinctly many years ago to the queries of Alan Ayckbourn, then a young actor playing Stanley, as to what the character thought but didn't say: 'Mind your own fucking business.' I read his code on *Taking Sides*. Since we hadn't worked together before and the rehearsal period was not long, he was fearful of getting bogged down. He was reassured in the event to see that once we got started I simply got on with the job: I learned the long driving part in a couple of weeks, which made his work avowedly easier. I reflected but didn't say that if I showed a certain confidence and efficiency it was due to the discoveries which I shouldn't have burdened him with. So the lesson is: research, but keep your findings to yourself until you're asked for them.

The only thing I did wrong at West Point was to be late – an hour and a half late, for reasons pretty much beyond my control. It provoked not so much disapproval as innocent bafflement that such a thing could be: it was very foreign to a soldier. However it would have been well understood, and approved, by a Neapolitan. For the production I mentioned earlier of Eduardo de Filippo's *Filumena*, as well as doing what I now call the Gavin Fowler Tour, I attempted to come to terms not only with care-free unpunctuality but with how much closer southern Italians are to a Moorish fatalism than to the worldliness of northern Italians. Domenico Soriano was a confectioner by profession and a ladies' man by instinct; I concluded that his pride and *amour propre* would have taken the form of dressing rather con-servatively, with splendid dignity, not with gold all over him as a Roman or Milanese might have done. At the moment of his greatest outrage, he defines himself thus:

> Do you really think that Domenico Soriano, the son of Rai-mondo Soriano, one of the most respected confectioners in Naples, would have let you down and left you without a home?

(There's the clue to him: he says 'confectioners' as others might say 'priests' or 'statesmen'.) Having got this hint of Domenico's mindset, I read Peter Robb's wonderful books about southern Italy, especially his account of the importance of coffee, ice cream and fireworks. It's an obsession – similar, as he says, to that of the Milanese with aperitifs, the essential difference being that the more affluent Milanese see the aperitif as a promise of a stomach-filling meal, whereas in Naples the meal to come is his-torically in doubt. It also has to do with a sense of being robbed by the north of the big things in life – pasta and fashion – and being left with the trivia, despite an immense pride. The result was that every time I spoke I knew what street I was on, where I had just come from en route to where, what I most wanted.

For King Lear, on the other hand, which I've just now played in New York, I did nothing at all.

6 The Time of Your Life

Rehearsal Weeks One to Four – The Technical – The Dress Rehearsals – Four Previews

> ARKADINA: To sit in a hotel room somewhere, learning your lines –
> what could be better than that?
> NINA: Oh yes, yes, I do understand.
>
> CHEKHOV, *The Seagull*

29 April 2013

Outside my local Tube station a substantial crowd is spilling out onto the quite deep pavement: they are completely, unnervingly still. An incident, perhaps: a public address or a murder on the forecourt? It turns out later that it was only that old friend, a signal failure at East Finchley. Without breaking stride I veer off to the bus stop, and catch a slow-moving bus that's taking the overflow of commuters down to King's Cross. I reckon to get the Victoria Line there to Green Park, then the Jubilee to Southwark, thus travelling west and then south to go east. At King's Cross we queue to go through the barrier and end up horribly overcrowded on the platform, like a great belly bulging out over the rails. Now there's an announcement that there will be no further services 'in the foreseeable future' on this line either. We all surge back up the escalator, wondering why we weren't told this on the street side of the barrier. I'm running along the underground corridors by now – I detest being late and this is the first day of rehearsals for Strindberg's *Dance of Death*, to be mounted at the Gate Theatre in the summer of 2013. I am full of accumulated spite towards both London Transport and all innocent bystanders, like the misanthropic character, Captain Edgar, I'm about to play. I eventually make all my connections and get to Southwark, grateful that I've left myself an absurd amount of time on this first day – after a Sunday considering all sorts of alternatives, including a now abandoned leisurely bus and walk over the river. I plunge through a stationary crowd of baffled commuters, not quite minding if I mildly bump into one or two of them, out into the street, and bustle along to the rehearsal room. Opposite it, I see Howard Brenton (who's done our adaptation of the play, which is now titled in the plural, *Dances Of Death*) enjoying a coffee at a pavement cafe. Calming down, I join him and add caffeine to my adrenalin. In fact, I suddenly have all the time in the world. Because of course the call at 10 a.m. is only 'for' 10.30, whereupon there's a Meet and Greet and then we start – it's like a civilised party. Meanwhile my sweat-rag of a shirt is drying out fast. Howard, like my colleagues at the Meet and Greet, is not much interested in my experience getting to work, even though it seems a remarkable story to me; after all, what is more ordinary to listen to than such a tale? An hour later, deep in Strindberg and learning everybody's name, I've forgotten all about it.

~

Rehearsing is the oddest business, and difficult to describe to anyone not used to it: in one way it's all practical, in another almost too abstract to explain. Around you for a few weeks a sort of scaffolding rises, a small library of paper and electronic schedules, daily briefings and records of what's been done the day before; the relevant features of what will be a set are marked out on the floor in various colours of gaffer tape, suggesting a network of pathways and obstacles, entrances and exits, calculable sightlines, sharp angles and maskings. After a time, they will begin to feel like metaphorical pathways too.

Each day you'll stand in the midst of it all, wide awake, disciplined, but also in a dream: as you navigate it, you're plunging into your memory and imagination. Sometimes your nose is in your script, looking for plain facts from which to build up the character; at others you gaze speculatively into the middle distance, thinking what you might do in certain imaginary circumstances and guessing at what an invented somebody else might. You're beginning to keep company with a person you don't yet know and who in fact doesn't exist. You hope to be taken over by whoever they turn out to be; you offer yourself to them in the act of inventing them. The hope is that Juliet or Romeo will end up playing you rather than you them; that they'll make you do something new one night without thinking about it, off the cuff, and then you'll realise it's exactly what they would have done. This, after all, is what happens in a dream – you create a world, sometimes bizarre but with familiar features, at the same time coping with its surprises. An actor in rehearsal is both the inventor and the raw material.

In *A Midsummer Night's Dream* Theseus hauntingly comments of actors that

> the best in this kind are but shadows, and the worst are no worse, if imagination amend them . . .

– and the Japanese acting teacher Zeami Motokiyo says that at his best an actor is like a rock with a flower blooming on it. An earnest American colleague once asked me about my method of preparing a part in the theatre. I baffled her by saying it depended on the circumstances – the director, the range of the part, whether it needed much research or unusual physical fitness, and above all the length of the rehearsal period, which can vary from two weeks to six and more. She already looked a little shocked, and in a burst of mischief I added that it also depended on how much I was being paid. A cheap industrial joke, but it had an ironic centre: you do seem to get remunerated the least the harder you work and the more worthwhile the project, as if artistic reward disqualified you from any other.

There's every kind of rehearsal period, every type of project, every kind of director, and some of what follows you will already know. You'll be in casts of twenty, casts of ten or casts of three. Apart from the fact that the smaller the cast, the closer, for better or worse, it's personally going to become, the traditional ground rules are much the same – about four weeks' preparation, probably in a location some distance from the theatre that will house the play, unless it's blessed with rehearsal facilities. When the RSC moved into the Barbican in the early 1980s they found an incomprehensibly wretched provision of rehearsal space in their splendid new home and had to move that part of the operation out to Clapham; although I like the National Theatre rehearsal rooms, some find them airless and prefer the Jerwood Space along the road; on the other hand the main in-house RSC rehearsal room overlooking the river at Stratford is so beautiful and well equipped it's a wonder anyone concentrates on their work at all.

Week One

> You should pay careful attention to everything in preparing a play.
> ZEAMI MOTOKIYO

Day One is like the first day at school, and it gets no better with age, not really. Everyone is nervous or overexcited – actors, stage management, and director too. I've noticed an odd thing: sometimes this is when the concept of Them and Us unexpectedly arises. A knot of actors stands uneasily on the pavement. One actress on a recent first day stood at the closed door of the

rehearsal room and said, 'They told me we should be here at ten
. . . They want us to wait outside . . . Are they locking us out?'
I pointed out that another, open door was next to it – with the
coffee and buns just the other side. You'd think 'they' were ward-
ers at a particularly nasty prison rather than well-trained and
helpful stage managers. Then 'I hear (s)he [the director] wants
this,' sometimes with a little moue of incredulity. There's a subtle reversion here to gender roles. If the director's a man, the
women may be implying he's a bully; if it's a woman, the men
that she's a bit mad. In a way it fortifies us as actors, this idea
of clanship against a hostile world, but it's false. And odd: we're
supposed to be beyond all that Them and Us. It's just that directors have different pressures from ours, and other judgements to
make; producers different ones again. All this ganging up is just
an outcrop of nerves. It's time to go in and break the ice.

Unless in your eagerness you're quite indecently early, the
room is already full, as if everyone else has been there all night.
If the company is well enough funded, there'll be (real) coffee on,
and even (an excellent imported American habit), some crois-
sants and Danish pastries. Grab one now – they won't be so suc-
culent by the time the readthrough's over. I used to arrive primly
ready to work, opening my script at exactly ten of the clock; I
now look forward to the refreshment and know a quarter of an
hour's gossip is not going to wreck the production – might even,
in some subtle way, make it better.

Who will be there? The 'Creatives' – and no, that's not you.
The new phraseology of 'Cast and Creatives', as if the former
weren't also the latter, is a little surprising. 'Creatives' now
means Writer, Director, Designer, Lighting, Composer, Sound
and Movement; which just leaves the foot-soldiers – the actors
and stage management. As modernisms go, I suppose it's no
odder than Casting Directors having letters after their names
that sound like honorifics, and sometimes the longest CVs in

the programme. Anyway, don't be put off. The precious adjective 'creative' is already thoroughly debased; when the Internet encourages you to give rein to your inner creativity in the way you cut your toenails, it's hardly a distinction.

There'll be a Stage Manager in charge – maybe a Company Manager as well, whose job is pastoral (getting you a doctor, a taxi or a sedative) as well as practical (reproaching you for being late, reminding you to return your Equal Opportunities form); but these two jobs may be combined to become Company Stage Manager. There'll be the Deputy Stage Manager (script and cueing) and two Assistant Stage Managers (everything else, including prop-setting and errands and sometimes a bit of acting). They're at one great humming table, like a small bourse – a director friend of mine calls it the Hub. Do respect these specialists: they're the construction team and working sinews of the production, and they don't like being flippantly called Stage Damagement, any more than we like being called Thesps. Learn their names early as well: they're tired of being called 'darling' (as in 'What's that cue, er . . . darling'); and your affection will make up for the inevitable moment when you forget your lines and ask them snappily for a prompt as if it were their fault (as in 'YES???!!! . . .'). Often, when then given the correct line, actors for some comical reason say, 'Yes, that's right!' as if they'd just set Stage Management a test and they'd passed.

The cast is called into either a great circle of chairs like a circus ring with nothing in the centre, or half of one, facing a long trestle table such as an interviewing committee might use; or perhaps to a long rectangular table for everyone – better probably, except that when you come to read the play through you won't so easily see the actor you're addressing even if you're brave enough to lift your eyes from the script (which in fact I recommend), and peer down the row at them. The director introduces himself, then generally asks you to do the same. What cowardice, you think

– he should do it himself! Imagine it though: what if he forgets someone's name in the heat of the moment when he's agonised for weeks over their casting and even told them they're indispensable to the show. You await your turn. Actors are supposed to be eager to promote themselves, but you never saw a more nervous group of wallflowers than the average cross-section of us at this moment. You may have spent half a lifetime bellowing 'Alone I Did It' or 'I Am Thy Father's Spirit' and still have real trouble pronouncing your own name. In any case the idea that anyone will remember any of this is a joke, because we're really only listening nervously to ourselves. Ask the director to give his name too; on second thoughts, don't. Likewise if you make a joke while you introduce yourself it won't be noticed, except by those who've already done their self-announcing and can relax. As wallflowers go, we're intensely self-conscious.

When I first did a Chekhov the director, who had a stammer, spoke fearlessly all morning without notes about the play – it was moving and transfixing and I've never forgotten it. Another director might just have said, 'OK, let's read this thing'; and I can't prove he wouldn't have made as good a production in the end. If he does start speaking for himself and seems to be settling in, you'll be doing the readthrough in the afternoon and not imminently; this may or may not be a comfort.

It's difficult to say how much these opening ceremonies are designed to satisfy an emotional need and how much as a practical preparation for building a wall. From the start, apprehension is a constant for everyone, together with the desire to turn it to useful purpose. The Readthrough already mimics a performance. A director will encourage a company towards it in two opposite ways – on the one hand: don't feel you have to deliver anything final, that would be absurd; but at the same time: don't mutter into your boots as if to announce that this is, after all, just a readthrough and you're not taking any decisions yet.

Undeniably, a process of assessment and calculation begins as soon as the scripts are opened and the first line bravely spoken. To do their jobs well, everyone in the room needs to hear what this unfamiliar beast of a play feels like – not what it means, but how it feels on the palate and nerves. The director is listening to the timbre of someone's voice; Stage Management is provisionally timing each Act; the Designer – perhaps most nervous of all, as her turn comes last this morning – is wondering if her idea for costumes is going to sit happily on the human tissue in front of her, and, if she's done the set as well, imagining these voices singing out from the toy-theatre model standing shyly in a corner of the room. After the reading she'll present her costume sketches – sometimes little works of art, sometimes just hints to be discussed – and explain the model: a fearsomely exposing thing that provokes the actors' imaginations and also starts them thinking practically. On ninety-nine per cent of occasions the cast will, whether sincerely or not, declare themselves delighted with the design – it would be ungallant not to, and it's a coded form of bonding. If the anthropological need in any group is its own survival, this small human organism, a theatre company, is already beginning to support, nurture and protect itself.

Assuming all this takes up the morning, after lunch any clear path through the woods disappears; or rather, there are many paths, all of them equally good-looking. It's impossible to know what this director will do. Some even postpone a readthrough for several days yet; some, having done it, immediately start staging the play, imagining compositions – naturally, they've been looking at the set model for weeks – though that's less rewarding for you: it deprives you of the playful privilege of improvising a little first.

Some actors are better at staging themselves than others. Left alone, we may do oddly unlifelike things: we stand nose to nose to argue with someone even though the area is big and even though we'd hardly ever do it so aggressively in life, unless a punch or a shove was on the way. In Shakespeare especially, too much physical proximity can cramp the language, which is usually designed to arch across space even if only two people are involved; most stage arguments are liberated by a bit of distance between the arguers. Sometimes we fall slavishly into patterns. Recently I saw a new play that consisted largely of duologues. There was very little furniture on the set – the play, though realistic in manner, happened in an open imaginary space. It was surprising (the director was quite eminent) to see actors striding up to each other to deliver an insult, then crossing theatrically in front of their antagonist on a diagonal to downstage left, say; then, after the intervening speech, making a strange curving move round the back of the speaker to the other side to make another point. All this recalls an old-fashioned wish to be upstage when you're speaking and to keep criss-crossing so that both sides of the house get enough of your face. It was very unrealistic, and suggested that the actors, uneasy with the material, had fallen back on some ancient motor memory. If they'd been helped to feel the argument better they'd have moved more interestingly; and one of them would surely have asked for a chair. The fact is that a move that only exists on a stage shouldn't exist there either.

The cast may occasionally be asked, rather than reading from the text, to improvise the situation beneath it, particularly if its topsoil is at all classical and remote. Quite an alarming way to start, and fairly unusual these days. Most actors are not very confident in themselves: being asked to make things up, especially before they know each other well, is a fearful business. Let alone if it requires special knowledge. I workshopped David Hare's *Stuff Happens*: it was very hard to improvise a family breakfast in George Bush Senior's house unless you were quite well informed, as it's difficult to imagine that family off-duty if you don't have much impression of them on.

Another director will start playing games – a thinly disguised way of creating trust. I have, in my time, run across a school playground as fast as I could with my eyes closed in the knowledge that before I hit the wall ahead my colleagues would stop me; or I've myself caught one of them falling backwards off a four-foot platform trusting that I'd save them; I and they are here to tell the tale. There are, or have been, eccentric variants on this: hand-holdings, company hummings, medicine balls tossed across the room, wordless assaults, shouting matches without consonants. I've always admired older actors brought up conventionally who throw themselves into this: it's a real sign of grace, and they sometimes turn out to be the best at it – whatever they then say when they get home.

You may be asked to tell everybody five things about yourself (it's genuinely a good one, this) and at the same time to remember what your new colleagues reveal about themselves. You may be asked to share some recent experience when your own reaction surprised you (like my circular journey to Southwark) as a means of breaking the ice. You might imagine this would make the thawing ice freeze over again, but it's a good idea, not too embarrassing and a way to begin appreciating each other. Some directors are mildly provocative: Peter Stein once declared off the bat to his English cast of *The Seagull* that only Russian actors knew how to do Chekhov; a bond like Araldite was immediately formed among them.

The first day may end a bit early: by teatime everyone's too tired to do much further good. Go home.

As the First Week develops any games generally fall away. More probably, the company will sit around a big table, reading slowly through the text, until, by Friday, they're bursting to get up and act, like dogs wanting to be let out. It's just the moment when they should be allowed to. Still, no one's invented a better way of opening up a play and making a group of strangers into an ensemble than this civilised brainstorming. You may be asked to research something related to your character, or indeed the whole play, and come back to tell it to everyone: about wire-walking techniques, say, or rural church-building in nineteenth-century Norway. This last was on the production of *The Master Builder* that I mentioned earlier. On this show the director was excellent, the translator the top of his line, the designer likewise, and the casting was perfect. It was a company with an age range of twenty-five to seventy. By the Wednesday, as we exchanged all sorts of intimate reminiscences that might apply to the play, attending to each other across the decades, it occurred to me that when it works, there's no other profession like this, and how fortunate my life has been.

There are variations of course: you may be asked to break the script down into short units and give them titles – 'In which Jane tries to get Tom to do the washing-up.' This is related to Stanislavsky's Units and Objectives, and also to Max Stafford-Clark's 'actioning' process, which pins down exactly what a character wants from every phrase he speaks. It may feel like turning the play into a series of very small chapters, but it does start you thinking precisely.

A director tends to be an idiosyncratic loner who may not often talk to other directors, let alone see them work. Actors develop great strength from being flexible; they're garrulous and always milling about at close quarters, adapting to different circumstances. We are indeed like dogs and prefer plain talk to metaphors; though conversely we suspect a director who tersely blocks the play and gets on with it, like the old repertory hand who once described to me his ideal three-week rehearsal period: Week One – Block it; Week Two – Psycho it; Week Three – Zhoozh it (See A–Z). I guess that makes us feel *too* much like dogs. Anyway you should be prepared to work in any way you're asked to – an actor insisting on his own method (*pace* my American friend), can be problematic. I happen to have worked with two highly individual directors from different cultures, the Russian Yuri Lyubimov and the German Peter Stein. Both wanted fast and spontaneous outcomes at each rehearsal: I was startled that one or two of the English actors wouldn't be rushed from their steady, accustomed way. I couldn't quite see the point of working with such exotic figures and then insisting on your usual routine. Occasionally, on the other hand, a director will ask you how you'd like to rehearse – especially if you're older; what will help you most? This is more a form of courtesy than a real offer, like offering you a seat on the Tube, and a bit unsettling: best to demur, insisting that it's really up to them. After all, he or she is more lion-tamer than friend.

By the end of this first week, you're on some kind of terms with much of the play and already a vague shape is appearing. Provisional alliances are forming in the group – those who suggest lunch together, those who one day might suggest more than lunch together, those who go off on their own, those who've brought sandwiches with them, the smokers and the non-smokers, the ones who've found they have a friend in common or agree that some show they've seen isn't as good as it's cracked up to be. And so an eccentric human machine, temporary but powerful, begins to stir.

Week Two

From now on, much depends on how long you've got. If it's four weeks, you're probably best getting off the script by the end of this second one. Learning is in any case only the start of a long process, accompanied by many disconcerting failures. The moment you really know you've learned your lines is when you can go through them without somebody reading in the intervening text or yourself looking down at it in the script. By then you pretty much know the whole play, and can get through it with your eyes and ears shut, as familiar with what comes between as with your own bits. (Of course you need to check with the script afterwards that you haven't missed out a great chunk.) If your colleague then dries, you'll know what they've forgotten and can do something about it; you're not dependent on anyone else.

It used to be said that learning a script early, almost mechanically, rather than just letting it come in the repetition of rehearsal, tied actors down too much to certain rhythms, inflections and choices. That seems a little old-fashioned now. More compellingly, directors are asking that the lines be learned before the first rehearsal, as opera singers do (a bad comparison, actually). So increasingly actors who aren't coming straight off another job will have done a good bit in advance, all the more so if they're getting on a bit in years and don't trust their memory as they once did. But some positively resent the request, regarding the advance time spent as unpaid rehearsal (not a good argument either) or even as a sort of vulgarity. They probably sense that it's for the benefit of the director, one of the most boring passages of whose life is watching actors blundering about in rehearsal half-knowing their lines, all their energy and passion going into correcting themselves, accompanied by extravagant expressions of self-loathing. But those who've learned in advance can become frustrated because the words elude them nonetheless as they tie them to moves, the other actors' work and various 'distractions'. The only difference is that their blundering-about period happens straight off, in the first week, not the third.

What's really important is that you start to 'play' with whomever you're opposite, inventing and perhaps paraphrasing: it's a precious opportunity, and if you're preoccupied with remembering what to say next, it's squandered. Memory won't be bullied in any case: it's going to be a long repetitive while yet before the words are truly, deeply bedded in. On the other hand, don't postpone the mechanical part of the learning, and do open the script between one rehearsal and the next. Remember what happened during the day: no director likes it when the blundering is exactly the same as it was last time. Much of learning is drudgery, like installing small new apps in the brain as reminders of what word comes after what, and not always for any compelling reason; dramatists use non sequiturs, as a prosecuting counsel in court shifts his argument to baffle a witness. When you get home at 6.30 or later this homework compares unfavourably with opening a bottle of wine. You may have a family or a partner, or errands to run; you may be planning to go out. See if you can't do an hour's work first. There is an alternative – get up an hour earlier the next morning. Unfortunately, it seems that by far the best time to get lines lodged is last thing at night, so that they sink slowly down through the hours of darkness. But that depends on your chemistry at 11 p.m.

The cookies in this process are the mnemonics you invent – such and such a sequence of abstract nouns does or doesn't run in alphabetical order in this speech (ah, but which? – more mnemonics needed to remind you); you repeat the question you're asking three times because this is the third scene of the play, and so, meaninglessly, on. You sit there muttering, your bit of paper covering the next line of script as if you were at school, testing yourself. But whatever, this is a kind of purdah till the job's done. What I do now is to divide a script into sections according to how many pages I need to learn every day to get the whole lot done by the midpoint, say, of rehearsals. Some evenings are easy therefore, and some very hard work. Then closer to the opening, oddly enough, I can go out and have fun, even after a run-through.

8 May 2013

This week on *Dances of Death* I have become very observant, and all roads lead back to the play. Down in the Tube today, a Caribbean man has stepped onto the train, which is very crowded, and made a loud announcement that the gentleman reading his newspaper could free up some valuable space if he lowered it – unless of course reading his paper is more important to him than other people's comfort. Unperturbed by his remark until the flick in the tail, everyone now looks at the ground and hopes the newcomer will get off soon. The paper is the *Daily Telegraph*: its reader, silently resentful rather than hostile, eventually lowers it – it makes no more than six inches' difference, but honour of sorts is satisfied. There is class hostility and a little mutual racism in this. Instinctive antagonism and silent grudge – Strindberg's Captain Edgar is like both these men combined, I think to myself.

~

The end of the second week of a rehearsal period has always been a significant time. There used to be a clause in the Equity West End contract which allowed a producer – like a customer changing his mind about buying a product – to fire an actor at this point if he or she was a casting mistake. This nearly happened to me in my first major West End job, playing a young lawyer, because I came to rehearsals in jeans (not so common in those days), whereas the part was that of an upper-class boy. At just this moment, I was rung one morning by the producer and instructed, under duress, to get a haircut immediately (at his barber's) and always to wear a suit to rehearsals. He also, as I began to boil up rebelliously, said how glad he was that I was playing the part. I learned later that the director had been to him in despair about me, so he'd come down to see a rehearsal but decided not to fire me: he saw, better than his colleague, that there was a perfectly good performance in there being muffled by the wrong clothes. The moneyman, in other words, proved himself a lot smarter artistically than the very experienced director – who, relieved, then gave me the lead in a TV play (playing a Russian student revolutionary in the equivalent of torn jeans).

My real mistake had lain elsewhere. I wasn't imagining my posh boy physically but just sloping and slumping about, figuring that I'd add the physical life later, once I'd got the 'reality'. That's inexperience for you. There's a genuine anxiety among young actors, and sometimes older ones, that by thinking about the externals you'll somehow become untruthful. It's a respectable worry but best abandoned: imagining a character is bound to include the outward expression of their personalities, after all. You can suddenly get a physical hint from someone glimpsed in the street or in a dream. Or especially, I think, on public transport. Preparing Malvolio in *Twelfth Night* I looked one day along a line of city gents sitting suited in the Tube, and imagined cutting the bottom half of one of their pairs of trousers off and how they would look in suspenders and bright yellow stockings. It was funny largely because of the self-satisfaction with which they might carry it off, as if it were the chosen style of all good venture capitalists. What is likewise funny about Malvolio is his sublime confidence that he's become the sexiest thing on two yellow cross-gartered legs; everything else about him should be completely normal, down to the knotted tie, and even (John Cleese-like) the bowler hat.

I hope you end your second week, now the Equity clause is a thing of the past, with no bigger issue than whether you should perhaps start dressing to suggest the part. There are theatrical forms in any case – Restoration Comedy for one – where posture is so closely connected with class and personality that you'd do well to get up on heels as soon as possible as a man or get a fan into your hand if you're a woman. In other classics, if you're going to be in a full dress, use a practice skirt pretty soon; wear a coat if you're headed for a robe or a gown. You can sometimes see an actress in performance in full Restoration fig but still moving from the hips as if she had jeans on, and a young man playing a soldier with a slouch in his shoulders: in both cases they may have missed the good moment in a rehearsal room when, scripts finally put down, their body could have started thinking for them.

Appropriately, Costume Fittings, or discussions at least, have been beginning to filter into rehearsals. If this is a big institution, and it's all being done from an in-house store or makers, fittings are a sort of heaven. You may be attended to by four or five people who are in charge of different parts of your body, from hat to shoe, and be thoughtfully handling the best velvets and old linens. Or you may have to go to Hendon. Unless the run is guaranteed to be long it's far cheaper to hire than make, so you find yourself at a hire firm somewhere on the North Circular, trying something on in the middle of the day before coming all the way back to continue rehearsing. This is tiring of course (lack of air and about half a ton of material in the building): as you slip in and out of this and that approximate outfit, your feet sing as if you were spending too long in a museum. However there may be a pleasant surprise: some bright idea you or the director had at one rehearsal – purple gloves for Act Two – has miraculously spawned six pairs to try. The reason for this is the Hub – the DSM is tasked with making a note of all ideas that arise in the day and passing them on to the Heads of Department.

Through all this, do be on time for rehearsals. You can always get a coffee if you're early. Better still, go through the lines – lightly, not working them. Some excuses for lateness are charming – Ian Charleson once rushed in, declared that the wind had been against him and got down to rehearsing before anybody remembered he'd been walking, not on a bike. (This is a slight improvement on the old-fashioned excuse – particularly favoured by radio actors who I think liked the rhythm of the words – that there was fog on the line at Tring.) The theatre is ferociously disciplined about punctuality, far more than more orthodox professions. Lateness screws everyone up. It'll happen one day in any case – your train will be stuck in a tunnel – and though you'll be forgiven, you'll feel bad most of the day.

Week Three

13 May 2013

On *Dances of Death*, we're having momentary successes in getting hold of these characters but nothing much is sustained. However, when Alice or Kurt pause for a moment and walk over to the stage-management table for a drink of water, they suddenly *are* the person they've been so diligently searching for – at the very moment they've stopped looking for them. Alice becomes discontented, highly strung and anxious, Kurt perplexed and honourable: perhaps because the lines aren't quite secure, we're becoming the characters, but not yet through the language – we could have, in fact, a perfect silent movie of the play. I wonder if this often happens, this going into character just as we've come out of it: for the present it's an invitation to work less hard. What it does mean is we're well cast: the actors' and characters' temperaments are matching up.

I seem to know the lines rather less well than I did last week. And I haven't done anything about the series of mini-strokes that Edgar seems to suffer during the play, maybe six of them (one of them faked). What is their warning sign, what's the impact and how paralysed do they leave him? The play's second half is two years after the first – has he recovered entirely or only partly? It commits me to having only one practical hand (which soon emerges as the left), and is thus a big decision. I start putting it in today, a bit late.

~

Not so long ago the playwright David Mamet, showing his annoyance with a certain kind of navel-gazing American acting, felt obliged to write *True and False*, a blistering piece of propaganda about actors obsessed with the unnecessary. Mamet's a great playwright but *True and False* has worried and confused young performers on both sides of the Atlantic – I'd call it an inglorious moment in a great career. When the book came out I was in a play of his with young actors who were all reading it and, as a running joke, I threw every copy I found out of the window of the (second-floor) rehearsal room – it ended up, as a matter of decency, costing me a good deal. This gesture of disrespect was certainly not for Mamet's plays, but for the disingenuousness of his book, which was so knitting all brows. The job is difficult enough as it is.

Times have changed. Some of the self-conscious American methodology he hates wouldn't have come at all amiss in the old days in a British industry where an old-fashioned (and mostly pretended) amateurishness prevailed – a sort of passive-aggressive self-denigration: 'I just learn the lines and try not to bump into the furniture, dear boy.' I knew an elderly actor in Stratford in the 1960s who prided himself on being out of the building before the audience at the end of the show: he always asked to be dressed in a long Shakespearian gown, regardless of role, so that he could wear his getaway trousers beneath. I once incautiously asked him why he did certain subtle details of his eye make-up: he said he had to be in half an hour before the show anyway and needed to fill the time somehow. He was a charming fellow (and a good actor) but perhaps not a good example.

Mamet's book was fallen on with special glee by the Press since it seemed to debunk 'luvvies' – a wretched misnomer for a hard-working profession; but then the Press love to take the mickey out of us almost as much as they love to whoop at the broken bra-straps of celebrities. *True and False* was really superior journalism, with Mamet's cheek full of tongue: from what I hear, it has little bearing on how he himself handles actors when he directs. Still, the book is implying to young performers who aren't lucky enough to work with him that it may not be important to ask themselves such questions as what the airline pilot in whose hands their life rests had for breakfast, or in *Hamlet*, what Horatio might or might not feel about his mother. In this rather mixed-up simile, I would say that what the pilot had for breakfast might be relevant to your safety; and likewise a Horatio whose imagined life is real, at least to him, is going to be a more convincing Horatio. Actors are entitled to their private radar, flashing away between the part and their own secrets – but it's their own business, and you don't want the director putting it in a book. As a result of my and Gavin Fowler's research on Naples, did we not play Eduardo de Filippo better, his every line fraught with a sense-memory of streets and sounds? Didn't the show maybe benefit a bit from our knowing that a Neapolitan can be moved to tears by a chocolate ice cream?

The most timely reminder in *True and False* is that putting on a play is a collaborative process, not an excuse for private therapy played out in everyone else's time. In filming, your prime relationship may be with the camera, but in the theatre it's always, always with the other actors – or if you're in a monologue, with the audience. Collaborating goes beyond being nice, though being nice does no harm. I've had very few tussles with colleagues: occasionally you'll find yourself with someone who takes a little more than they give or who might look for momentary advantage, but you can handle that. Overwhelmingly, the

pleasure of this profession lies in the frankly co-dependent relationships you make.

It all, in any case, depends on the director, and part of your job
is to figure out, as far as you can, who you're dealing with. There
aren't too many bullies around these days, eloquently sniping
from the darkness of the stalls at especially vulnerable victims;
they'd probably be had up for harassment now. In fact directors
have a multiplicity of attitudes towards actors, from profound
affection to utilitarianism, and everything in between. They're
not generally teachers, as interested in you as you are: except
perhaps the remarkable Declan Donnellan, of whom Lydia Wilson, who played Annabella in his *'Tis Pity She's a Whore*, says:

> Declan wouldn't give notes about how to deliver specific
> things in the short term, rather he'd give us principles for per-
> formance which could potentially change your work for the
> rest of your life.

The bottom line is that they do want you to deliver, however
you can. What they don't much enjoy is the moment when you
wince and shift in your seat, clench your fists, do a little twitch,
and say, 'The difficulty I'm having with this bit . . .' You then
stumble time-consumingly through an explanation of how
something isn't working for you psychically, gender-wise, emotionally: you just don't know what it is, but you need their help.
The director's tolerance of this varies, but it's safe to say it's far
from infinite. On a good day, they may be sympathetic, but the
truth is you must solve your own problems your own way; to
that extent David Mamet is exactly right.

If you can talk in practical terms – that you're a bit uncomfortable sitting and would like to try standing or walking – you'll
get a much better response. The director may feel you're always
going to be better off sitting, but he'll probably humour you, as

he might allow someone very young to conduct an obviously ill-advised experiment. If you want to stand on your head in 'To be or not to be' it's probably better to let you try it – and then wait; chances are, you'll come back soon before the opening night and say you don't think he was right about asking you to stand on your head.

So keep it practical: simple solutions can unlock psychological processes. Vsevelod Meyerhold, the original Tusenbach in Chekhov's *Three Sisters*, was having trouble with a particular moment in rehearsal until he and Stanislavsky (whose thinking was always surprisingly practical) hit upon the idea of his opening a bottle of wine and coincidentally struggling a little with the cork. Strangely enough, this displacement activity helped him as he talked about his dreams of a new Russia.

All your life directors will enrich and inspire you; a very few you simply have to survive. The best are simply wonderful. Their job involves myriad skills, including sensing whom to push, whom to nurse, whom to give their heads to (sometimes all three in the same scene); which problems to tackle now and which to leave for later, and how much later. A reasonable degree of patience with the actor who talks too much and too far off the subject; who, having made a mistake, explains at length why they made it, what it was that triggered a series of mental events that led to the error – which can be of no interest to anyone else. The good director also knows that in losing their temper they lose trust; at the same time all actors need firm orders at some point, since we like coming to heel as much as barking.

So offer yourself up, every way you can, but protect a little corner in which to keep your own counsel. Never mind the mighty Mamet: you do have to know what your character had for breakfast. Just don't tell anyone else.

Week Four

Ten days to the first preview. You're simultaneously painstaking and reckless. You've already run whole scenes at a time, maybe two or three of them in a sequence. It's time, with a great clearing of the throat, for the first runthrough.

Forgive yourself – the second one will be better. You were ready to start it ten minutes early; you warmed up for it that extra bit. There were moments of exhilaration, but nerves kept striking you down; you felt exposed as a bit of a sham. You particularly felt this as there were some new people from the production team in the room; you'd been officially hoping that this first run would be in camera, just for 'the family', though secretly you may have rather looked forward to having a bit of an audience. In fact the presence of the Musical Director and some Wardrobe staff is likely to bother even the most experienced performer – especially perhaps the most experienced. But they're only there because they have a job to do, preparing one thing or another, and they usually leave at the end without comment. The actors tend to feel a little hurt, but what could be dafter? These are not fans, after all. As ever we're redeemed by self-mockery: a scandalised reaction to this, like sometimes admitting extreme professional jealousy, is part of the actor's repertoire.

Certainly, outside forces are bearing down on the production with some sense of expectation. You assume that before a second run, there'll be a chance to rehearse what needs urgent attention, now that its threadbare state is exposed. The problem is, nobody can agree on what bits these are. In fact there is unlikely to be enough of this kind of work, and you may feel, starting the next day's runthrough, that nothing has been fixed since the first. But most plays benefit from being run a lot, so that a thing that seemed huge and uncontrollable can begin at the very least to turn into a manageable proposition.

And remember that in the midst of all the shaming anxiety to please, once or twice you did feel a lovely centredness, as if you were improvising, the character living a life of which only part is seen in the play. Not to mention a few encouraging words afterwards and, by an unspoken company ritual, maybe a glass of wine across the road. Few things bring a group together more effectively than the anxiety of a first run.

The Second may be more assured – but there are new strangers in the room, for this may be 'for the Creatives'. The presence of all those Creative people makes for nervousness all over again, and you mentally take it out on them (another glass of wine?) if they don't say anything nice afterwards. Of course they won't: they're too busy thinking of how to make you look and sound good. The Third Run may be for the rest of the theatre's staff and perhaps the Producer, traditionally the most judgemental and practical eye, but quite often now the youngest person in the room. As with many things in the theatre, what's really happening is not exactly what seems to be, just as you can sometimes take your eye off something for a time and find when you look again that it's moved. For beneath the whole harrowing business of one runthrough after another a sort of strength is gathering, an imperviousness even, a sacrifice of your less glorious qualities for the sake of the matter in hand. To put it simply, you're getting used to an audience now, and you begin to take it in your stride. Your engine is built. You're ready to go into the theatre.

22 May 2013
On my way to the first runthrough of *Dances of Death* a man on the Tube stands with a badly burned face, grievous and blasted – his features are therefore set in an emotion he may not feel. Like me, he is listening to two men talking with Boris Johnson voices. One declares an aversion to opera and large sheepdogs. Then he asks his friend about 'Wendy's bump'. It takes a moment

to realise this refers to the other's pregnant wife. The answer comes back that Wendy's frustrated that she can no longer do Pilates; she's on her third 'trimester' now. 'Trimester?' says the first fellow – 'Is that a new kind of car?' He then swiftly goes on, with evident relief, to describe his own car. Later, he answers a question about his own children by saying he hopes to 'get shot of them' by 2020. It sounds as if they're skin infections, or that he plans to murder them. I'd like to catch the burned man's eye, but I don't know how he would be able to acknowledge the black comedy of this. Two days later two men assassinate a young drummer in the street in Woolwich.

Charging through the underworld every day to get to and from work, I seem to have been in the world of the play. The Edvard Munch-like figure on the Tube, the comically suppressed misogyny of the two George Grosz-like men, me as the narrator, all hurtling through London's subterranean chambers – I think Strindberg, and his Edgar, would understand this bizarre vision, as they would the horrible imminent crime.

Week Five

The Technical Rehearsal (the 'Tech') is a period of perhaps two days (more, with luck) once the company has moved out of the rehearsal room and into the theatre. That may simply mean going up- or downstairs in the same building; or it may mean travelling to a distant address in the same town (new bus routes, new timings), or perhaps to quite another part of the country. In terms of comfort, it can involve up- or downgrading. You may have rehearsed in some squalor but be stepping out into a beautiful Frank Matcham-designed auditorium such as the Theatre Royal Newcastle, wondering who may have stood on this spot in the early nineteenth century and whether they still haunt the building. Or, oddly, you could have been working in relative comfort and be moving to a venue where the smell is of old socks and yesterday's boiled cabbage; where the sound of hamburgers being beaten out in the pub kitchen on the other side of the wall could be confused for some musical cue for the show; where the only loo is in the front of house, so that you'll have to wait for the audience to be all in and then make a run for it (petticoats, farthingales and all) and then back in time to start. (Maybe not the men – such a theatre strengthens the time-honoured tradition that a male actor is not really a pro till he has availed himself of his dressing-room washbasin.) Once the show is up and running, there may be so little money available that you end up ironing your own costume.

Needless to say, neither scenario is a guarantee of good work.

Dressing rooms are not a high point in most theatres. A few – the Haymarket in London, all wood and shades of Irving – flatter you; most put themselves at their visitors' disposal with something like ill will, as if looking forward to a better tenancy later. Some West End theatres are shockers – 'star' dressing rooms you can hardly turn round in, let alone stretch out for a sleep. There may be rat-traps under the working surface, hefty old radiators that don't work or work too well, basins with one tap and a little cistern above them for the hot water. Or they may smell of disinfectant, be very hot and boast one coat hanger. There may be only a small mirror on the wall of whitewashed bricks, ancient piping and an old cork noticeboard with some dire warning on it, a fire blanket, a deal table painted white (why?), a drawer space with no drawer in it, and a couple of other drawers with two lonely hairpins in one of them. These have no atmosphere at all, and many male actors leave them that way: the women soon transform theirs into beguiling parlours into which approved men may venture for fruit, the scent of flowers, and exquisite female solicitudes; they're getting away for a few minutes from their own, which generally resembles a rugger changing room.

Many of the smaller theatres have just one room for each gender, so for once the women do better (compensation for the relative shortage of parts): perhaps four of them in a room, as opposed to seven or eight men next door in the same dimensions. Other theatres have a handful, and the task of allocating them lies with the Company Manager, an unenviable job that lies halfway between a rock, the acting company, and a hard place, the management. In doing it he or she has to keep in mind contractual arrangements that may have been made for the star(s) which stipulate that they will be on their own, naturally enough, but may also call for new carpets and other inexplicable easements. An extremely famous Hollywood movie star (name on request) once had a furious row with the Chichester management because they wouldn't get the cathedral bells, which had presumably rung out since 1100, to desist on a Sunday morning, so who knows what she was like over dressing rooms.

Though there's much to do yet, the last weekend before the technical has felt oddly final. You thought you could put the show to one side and attend to all the deferred business of life and not obsess about the play. You certainly needed to rest: those runthroughs were a strain, and the next few days will be tough.

27 May 2013

Over the weekend, Tom Littler, who directs *Dances of Death*, has told me a story about a compulsive liar with whom he recently shared a train carriage, who made a series of loud mobile calls – to her brother, her mother, and a boy she was interested in, telling blatantly different versions of what had happened that day with her current lover. Having deafened everybody with her dazzling mendacity she said that she had to ring off, because 'something's happening at this end'. In the play Edgar lies continually, unnecessarily, self-defeatingly; his first instinct is always to tell something other than the truth. Like a bigamist, he gets his own perverse reward from this.

In the rarely performed second Part of Strindberg's play, which has become the second Act of our new version, Edgar also talks a lot about the Bible story of Judith and Holofernes. This is because he is in constant strife with Alice over the allegiance of their teenage daughter Judith, and he clearly fears at least symbolic decapitation. Anyone who knows Caravaggio's wonderful painting (or indeed that of many other artists) of the beheading of Holofernes will have noticed the sexual charge in the dramatic moment when Judith turns from victim to revenger; Caravaggio (who was after all a man) goes further by implying that at the moment of decapitation Judith falls in love with him. Whether that's meant or not, the erotic content of violence is there, as it must have been for Gustav Klimt, who painted his version of the Holofernes and Judith story the year after the play was written.

$\sim$

Thinking about the last run you remember you took a prompt. It doesn't seem to matter now, and indeed it doesn't. There were good things as well: will they translate to the stage? Apart from the technical sessions, there should be two dress rehearsals. Meanwhile the Production Manager and HODs who sketched cryptic little diagrams during the runthroughs – calculating stress and distance, safety and practicality, circuits and costs, materials, budgets and delivery dates – have finally stepped out of the shadows. Racks of costumes have assembled themselves like a ghostly army in dressing rooms; a bobbing sea of wigblocks – those strangely unnerving faceless heads that once caused a very young friend to run screaming from mine – have allocated themselves; and on the stage itself, what was a D-shaped strip of gaffer tape in the rehearsal room representing a door and its direction of opening (over which you used to pass, mimicking its action by doing a strange little shuffle and stamp on the floor) has indeed become a door on its hinges. (Not usually a shuttable one yet: the catches for some reason come later, with luck by the dress rehearsal.) The canvas floor that was easy to kneel on is now a less forgiving bed of shiny tile, perhaps, causing a skid or pain if you fall; it may be on a rake, which you were mentally expecting but not physically prepared for. The scaffolding pole you used to lean on is now a convincing, semi-stable pillar. There it all is, as beguiling as your toy theatre when you were a kid.

It's no one's fault in particular, but things are a bit behind schedule. 'How's it going?' actors cheerily greet the designer on arrival at the stage door, and get a rueful, friendly, just-about-hopeful shrug in reply. In fact, the structure rearing up from a forest bed of cables, boxes, ladders, iron flying bars, detritus of every kind from which no order can be imagined to come is about to be presented to you as your enchanted circle, the bullring where you'll seem to fight for your life and with luck brandish the bull's ear at the end. Not to be too carried away by metaphors: these will be a few days outside time, in which the TV news is of very little importance and emails get neglected, though you may wistfully gaze at the civilian world around you and look forward to eating at normal hours, no longer a mole in the deep dark. How you'd love to read a book, go on holiday, see a friend, or just think about something else. Or so you think. In fact, you are excited, regardless of age, and also feel mildly sick, all the time.

Morning, noon and evening, the company crawls through the play for purposes of lighting, sound, repainting of the set, fine adjustments to props and positions, before dress-rehearsing on Tuesday night and, all being well, Wednesday afternoon. There seems to be both endless time and nothing like enough: the days combine acceleration and thoughtfulness, longueurs and panic. The set can hold some surprises and the work may need adjusting. Civilians sometimes ask irritably: Why do you change it all at the last minute – surely you're all professional enough to know what it's going to look like in advance? (They're thinking of the money, their money in a sense, which they're convinced we squander.) Sadly, no: everything is up for reconsideration and may, rightly, change. At the most extreme, entire sets are junked – Peter Brook abandoned his for his legendary *Cherry Orchard* in Paris on the morning of the opening, leaving the actors with a carpet and a wardrobe, and the result was a triumph. Costumes may be cut, new and suddenly vital props hunted down, and countless little staging flourishes exposed – now they're in the theatre and about to take up an audience's time – as not having earned their keep: in a couple of days you won't even remember what they were. This is why theatre isn't rocket science; and you can't explain to a first-night audience that something worked fine in the rehearsal room but hasn't translated.

In this period, contrary to expectation, the actor seems oddly unimportant, but there will come a moment when, alone and with time to kill, you sit in a dressing room with a sandwich and play with your face. You've scrupulously prepared your look, but it will still be a shock and very likely a pleasant one. If not, there's time to fix it. Maybe the false eyebrows were a mistake.

Above all, please, please, use the technical for yourself. Actors can get bored by the long hushed deliberations from the production desk in the middle of the stalls, and tend to horse about a bit, as if showing off to a teacher who has far more pressing things to attend to. Don't do little tap dances and swap noisy anecdotes in the pauses. Most actors know very little about lighting beyond a general impression of it being too dark or (not often) too bright. This can make them infuriating in long technical rehearsals, when they may ask – as children might about some worrying thing threatening their sleep – if the lighting's going to be 'like this', just as its designer is in the very middle of his laborious work. He's not going to leave you in the dark.

169

Think of it differently: this is the longest time you'll be on the set in the whole run, and extremely precious. Adapting to circumstance can be a pleasure, and you're learning a lot now, fast. You might come offstage and not know at all where to go or even what happens next. Is this your quick change now, and will you have any help with it? How much time do you have anyway? Check things for yourself, practise small actions, think everything through. If you need the telephone cable to run in a slightly different direction ask stage management; if you're going to need rubber soles on your shoes after all, the costume supervisor is at the production desk and there'll soon be a tea break in which to speak to her. Use every minute. Keep your mind on the job. Think, and only gossip a little.

By the time of the Dress Rehearsal you've forgotten quite a bit of what you learned in the early stages of the technical – much has intervened. Of course you feel ashamed of this, but everybody does it. You forget having discovered in Scene One that you should be sure to close the door behind you or leave it open or ajar, or to go downstage on your colleague's left side, not right. Those sound cues for coming on are now a reality: but what moment within them is the ideal one to enter on – when that zoomy bit happens, or at their end (which you have to learn to recognise)? Is there a green cue light to go by? Does the theatre even have cue lights? Is it better to wait for the onstage lighting state to change or to anticipate it? The rehearsal room feels a long way away. Your new route map through the production will gradually become a muscle memory (and then be completely forgotten the moment the run ends). You make little notes all the time; but where to put the piece of paper, especially if there are no pockets in the costume and you're sharing a dressing room that's like a small broom cupboard with four other people? Even if the room is better than that, is there time to go back to it at a particular point or is it better to stay around the set?

For all this, by the Dress or First Preview, you may recover a clear crisp view of the text, renewing your relationship with it, even remembering its layout on the page. Now, like death, an imminent audience wonderfully concentrates the mind; the fear of messing up in public turns into a vicious determination to do it well, for everyone's sake. Nevertheless, you will make mistakes in this period, some of them in public. Both forgive and don't forgive yourself – that's a characteristic position in the theatre, where our worst cock-ups become the stuff of our jokes. Which doesn't mean we take them lightly: they're a sort of agony, relieved by the wonderful absurdity of the job.

After the slog of rehearsals the company has seen itself through the technical period with a necessary if unreliable air of mutual encouragement. Everyone's look, costume, acting may have been greeted with determined rapture; an older colleague may have quietly mentioned how much he's noticed your performance 'growing' in this final stage; kind friends who've gone out front to watch the dress rehearsal during scenes they weren't in themselves have congratulated you, in the private hope that you'll do the same for them.

Needless to say, the first Dress Rehearsal may be the only one, on the afternoon of the first show. It could be worse: there could be no dress rehearsal at all. When I did *The Madness of George III*, a play of very many scenes situated in different places, many mechanically realised, we were still trying to finish the technical as the audience waited to come in for the first night. That evening the wings were littered with little pieces of paper – aides memoire to remind actors where to go next, since no human agency could help. We'd come off, look left and right and left again as if nervously crossing a highway, before plunging straight back on the way we'd come from. Stage management and dressers endured the same nightmare, but without the pleasure of being onstage, which seemed the safest place to be. The galling fact that, like any good company, we managed to pull it off, is exactly what emboldens producers to assume that they don't need to allocate so much technical time on the next show.

If there are to be two, the first Dress Rehearsal, like the first runthrough, is likely to be a halting and self-conscious affair followed by unconvincing good cheer – 'No really, it's getting there . . .'. You're trying to remember a hundred things; your wig still needs attention and your shoes are too tight. You think you look like an ass, and incompetent. You'd rather be almost anything but an actor, you lie to yourself.

The quantum leap into the Second Dress can be startling and there will be a photographer or two present as if to emphasise it – this is the latest time his or her work can be done if there's to be anything up at the front of house within a day or two of opening. And then, with the First Preview, it all changes again. You come on at the wrong time and have to beat a retreat, after doing it correctly for weeks. It's also when the playing cards are stuck together, the lighter doesn't work, and the door handle comes off in your hand. But you feel unaccountably happy.

It's hard to remember now that generally we used to open to the press after one Dress Rehearsal. Previews in Britain were pretty much invented, like much else, by Peter Hall. It's true, as he has said, that a play that doesn't interest its audience on a first preview is unlikely ever to interest them, however much work is done on it; also true that in the commercial theatre a huge number of previews are less for creative perfection than because of an obsession with courting good notices. *Spiderman: Turn Off the Dark* did 182 previews on Broadway before the official opening night the following year.

For the actors, however many previews there are, they're never quite enough – except that by now they also want to get the thing on and running. As a general average, there might be five, enough to create the feeling that there's unlimited time as the company comes in for another long day of Rehearsing in Preview – the strangest period, a slow-motion hurtling towards a deadline. The most terrible setback of one night can, in the light of the next day, be easily fixed, no problem at all. As time goes on, everyone agrees that the audience has taught you a lot, especially not to let them get ahead of you, either in terms of plot or unfolding character. Some things have gone across effortlessly; others, seemingly surefire, have met with incomprehension. Some laughs have been unexpected, some grievously missed. There's still time, with these daily post-mortems and re-rehearsals. You want to review interpretative things you're not sure of, only to find that technical matters take overwhelming priority: there may be a hundred and fifty sound and lighting cues to lock off. Long afternoons (not usually mornings) are spent tying up finicky matters of cueing, scene changes, all the minutiae. There is a distinct blood-sugar dip at about 4 p.m (or is that just me?). And some panic: sometimes the director has become so tired of listening to parts of the text that swingeing cuts start appearing in it, which the actors inevitably take personally.

It's startling how quickly a performance can be transformed. You despair, then go back to the beginning at the next preview, which seems much easier. Paradoxically, the process seems to be slowing up: oh, we'll sort that out tomorrow, or maybe the day after. A good director knows in what order to fix things. There's unlikely to be a rehearsal after the final preview – the ship is assumed to be as steady as it will ever be and the job done – though I have also anxiously rehearsed down till 6.30 p.m. before a Press Night.

The Second Preview is when you change into the wrong costume and the opening sound cue misfires. You tell yourself that the enterprise is not all just a matter of the Press Night but the whole run; it's not printed like a movie when you open, but will presumably get better and better with time. This doesn't seem to help much. The Third Preview is when the most pacific member of the company throws a fit – incomprehensibly, until you remember his partner is in tonight and he is nervous. Or the partner was in last night, and now he's discouraged. Either way it has nothing to do with what he's ostensibly complaining about. The only thing that matters about this is that he doesn't say to the director: 'I had a friend in last night who thought it might be better if . . .' That's worse than quoting *Macbeth*. The Fourth Preview is when your costume loses its moorings: the cloak slung over my shoulder in *Dances of Death*, tethered to my other side with gold ropes, somehow untethered itself and slid gently down me like an encasing tube of blue wool. Having cunningly prepared my stroke-paralysed arm, I could do nothing about it as my other arm was busy pulling necessary props from my opposite pocket within the tube. I was like a moth in its cocoon.

Press Night. Here it is, rearing up in front of you, the moment you can't see beyond, the day when you'd rather work in an office. No you wouldn't. As for nerves, the director Peter Wood once told me to get my ego out of the way and serve the author. Some things are easily said.

The day feels like a drawn breath. The only answer to it is to get working. Basically it's now a matter of remembering the lines: you know what you're doing and others can form an opinion as they will, but you very much don't want to dry. You buy good-luck cards and sometimes presents, distractedly: there are no more rehearsals, only a meeting to warm up a bit around teatime. This ceremony (perhaps an hour before an early curtain), however it's used, is gold dust, and you extend it as long as possible before leaving a stage to which you will only return under the beady eye of the Press. Fortunately stage management provide a deadline, or you might never leave: they have to set up and you have to get out of their way. Shortly there will be the nightly sound-check on all the speakers, and the almost provocatively untypical music track used to balance them will at least give the ASM a chance to bop a bit: Dolly Parton may precede *Hamlet*, the Rolling Stones *Hay Fever*.

All day you've resented the good weather and the people going about their business in the street. Myself, I become quite sentimental, nervous about everything else except the play. Missing a bus becomes a bad omen, let alone dropping a plate. Most of the world doesn't care what you're squaring up to now, but you make up for their indifference. The fear is far more to do with the prospect than the doing, which may even be highly enjoyable. Once you're on there's nothing else for it: this is an object lesson in living in the present. In your own way, against the odds, feeling ever unready, facing yourself in the mirror, doubting and being reassured, you've got to the point. *Merde*. Break a leg. *In bocca al lupo*. Good luck, to all of us.

7 First Night to Last

Opening Nights – Playing It In – Who's to Judge – Repertoire and Runs – Touring – The West End – Did I Leave the Fridge Door Open?

> NINA: I felt so completely vulgar and bogus. I couldn't decide what to do with my hands. Or how to stand. I couldn't control my voice. You've haven't any idea what it's like, knowing that you're acting badly . . .
>
> CHEKHOV, *The Seagull*

Don't be upset. It happens.

Dances of Death opened strongly, but I was reminded of another Scandinavian outing of ten years ago and playing another iron figure, Ibsen's John Gabriel Borkman. We'd toured the play for several weeks and got it to a good point, so that I stepped with some enthusiasm onto the stage at Greenwich Theatre in front of the national press – and was immediately unsure whether I had the slightest right to be there. Far from being in the moment I mentally returned to haunt every line I'd just spoken, reviewing it so obsessively that the next line only just came to me in time – with the result that it too was spoken without much specific meaning, its echo analysed in its turn. This backlog of self-judgements gradually built up to the point that I was close to stopping altogether: I wobbled as if on one leg, all but toppled, just regained balance. My attempts at character seemed patched on to the lines rather than giving rise to them; my vocal pattern was like the unaltering tune of a mobile phone, steady, annoying and shrill. How I longed to start all over again.

In the interval I battled to understand it. We'd been playing for six weeks, so this was hardly an opening night: it was all to do with the press. I hadn't been in front of them for a year or two. Some like my work more than others. The part of Borkman is a rarity – at that time only Paul Scofield and Ralph Richardson had done it in living memory, by which I mean the merciless memory of those older critics who were now looking balefully at me, it seemed, over their spectacles. Even so, what sense did this make? I'd been doing my job for a long time, and I was supposed to be as at home on a stage as a fish in water. And here I was on the end of a hook, floundering.

There are several reasons why this sombre farce might happen to you. Perhaps you were thrown off balance by something at the beginning of the show, known only to yourself: some metaphorical stumble or involuntary thing, some moment which seemed less good than it was at last night's show. You may be, facing the critics, suddenly seeing the play with the eyes of the enemy, as if you'd brought a dodgy friend home for approval: you again feel the doubts you had all those weeks ago, when you wondered if it might not be a bit of a leaky vessel. Then, as if corroborating you, the audience is very quiet – of course, it's full of critics. Actually most of them aren't there for blood, and would much rather have a good evening than a bad; they're therefore not that different from the punters who've paid, except that they're being paid themselves and will remember the bad night without any of the punter's bitterness. They don't laugh much because they've seen most things before. If they approve, it's in impassive silence. Nothing could be less conducive to comedy than a house full of reviewers, especially in a small theatre; and if it isn't a comedy, the silence is not that of rapt, almost tangible attentiveness but just that of an empty room. So you tighten up and pretty soon start listening to yourself, and the illusion that you're having a conversation with the other character is shot:

you jump in on her line before she finishes, so you're replying to something you haven't even heard yet. You're convinced
that every man, woman and child out there has seen and been
shocked by this elementary gaffe; actually they're too busy trying to follow the plot.

The symptoms may have started when you came into the theatre hours (no, light years) before, relaxed and confident, and
were immediately rattled by the sight of first-night cards and
gifts. When you made up, why did you smudge your mascara
as you never had before – was it an omen? Why did the spirit
gum fail to stick properly, or drip from the wig-join in viscous
threads, just catching the tip of your nose (at least it missed
your eye, where it would have welded to the retina in seconds)?
Why, after getting in much earlier than ever before, did you end
up running late? Because you gave yourself too much time in
which to worry. Ellen Terry, the great Victorian actress, taught
Henry Irving a big lesson: always have a cup of coffee half an
hour before the show and then make yourself a little late. Be
obliged therefore to run down the stairs, through the wings and
straight onto the stage. Above all don't stand offstage thinking about what you're about to do. Irving's acting immediately
improved: less calculated, less po-faced, more, well, natural. This
was a woman ahead of her time.

In my example you do immediately have another chance, the
show's second half: you can hardly wait to get back on and take
a grip on things. What's to lose any more? A prizefighter can
be decked in the early rounds and still end up the champion:
England can drop catches and win the Ashes. Look carefully at
the face of a Wimbledon finalist, two sets down, swigging his
Gatorade before winning three sets in a row. So, the first half was
a bit down: most audiences remember the later stages of a play
better than the early, and at the interval most minds are, if not
open, at least ajar.

By the time of *Borkman*, I fortunately knew something about pulling a chestnut out of the fire. The second half was an hour not of inspiration but of hard graft and sheer bloody-mindedness. And I just about got away with it. Or, to be accurate, the critical reception was the usual free-for-all. The *Daily Telegraph* thundered, 'He totally fails', while *The Times* purred that I was 'spot on'. So, business as usual. I was slightly appeased; but I wondered what the outward effect had been. Though the reviewers wouldn't have known the reason, there may have been a slight puzzlement about the performance's remoteness; it had probably seemed muffled (as it was, by technique, my means of getting through); not a light shone into the mind of Borkman but something private, hermetic. A thin varnish of evasion had settled on quite a good piece of work. At least I now knew what the effect was when I was really bad; and that whether in your first year or your forty-first, paralysis can strike.

If it's of interest, now I've turned seventy, the extremes have become more extreme. The last two shows I've done have, on the afternoon of opening, reduced me to a nauseated fear worse than any I can remember – which then vanished the moment I stepped onto the stage, replaced by a certainty greater than I've had before. The gradient between increasing self-doubt and accumulating self-confidence has just got steeper.

However your first night develops, you finish the show. Maybe nobody much comes round to see you. What does this mean – is a secret being kept? Is the play not liked? Is X failing to deliver? Am I? Keep your reservations to yourself, and don't look for reassurance. As often, Chekhov offers comfort. Of the disastrous first night of that *Seagull* of his, in St Petersburg in 1896, he said: 'People I knew well, people I'd had dinner with, looked at me with odd expressions, very odd.' Your colleagues, having perhaps felt the same doubts, are hopefully lying, to you and themselves; in fact there's nothing, absolutely nothing to say. Not even the odd ecstatic customer can relieve this anxiety. There's a knot of people in the corridor or at the cast party: author, wife and agent, assistant director, company manager. You veer towards them, to greet, then immediately think better of it. There's a smell coming off them: they know something you don't.

~

A really good First Night may be described by means of a bad: instead of battling the tide, you rolled like a dolphin in warm waters. It's also a far rarer event, and a credit to our profession. With exactly the same benedictions and gestures of mutual support that went into the failure, a group of professionals say, Fuck it, what are we here for? Why work all this time only to throw everything away now through self-regard? Nerves would be an insult to the author, the director and each other. So they work as tightly as a champion team indifferent to who scores the goal. Everybody listens not to themselves, but to each other. It's one of the best things that can happen and, as you see, there's far less to say about it. As for the press, who knows, ever? I knew of the critic of one leading national newspaper who used to make a habit of standing up and cheering, then going home and writing a stinking review. Perverse, or what?

~

Try again. Fail again. Fail better.

SAMUEL BECKETT, *Worstward Ho*

Whatever's happened, you have to climb back on to the horse. On the morning after an opening you may feel as if you'd been hit by a truck – or, as a friend said recently, like a stunned mullet. You may have a monster hangover from adrenalin depletion and pub wine, or teetotal exhaustion. The pleasant horizon you so looked forward to at this moment remains cloudy; all the dear postponed ordinary-life things you would suddenly be able to do stay undone; the dyspeptic fear that you might not be able to rise to it all again on the second performance begins to pre-occupy you.

In fact this may be the first matinee – with rehearsals con-tinuing, matinees in previews are rare. Personally I like them, especially on a Saturday, once you've got going. They're for truly dedicated theatregoers who really want to be there rather than having gone to the half-price ticket booth to book anything that's going. Whether afternoon or evening, the adrenalin comes back: it can't be stopped. Actually adrenalin is the last thing you need; dogged application, more like. If the opening night was good, whatever made it so is irretrievable; if bad, there's everything to play for and the slate is clean. Still, you kick yourself to find how easy this one is – you seem to have all the time in the world, and the audience is quick-witted and willing.

The progress of a show through its life is oddly self-govern-ing. Obviously the actors work hard, hoping to grow, deepen, in every way improve: they want to feel the difference every night. But the show may not oblige – or rather, it'll obey some mys-tery of its own. The one constant is your own discipline, which has to include a certain tolerance: a production will grow at its own pace, like a plant, and we sometimes spoil it by overwater-ing. The director's gone but in due course they'll be back and may have to 'take out the improvements' – all the elaboration and lily-gilding which we thought was nightly reinvention. It's no fun for a director to return to a success and feel a whiff of self-satisfaction coming off the stage: someone doing a meta-phorical backflip in the middle of a line, so at ease is he, the unassuming quality that once made the show good mysteriously lost. In the case of a less-than-success, there may be a slightly desperate striving for effect.

For the time being though, he or she has gone, no longer paid and needing to earn a living; the Assistant Director may be young and hesitant to criticise. So who's to say how you're doing? There's a story of Laurence Olivier storming off to his dressing room after a show, not because he'd been bad that night, but because he'd been exceptionally good, couldn't for the life of him work out why, and so couldn't be sure of doing it the next night. But was even Olivier the best judge? The pleasant fact is, maybe not. As friends begin to come in, you look around for corroboration and get surprises. You might be castigated by an honest one after an evening you think has gone well (and how you were looking forward to their visit!); or there might be a knock on the door, and as you start apologising your visitor announces, straight off the bat, how delighted they were. Don't refuse this praise, by the way, or seek to limit it: that's grace-less and sounds like fishing for more. I once did this when Tom Stoppard – nobody's fool, after all – told me I'd been wonderful. I pulled a self-doubting face. 'All right then,' he said, 'you were shit. Whatever you like, Michael.' Quite right.

There's no objective fact in the theatre, only individual responses and a mild consensus. Your own Geiger counter may not be infallible. I recently had to look at two filmed versions of a solo show of mine, shot on successive nights, to decide which bits from which to use for a master version. I thought I had quite a fresh memory of both performances, and what was better at which; but I was wrong, every time. The performance I thought was not quite in the zone had the odd virtue of uncertainty, the favoured one seemed glib.

So, Sir Laurence, you were generally pretty good, but you couldn't control everything. And thank you, Sir Ralph (Rich-ardson), for putting the same thing in your mellower way: that a good night feels like driving a golf ball clean down the fair-way, the next is 'nowhere to be seen'. (Even the joke's grammar is eccentric in the Richardson manner: what exactly is it that is nowhere to be seen? The ball? The fairway? His talent? All three?)

Don't worry if an audience coughs a lot – it may be the middle of the winter, they have colds, they wanted to come so much, they've paid a lot of money to be there, and they may be mortified by it. So for goodness' sake don't take it personally – that's just your vanity. All in all, don't give yourself too hard a time, just a hard enough time. Try not to take the worry home with you, not more than you're bound to, anyway. By tomorrow, the evidence is gone: set to work again. Any run is a mix of absurd repetition and reckless adventure: something interesting is going to happen every time. And if you have a bad night – accident-prone, timing gone, self-conscious, even drying – please note: Alfred Brendel, with the gallantry of the truly great, once told me he'd done an unaccountably bad concert in Berlin a week ago and still couldn't get over it though he'd done half a dozen good ones since. So you're not alone. And what, in any case, is Alfred Brendel's idea of a bad night?

～

For the actor, repertoire is the ideal fix, a sort of heaven really. We owe its arrival, as with previews and much else that we take for granted, to Peter Hall's decision to model the RSC from its inception on the Moscow Art Theatre and the Berliner Ensemble: a semi-permanent company and a rolling repertoire in which the play changes every night or so.

If you're in only one show in a repertoire company's season you have plenty of time off, so you greedily hope for lucrative other work fitting in perfectly with your schedule, though, frustratingly, it rarely quite does, clashing by perhaps one infuriating day. If you're in four, you're busy but stimulated, developing an infinite variety which you may not have had before. There may be a financial consideration: the National Theatre pay a basic salary augmented by a per-performance fee, the RSC a steady rate, come what may. You could therefore do better at the NT, but only if your show or shows are scheduled to play a lot. In a busy repertoire there's also a question of stamina: you could be rehearsing a new production while playing an established one at night – or, on certain memorable days, rehearsing Play One in the morning, playing a matinee of Play Two and then an evening show of Play Three; this is fine when you're young and hungry, but further down the line you might look at such a commitment more warily. A management will always press an actor towards it, for understandable reasons.

If your show has been out of the rep for a while, as it can be at the NT (though not to the extent of the Moscow Art Theatre, which sustains an enormous programme and sometimes rests a production for a year or more), time has to be found for a line-run on the day of its return, even if a new show you're in rehearsal for is about to open and under pressure. In fact line-runs only help up to a point – as do speed-runs (everything at double speed), which are loved by some but about which I'm sceptical. The problem is more a matter of imagination: every show has its own *genius loci* and you have to re-enter it; like a dancer, you need to recover its required muscle memory.

The logistics of repertoire can be complicated, with certain anthropological inevitabilities. When Peter Brook came to do *Antony and Cleopatra* at Stratford in 1978, he was scheduled for the last slot of the season and he found a very weary company who were, variously, playing up to three matinees a week as well as their evening performances; so the actors (all of whose individual spread of shows was different) weren't able to start as early in the morning as he would have liked (Equity overnight breaks), and he had to release various combinations of them in good time for their matinees. His six-week rehearsal period thus boiled down, in effect, to something like four. It's a pity he wasn't one of the season's openers. This of course presupposes a company operating like the RSC at the time, in which almost everyone was, bracingly, in two or three productions at once; sometimes in its early days an actor would play a matinee in Stratford and be rushed to London for an evening show of another play at the Aldwych, the company's London home. Nowadays the RSC sometimes does straight runs as well as repertoire; at the NT the public gets the benefit of a repertoire, but the casts tend to be separate – more expensive on salaries, but a lot easier to programme.

In whatever form, who wouldn't like repertoire, the luxury end of the job? One of the pleasures of my life is to have played Hamlet for a period of two years – but not every night, so that I notched up about a hundred and fifty performances overall and felt the life of the part gradually bending and shaping with my own. Early in the run there might have been four performances in a week, thinning out to two or three later as more shows opened, and finally to one. The benefit is obvious: you come back renewed, on your mettle, work refreshed by life. Other people's lives too: with the Peter Hall Company at the Old Vic I played in Harley Granville-Barker's *Waste* for a whole year, but only a handful of times in a month – such a play, brilliant study of political graft as it is, would have had trouble sustaining a straight run for that long. Its first couple of months were in the run-up to Tony Blair's triumph in the 1997 general election; the political and human sleaze Barker exposes in the play appealed hugely to a public generally sick of Major's government and preparing to welcome the fresh-faced boy. However, after the election the euphoria was such that nobody really wanted *Waste*, and the bottom immediately fell out of the box office. Unusually, we were able to do something about it. In most theatres, the schedule would been long set and booking, but by delaying the start of each booking period as long as possible, we were flexible

enough to re-programme quite late and avoid the embarrassment of empty scheduled performances – just as we would have
been able to exploit an unexpected hit. We only just scraped
home: there came a day when, because of some database glitch,
I got a duplicated letter addressing me as 'Dear Theatregoer'
and offering me half-price seats for *Waste* featuring Michael
Pennington.

~

A short straight run, meanwhile, represents honour satisfied.
Four or five weeks, perhaps; so by the time you've done a handful of previews and a couple of nights for the press you may
already be quite a long way through it. This kind of continuous
season is about the norm at Birmingham Rep, say, or at the Lyric
in Hammersmith, or any other theatre that schedules a season of
plays at a time and can make only an educated guess at how long
each might attract an audience. Very successful smaller theatres such as the Donmar and the Almeida in London generally
feel comfortable in scheduling eight or nine weeks, especially if
it's a particularly tasty prospect (big American actor or popular
Shakespeare), and if they feel sure enough of their regular audience as well as their stargazing one.

What happens as your eight-show week now unfolds depends
on the circumstances: whether you're straight away rehearsing
another job or have a day full of voice-overs (assuming you're in
London), or more probably just idly living life till the evenings.
It should feel like sailing on an open sea; the pleasure of coming
in rested each night to do a show you feel on top of is obviously
great. It's accompanied by the strange fact that you may only
now feel you're being properly paid: in many contracts, your
respectable playing salary only kicks in now that you're working
for three or four hours of the day rather than during the hard
graft of rehearsals, when you earn a pittance.

Casts vary, of course. Some people commute from far away and arrive just in time for the traditional half-hour call before the show (actually thirty-five minutes, since you're supposed to be standing by five minutes before the show starts); some warm up physically and vocally at length at about 6 p.m. on the stage, some not at all. On some shows I've stretched and rotated for England; on others I've strolled into work. If you come in early enough and you're in a producing theatre (rather than one that buys its product in), you'll sense the next attraction rehearsing in the building, like a suddenly more important train being prepared in a siding; the corridors and green room are full of people who seem like intruders, until you recognise some of them and realise you may even have worked with them.

While a play is running it seems imperishable: same place, same routine, same absorbing world. But it evaporates in a few hours late one Saturday evening, gone beyond recovery unless the costumes and set are, unusually, being stored. A group that's been together for three months disperses, some to other jobs, most, generally, not. You feel you were just getting started, and now you're done. Those who are most saddened by this moment are often, oddly enough, the ones who crossed off each perform-ance on the schedule stuck to the dressing-room wall, as if they couldn't wait for it all to be over. I've no explanation for this, except to assume that an actor's forward compulsion towards being one of the ninety per cent out of work can be almost as great as his desire to be one of the ten per cent employed. You play the final night as if it were the first, since you badly want it to be the best, which more or less ensures it won't be. There may be a little devil at work, in recognition of the event: on the last last night I did, I was advised by another character not to fly off the candle rather than the handle, and I almost asked another if he was still in love with his mother rather than if he was still in touch with her. I also fused all the lights in the dressing room.

If the show has gone well, you want to blame someone for its short life; you inveigh at the theatre's inflexibility, which hasn't allowed your success to be extended (but how could it have been?), or pursued a transfer to another theatre vigorously enough (case not proven). But at least you've played the play for longer than you rehearsed it. If it's the other way round, it feels like unfinished business, which is what's wrong with the three-week run (or Broad Hint), which is surprisingly common these days. Chichester do it as part of a policy to stimulate their box office by having one or even two more shows in the season than you might expect. Despite the capital cost of mounting them, eight shows each of which runs for three weeks seem to do the trick better than six that run for four or four for six. But the implication is obvious: if the play seems, even in early rehearsals, to be developing any sort of legs, there will already be talk of its future, especially in the West End of London. This is called Going In. Friends come round and say this really must Go In, and you begin to think: yes, that's right, It Should, in fact it would be a Great Wrong If It Didn't. Occasionally critics say it as well. But it usually doesn't happen: the economics have become so hard that a producer once told me that only if the reviews were a hundred per cent favourable would he consider such a thing – not even ninety per cent was enough, he had to have unanimity as a starting point. Invariably too, a transfer to London, even if a theatre is available, will need to be shored up by the guaranteed income of a few weeks on the road first.

~

So: touring, which is what the playwright Ben Jonson described as 'going with shoes full of gravel . . . after a blind jade and hamper and stalk upon boards and barrel heads to an old cracked trumpet' – and perhaps, for all of Luckings Transport, Raileasy and a Marks and Spencer in every town, it's not changed much.

For Ben and his actors, the strain was on the feet and the horse's hooves; now it's on the pocket. It's ruinously expensive these days to get comfortable accommodation on the road, whether you're up at the three-star end or looking for the legendary five-pound-a-night digs of ancient theatre repute – which, like their celebrated landladies, don't really exist any more, having yielded to short apartment rentals and anonymous self-catering of various standards. Whatever the nature of the tour, the touring allowance wrung by Equity from most managements is unlikely to cover your costs; and the question of whether to share and with which colleagues, in an apartment you're getting off the theatre's digs list but which you're unlikely to have a chance to see until you arrive, could make you want to run home to mother. The sharing decisions have to be made at a bad time as well: unless you like living dangerously you're going to want to secure somewhere in the early stages of rehearsal when you may not know anyone very well or whether you would care to bump into them at breakfast.

There was once an actor who slept in his car in a layby rather than pay for digs; another bought an ambulance for the same reason, though it's hard to see how he broke even that way – free parking near hospitals perhaps. Maybe he was the same fellow who travelled with a tape measure to check the size of his billing on each new theatre's posters – it sounds like the same mindset. Digs, meanwhile, used to be one of the most fruitful sources of theatrical lore, largely because they were linked to seasonal reps with permanent companies, and you might be in them for months, not a week. Let's roll several mythical landladies into one. In a town that ran a weekly rep she would always come to each new play on its first night and praise you because you were so reassuringly the same as you'd been last week in the previous show. She would regularly greet a friend of mine when he came home with 'Oh, Mr Kay, you were absolutely . . . adequate.' She

celebrated Christmas with her pantomime artists by at last giving them a breakfast sausage in addition to their usual baked
beans; she kept a visitors' book in which she didn't notice that (or
understand why) the regular recommendation 'great digs' was
sometimes followed by 'quoth the raven'. The disgraceful entry
in the same book, 'LDO' ('Landlady's daughter obliges'), was not
uncommon – and, in the same vein, she herself was once caught
in flagrante with a famous lodger on her own kitchen table when
her other lodger came through the door, at which she called out
to him from beneath the great man's weight, 'Ooh, Mr Smith,
you must think I'm a terrible flirt . . .' All these anecdotes are part
of your equipment in thespian life, the only trouble being that
we all know the same ones, and have our own variants.

On the weekly touring circuit in those days actors from a
variety of companies would expect to run into each other in
transit on the Sunday on the platform of Crewe Station, then
the busiest interchange in the country, and swap notes before
fanning out variously for their next week's date. It was said that
Moss Empires had access to the best weekly digs and that those
in Ashton-under-Lyme were the worst. Nowadays Equity gives
you a digs list, with genuine opinions instead of the theatres'
non-committal ones, and confirmation of wi-fi.

You'll certainly be opening on a Monday – most venues won't
countenance a Tuesday opening since it sacrifices a night's revenue, and they'd rather put up with the overtime costs of loading
the show into the theatre on Sunday for the sake of getting the
turnstiles moving on the Monday. This is tough for you in other
ways. You'll have been travelling to and fro, almost certainly,
unless, having no other home to go to, you like arriving directly
in a new town on a Sunday. Quite swiftly, you then have to work
out how to get to and fro, and once in the theatre on Monday
afternoon – this is to confirm that you've arrived – there's very
limited time to sense its dynamics. The set may be up but the

lighting, work on which involves regular plunges into blackness, may only make it by a whisker in the evening: the angles and sightlines will always, surprisingly, be a bit different from last week, and you'll become preoccupied with them. Though all this has been carefully planned for by the production team, it can still feel disorientating. The company rushes into the first show, still finding out about the acoustic, and only gets into its stride around Wednesday.

There'll be a midweek matinee and a Saturday one too. The entire week sometimes feels easier to get through than a typical single day: although there are only three empty days to fill in, each can seem long. If it's somewhere you've not been before, you may bump into a colleague or two in the local museum or gallery or health club, likewise feeling that the new place demands you pay some perfunctory respects – if you're in Hull, you might as well learn about the trawlers. But how many movie matinees (starting around 1.50 p.m.) can you do in a week? You do the rounds all day, have supper at teatime at the local Strada (where you may get a discount), then at 6 p.m. you're back in the theatre, feeling that it is, after all, the best place to be. 'What did you do today?' you ask or are asked, as if you and your colleagues had been apart for weeks. You may have much to tell or you may have stayed in bed all day, it doesn't matter, it's a bonding. Now, with relief, work starts. It feels oddly like home.

As always, you warm up physically – or not; it can't do any harm, and it has nothing, by the way, to do with the size of part you're playing. Someone with three lines is as entitled to this re-immersion in the life of the show, the physical sensation of being on the stage, as the lead. If you have a fight or a dance, however, you must – must – have a Call to run it before the show every night – the risk of injury (and not only to you) or muscular disaster is obviously much higher. The two are really the same thing: a stage fight is like a dance for two or more people

– intensely collaborative, entirely dependent on eye contact and precision (and certainly not on savagery with the weapon), a sort of *pas de deux*. And a dancer would never go on cold.

However things go, afterwards you might go to the pub, which may or may not be nice, and may or may not have a soft spot for theatricals, so you may or may not get a welcome. In a modern theatre, you might have hoped to be heading for the front-of-house bar for your recuperative drink. These days they are rarely open; most theatres now run them as concessions and so don't control either prices or attitude. You may pay the same as the public and be treated with the same contumely at that end of the evening. When I played mad King George III at Birmingham – a part, I must say, not far from King Lear in its demands – I would stumble into the foyer bar for a glass of wine and be yelled at as if I were trying to get into a pub at closing time, while my director – an Associate Director of the theatre – was refused a drink unless she produced her ID. I hope it's different now – it was a sort of nadir.

Rather than risk such unhappinesses, you might sit in the dressing room with a colleague or two and a bottle of wine, and, if you're old enough to remember the opposite, deplore the regular tannoy announcements saying firmly that the stage door will be closing in forty-five/thirty/fifteen minutes. What philistinism, you protest. Don't they realise what we've been through and our entitlement to drink the night away, while some unfortunate stage-door keeper sits waiting, like a movie star's chauffeur, to lock up? The fact that it's usually a young person's voice – a temp, work experience even? – seems to make this worse.

Stage-door keepers, by the way, are not quite what they were. Nowadays they're usually retired automatically at sixty-five, even though they may have as many years of their idiosyncratic work left in them as I would hope to have as an actor. Their uncanny gift for keeping the wrong kind of visitors out, and their sharp nose for recognising that people who announce themselves as unexpected friends should perhaps be let through, is an instinct as sharp as a watchdog's. Nowadays, though, stage-door keepers can be maids of all work with no such sense of smell. I was once yelled at by a teenager running the stage door in Bromley because I objected to coming to it – a considerable distance – to identify my visitors rather than having them sent through or politely turned away. What if, after such a journey, they were unwelcome? You really don't want a stage-door keeper with Attitude, let alone an active dislike of what they're doing.

Then, come what may, you're back in the digs – a moment so subconsciously feared that you may have stayed alone in your dressing room till the last moment, reflecting on this and that and the other thing. The light was still bright there and the air hummed with echoes of the play, its ghostly shreds of laughter and vivid language. But in the end you're back in your Accommodation. Instead of the cup of tea and the cheery congratulations for being, like Mr Kay, always the same, you're likely to be in an otherwise darkened house, looking at wallpaper you wouldn't have chosen, flipping on the TV without much interest because your heart is still somewhere inside what you've just been doing. You're hoping for a wave of fatigue. When you've been trying to perform well, who wants to see politicians acting badly in the face of Jeremy Paxman's histrionic bullying for more money than you're making? Or more bad acting in some American Soap, also for more money? Sport may be the best option. Who, after all, quietly reads an improving novel after a show? If you have a partner, you'll text or call them, hoping to goodness for a benediction in return. If you haven't, you may text a couple of people you normally don't, looking for human contact, before sinking into lachrymose oblivion.

~

There are refinements on this model – the post-West End tour with a new cast, or the dedicated touring company that does little else. But whatever form it takes, it can be a fight with loneliness combined with an odd sort of elation, as if you're proving that Touring Is What It's All About. Donald Wolfit did it all his life, including when the bombs were dropping: he also paid for his dedication with a certain metropolitan neglect compared to his acting peers. You may get a flash of this on Sundays, when you're briefly in London, feeling dislocated, doing the laundry. You might bump into people at some event or other. No one knows what you're doing – 'What are you up to?' they say, with a puzzled air, cautiously, as if imagining you're out of work. They haven't heard of your project (it hasn't been nationally reviewed), and wonder how you're filling your time. Not for the first time you realise how London-centric British theatre life still is: despite the vigour and, often, supremacy of the 'regions', the capital is what matters. When I would return periodically during the five years I spent on the road with my own company, I felt like some ragged pilgrim back after half a lifetime to a place changed beyond recognition and with no memory of him. Being out of the loop is chronically felt by anyone who tours a lot, and it can deepen into real pessimism if the process of getting good freelance work afterwards gets off, almost inevitably, to a slow start.

And yet, and yet, and yet. You'll go on tour over and over again and even look forward to it. You wear a special badge, or scar: wear it proudly. Regional audiences pay their taxes as well, and even now don't always get the best provision. You've done a fine thing, and your sinews are tough as rope.

Meanwhile, if your tour brings you within the M25, a new metropolitan gossip begins: What Important Person Might Be In Tonight? Doesn't he live down here in Richmond? There's a dressing-room etiquette about this. Rather than declaring to everyone in earshot that Cameron Mackintosh is indeed on his way, experienced actors will quietly ask each other if they like knowing such things or not – rather as they might ask if you read the reviews or not. But you may sometimes need what Judi Dench calls an Adrenalin Booster – eight shows a week for several months is quite a big call on your enthusiasm, and if a whispered name or two runs round the building it may wake things up. If ever for a moment you shamefacedly lose interest – for all that your training tells you that every audience deserves the best – you can give yourself a shock by thinking who might be watching: a producer, a director, a talented colleague, any number of unexpectedly potent people. The habit of thinking this then gets so embedded that in the end you determine to be at your best every night, come what may.

It's surprising, by the way, who makes you nervous and who doesn't. I have a friend who loyally comes to see me in everything and is always supportive and enthusiastic; I'm a bit nervous meanwhile because I secretly think he may be a better actor than I am. Thus, because of nerves, I fulfil my own prophecy. Perhaps there's someone in who's known you for a long time, back to your childhood, for instance. It took me years, certainly into my thirties, to get over a funk of terror when my dear parents would come – they knew me even before I was in nappies, after all, and remembered my foolishnesses. Then at a certain point, perhaps because I knew they wouldn't be there for ever, I became utterly determined to prove to them, even at that late stage, that I'd made the right decision in life. So these egotistical anxieties can come to good; and perhaps in a way you always need someone to dedicate a performance to.

~

And so, hope against hope, to the fabled West End, with its dilapidated seating, its inadequate toilets (yes, I know there are exceptions), the necessity of going to work each night in an increasingly déclassé and rackety Soho. Shaftesbury Avenue, our equivalent of Broadway between Fortieth and Fiftieth, must be a huge disappointment to visitors, but then so is Broadway. For the actors, in place of what you imagined (and I think used in fact to be), a sort of community of West End shows, including cheery post-show meetings in the bars – 'How is yours going?' – has been largely replaced by an uneasy resentment of those doing better than you are, and the fear that some heathen producer will pull your show off for no discernible reason. The fact is, everyone is extremely insecure: this is a place of insult and sudden, unexplained decisions. Casual labour changes by the week, so that instead of the consistency of staffing you would find at the National or Manchester – genuine collaborations with costume and wig specialists who have a stake in proceedings – someone new, like a babysitter, seems to introduce themselves every couple of weeks. And the money is most certainly, and laughably, not what it was. And yet it remains a kind of Mecca, and you want to do it.

From a producer's point of view, the tour preceding this moment has been the means of getting enough money back to pay off the production's capital costs before risking the major reinvestment of a transfer. The set-up might have been this: one of the handful of regional producing houses with adequate means (currently Bath Theatre Royal and the bigger reps) sets up a show to open at their venue and then tour for six to eight weeks in preparation for London. A West End producer might have put in fifty per cent of the capital in return for first refusal, and the regional theatre the same percentage: so the touring income is likewise split. Bath, we'll say, will pre-sell the show to the touring theatres, either looking for a proportion of the box office or a guaranteed figure to cover their running costs (paying the actors, carting the production around the country), plus a management fee (a polite name for profit) on top of that, as high as they can get away with. If the host theatres are excited about the commercial possibilities, they will bid against each other for a particular week and so it becomes an auction; in the end the original producer may make a clear ten or even twenty thousand a week above his direct costs. If that happens across eight weeks, he'll be able to pay off much of the original costs of building the set, rehearsals, publicity and all the rest of it. The auction has become so sophisticated in recent years that producers some-times hire specialist independent agencies to book their tours for them and do all the deals. They will charge whatever they think the market will bear and encourage competition some-what in the manner of estate agents, pushing the price up by implying there are many rivals also sniffing around the show. I've heard tell too of some dirty tricks I'd rather not believe: since a producer needs to secure a number of weeks a year from the touring theatres, he may even sell them an imaginary produc-tion loaded with stars, thus blocking off certain weeks, then ring late in the day to say the production's cancelled but, not to panic, he can offer something else instead – the less starry show he per-haps planned to do in the first place.

If the tour is long enough and the deals good, both parties may make some money; but this still doesn't mean you'll get to London with your cherished work. Like a poker player who gets up from the table as soon as he's winning, the producer may decide to quit while he's ahead and not risk the reinvestment of re-mounting the show in the capital – an increasingly exorbi-tant enterprise, especially in terms of publicity, advertising and front-of-house displays. This is of course depressing for every-one else. Especially the actors: waiting for news about whether you're Coming In, week in week out – 'Has anyone heard any-thing?' – is one of the most enervating parts of life on the road. And sometimes you realise that the prospect of the West End may have been a cultivated mirage to attract the actors: the advertising phrase 'prior to the West End' covers a multitude of half-truths.

However, this time, in you come. You're pleased of course, but in another way you're facing a peculiar kind of life. This is to be the open-ended uncertainty of London, a thing that can be terminated by the management at only two weeks' notice if they start losing money, but which you're stuck with for whatever length of contract you've managed to negotiate. Nowadays that's unlikely to be less than six months, or three months sometimes for the stars, and more probably will be a year, assuming the show survives that long. You've no control – you could be out of a job in two weeks or twelve months, so can neither book a holiday nor make plans. There's not much quarter given in this negotiation – the cost of re-rehearsing and reprinting the posters is significant for any management. In any case you may want the security. It could be worse: in the old days you could be caught on a 'run of the play' contract, come what may, but since that could technically be for the rest of your life, Equity managed to get rid of it. They also got rid of the clause that required a man at a certain level of salary to provide his own lounge suit, another at a slightly higher level a dinner jacket, and one at the top level full evening dress.

Sometimes none of these questions arise. I once played Oscar Wilde in a play about his three trials called *Gross Indecency*: it was a good piece of work but didn't consolidate its West End audience, and closed after three weeks. After the final night I went for supper with a friend at a restaurant immediately opposite the theatre; by the time we came out to go home, the front-of-house display was entirely gone apart from an eight-foot picture of me against which a Saturday-night passer-by was performing an act of, if not gross, then urinary indecency. The picture, scrubbed down, now hangs at the top of my house to remind me of John Gielgud's maxim that you can learn more from your failures than your successes.

Assuming you're going to be in a substantial run, you'll fall into a certain pattern, or rather a variegated vagueness which becomes an intent routine at about 5 p.m., when the air begins to change around you, the whole point of the day approaches, and, against the tide, you go out to work. Ninety-five per cent of the people surging in the opposite direction wouldn't, by the look of their tunnel vision, be much interested to hear what you're doing. As you arrive in central London twenty or so other shows are flashing their neons and pushing themselves out onto the sidewalks for attention like importunate tarts. You're thinking a bit about what happened last night and whether there are metaphorical repairs to be done. You may go over your lines, particularly in the early stages, mainly to jog your memory of last night and certainly if the text is one of those inexplicably tricky ones that's still proving tough to retain. You remember that Stage Management, by a standard convention, announced the show's running time at the end of last night's performance, noting whether each half had speeded up or slowed down. Most shows are remarkably stable in this way. If it's a matter of a minute longer, I hardly think it's important – I'm not sure it matters if it's up to five minutes, unless it's a farce, which has rather stricter rules. Elsewhere pace isn't everything: still, it's worth a moment's thought.

You'll become so used to not having an evening free that much as you'd like one, you sense that when you finally get it, life will have lost some meaning. Compared with touring, the West End is a relatively unsociable life: after weeks of being in each other's pockets and mutually dependent, the company scatters after each show, heading for home. Still, there's a continuing mild flux among you; sometimes you get irritated with a colleague, however close you are, then, for no particular reason, you get un-irritated and continue. It's like the ebb and flow in a marriage. You may start counting the house, taking an unhealthy interest in the box office in an attempt to work out whether the show is still solvent; very hard to do unless it's really empty, since there will have been concessions, free seats, and it's difficult to deduce accurately what the box-office take may be from the number of people out there.

If you've done this before, you'll know of a far worse thing which can happen after a couple of months or so – a creeping sense of unreality leads you to forget your lines and develop early signs of stage fright. It's logical really: an ever-repeated word or phrase becomes meaningless, and the same can go for a whole speech. Some people, having dreaded this so much, recover with perverse stylishness. I knew an experienced actress so afraid of forgetting her lines in a long run that when she did so one night she fell to the ground in a faint. We brought down the curtain, put on the understudy and sent her home in a cab – a cab that, as it turned out, she then commandeered to drop her at a restaurant close by, where she was seen by a passer-by at the end of the show enjoying the remnants of a dinner *à deux*. Apart from her gall, the interesting part of the story is that the faint was absolutely genuine, not thrown; her dinner was not pre-planned but a rapid and I'm sure satisfying response to the new situation.

Even without such drastic solutions, this problem clears in due course like a harmless enough illness. In fact, such dangers are part of the reason I like straight runs – they're cautionary. Some actors see nightly repetition as a challenge to do exactly what happened the night before (as if that was a definition of professionalism), followed by an untroubled night's sleep: if they fail in this aim they kick themselves. These are good actors, I don't mean they're not, but their performances are liable to congeal. The temptation merely to repeat what is known to work is so strong that it takes some strength of character to reinvent, and there's therefore much pleasure in doing it. What happened last night is only one possibility. It's not a matter of consciously avoiding being the same, but of being sure that the route being traced to each moment is found freshly. If it's not, and you cheat a change, that's when you kick yourself. For we all kick ourselves for one reason or another, that's for sure.

And you know what? This time you're a hit.

A Reverie: Did I Leave the Fridge Door Open?

Now it's second house on a Saturday in July 2009, about nine o'clock and well into the second half. After a hundred nights we're running well. Looking across from the stage left wing into the right I can see Jan, the Wig Supervisor, sitting lost in thought. She wears a little apron with pockets full of hairpins, combs, adhesives and a pocket torch: she looks like a nurse, ready for anything. She has yellow plimsolls on, and she pensively lifts first one foot then the other a few inches off the ground to do ankle-circling exercises: left, right, left. Technically, I suppose one side of her brain controls one ankle and the other the other but tonight I like to think one side is taking in what's happening on the stage and the other handling her own thoughts. Jan might not be able to tell you all the details of the play – she only arrived for the dress rehearsals, when her attention was rightly on hair and wigs rather than the unfolding drama. However, circling her ankles and well into the run, she's alert for anything unusual – a line or two being cut, say, that would cause David to come off for his brief wig-check a moment sooner. If everything sounds just as it did last night, it's a good show for her: her torch will go into her mouth, David will rush towards her and be tidied up by its light, and back on he'll go.

Tonight though, Jan's balance could be a little out: she certainly looks preoccupied. David, who knows her better than I do for the simple reason that I don't wear a wig – for someone who does, having it put on every night is a personal ministration leading to shared confidences – says she's unhappy about many things in her life. He is thus a good colleague to her, and tolerant of her sometimes getting the night wrong and bringing him the wrong wig at a quarter to seven (we're in a repertoire of two plays) – if it were me I'd get a bit tight-lipped.

His wig check is combined with a quickish costume change – not Jan's responsibility but that of Chrissy, who is sitting beyond her, deeper in the wings, next to a rail of clothes which holds all the evening's changes for which going back to the dressing rooms would take too long, as well as the used costumes that haven't yet found their way back upstairs. She too is anxious tonight: she has her third audition on Monday to take over as an understudy down the road in *Oliver*. She gave up performing – she's a singer and dancer – to have her daughter and is having some trouble getting back in, though she does teach a bit: she's filling in with us as Wardrobe Assistant and Dresser. Today she asked my advice on tactics: whether to go for this third meeting or just tell the producers that they've surely seen enough of her by now to make a decision, and that on Monday she is just too busy. I advised a middle course – to offer to go, but at a time that suited her better, when her daughter was at nursery school, rather than when they'd suggested – and that's how it's ended up. She was pleased, and mentioned as she left my room that my trousers needed a bit of darning on what she called the right butt-cheek.

Chrissy knows every button (and butt-cheek) in the show, as Jan does every curl, but, like her, only some of what the audience gets. When I started at Stratford, three matronly dressers used to sit in a row on the first-floor landing like tricoteuses – they always knew what plays were scheduled for the next season long before the hopeful actors. They'd say, Ah, *Love's Labour's Lost* again – that's three changes for the women, two for the men, plus the quick change into the Muscovites' scene. You might say, Well, that will surely depend on the production, but they were usually right in the end. My own dresser in those days was, unusually, a man, Phil Trueman, who worked in a car factory all day and so arrived looking grey in the evenings. Once he sent me on as a Trojan hero in my long white flowing robe with a coat hanger hanging off the back of it. I said, Phil, really, you'd have me going on in front of all those people looking like a fool (not the word I used); he said, It doesn't take a coat hanger, mate. I loved Phil and am sad at his passing – the greyness in his skin came direct from his overworked heart.

I keep thinking of those Stratford days these evenings two generations later: there's a scene in the current show that unaccountably takes me straight back there. The most likely explanation is that some haphazard thing reminded me of them during the couple of days when I was originally learning the scene, so the memory got printed as well, in the shadow of the lines. Now, every night at this point, I can catch the backstage smell of the old RST, a mixture of disinfectant, home cooking and damp wool: there was I, new married, new employed, eyes wide open, still curious about all of it, living on the Tiddington Road and declaring I couldn't love anyone who didn't love the Beatles (she did).

This quick change has always been a little problematic because the clothes are hung on their rail on metal coat hangers rather than plastic ones. A quick change is difficult to keep quiet anyway since even subdued panic creates incidental noise, and when metal hangers clatter and fall to the ground in all the haste it's audible: the scene on stage meanwhile is very quiet, very concentrated, and for Amy very emotional. She was so upset last night at this point that she, unusually, cried when she came off. I stroked her face, and she thought I was being tender – taken aback, she genuinely smiled, then took refuge in an acted smile when she realised I was clearing the mascara that had run down her face, *Pagliacci*-like, as I knew she had to go back on a few seconds and, in the story, several years later. This was like the moment in Ronald Harwood's *The Dresser* when, amidst much company gossip, Sir, the actor-manager, summons a young female stage manager to his dressing room. She approaches cautiously, fearing the worst, and the company holds its breath. He sweeps her into his arms and lifts her in the air. Scandal! In fact he's just checking whether she's too heavy to take over the part of Cordelia and be carried on by him in Act Five of *King Lear*. So what kind of older actor does this mascara-wiping make me?

The fact is that Amy is upset by the noisy change; but it's her first time in the West End and she's reluctant to make a fuss. I wonder if it's worth asking Sarah about it for her. Sarah is a really good Company Manager, a job set at the crossroads between management and cast, decidedly a hard place if things get tough. She's good in exact proportion to how little she takes sides in any small skirmish. She'll judiciously sort out the matter of the noisy change, just as she does the matter of talking in the wings, of actors being late arriving at the theatre, the noise of the staff's card game drifting distractingly up from beneath the stage. In other words, she is sensitive to every sensitivity in the building, and even though, like Jan and Chrissy, she only joined us as we went into the West End, she is a degree more familiar with the show than they are, since she was at most of the rehearsals for its transfer.

But not at as many as Judith, Deputy Stage Manager, who was in daily attendance from first to last, from the original rehearsal period through the tour and into town. She is now perched in an improbable gantry offstage left – very crowded, but on the traditional side for a prompt corner, so much so that it's a surprise occasionally to find it on the right, as if the theatre was, so to speak, left-handed. In newer theatres she would be running the show from a control box out front, above the stalls, less friendly but more efficient and probably more comfortable for her; but it's good to see her in her crow's nest. She's the best DSM I've known – fanatical about the split-second timing of an electrics cue, and tonight guiding a young assistant through the show (since she too needs an understudy), and thus handing on her mysteries to a new generation. With us she's a mixture of motherly and respectful, would defend our reputations to the death, and is very firm if we change a line – but only if it happens several nights running and is clearly a developing habit rather than one night's aberration. She is thus proud of the production but not as proud as she is of the civil partnership she's just achieved in middle age, topped off with a Venice honeymoon.

She and Sarah see the show through a practical lens, of course, as the actors do through theirs. Nobody in a theatre knows all there is to know – not dressers, performers or technicians. As for the actors, no wonder they're only nominally aware of the other trades: they're in a permanent state of self-division, both in the play and not, there and not there. That's not all: I've never been able to account for the fact that the harder you concentrate on the job the more open your mind is to other possibilities – other ways of playing the scene certainly, but also such heresies as whether you left the fridge door open when you set out for the theatre. If you imagine a lens widening as you step onto the stage, it's easier to understand: you can think extremely hard of what you have in hand but you're also letting in peripheral light. The other day when David's character talked about the importance of having coffee at the right time, it reminded me intensely of a scene from quite a different play. It's not a matter of not concentrating, only that you have more concentration bytes available than you really need. I'm sure there's a neurological name for this. It certainly defies all known solemnities, and Stanislavsky would be shocked – except he wouldn't have been, he who said you should always have a year to rehearse a play but, told once that he could only have two weeks, said yes, that would be fine. Many great men of the theatre have unshakeable principles that can be abandoned at a moment's notice.

Dangerous things can creep in through this open lens, of course. A little demon nudges at your elbow, murmuring: Ignore what you're saying, look, that's interesting, that man at the end of the third row may have dropped off . . . and why is every-one in the front row wearing ties? . . . Of course in the old days more people did wear ties in theatres . . . and nobody brought in their drinks in plastic cups then, let alone mobile phones . . . STOP! This familiar spirit wants your downfall: forgetfulness. Mind you, it's an odd paradox that there are few things that look more like good acting than an actor momentarily drying up. The audience (apart from the actors among them, who sense the fear like a bad smell) is only aware of a mind at a loss and fighting at speed to reconnect. Nothing between the player and the specta-tor – no technique, no effect, just an exposed brain: it's a thing we work hard to achieve and rarely do.

Back on after his wig check, David slips infinitesimally over a phrase. I wouldn't even notice except that I've heard it a hundred times, plus many more in rehearsals. It certainly doesn't matter, but may just be a symptom: Is he tired tonight? Should I be extra alert?

It turns out the reason the front row is wearing jackets and ties is a charming one. They're Sandhurst cadets starting officer training, in their blazers and club ties (not the Australian cricket team as David and I had fantasised, imagining drinks after-wards with Shane Warne). This is part of their schedule – a dead-serious West End play, no doubt sandwiched between the Velasquez exhibition this afternoon and the Festival Hall tomorrow. I like this innocent oddity very much: I'm touched to think of them sitting there guilelessly watching the play, interested because of their discipline – after all I'd be unlikely to take much interest in a passing-out parade. How smart they look too, members of a profession that seems to be in costume even when off-duty. Not like us. Last night, I couldn't find my socks after the show: Chrissy had swept them up with the laundry and put them in the overnight wash. It so happened that I'd resolved that night to take home a mattress I didn't have room for at the theatre: so I walked through Covent Garden with no socks and a mattress under my arm, through streets which though named after actors – Kean Street and Kemble Street – are now mostly dotted with homeless hostels. A copper who passed me didn't turn a hair – though he might have been surprised if he'd seen me get suavely into my Vauxhall Astra a moment later.

I think the show's a bit thumpy this evening – probably fatigue after the matinee, and the last day of the week too. Rushed as well, a corruption of the virtue of pace, unsteadily timed and rather loud. I also think we're all looking at the audience too much, instead of imagining the fourth wall of the room where there might be pictures hanging and a window, say. What people who like the movies sometimes find tiresome about the theatre is the fact that we execute certain devices so that two people talking in a room can both be seen fully by the audience. There are many ways of achieving this, some of them quite subtle. Not done well it's like watching squash players, entering at one end of the court and then watching the ball's impact on the wall at the other end and hardly ever each other. Sometimes the priority seems to be to get both eyes visible to the audience, always. When I watch this I want to say: Stop! What are you looking at me for? Leave me alone, you're not supposed to know I'm here. Audiences like their privacy: they don't want to be got at. Like the thumpy delivery, this general loosening is all to do with our longish run. We've become like a book too large for its binding, displaying its contents rather than letting the reader find them for himself.

Max is straining to find new meaning in his part: he kicks himself if he doesn't discover something each evening. Unfortunately it's beginning to make him elaborate. His character works by sustaining an impenetrable mask of amiability which you know hides the most vicious intentions. Now Max occasionally lets the viciousness out for a moment, in an inflection or a look, as if he doesn't trust the audience to get it. But audiences are bright: they're usually there before you, understand the context, and know from the plot what lies behind such a character's smile.

I simultaneously want tonight to be over and dread it being done. We all know this. Whatever you look forward to – the glass of wine, the company, the comfort – the washing-up may still be in the sink. I have friends in tonight who I'm hopeful will have enjoyed it. What bliss to sit down with them in half an hour's time and order something and talk. The trouble will be that there's nothing to discuss except the show – it's just more interesting than most things, to me anyway. The conversation will drift on to their children, reminiscence, all of it – but I'll only be happy if the background music, briefly heard in the pauses, is the gentle murmur of acceptance. And within the hour I'll be tired, wanting to go home after my eight shows, however much I love them.

Last night (having got my mattress home, sockless) I dreamed a strange, extravagant variant on a familiar theme. I was in either Congreve's *Way of the World* or Molière's *Misanthrope* – or perhaps simultaneously in both. Anyway I knew it was an evening of big speeches, but I suddenly had no costume – so far so familiar. Up to Wardrobe I rushed, where someone not at all like Chrissy looked up from her newspaper, shrugged her shoulders and did nothing. A friendly ASM type found a bulbous suit for me, all padded like the Michelin Man, which she thought might do. Also a square yellow comedy hat turned up at the edges with wire sticking out like springs in a theatre seat: I last saw this kind of hat on Shakespearian clowns in the 1950s. I put it on but it was inside out. I reversed it, and discontentedly went onto the stage – which turned out to be an elegant wood-panelled library (four walls, no audience). I went plunging on, improvising in rhyming couplets, and for once the lines have come out of the dream with me:

> You talk to me of all your love
> To be like me is awful tough . . .

Not a bad sentiment for Alceste in *The Misanthrope*, but I couldn't think of any more, so started to talk gibberish. My trousers had now fallen as far as my knees, making movement difficult. So – a brainwave – I subsided onto a bench at a long refectory table, where I found myself sitting next to my old pal Roger Rees, whom I've barely seen since the RSC days of the 1970s. This was an odd dream because, apart from the couplet surviving, I was convinced throughout that it was definitely not one of those regular showbiz dreams when you lose your costume, can't remember the play etc.; this time I knew it was real. Long runs are obviously doing me no good.

Another night I found myself coming on at Covent Garden in the white tights and floppy shirt of a principal ballet dancer – in my dreams indeed. As I came tittupping to the centre there was a huge ovation, as if a hero had returned from the dead, Rudolf Nureyev perhaps. Acknowledging the applause I realised with a start I had no idea how to dance – not ever, not for a moment; I could hardly waltz. What to do? I started – and the *entrechats* and the leaps were suddenly like second nature. It was a fabulous performance – I'd been doing it all my life. Landing after the last *jeté* – perfect – I bowed, or rather curtseyed, low, and waited for the huge reception again. There was a pause, then a single pair of hands began to clap, slowly, in the most grudging acknowledgement. From the rest, silence, as if they had been subjected to an unspeakable fraud, to someone who indeed didn't know his left foot from his right, a non-dancer at Royal Opera House prices.

This dream took all the familiar elements and reordered them. It started with confidence, moved to panic, then triumph, then mournful defeat. The more usual dream just dramatises your fear that despite your qualifications you may not be able to do it again tonight, not this time; and just as you realise you can, you get kicked back into consciousness.

For the sober fact is that Yes, I Can, and as a result of knowing that, there's really nothing I enjoy doing more – I wish there were. After all, I told my anxious mother I'd be OK in this profession, I could handle every bit of it, so I've spent my life inventing someone who could: some fellow I don't always recognise, whose reactions are faster, mind more open and emotions more candid on the stage than they are anywhere else, someone decisive and quick, who takes charge, who rarely feels tired when acting though is liable to feel tired doing almost anything else.

Through the door that stands open on the set, a corridor of light spills diagonally back to me in the wings from the stage: I'll soon turn left into it to come on, as if from round a corner in my house's hallway. I like this scene coming up: there's a lot of unacknowledged movement inside it as I reorder my deepest beliefs without admitting as much. Small gestures mark profound changes. Altogether, in fact, the part is a good fit and I love the character – a man who actually lived, a great musician, so I've learned some things I didn't know before, and grin at his picture on my dressing-room wall, and wonder if he'd be pleased.

I'm tired already, as tired as David, and therefore slightly apprehensive, determined but a little unwilling. How to get willing enough? Draw deep on whatever drives you on. Rostropovich used to say of his audience that he wanted to make love to every one of them (not the word he used). But also there's everyone you've promised your best to over the years, not only your mother but anyone you've mistreated in the name of talent, the little ones you hope will remember you, the critics you've never pleased, the pricks who said you'd chosen the wrong profession. Maybe even that Sandhurst cadet at the front, concentrating hard on something foreign, who might take some unexpected memory away with him; and, beyond all that, some nameless thing to do with no one else, some idea of yourself, some way of holding your head up. And remember: the girl or boy you love is up in the gallery, or might be.

There's the cue. As I turn left down the shaft of light I forget all the above, instantly. David's head turns to greet me: he momentarily looks as if he's never seen me before, but I also hear the small comical sound of a dislodged hairpin leaving his wig and hitting the stage. I knew Jan wasn't quite herself tonight.

8 Musical Theatre

Yes You Can – Three Remarkable Women

I always wanted to be the singer with the band, but turned out to be better at Shakespeare: I who knew *The Music Man* and *Guys and Dolls* (and horribly sang them round the house) before I ever went to the Old Vic. Having like all children been able naturally to sing, I was felled by a teacher in a choir when I was eleven who said I was tone-deaf – God rot him. Because of course I'm not; virtually nobody is. There is such a condition, rather clumsily called dysmelodia, to do with the temporal and frontal gyruses, but it is extremely rare, far less common than being colour-blind. If you can hear the difference in pitch between a motorcycle in the street and a pigeon you're not tone-deaf. If you can imitate them reasonably, you can sing. So when I say I'm no singer, I mean it, as many of us do, as a shorthand: it would be better to say, I need a lot of help if a musical part comes up, and there are many people who do it better.

Anyone can sing in their own way if the circumstances are right: in the famously favourable acoustic of a bathroom, or assisted by wine, which reduces the inhibition quite a while before it damages the musical judgement. Most of all, when something comes direct from the heart – such as a favourite song or when there are a lot of other people doing it at the same time: *Bridge Over Troubled Water* always brings out the best in non-singers.

To go further is mainly a matter of getting quite a tangle of self-criticisms out of the way – there's no more or less special magic in singing than there is in acting, and each is part of the other. I'm quite a good mimic, so if I have a character I can identify with who sings I can probably do it – as long as the character is just an ordinary person having a sing, and not a virtuoso. I also have a musical vocabulary and musicality in speech: I know what a breve and semibreve are when applied to prose and verse, a ritard and accelerando, and how to use them (especially the latter – it's usually better to be a fraction ahead of the beat, and hence of the audience). But I've never played in a musical – unless you include Archie Rice in *The Entertainer*, which is really an acting job, even though Archie's signature song 'Why Should I Care' has an echo of 'One Beautiful Day' in Puccini's *Madama Butterfly*.

To digress for a moment: from the hoofing point of view, the trick with Archie is to become as good a tap-dancer as possible and then let yourself decline; he's someone who can't be bothered any more to do what's second nature to him, rather than someone who can't do it. If you come across any clips of Laurence Olivier in this part on stage (not from the film, which is less good) you feel one of the magical ingredients in his legendary performance: not only that Archie used to be quite good before we meet him, but that behind the shoddiness lurks a hard training, now neglected, and a certain mastery – the very same mastery and discipline that you sense in Olivier himself, the pre-eminent classical actor become song-and-dance man. It's unsurprising that subsequent interpreters of Archie Rice – though there haven't been many – are invariably actors known for their classical work: the enormous part is built on an heroically unheroic scale, like Richard II. Always, in fact, when you sense an infinity of training behind the casual, you have magnetic acting: when you see the great Adam Cooper playing Gene Kelly's old part in *Singin' in the Rain* his body line – the way he uses and extends into the space around him – remains, and this is entirely a compliment, that of a Royal Ballet principal dancer who used to partner Darcey Bussell, and it doubles the effect without in any way compromising his performance as Dan Lockwood.

As for Archie Rice's songs, it puzzles me that I could do them – they're not all that easy – I, who have no particular confidence there; but the style, 1950s music hall, is so particular, such actable pastiche, and I felt so sure of Archie, that I was able to do things musically that I had no idea I could. This is not of course like holding down Jean Valjean in *Les Mis*, or any other musical challenge in which judging the actor's inherent ability is part of the blood-sport. I've had other brushes with Melpomene. Edgar in *King Lear* improvises songs and tunes and little chantings in his assumed madness: that was easy too, and even praised by some for its musicality; but there they sat, right in the middle of lengths of Shakespearian prose – an extension of it really. I was asked to be in *Dirty Dancing* and sang 'Tea for Two' for a very large room of sceptical American backers who needed convincing: that was all right too as I was thinking of it as coming from a man (Baby's father) who could just about hold the tune for the sake of appealing to the girl, but not necessarily sing.

That wasn't the reason I ended up not doing *Dirty Dancing* – or the premiere of Alan Ayckbourn's *Chorus of Disapproval* at the National, in which a young widower, Guy Jones, joins an amateur operatic society putting on *The Beggar's Opera*, rapidly progressing through the ranks to play Macheath, the male lead. I practised and practised and went in to sing it for Alan Ayckbourn as if I was indeed offering him my Macheath. As I did so, I saw a shadow passing across his courteous face. He then suggested I played it – obviously enough – as Guy, who was just about good enough to be in the society though not brilliant and certainly not a pro. So I imagined this character, became more tuneful, and he was reassured. On the other hand I was scuppered when I played in Mikhail's Bulgakov's *The White Guard*, set in the Russian Civil War. This was in the delightful character of Shervinsky, who aspires to be a great singer, though we never see him perform; I had the idea that he would, in the midst of the misery of the conflict, casually sing snatches of *Eugene Onegin* as he went about his domestic business. I went for several lessons with the legendary teacher Chuck Mallett, whose technique was to sing pretty badly himself in demonstrating what he wanted so as not to intimidate his student, and would likewise declare that he'd rather hear Maria Callas sing out of tune than anyone else in tune. Though I momentarily saw myself as the diva I was defeated this time and we cut the idea because I couldn't do it well enough: the character was, after all, a trained opera singer.

It's worth remembering too that with a few exceptions – such as when Maria and the Mother Abbess acknowledge that they're singing when they do 'My Favourite Things' in the original stage version of *The Sound of Music* – characters in musicals aren't conscious that they're musical. Rather they're getting their point across to the audience much as a Shakespearian character does, either in soliloquy or dialogue: the same need, the same energy and urgency. They just happen to be speaking up and down a diatonic or chromatic scale across two or three octaves; thirty-six notes at maximum, all of which a singer must have an intimate knowledge of and even recognise out of context. At least as important, they have to join them up, which takes planning; that's the difficult bit, with its implications for the shape of the mouth, the belly, chest and head, and how they navigate from one to the other in a way that pleases the hearer while leaving them with enough breath to carry on. The difference between this and a straight play is that if Cleopatra or Hamlet develop an upper respiratory-tract infection or are simply inspired to change the notes, they can: the most a singer can do is sing the same note an octave higher or lower, but it will be noticed and probably not liked.

I'm fooling myself with all these practicalities of course: the worry – and the special mystery of music – lingers on. People who really can do it, can hit the plumb centre of the note, night after night, and hold it for exactly the right length without a wobble, while all the time suggesting they've only just decided to sing it at all, seem to me to have an extra gene.

Does this ring any bells (of any pitch) with you?

~

Janie Dee's grandma was doing the can-can at eighty-four; her mother hoped to be a dancer too, but one day Janie's brother, meaning it for the best, put their mother's one pair of point shoes in the washing machine, and that was that – she could never afford to buy another pair. Janie's dad races a motorcycle at eighty, he and her granddad were both enthralling storytellers, and her Irish uncle did magic tricks.

One day when she was about six **Charlotte Wakefield** was lying on her bedroom floor, singing along to 'You Are My Sunshine', when she looked up to see that her father had climbed down from the loft and was standing looking intently at her, followed soon afterwards from downstairs by her mother. She didn't quite know why, and so became a little confused and tearful. Perhaps they shouldn't have been surprised by what they heard – all her grandparents could hold a tune, and her grandmother had sung in the Hallé Choir.

At fifteen **Elaine Paige** was at school singing Bastienne the shepherdess in Mozart's *Bastien and Bastienne*, written when he was twelve. It was her first solo aria about unrequited love, and she decided to put an extra little telling sob of emotion into it. The audience gasped, thinking Elaine herself had broken down.

216

Had there been a loft to come down from, no doubt her father, who was in the audience and gasping the most, would have done that.

You could of course put these stories straight onto a stage.

~

In 1978 Elaine completed her eighth audition for *Evita*, and thinking there was nothing more to be done, went to see her parents on the south coast for the Easter weekend. As she arrived her agent called saying she had to come straight back for a final (final) audition, to sing it all again, immediately.

For a year or so Dustin Hoffman had been an admirer of Elaine's singing and had given her some advice, starting with a question: what time of day do you sing best? In the afternoon, Elaine felt, when her voice had woken up. Then, he said, that's the only time you must agree to audition. But, she objected, she didn't have that kind of control over events. Oh yes, you do, said Dustin: you've got to take charge. He himself used to mumble at stage auditions but would explain to the director that if he projected any more he would lose the truth; seemingly that policy has hurt him none. He persuaded Elaine always to stand her ground – to be brave, but canny. So she now told her agent the truth, that she was out of town and couldn't easily get back, but she'd come for the recall tomorrow afternoon. The agent reminded her that she was close to landing the role of a lifetime and to be co-operative. Elaine, who knew she was right, faithfully promised to come back and sing whatever and wherever they wanted – but only on the following day. And so it was agreed.

The next day she got home and pulled out the hooker shoes and little frock she'd worn for each previous recall, giving her a 1940s look that slightly suggested Eva Perón: no reason to change it now. Warmed up and focused, she went in for the audition, did the song the best she'd ever done it, got the job, and the rest, unless you're very young, you know.

The showbiz story of the nine auditions is good precisely because it doesn't translate easily into advice: you could take the same attitude and lose out entirely. But perhaps Elaine had a hunch that this was something different and she might have a little more traction than usual: that she wasn't just close to getting the job, but very close. You can have an instinct about such things, though it's one in which you can be horribly deceived. And she knew when her voice would be at its best. This is a consideration an actor auditioning for a straight play wouldn't have had to have: he or she could probably rush up and do the audition in a hurry, and it might even be better for it. But for a singer it's different. Elaine's other weapon had been sweet reasonableness: she had parents and a life of her own but at the same time was dedicated to the job almost in hand. What would not have been so canny would have been to pretend she was away on holiday and could only be back to audition next week: that would be just silly, suggesting she wasn't really interested.

She is thus the unknown who plays an ace by simply being herself and becomes a star.

~

When Charlotte Wakefield saw Steven Slater and Duncan Sheik's musical version of *Spring Awakening* on Broadway on a school trip in 2007, she decided she had to play Wendla, its young female lead, if it came to London. She was seventeen and had been acting since she was ten. She'd done stretches on *Holby City* and *Waterloo Road*, and once danced for the county of Cheshire; but apart from a school production of *We Will Rock You*, no musicals. Still, her parents were right – the voice was remarkable. In fact general auditions for the London *Spring Awakening* had already started – all in all they were to last eighteen months. Her agent got her in at a later stage, whereupon she did four weeks of workshops, including text sessions on Shakespeare, with a shortish shortlist of candidates. Every time she went in to read she was asked to come back again: she read for the American backers, and made Tom Hulce, who was an Executive Producer, cry at one of them. Then there was another week-long workshop on the music and the script with Kimberly Grigsby, the Musical Director. She had to leave the last of these sessions early as she had some filming to do in Ireland and needed to catch her flight, and became superstitiously afraid that that would scupper her chances; worse, the production team hugged her goodbye as if it was for ever. Two weeks later, as she turned eighteen, she had a solemn call from her agent asking her if by any chance she'd like to play Wendla, because it was now an offer.

So Elaine Paige and Charlotte Wakefield got their most important break after making themselves just a little scarce in the final stages.

~

Elaine reckons she couldn't have sung Eva Perón sooner than she did: in life terms, she needed to put a few years between herself and Bastienne. Meanwhile she'd played Miss Sheep, a very small part, in panto at the Westminster Theatre, and despite its being a Moral Re-Armament house, spent much time in the bar – not an unusual occurrence in those days as many theatres had a licensed backstage green room. She'd been one of the 'tribe' in *Hair* and in the Chorus of *Jesus Christ Superstar*: this was the early 1970s and in the interval there was sometimes a whiff of marijuana among the disciples. She'd modelled for Marks and Spencer, played a small part opposite Jack Hawkins on TV, taken over the role of Sandy in *Grease – the Musical*, and the first role she originated was Rita in *Billy* opposite Michael Crawford, in 1974. She'd also worked with the great Joan Littlewood Theatre

Workshop in a revue called *Nuts* and sung 'Summertime'. Little-wood was allergic to anything that came out the same way twice in a run, so Elaine wasn't surprised one night to find another actor throwing a variety of wet fish at her from the wings which she then had the presence of mind to catch and throw at the audience in turn whilst continuing the song.

More to the point, she'd learned intercostal diaphragmatic breathing, watched the old-timers from the wings and worked weekly with the late great singing teacher Ian Adam. Fortunately Andrew Lloyd Webber and Tim Rice were learning their craft at the same time as she was, and the three came together on *Evita* as if they'd been waiting for each other. *Evita* is a modern opera, an exhausting sing, covering Eva Perón's life from fifteen to her death at thirty-three: the edgy score is not easy to deliver and written for a mezzo with an unusual two-and-a-half to three-octave range, which Elaine had. For all three artists, the timing was perfect.

~

As Janie Dee watches her daughter playing the guitar, she sees herself: the music is in her. Dancing was the way Janie naturally expressed herself, how she told a story. She would invent the music, then get up and dance it: her every plié had narrative meaning. Once she watched Nureyev and Fonteyn working; during a pause, the way Nureyev put his hands round Fonteyn's waist made her realise that this was the intimate story of two people, beyond what they were rehearsing.

She went to local ballet school, then to Arts Educational; she took class with Arlene Phillips. Pretty soon she realised she could be funny as well. She got her Equity card at sixteen in Guernsey with *Trendsetters*, a stagey version of *The Younger Generation* – she'd hated leaving Arts Ed but her parents were short of money, she was one of four, so she felt she had to get out and earn. She came back to London to work with the Krankies, the Scottish comedy duo – what she calls a bikini-and-feather job. (It must be said that not many of those who worked with the Krankies went on to do Harold Pinter.) Then she went to Italy to teach dance, but also to study art and architecture; she went to the ballet and opera in Rome, and was taught to sing properly by Michael Aspinall, a British semi-baritone with a deliriously extended falsetto range who lived on the Spanish Steps and worked in drag, singing the likes of the Mad Scene in Donizetti's *Lucia di Lammermoor*.

Gradually Janie was coming to terms with being a curvy, funny singing blonde, not a ballerina as she'd imagined. Back from Rome and proud enough of her shape to give up sacky T-shirts, she knew she also had a good voice and was ready. She got a job at a West End nightclub singing with a live band, two shows a night: the legendary Gillian Lynne heard her and auditioned her for *Cabaret*, in which she understudied Kelly Hunter and then Toyah Willcox as Sally Bowles. Normally as a 'swing' (an understudy in musicals) you get to go on sometime, but Janie didn't: the musicians went on strike just as she was about to. But then Wayne Sleep took her on tour as a singer. And on she went, through *Guys and Dolls*, *Can Can*, *Oklahoma!* in the West End, Alan Ayckbourn's *Dreams from a Summerhouse*, and finally arrived at the National Theatre for Nicholas Hytner's production of *Carousel*. The one thing she had no training for was acting. But the National being what it is, she went to classes with William Gaskill and Peter Brook and read David Mamet and Stanislavsky. And so she achieved her Nap Hand: now she's playing Shaw, Pinter, Coward, Chekhov, Ayckbourn, Frayn, and, in case you were wondering, Shakespeare and Euripides. Or, if you prefer, Rodgers and the Hammersteins, Hart, Hamlisch, Laurents, Porter, Kern, Kander and Ebb, and, oh yes, Shostakovich and Duke Ellington – not to mention Andrew Lloyd Webber, who once advised her not to be so flexible; but she loves to do everything, and hates saying no.

~

I ask Janie to explain her warm-up, which she does early every morning, whether she's working or not. She says: first of all, you must take a breath, and no more than that. Breath is the beginning of it all. You should do three sets of breathing exercises before making a sound, so you can gain relaxation and control. In – and gently out. Don't sing a note till all these exercises are done, in and out, and you've felt your ribs opening and the diaphragm working. This is a miracle you don't normally think about: you don't have to remember to breathe, the body takes that decision for you, but this way you notice when it's ready. This warm-up would suit an actor just as well; but if you want to sing you have to know there's enough breath to call on to get you to the end of the obligatory phrase. In again – and out, feel the process; then a small noise, barely more than a breath, and in again. Pay attention to the detail inside the notes. If you want to make a big noise, make a smaller noise first and see how big it becomes.

And you may still not be any good, I say. She smiles encouragingly.

I ask Charlotte about hers. 'Warm-up?' she cries. 'It just happens – I have an iron voice!' This isn't conceit, just the plain fact of being twenty-two and a healthy country girl, fit and well as long as she can get ten hours' sleep a night. But I know that in musicals pre-show warm-ups with the Musical Director or Assistant Musical Director are compulsory, as are physical ones with the Dance Captain (they only very rarely are in straight theatre). Pressed on the point, Charlotte admits to being in a permanent state of warming up, all day long. When she finished her run in *Mamma Mia* (which she describes as 'pop belt' – that is, singing from the chest, with no vibrato but a pingy, pure top-of-the-line rock sound) and started auditioning for *The Sound of Music* (classic musical), she worried that she'd long neglected the head notes she needed for it – she who had always been able to sing anything. In fact she worried about the overall health of her voice. As she always does if she thinks she's in trouble, she went to Jacob 'the Strangler' Lieberman for voice manipulation: to relax her larynx, he painfully massages her tongue. She explains to me that her cords need to become like short elastic bands if she's to do pop belt, and long ones if it's classical singing. Jacob gets them into neutral, ready for both. This reminds me about the precarious physical health of a singing as opposed to an acting voice. For an actor in trouble with laryngitis, for instance, there used to be two cures: either cocaine derivatives of one kind or another or Melba's Paint, attributed (like many things) to Nellie Melba and more or less completely opiate – all any of them did was take the pain away. Now you might fix the problem with steam at home. Or antibiotics or, exceptionally, with steroids. Or, if you like, acupuncture, though I'm sceptical. While you're mending, you can to a degree adjust your performance: go high or low as you choose at any given moment, quieten down, take a tactical pause or speed up at will. So you can usually work reasonably well with what you've got, even if your voice feels like a guitar that's lost a couple of its strings. But when you sing you're pretty much stuck with the music: if you don't have the full set tonight, you have to let the understudy go on.

As a result of her momentary problem, Charlotte set about becoming a technician – a surprising number of singers don't know very much about their own voices and can get into trouble, particularly with nodules on their vocal cords. Now her understanding of it as a piece of physiology is well ahead of most singers of her age, and she is fascinatingly scientific on the subject. These are days of far more precise analysis of the complex activity of the vocal folds (cords) than before; a study of the Estill Voice Training programme would probably make an actor too voice-conscious, but for a singer can be a huge advantage. By the time Charlotte had – triumphantly – reached Julie Andrews's old part in *The Sound of Music* in the summer of 2013, she had discovered how to use thin fold control (as opposed to thick, stiff or slack) which in practice brings you long, lyrical, emotional lines right in the middle of the note, clean and straight in the difficult area between chest and head. Some singers look for this sound for years.

~

I ask Elaine for a day in the life and learn a fiercer version of an actor's anxiety. As a singer your first thought on waking, whether you're working that day or not, is to go *la-la-la*. Is the voice there today – how free are the cords? You might wear a scarf even though the wind is down and it's not really cold – the weather might change. *Mmm*, you go, and *mmm* up an octave. You practise twenty minutes twice a day, to keep the muscle sleek and oily, the muscle of an athlete. Otherwise when you go for the big note not properly prepared you could lose control.

She thinks, and I agree, that musical theatre – including dance – is the toughest and most life-shortening thing you can do in our industry. Quite apart from the constant costume changes, there's the caring for the voice, the technique and the emotion invested in the songs. There's probably no other life for you during the day, apart from what's absolutely necessary, and not much life overall. For those with children, the whole achievement is a miracle. I can bear witness to Elaine's dedication: I once worked with her on a straight play – Molière's *Misanthrope* – which must have been a breeze for her, compared to a musical or a concert tour, and we've been friends ever since. Apart from having the dirtiest laugh I know, her belief that every performance could be both fun and a matter of life and death was terrific to be with.

The central part in Pam Gems's *Piaf* was created by Jane Lapotaire thirty-five years ago; it was an exceptional example of an actor who sang, rather than a singer rising to the acting side of the challenge. Elaine later did it for Peter Hall, who saw that she had by nature the muscularity and skill to sing as *la petite môme* did on the street corners of Paris. Rather than look a gift horse in the mouth, he added more Piaf songs to the script: the show ended fatter by fifteen of them and by forty-five minutes. Like that of Perón, this life story (age fifteen to forty-seven) was terribly gruelling, but completely fulfilling. Imagine playing Piaf's rollercoaster emotional life (including her disillusionment with the world of music), and singing her repertoire whilst embodying her physical decline: arthritis in the hands and knees and a broken jaw which called for a special plate being made for the actress's teeth. All this on a seriously raked stage. Initially Elaine played eight performances a week, but after a month found it too gruelling, and it was agreed that the understudy would play matinees on tour.

~

There's nobody quite like Elaine Paige, and I for one am at her feet: she's quite literally incomparable. I don't know of a more thrilling piece of popular theatre than her in full voice in 'Don't Cry for Me, Argentina' or 'I Dreamed a Dream'; this is when the classless appeal of pop, the stamina of opera, and the fullness of theatre emotion meet in a three-minute song. I admire operatic singers but if I'm honest prefer them through a microphone with less pulling about of the vowels and rather better pose-striking; the theatre is my life but sometimes I wish it could make the fast and electric connections of rock 'n' roll. Musical theatre can be Shakespeare with strings, and Elaine is a virtuoso.

I also know no one in whom the talent for straight and

musical theatre is separated by such a narrow margin as it is in Janie Dee. And I never saw a career so certain, barring acts of God, as Charlotte's, who seems to have everything. All three possess, apart from prodigious talent, a self-confidence that nobody could call boastful: they are at the glittering heart of show business, and I stand at the gates and watch them. And many besides – there are male equivalents of course, but this chapter is for the divas rather than the divos. While Elaine is on the road and Charlotte heading for where Elaine was, Janie is simultaneously considering the parts of Phaedra, Low-Dive Jenny in *The Threepenny Opera* and Mrs Alving in *Ghosts* – the latest stage in a career that has moved between the forms with so little strain that it's hard to deduce which she prefers. And she may take up none of these offers as her daughter Matilda is doing her A-levels and will need her at home rather than waving goodbye to her eight times a week. Apart from her early morning warm-ups she reads Stanislavsky's *An Actor Prepares* in bed. Singing and dancing and acting are as deeply in her bones as the ability to sing anything required is in Charlotte's and making drama out of a song is in Elaine's.

They're all three doing something very few of us can reach, but that can be an inspiration for you rather than a deterrent. You ask any of them how they were first aware of having talent, and they just say they don't know but they always enjoyed it (musicians can be disarmingly practical and not precious at all). I understand Janie best because she acts more than the others in plays that I know: so I'm familiar with half her territory and sense she is helpfully knocking down barriers that obstruct most of us. Hers is a triumph of open-mindedness operated by single-mindedness. Charlotte seems to have no fear at all, except of fear itself – but when she describes the streets round the Aldwych Theatre being blocked with people chanting her name on the last night of *Spring Awakening* I recognise her need for validation in return for what she puts in. Like Elaine waiting quietly, as she does, before starting a concert, I imagine that for both of them, as for dancers, there must be an awareness of the lifespan of the instrument, just as I wonder when my memory will loosen.

~

When Trevor Nunn implies to me, ironically or not, that he perhaps prefers *My Fair Lady* to *Pygmalion*, I rather agree. I'd sooner have the harmonies of Lerner and Loewe and the ghostly sound of Rex Harrison talking his way through being accustomed to her face than Bernard Shaw, all the time pushing into his own plays with his confounded buttonholing wit and irony.

Of course musical theatre manipulates you too, shifting you wholesale into emotions, not always for a noble cause, by means of this crescendo, that harmony and counterpoint, a change of beat, the sway of a melody that moves you against your will. I was at the very first night of *Les Misérables* in 1985 at the Barbican, and just as the auditorium lights were going down at half past seven, in the last few seconds of the musical's pre-existence – the conductor's arm up, the actors drawing their first breath, before the reviews, well before any West End transfer – I noticed the man sitting next to me had a reprinted version of Victor Hugo's novel on his lap, the words 'Now a Smash Hit West End Musical' blazoned across its cover. Within five minutes I saw the publishers' reckless confidence had been justified: the show was unstoppable and just insisted on your love, almost whether you would or not.

Shakespeare does the same with his sudden heart-stopping monosyllables, the swing of his verse line, the undercutting of his prose clowns. In lyric theatre, the music is an extension of the scene, a highly disciplined form of passionate conversation: it takes over, as a song does in Shakespeare when speaking won't suffice for the emotion. (Conversely, in a sung-through piece like *Les Misérables*, and in some operas, the singing of very conversational dialogue as recitative can be a little alienating.) Given the height of the emotion being sung, imagine its pressure against the structural boundaries. And of course the clarity of a singing voice can be affected by the performer's emotional state and even the weather; just as orchestral brass players go out of tune when it is cold, singers hope not to get too wet (colds), windswept (dry mouth) or hot (lethargy) – warmth is good but thirty-seven degrees is a struggle. The muscle being used is highly suggestible: it also fears humidity and hay fever, air conditioning and lack of sleep – and also, some people mischievously say, insufficient sexual activity – though singers, from Nellie Melba onwards, who say this is necessary before they go on probably only mean they wish it were so.

Musicals are a cruel battleground, on which the fact that Hugh Jackman played Peter Allen in *The Boy From Oz* for a year and never missed a show assumes the status of myth, just as Adam Cooper dancing *Singin' in the Rain* for sixteen months in the West End smacks the gob. Adam says he wouldn't have missed it for the world, but remains astonished that he was able to do it. He managed it by treating his life more simply, though it was complicated by protein shakes, ribbed physio rollers to loosen tight muscles (their foam surface feeling sometimes like concrete), yoga and Pilates and more or less constant physical niggles, the sense of being always mildly crocked. More than that, it was possible only because of the unique joy felt by performers and audience. Somehow the public perceive what goes into such a performance as they sit around the arena, sensing the improbability of it all. No wonder they spend the money on musicals: at best, in terms of affirmative energy, the return matches the investment. No wonder the latest revival of *Chicago* ran for fifteen years, that *Billy Elliot* is now eight years and running, that

Jersey Boys is five and moving its theatre, that *Mamma Mia* has done fourteen years and *Les Mis* twenty-eight. Musicals make you feel wonderful. If straight theatre wants the audience back it must fight for it; and in fact, after the intoxication of musicals, it may now not be quite the same audience.

~

So when the audition comes up, it would be an awful shame not to go to it out of uncertainty. If you're nervous, invest in some lessons if you can and practise – but spend as much time on the character as on the music. You may not get the part, but then often you may not get the part. If you do, it's good work, even if you don't become Hugh Jackman or Maria Friedman. And if you do, all the better. My point is, you can work in musicals even if you're never going to be one of God's elect. Don't think of it as a foreign language or a second sight; it's just another skill, and probably within your range.

As for me, I've approached this enchanted world as close as I could. I've been on stage with Janis Kelly, reading from Strauss's letters, and likewise for Berlioz's *Béatrice et Bénédict* with Simon Rattle and Maria Ewing. I've watched Bryn Terfel rehearsing at Kenwood, noticing what a fantastic sound he produces even when he's just lightly marking out his moves and joking as he does. I suppose that's his version of mumbling. And I'm smug that I once suggested a song to Elaine Paige for an album and she did it. It's probably as near as I'm going to get, and that's fine. As the rock 'n' rollers used to say, I've got my own album to make, and it's in my head.

PART THREE – Three Essays

9 Sex and Drugs and Turning Up

There is one scene that lies in wait for us all.

John Mortimer's *Summer's Lease* covers the Tuscan holiday of a harassed wife, Molly Pargeter, her flaky husband Hugh and their three children. Molly works fourteen hours a day to make the whole event good for everybody; Hugh languishes for lunchtime profiteroles in City restaurants with his London secretary, and is at one point caught writing sneaky postcards to her; meanwhile Molly's roguish father Haverford Downs (John Gielgud) has the drop on Hugh – having witnessed a kerbside kiss after one such City lunch just before the holiday, he is able to do and say any discomforting thing he wants to Hugh, a licence of which he takes full advantage.

After many twists and turns, the four-part series ends with a sweet reunion between the hitherto dispirited couple. Molly and Hugh see each other anew in the setting sun across the swimming pool (good dappled underlighting from the water on both faces). In the next scene they are making love as if they've only just met; Haverford is confounded, the children, as children will, sense a new peacefulness in the air, and the holiday ends happily, all secret smiles and renewed well-being. It perhaps goes without saying that the crucial love scene needed to be planned in as much detail as, say, the murder of King Duncan. Susan Fleetwood, myself and the director, Martyn Friend, had a provisional rehearsal before leaving England for Italy, determining, much as you might some military strategy, precisely what intimacies, and

233

at what angle, might result from John Mortimer's tersely gen-
tlemanly stage directions sending us to bed. The BBC rehearsal
room at Acton had been emptied for our purposes to spare any
blushes. Then the whole business was shelved for three months
while we shot the rest of the series around Siena and Florence.

The scene in question was scheduled as the very last of the
shoot, by which time we were back in England and in a studio, having got thoroughly used to each other as a unit. Susan
and I already knew each other well, from RSC days of old; we
were something between colleagues and friends, having never
actually worked together before – which is of course when you
really get to know someone. Susan was a brilliant actor, inventive, professional, thorough and comradely; my luck having
held for twenty-five years, I was now facing up to my first bed
scene. We earnestly renewed our discussion about ways and
means – refining the search, you might say. The exact order of
events; where should the legs go, particularly Susan's; the level
of energy; who should take the initiative when, and should it
pass to and fro between us; should there be any reposition-
ing, and should the lovers arrive at heaven's door at the same
time or, in a variation of good manners, should one usher the
other in before joining them there. We were after all trying to
concentrate the couple's long history, the necessary depth and
complexity of their relationship (three children) into what was
always going to be about a minute or so of intense and mostly
wordless experience. It was to be a brief snapshot to tell the
audience all it needed to know.

The set was cleared to a minimum crew; but it was still a very
small bedroom, and it didn't feel particularly empty. The camera
was suspended from the ceiling above the bed, looking straight
down at the lovers: it might zoom in and out, but that would be
the only angle used. So off, you might say, we went. After a couple of takes, it wasn't going right. For some unfathomable rea-

son, the character-based activities conjured by Susan and myself, professionals if nothing else, weren't registering significantly from the camera position above – not on that angle, not with that lens. A solution arose, and it involved the First Assistant Director, a post which, as you may have gathered from another chapter, is recruited as much for sergeant-major authority and macho manners as sensitivity. John was one of the best, but he'd never been faced with what was now proposed to him – that he take hold of the foot of the bed, just out of shot, and gently rock it to and fro, accelerating by degrees to a pitch that matched the frenzy between the sheets. Simple enough, but in some subtle way he was about to reveal something important about himself. I never saw a tough guy go so red, take after take after take.

The heroic discussions, the deep breath taken, the embarrassment of John, are now lost in the ether. The fact that only a few moments of the scene survived on the screen – rather beautifully in fact – is neither here nor there. The feeling between the actors was, I should say, tenderly professional, a matter of mutual protection – the covering each other with sheets between takes as you might a child, the strategic holding up of dressing gowns, before and after. Though Susan was exceptionally beautiful, I need hardly say that there was nothing erotic about it for us – even if something were brewing between the actors, it would be unlikely to survive the mechanics of this strange ritual.

This story is tame by today's standards. Now you might be doing such a scene without a blanket over any part of you and the camera more actively interested in the details. For the fact is that you, a twenty-first-century generation, are going to be asked to do more and more merciless things. Having got yourself on occasion supernaturally fit, learned to sing/dance/juggle and speak in an infinity of accents to earn a living, you're now asked to offer yourself up at your most personal, in a simulation that has to come extremely close to reality. Afterwards, you will see the unasked question forming on the lips of your acquaint-ance: How did it feel? *Was* there anything? Did you perhaps . . . ? This is an impolite query, like the equivalent question in life, and your revenge can be a Cheshire Cat smile: you couldn't possibly comment.

Now some people are untroubled by nudity and sexual can-dour – you may be among them. Maybe you're just too cool to worry or you have a helpful streak of exhibitionism. But most people don't see themselves as particularly gorgeous and are mildly appalled by the prospect, especially after a certain age, of revealing everything. I did my first nude scene (the above being, technically, not quite that) in the theatre in middle to late-middle age, a fact noted with disgust by one of the national critics who had even gone to the trouble of Googling me to check my age: he didn't see why he should have to endure the sight of a sixty-year-old bottom. And there is as much trade wis-dom about this as about voice exercises or warm-up routines: telephones sometimes buzz between actors about to do such a sequence for the first time and those who have done it before, for tips on how to, shall we say, look your best. This, by the way, applies to men as much as women.

It's worse for the women, for sure, as it always has been. This is despite the fact that there is now an official tissue of guarantees against exploitation at work, as there is in many professions. In show business, however, it's all a bit vague and unenforceable. Theoretically, your industrial rights are enshrined in contracts: Equity has determined that an employer must warn you before you sign up that nudity will be called for – and how much and how persistent. Angry actresses have been known to call the union if a director then asks for more than the contract speci-fied, or a variation – even if it's a genuine change of mind about what the scene needs in the light of rehearsals, which it could be, just. It's hard to argue with a director who says, You're two characters in an intimate relationship in a room together, aren't you going to touch each other believably? In these circumstances, standing up for your contractual rights takes some courage, and can be seen as finicky. As with tax, National Insurance and hours of work, legislation in our industry is an ill-fitting glove, especially so when it comes to pinning down definitively what is to happen in a scene such as this. An awful lot has to be taken on a good faith which can be betrayed.

The truth I suppose is that this isn't in general a profession for the very sexually squeamish, any more than it is for someone with a high standard of living. In an odd inversion of, say, a politician's life, you can be as straitlaced as you like at home, but in the normal line of business, if you're gay you'll have to kiss, convincingly, the gender that does nothing for you; if straight, increasingly, likewise. From this has arisen a certain low-grade media Attitude. I was once lambasted for being cast as Oscar Wilde by the *Evening Standard* critic who shall remain anonymous (Nicholas de Jongh) because I was a 'known heterosexual' – well, how did he know that? Had he been hanging around theatre bars? He sounded as if some personal betrayal had taken place. He went for me again in *Timon of Athens* for refusing to play the gay subtext he thought he glimpsed (quite wrongly) in the production. All this was ridiculous: but in these matters there is such a thing as delayed revenge, and maybe we heterosexuals had it coming.

Young actresses in training can also be vulnerable to a certain kind of freelance teacher who sees the job of instructing a group of young women as an implicit *droit du seigneur* – or at least an opportunity for discomfiture. They will repeatedly remind their students of the sexual meaning of the word 'die' in Shakespeare, even though it does sometimes mean to end your life. Beware such teachers as you would a heating engineer who's not Corgi-approved. There is also an undercurrent to some drama training which implies that any student's talent remains provisional until his or her sex life develops – an idea that can be expressed gently or coarsely. The oppressive diktat that you must extend your sexual experience if you want to be any good at the job is obviously unfair, since you could, as a matter of obligation, sleep with everyone you can find and still not have very much sexual presence on the stage. The difficulty of course is that there is also something in it. The uninitiated in life are unlikely to become good actors: the job calls for as old a head as a pair of young shoulders can carry.

There is something intrinsically sexual about standing on a stage and performing anything, by which I mean little more than that the whole personality is engaged. And you are, as always, on the catwalk. The movies give high desirability ratings to those whom the camera, in its mysterious way, favours for the set of their eye, their bone structure, their general air. Which of course can be an illusion – who would have thought that Humphrey Bogart was a rich kid whose mother used a picture of him in a baby-food ad and was the first actor to say 'Anyone for tennis?' in a play? Movie stars have always been figures of fantasy; though should they become involved in a real-life scandal, the revenge of the public, somehow betrayed in their sense of ownership, can be very sharp indeed. The theatre has a milder version of the same thing: an audience, unobserved in the dark, becomes more or less intrigued by the figures executing the brightly lit dance in front of them, and slips into something of an alternative universe. Sometimes the cruellest characters are the most attractive, though they would be intolerable in life: actors, young ones particularly, may develop a fan base because they always look the fanciable same rather than because they're good. A performer can be blessed with a magnetic natural presence or not in the same way as someone at a party can get along well with everyone, and another not.

Comically, there used to be a slightly envious public idea that

actors were all 'at it like knives when the curtain comes down'
– a quaint phrase since there isn't usually a curtain these days,
and the idea of knives scraping away at each other is disconcerting. The prospect of bacchanalian revels is quite hard when
you've done two shows in a day, but a certain raffishness has
always hung about the theatre since Edmund Kean had regularly
to be pulled out of the brothel by his stage manager and John
Barrymore used to make up his lines as he went along. Nowadays all that's been more or less taken over by rock 'n' roll, while
actors worry about their VAT returns and Health and Safety. The
oddity is that even as the culture asks you to perform more and
more extravagant sexual acts, it also insists that you swill and
gargle with TCP first and remember the virtues of punctuality,
toothpaste and tea. Soon you may not even be allowed to smoke
on the stage, apart from herbal cigarettes, regardless of what the
author requires: actual devotees will miss this, like the promise
of a practical onstage meal during the action with which managements used to tempt hard-up performers as compensation
for their paltry wages. The best performers are in easy touch
with both the male and female sides of their natures and are
unafraid of them. Heterosexual actors are notably good at playing queens, at least in Britain; cross-dressing and travesty are
quite deep in the psyche. The public has always been a bit puzzled and intrigued by this, but it's humorously taken for granted
in the trade. And the fact is that in the theatre you can live any
life you want, licentious or demure, as long as you learn your
lines and turn up. That's all anybody minds about: ferocious
discipline releases good fellowship. For the peculiar pleasure of
what we do, I'd say, it's worth kissing a lot of frogs in front of a
thousand watching strangers; putting up with impertinent questions from the press if they show an interest in you; and endur-
ing some odd proximities and surprisingly intimate knowledge
of complete strangers.

There's a funny side, of course. An actor friend, an older gentleman of unimpeachable respectability who always came to rehearsals in a pinstripe suit, once told me that he had taken part in what, by the tamer standards of those days, amounted to a porn film. When he told me what he'd had to do, I was quite shocked, and tried to still my imagination. But why did you do it, I said – you're always in work anyway. He turned a gaze on me of infinite wisdom and patience, that of a bloodhound or a melancholy gorilla, and uttered a simple phrase: 'My granddaughter's oboe lessons'. Then again, if you've ever done a quick change in the darkened wings with dressers, you'll be familiar with having your clothes torn off you by complete strangers you might not recognise in the light – the turnover in wardrobe staff being so high that you get to know few and they will soon be replaced by other passionate strippers. And I was once asked at the outset of a very serious interview with the literary editor of the *Independent* what it was like to kiss Felicity Kendal on the stage. He was apologetic about it, but said he simply wouldn't be able to run the article, however brilliantly it probed the deepest recesses of my art, unless this could be flagged on the front page. The alliteration was especially valuable: 'Kissing Kendal' would do nicely. I thought, Well, either I haughtily stop the interview now or roll with the punch in the interests of getting the piece published and tickets sold. So I gave him an enigmatic answer which seemed to excite him greatly. He then wanted to know whether it was normal practice to 'do tongues' in a stage kiss. Not unless you really are up to something, I said, otherwise it's very bad form indeed, a sort of betrayal. Looking at his disappointed face, I felt like a vicar being asked if he normally finished off the communion wine.

Which brings me to the drugs.

~

And, most dear actors, eat no onions nor garlic, for we are to utter sweet
breath; and I do not doubt but to hear them say, it is a sweet comedy.
SHAKESPEARE, A Midsummer Night's Dream

If only it were that easy.

Most actors don't mind the smell of garlic on a colleague's
breath, preferring it to that of alcohol, which is a truly alarming
thing, and almost unheard of nowadays. In the 1960s we used,
many of us, to sit in the pub before a matinee and go to the show
much in the state that you might go to the football. It was also
normal to have a liquid lunch during rehearsals. The firm rule of
course was not to mess up afterwards: we were like poker players
raising the ante, and heaven help us if we screwed up. The puri-
tanism that these days generally stops actors doing this was thus
at work in another, slightly macho way: you could sway on your
feet in the wings, you could be bilious with hangover, but you
couldn't make a mistake once on, or you were done for in everybody's eyes. The fortunate or unfortunate fact is that there were
heavy-drinking heroes then who seemed able to do the whole of
King Lear on a bottle of wine and never drop a stitch, and where
there are heroes there are less noble acolytes. At that stage of my
own career, I lived a life of – what? – routine disorder, a standard
young actor's behaviour which sometimes edged into rock 'n' roll
excess. Nothing unusual there, and it certainly chimed with the
times. I wasn't playing the biggest parts, but they were important
enough: Laertes for instance. I remember looking in the mirror
before one matinee and literally not being able to see one side
of my face: all the same, I never gave or received a scratch in the
duel in two hundred performances. So my card stayed clean of
penalty points – though I was sometimes sent to sober up a less
disciplined colleague because it was felt that I would somehow
know the lingo. This is a matter neither of shame nor pride, even
if it now seems out of date.

As the decade turned over, mind-alterers appeared, especially those that accelerated rather than stupefied. Brightly fizzing performances replaced those tending towards somnolence and introspection. Some may have been good, but the odds were always against it. To state the obvious, amphetamines and cocaine make you race with borrowed energy, sedatives slow you down, and alcohol skews you out of shape; leave alone what their domineering rule does to your ability to bring an imaginary person to imaginative life. In fact the more fashionable drugs have never made much inroad in the theatre – as opposed to Hollywood, where their cost is more manageable by the stars and their effect may be more containable in the working day, with its repeated takes and many pauses. In the theatre few people make enough money to get far beyond the milder pharmaceuticals, and anyway a junkie stage actor is as hard to imagine as a junkie high-wire walker: alcohol has been the historic choice, since the alcoholic or semi-alcoholic still stands a chance of turning up on time and – just about – delivering. Also it's sociable – it is as difficult to be entirely teetotal for actors as it is for writers. Both are jobs in which introspection and loneliness need keeping at bay: what we all want after the show is a companionable drink or four. All this is recreation, a release and a consolidator, hopefully, of friendship. But even if you think you can handle it like a hero gone by, it's very unnerving for everyone if you bring the habit onto the stage with you, defying the tender co-operativeness that makes everything work.

Things still go wrong, occasionally. A significant actor in a repertoire company I was in evoked the tradition of John Barrymore one night to such an extent that he had to be kept off the stage by a quite young Stage Manager – she'd certainly never had to do such a thing before – and the understudy sent on in his place. Suddenly folk tradition collided with contemporary industrial practice. The next day, in quick succession, I happened to run into the Company Manager (the production's administrative head) whose subordinate had had to restrain the actor from going on, and then, a few moments later, a group of the offender's colleagues – though not, it must be said, those most directly affected by the scandal. Both groups' reactions were characteristic and remarkable. The Company Manager felt the actor should be fired immediately, no matter how senior he was, for setting such a dismal example; the colleagues were unanimous that we must all rally round the poor fellow because he would now be feeling so dreadful about having let everyone down, especially himself. Both responses are true. The sacking (which didn't happen) would have sacrificed a performance that, ninety-nine nights out of a hundred, was terrific; the tolerance of it seems to set the worst of precedents. Having been in management myself for a bit, I felt both reactions colliding within me: as a manager I too would have stopped short of the sacking, while feeling that something exemplary should probably be done, if only verbally. It's impossible really: what's the point of lecturing someone like a schoolchild about their behaviour the night before when they already feel the error of it? But then, what would happen if a perverse glamour were to attach itself to a middle-aged anti-hero and start a trend among the youth? And the fact is that in some performers' personality there is a compulsion to live dangerously, a need to snatch good practice from the jaws of bad. To be able to deliver a humdinger performance while throwing up in the wings with food poisoning, or in bereavement or pain, somehow argues a superhuman devotion, even if the obstacle is self-created. It's sometimes felt too that in this respect the good old theatre suffers by comparison with music – not the same vertiginous appeal, nor the reckless vitality. In fact musicians and actors are second cousins: they tend to enjoy each other's company and appreciate each other to the point of fascination. It's always a pleasure to be on a platform with an orchestra, doing a narration for instance. Meanwhile rock 'n' roll and jazz, our rogue relations, can be very instructive: an actor, after all, is always improvising within a structure, free within the time signature. I used to say I'd learned more from Billie Holiday than from any actor, though I might equally have said I'd learned the same things from Paul Scofield, who of all performers had the confidence to follow a sudden impulse while containing it within the frame. A live performance is really a matter of making choices very quickly, as late as possible – so late that the new idea and its expression appear instantaneous. In this sense acting, music and tennis are very close.

Musicians can be still more disorderly than actors, and not only in the popular field. Beethoven used to spit on the floor. Some turn up late, despite their ferocious Union. Yet others take advantage of admirers – some orchestral conductors notoriously. A young actor such as I was used to be very impressed by the fact that certain rock heroes seemed able to perform miraculous feats of cross-rhythm, of flawless capriccio, glissando and rubato, while full of confusing chemicals. But they did tend to leave the group and go solo in the end, a thing hard to imagine in the theatre. A theatre company, like a sporting team, is intricately collaborative, sustained by individual flair but vulnerable to wilful ego. There will always be leaders, but blind narcissism causes the whole thing to buckle. The sober truth is that your colleagues depend on you. The theatre carries its irregular traditions with pride while observing an ascetic discipline.

~

Public transport being what it is, everyone is late for rehearsals once in a while, and if you hate the feeling – the angry panic, the running through the streets, the imagined puzzled faces – then I'd say you're in good professional order. Use the delay in the Tube tunnel not so much to wear yourself out with curses but to check you know your lines, so that once there you don't waste any more of anyone's time.

As for *force majeure*, nobody would really expect you to play if you're coming from your dying mother's bedside, or, God forbid, your child is seriously ill – though 'seriously' might have to be defined. The industrial legislation intended to cover nudity now also enshrines paternity leave – a father-to-be has an absolute right to miss a show to attend the birth of his child, and to be there afterwards for a bit. The death of a husband, wife or partner should surely qualify for compassionate leave. On the other hand you probably should turn up to work even though a grandparent has died. Yes, probably. Death of a good friend – yes, you still have to be there, perhaps thinking that your friend would have it so. The death of a parent – borderline, hard as that sounds, depending on the circumstances and the survivor. My mother tilted into what turned out to be her final illness as I was about to take my own company to Canada for six weeks. Her sister I think never forgave me for not cancelling the tour – or sending on the understudy – and staying home to help look after her. It was a very hard call in fact, as the potential cost of not going – to our backers and to the working lives of a large number of people – was in its own way catastrophic. My mother characteristically solved the problem by staying alive until I got back – just.

In less emotional cases, I would say you have a contrary obligation not to play – if you have laryngitis that makes you inaudible you should be kept off, since only vanity would make you want to inflict your muffled croaking on an innocent audience. Spare a thought too for the painless damage you might do to your cords by subduing the symptoms with anaesthetics. I'm still not sure that I did well to continue playing Hamlet one night in a performance I had initially suspended because of vertiginous food poisoning. The audience loved it – the Dunkirk spirit and all that – but they certainly didn't get the quality I – or perhaps the understudy – was capable of.

You certainly have to turn up to perform if your life has gone wrong in some amorous way. But in that case you're probably better off as an entertainer than as a clock-puncher: acting gives energy as well as taking it and the body will care of itself. Think of Edith Piaf or Judy Garland. Your audience can save your life: theirs is a call to arms indifferent to your ego, your sexual behaviour, your recreations, your tragic or semi-tragic setbacks. The word is overused, but the theatre, penitential and unforgiving, is something like a religion, both a benediction and a cure.

10 The Scenery's Better on Radio

At least be glad that your bed scene wasn't on the radio. Then it would all have had to be done with the voices, while a possibly shy floor manager supplied the creakings and the rustlings, rather as the first AD on *Summer's Lease* did for Susan Fleetwood and me.

Strictly, such a floor manager would be in charge of Spot Effects, and she (as she usually is) is slightly less of a feature than she was. The major accompanying noises in a radio drama – the roar of the traffic, the pouring rain – are added in the control-box, formerly drawn from a huge record library of sound effects but now generated by computer software; the actors can't hear them (if they were folded back into the studio they'd be recorded for a second time) but still have to allow them to affect the pitch and rhythm of their speech. It's much easier with the more immediate effects – if, say, you're walking up a drive and Spot FX provides you with a little tray like a garden sieve full of gravel to crunch on the spot and then whips it away again; or if you're climbing through bracken, and become aware of miles of old recording tape being scrunched up beside you to make (oddly enough) exactly the right sound; or if you're supposed to be swimming, and are offered a large basin into which to raise and lower your head, even if it becomes difficult to know what to do with your script.

The man who's been through the bracken now approaches the microphone unzipping his windcheater with a telling little grunt of effort; upstairs a woman unzips her skirt preparatory to putting on a new one; beside them walks Spot FX, with a zip (different size for each of these examples), unattached to a garment and bought for the purpose from a haberdashers on its little fabric strip, doing the unzipping. The man then steps (with further grunts of his own) into a bath; Spot FX drops some loose clothes to the floor, augmented by an effect prepared in the control room of a body of the appropriate weight lowering itself into water. Occasionally – for in this scenario it's getting quite crowded round the microphone – the actors might banish Spot FX and do it themselves, for instance paddling around in bare feet in a rubber pool to simulate the Normandy landings. Some of them then have to go home and tell their children – who will long have outgrown paddling pools – what they've been doing for a living that day.

The criterion is really how many physical tasks you can be expected to undertake yourself when you're also carrying a script – inaudibly, of course. As you see, it will involve you in some odd behaviour, but no odder than the contortions generally necessary to express a feeling with your voice alone. An unkind photographer let loose in a radio studio could get marvellous shots of actors in front of the microphone, leaning in and rearing back, retreating from it and twisting their heads over their shoulders to suggest calling from a distance, kissing their own hands rather than the person kissed (the reality being a thing difficult to do without the scripts crashing into each other); snarling ferociously while turning pages over with great delicacy, grateful for the coarse-grained BBC-traditional paper that makes the least sound. (Already it's becoming iPads.) This is all part of the delirium in this seemingly stately medium.

~

My parents used to refer to the wireless as the Steam Radio, or just the Steam, as if it were something invented by Robert Stephenson. When TV arrived and we became fascinated by the great Bakelite cabinet with its tiny screen in the corner of the room, it so took over that, with wonderful contrariness, they started referring to the radio as the Silent. Compared to the whizz-bang effect and visual overload of *The Age of Kings*, or even *Double Your Money*, a radio play must indeed have seemed a quiet thing. At that time it might have sounded like this:

ANNOUNCER: Midweek Theatre. [MUSIC AND KEEP UNDER]. We Present: *This Gun That I Have in My Right Hand Is Loaded.*

[BRING UP MUSIC, THEN CROSSFADE TO TRAFFIC NOISES. WIND BACKED BY SHIP'S SIRENS, DOG BARKING, HANSOM CABS, FOOTSTEPS, KEY CHAIN, DOOR OPENING, SHUTTING]

LAURA (*off*): Who's that?
CLIVE: Who do you think, Laura my dear? Your husband.
LAURA (*approaching*): Why, Clive!
RICHARD: Hello, Daddy.
CLIVE: Hello, Richard. My, what a big boy you're getting. Let's see, how old are you now?
RICHARD: I'm six, Daddy.
LAURA: Now, Daddy's tired, Richard. Run along upstairs and I'll call you when it's suppertime.
RICHARD: All right, Mummy.

[RICHARD RUNS HEAVILY UP WOODEN STAIRS]

LAURA: What's that you've got under your arm, Clive?
CLIVE: It's an evening paper, Laura. [PAPER NOISE] I've just been reading about the Oppenheimer smuggling case. [EFFORT NOISE] Good gracious, it's nice to sit down after that long train journey from the insurance office in the City.
LAURA: Let me get you a drink, Clive darling.

[LENGTHY POURING, CLINK]

CLIVE: Thank you, Laura my dear.

[CLINK, SIP, GULP]

Aah! Amontillado, eh? Good stuff. What are you having?

LAURA: I think I'll have a whisky, if it's all the same to you.

[CLINK, POURING, SIPHON]

CLIVE: Whisky, eh? That's a strange drink for an attractive auburn-haired girl of twenty-nine . . . Is there anything wrong?

LAURA: No, it's nothing, Clive, I—

CLIVE: Yes?

LAURA: No, really, I—

CLIVE: You're my wife, Laura. Whatever it is, you can tell me. I'm your husband. Why, we've been married, let me see – eight years, isn't it?

LAURA: Yes. I'm sorry, Clive, I'm being stupid. It's . . . just . . . this.

[PAPER NOISE]

CLIVE: This? Why, what is it, Laura?

LAURA: It's . . . it's a letter. I found it this morning in the letter box. The Amsterdam postmark and the strange crest on the back . . . it frightened me . . . It's addressed to you. Perhaps you'd better . . . open it.

CLIVE: Aha.

[ENVELOPE TEARING AND PAPER NOISE]

Oh dash it. I've left my reading glasses at the office. Read it to me, will you, my dear?

LAURA: Very well.

[PAPER NOISE]

Let's see. 'Dear Mr Barrington, if you would care to meet me in the Lounge Bar at Berridge's Hotel at seven-thirty on Tuesday evening the twenty-first of May, you will hear something to your advantage.

[CROSSFADE TO OPPENHEIMER'S VOICE AND BACK AGAIN IMMEDIATELY]

Please wear a red carnation in your buttonhole for identification purposes. Yours faithfully, H. T. Oppenheimer.' Clive! Oppenheimer! Surely that's—

CLIVE: By George, you're right. Where's my evening paper? [PAPER NOISE AS BEFORE] Yes! Oppenheimer! He's the man wanted by the police in connection with this smuggling case.
LAURA: Darling, what does it all mean?
CLIVE: Dashed if I know. But I intend to find out. Pass me that Southern Region Suburban timetable on the sideboard there. Now, where are we? [BRIEF PAPER NOISE] Six fifty-one. Yes, I'll just make it . . . There we are. Well – [STRETCHING FOR FADE] Lounge Bar of Berridge's Hotel, here . . . I . . . come . . . [FADE]

In this imaginary play (in fact a wicked satire by Timothy West of the old-fashioned piece that suited action to sound and sound to action without end, as if for idiots), you should imagine the noise of the ship's siren and the traffic being generated from discs in the control box, the actor doing the sound of effort, and Spot FX doing the key, the door, the tearing of the envelope, the upstairs running, the pouring and the siphoning and the various noises of different papers. Clearly she was the overworked heroine of the hour. And who knows, she might in due course have turned into Jane Morgan, one of the great radio directors, who started her career in just that way.

Here's another kind of radio play, from me, in which she's one of the stars. Any resemblance to real people is entirely intentional: only the setting has changed.

Five of the Best

NARRATOR: Good evening. Around the microphone with me tonight are Jane Morgan, John Tydeman (Tydey), and Sasha Yevtushenko, three really good radio directors from different generations. And the telephone lines are open. Tydeman worked in BBC Radio Drama for forty years, including nearly ten as Head of the Drama Department; he discovered Joe Orton and also did every classic you can think of; a little later Jane Morgan started a career of the same length before retiring in the 1990s – some of you will remember her *Sword of Honour* and *Lord of the Rings*. Both she and Tydey are still at work, but generally outside the BBC in the 'Producer Choice' world of the last twenty years – that's with independent production companies that sell their programmes on to the BBC, such as Peter Hoare's Pier, Frank Stirling's Unique and John Dryden's Goldhawk. But they were at the fountainhead of radio drama for sure. Those were the days –

['HEAR HEAR' FROM ALL]

– but so are these, for nobody is better equipped to represent changing times in the new century than Sasha Yevtushenko, who has been at the BBC for less than a decade but has directed de Maupassant, Raymond Chandler, Kwame Kwei-Armah and Truman Capote; his next project is the entire Aeschylus *Oresteia* adapted by three contemporary playwrights. I've asked John, Jane and Sasha to come along and talk about their favourite medium, and why they prefer it to working in the theatre.

TYDEY [*Interrupting*]: Yes, well, because you're your own master in radio.

JANE: And the scenery's better.

[ALL LAUGH PLEASANTLY]

TYDEY: That's right. You know that vision of the Seven Kings in *Macbeth*, the descendants of Banquo? Have you ever known it to work in the theatre? It does on radio. And have you ever seen Birnam Wood move convincingly to Dunsinane? It always looks silly. But it works on radio all right, precisely because you don't have to see it. Shakespeare is the perfect radio playwright.

NARRATOR: What, because he has this gift for letting you see things that aren't there with words alone?

252

TYDEY: Yes, and the way he's always contrasting what the characters' inner and outer voices are saying; and he moves hither and thither in space and time. Lady Macbeth's sleepwalking scene comes with a running commentary from the Doctor, like stage directions – see, what is she doing with her hands? Shakespeare even helps by, even more than usual, naming people as they appear – here comes my Lord of Ross, etc. Yes, this is clearly a radio writer at work.

NARRATOR: Well, just to spool back, what I was going to say was that it's tricky to know what the career path generally is for radio directors. How did you all start? As a result of training, or almost by accident? Jane, weren't you going into publishing?

JANE: Yes, but as was the way in those days, I ricocheted, I suppose, from one contact to another. It was a sort of accidental networking, all a bit haphazard and circumstantial. My university tutor knew the producer Michael Bakewell, who kindly kept accompanying me round the BBC Club [FX: THE SOUND OF LAUGHTER AND DRINKING IN THE BBC CLUB] till I got a job as a Studio Manager, doing Spot Effects as you've described. [FX: THE SOUND OF CRUNCHING GRAVEL] I remember standing in as Piglet in a live Children's Hour production of *Winnie the Pooh* splashing in a paddling pool (it was that story when they're completely surrounded by water). You did all sorts of things in those days – editing too – I once spent the day editing with Louis MacNeice – we only achieved five edits in total because of the brilliant talk. In due course, without really aiming for it, I was trusted with a drama production of my own – *The Dales*.

NARRATOR: Formerly *Mrs Dale's Diary*. Sounds lovely.

JANE: Doesn't it? But it wasn't. We'd record one episode in the morning, another in the afternoon.

TYDEY: Those were the days.

NARRATOR: Didn't Tom Stoppard write briefly for *The Dales*?

JANE: Yes, he did, but he wasn't interested in Mrs Dale and Jim, and only wrote episodes for the mother-in-law and the quirkier minor characters.

[ALL LAUGH AT THE IDIOSYNCRATIC APPROACH OF TOM STOPPARD]

NARRATOR: Jane, I'd like to hear your episodes of *The Dales*.

JANE: They've all disappeared. No recording survives. Personally I think somebody nicked the tapes. I wonder who.

TYDEY: Yes, I worked with Tom Stoppard as well in the early days. Around the same time as I noticed Joe Orton's first play (he was just out of prison for defacing library books) – just as it was being sent back by the script department.

SASHA: Yes that was a big difference: you commissioned your own stuff then.

TYDEY: Yes I did. Once a friend sent me Sue Townsend's original script for *The Secret Diary of Adrian Mole*, and I put it out as a half-hour play on a Saturday afternoon, whereupon Methuen commissioned Sue to write a whole year's worth, and that was that: the *Diaries* were the *Harry Potter* of the 1980s.

JANE: Weren't you in them as well?

TYDEY: Yes, I played the radio producer to whom the thirteen-and-three-quarter-year-old Adrian sends his poems – 'Good try, but try again, eh?'

SASHA: For a producer today, there is a rigorous commissioning process. You often start by informally pitching an idea to the Commissioner, then all being well, you go back to the writer to develop it; you produce a treatment – and make a formal pitch, with a full plot outline, even though the play isn't yet written. And there's always a pressure: as producers, we're aiming to make around fifteen hours of drama a year.

NARRATOR: Radio 4 have a specific commitment to new writers, don't they?

SASHA: Yes, an informal one, to commission a percentage of first- and second-time writers every year.

NARRATOR: Where do you go to find them?

SASHA: Often to the theatre. I do prefer to look for writers who've had experience of having their work produced.

TYDEY: And you do get your commissions, I know.

SASHA: Not all of them. It's sometimes a matter of timing: for example, a writer once gave me a terrific idea for a play that started with a car crash, but when I pitched it to the network I realised that there were a number of other ideas already scheduled that began with the same premise. So good ideas are sometimes kiboshed because their subject matter is covered elsewhere – it's a significant pitfall because there is a lot of drama on the radio.

NARRATOR: Well, Sasha, you may have had your near misses, but I know what your writers think of you – this one at any rate you've done three plays with, Rebecca Lenkiewicz:

[THE VOICE OF REBECCA LENKIEWICZ IS HEARD AS IF ON A PHONE LINE TO THE NARRATOR]

REBECCA LENKIEWICZ: Sasha is extraordinary. His passion is conveyed not with volume but a quiet incision and beauty. He's not scared to show emotion within a project and is forensic in his treatment of the characters and words whilst giving huge freedom to the writer. With the actors he is so respectful whilst still leading them to higher diving boards with encouragement and grace. He is brilliant in directing and in editing, astute and full of care. And much of this is done with humour, which is rare.

TYDEY: Well, I'll drink to that. You can't say fairer than that. [HE DOES SO]

JANE: I'm doing the same commissioning rounds but now I've retired from the BBC, I'm going to the independent companies as well, like Pier and Unique, the ones that sell on. That's another difference, the independents.

TYDEY: Do you like dealing with them?

JANE: Yes, I do.

NARRATOR: What are the favourite programmes that you've done, Jane?

JANE: *Dada & Co* with Gerard Murphy, Struan Rodger and Julie Covington; Dickens's *Bleak House* . . .

NARRATOR: Jane, I must say it's interesting and rather gratifying that when you're asked for favourites, you immediately name the actors. [LAUGHTER] I'd also recommend for your consideration – apart from your *Lord of the Rings* in the 1980s and *The Sword of Honour* – Simon Gray's *Little Nell* and (in tribute to your – and Simon Gray's – love of cricket) *The Englishman Abroad*, about the 1931–2 Bodyline tour, and *The Champion*, about W. G. Grace.

JANE: Thank you.

TYDEY: And when *The Englishman Abroad* is mentioned could I butt in and say – that's a play that could never happen today – Christopher Douglas had never written a play before. So it's good to hear what Sasha's just said about the renewed commitment to first-time writers.

JANE: It was an unsolicited script that arrived in January and it was on the air that August. Oh, and the Shakespeares are other favourites: *Richard III* with Ian Holm and Barbara Jefford, *Antony and Cleopatra* with you, Michael, and Lindsay Duncan.

NARRATOR: Well, thank you too.

JANE: Don't mention it.

TYDEY: I was lucky enough to work often with Paul Scofield, one of the great expressive voices of the century (better than Olivier, who was vocally thin, or Gielgud, who was too unvarying); and I did *Othello* with him and Nicol Williamson as Iago. It was odd: though they were very different kinds of actors and men, their voices were too similar, so Paul generously dropped his down further into his boots. With Irene Worth, who was . . . well, tiresome – but brilliant; with Alan Badel, and Ralph Richardson and Alec Guinness, whom I found a shade too polite to pull off King Lear's 'Howl, howl, howl . . .'

JANE: I'm proudest of the actors I've managed to cast against opposition from upstairs, who wanted celebrities: I cast Hugh Dickson in the lead of the eleven parts of *Sword of Honour* despite all sorts of pressure to offer it to Alec McCowen. And Norman Rodway as Abthorpe, one of the great radio actors.

TYDEY: Yes indeed, and for me there was Ronald Pickup, who did Hamlet for me. And Michael Bryant who did Oedipus likewise – not stars, just brilliant actors.

NARRATOR: Jane, what was it like to work at the BBC as a woman when you started?

JANE: Well, I had to lie about my ability to sew and knit, which were thought to be proofs of manual dexterity, an essential quality for a Studio Manager working on the technical side. And later, because I had worked on *The Dales* and was a mere woman, it was thought that I only understood domestic affairs. It wasn't till I had done a spell in TV on Arts Features that it was thought that I could read as well as cook, and in 1970 I was entrusted with a classic serial – six hours of *The Mill on the Floss*.

[GAYNOR MACFARLANE, WHO'S BEEN DIRECTING FOR THE BBC IN GLASGOW, HAS BEEN WATCHING QUIETLY FROM THE

STUDIO DOORWAY AND BREAKS IN]

GAYNOR: I made *The Mill on the Floss* too!

[ALL GREET GAYNOR MACFARLANE WITH PLEASURE]

NARRATOR: Come on in, Gaynor. Join us. [HE PULLS UP A CHAIR]

GAYNOR: Yes, in 2003, but in four hours – in fifteen fifteen-minute episodes, so I'm glad it wasn't an initiation test! But I'm relieved to say that my knitting and sewing skills were never questioned. I've never experienced any discrimination. I think I was hired in part to balance an otherwise quite male department and was actively encouraged to develop ideas with women writers – and to do George Eliot indeed.

TYDEY: But now, Jane, you're an innovator, aren't you, in your methods?

NARRATOR: Yes, you have a quite unorthodox preference for rehearsals: if you have two days to make a sixty-minute programme you might rehearse the actors for a day and a half before committing anything at all to tape.

JANE: Sure.

NARRATOR: Well, you sound calm but it's a much riskier undertaking than to rehearse and then record sections from the outset, as in a film.

JANE: But of great benefit to the performances. They begin, with that much more practice, to develop some of the ease and depth they might in the theatre. The whole problem now is less and less time. On *Sword of Honour* it was easier: I'd have two-and-a-half to three days for a sixty-minute episode, and might not record anything at all until the second half of the third day.

SASHA: Yes, I think actors are invariably more comfortable and confident on the second day.

258

JANE: At the same time you're running a risk. I once worked with Bill Nighy, on *Lord of the Rings*. We rehearsed a very tricky sequence when he was moving through locations – across microphones, in fact – singing a difficult song. The first time we rehearsed it on the floor I naturally didn't even consider putting a tape on, but I wish I had: it went like a dream, whereas when we finally recorded it it took about a dozen takes to get a decent one; since then I've been inclined to run a tape on the technically trickier bits in rehearsal and keep it in reserve in case something goes wrong or I run out of time later. Apart from that, I still insist on the same proportion of rehearsal despite the ever-increasing pressure to get on with it. About other things, I've changed my mind a bit over the years. I used to be very keen on location recording, but I'm not so sure now . . .

TYDEY: Oh, I hate location recording. All that sound you can't control, the wind and aeroplanes and the dogs barking, make it very impracticable – and slow and cost-ineffective too; ironically, far more convincing exteriors can be created by the technology in a good studio.

JANE: Well, the writer Douglas Livingstone and I did once find the ideal compromise: going to an event with a sound-recordist, taping all the natural sounds, and then Douglas writing a play about the event, with the insight of having actually been there. The first one we did was the El Rocio Pilgrimage in Andalusia when maybe a million people across Spain process to visit the thirteenth-century shrine of the Virgin of the Dew, and we had some fantastically good recordings which really made you feel that you were there; so much so that Michael Kitchen, who was in the play, said that in future he would always travel with a recording machine instead of a camera. And when we went to Normandy for the anniversary of the D-Day landings we had the good luck of our boat breaking down mid-Channel: we really got to know the veterans of the Essex Yeomanry, who were on board, and their conversation gave us the play.

TYDEY: Oh well. [HE IS SILENT]

SASHA: Last year I produced two dramas in the studio which were set almost entirely outdoors – Elmore Leonard's Western *Hombre* and William Golding's *Lord of the Flies*. We have a great team of studio managers who are brilliant at creating exterior sound. Once I did a drama that followed a day in the life of a single mum. We followed the lead actress around with a boom microphone, in, out and around her house, and also attached a stereo one in her Alice band, and mixed between the two. If the location helps the natural rhythm, it's worth it though, and [TO TYDEY] as for the ambient noise, for a high street I'd go there but try to find a more controllable side street near it. John Dryden is a director whom I really admire and he records almost everything on location; he packs his equipment and goes to Mumbai to record *Q&A* (the novel that became *Slumdog Millionaire*), to Tokyo, to Mexico.

[JOHN DRYDEN MIRACULOUSLY MATERIALISES AT THE TABLE]

JOHN D: I do go abroad for certain productions – not only for the authenticity of the locations but because of casting. As well as *Q&A* I went to India to record *A Suitable Boy*, *The Mumbai Chuzzlewits* and *Undercover Mumbai*, both because they were set there and because I could work with Indian actors. If we'd made these dramas in the UK, we'd have been using British/ Indian actors and, however good, their voices might have had a little British element in them. Similarly we went to Mexico to make *Lost in Mexico*, about two British girls who get on the wrong side of the law during a backpacking holiday. We flew the two British actors out and the rest of the cast were Mexican and didn't speak much English: so immediately we got the tension of two English-speakers in a world where they don't understand what anyone is saying to them. We used a lot of improvisation too, and the local Mexican actors of course knew their country intimately and could do that. It would have been really difficult to cast such a project in the UK.

NARRATOR: So how physically do you set about it under those circumstances?

JOHN D: I block out a scene as realistically as I can, with all the moves, no scripts, and then rehearse and rehearse it until it feels like it's really happening and only then record it . . .

NARRATOR: No scripts?

JOHN D: Well, it depends on what it is, but generally I try to get the actors off script and we improvise a bit, especially when we're trying to work out what the scene's really about. Often the improvised sequences we actually record are short – maybe a few exchanges or it might simply be that a man gets into a taxi and says, 'Take me downtown' – and so even if the actor hasn't learned the lines beforehand, by the time we've rehearsed it, the scripts can be discarded. For longer scenes actors are usually on script in one form or another and we have to plan out the page turns. I've noticed a lot use iPads these days – which is actually really good as we don't need to worry about paper noise.

NARRATOR: And some scripts I suppose are more text-based than others, less desirable to improvise . . .

JOHN D: Yes, with Margaret Atwood's *The Handmaid's Tale* and Vikram Seth's *A Suitable Boy* we were mainly script-based. Though for *A Suitable Boy* there was quite a bit of improv in the scenes' background – street sellers, taxi drivers etc. – which was all layered into the mix.

NARRATOR: And that ambient noise was all completely authentic, of course?

JOHN D: That's right, yes.

TYDEY: How do you control the location?

JOHN D: Well, that's a big consideration: finding the right place to record in takes ages. For instance, if a scene is set on a busy street, we tend to record it on a quiet one, and then add the busy-ness by recording a lot of wild tracks of noisier ones and adding them in – in the same way that sound effects are added to studio productions.

NARRATOR: And I suppose, as Jane was saying, there's a time pressure too these days, less of it to get everything done?

JOHN D: Yes, but I can usually achieve twenty minutes a day of what will end up on air.

SASHA: Whereas in the studio you reckon on about thirty minutes a day nowadays.

TYDEY: They had much less time on the current redo of *Sword of Honour* than you had, Jane. For the Scofield *Othello* I had ten days, now it would be five.

SASHA: Yes, four or five days would be about right for a Shakespeare at that rate. You have a little more time doing a forty-five minute drama as you get the same number of days as for an hour-long one: two. So you're only doing twenty to twenty-five minutes a day.

GAYNOR: But for the Fifteen-Minute Drama series – five episodes in a week – it's also two days, so we record seventy-five minutes in that time. It can be flat out.

NARRATOR: Sasha, what are the big differences for you as opposed to these two? What brought you to radio in the first place?

SASHA: My background was film: Godard and Truffaut were my heroes since I was fifteen. I started making low-budget films – managing schedules and people, shooting on a shoestring. And all I learned in the making of short films applies to radio, in fact.

Then I worked in BBC Current Affairs, and made observational documentaries, before I started assisting in radio drama. In a way I like radio because it's a chance to be David O. Selznick in miniature. I can see a play all the way through from the germ of an idea I've discussed with a writer, through its commission and writing, to production, editing and transmission. And the audience is enormous: for an Afternoon Drama, it's often over a million, which is the equivalent of having all three stages at the National Theatre at capacity for a year.

JOHN D: Like Sasha's, my main influence is film and TV drama rather than theatre. So I treat the microphone as if it were a camera and make choices about who or what it follows. We'll often have to record several takes with the microphone doing different things: it's really very similar to having several camera angles. And then it's all in the edit: these productions require a lot more editing time than studio ones – weeks, not days. All the same, this way of working isn't really about location versus studio. I'd happily work in a studio in this way – with roving microphones – and often have.

GAYNOR: My background meanwhile is in theatre, so the speed of radio took me by surprise at first. As a director, you need to have something helpful and responsive to say to the actors, and the timeframe to prepare it is between the end of the take and your arrival in the studio from the control box, a few metres away! In theatre you can say, Oh, we'll look at it again next week, which you obviously can't on radio.

NARRATOR: And what about budgets and cost?

TYDEY: Drama's the most expensive part of radio of course, but it isn't really expensive in terms of scripts, actors, director, studio: *The Balkan Trilogy* cost £70,000 per ninety-minute episode, whereas an hour-long episode of such a programme on TV might be ten times that.

JOHN D: I'm sure, yes, and I also think that historically it's difficult to compare radio budgets with each other. £70,000 seems an extraordinarily high figure now – I would expect it to be more like £30,000 if it was made in the last twenty years or so, that's to say since Producer Choice came in. Before then, I don't think anyone quite knew what a radio drama cost precisely: producers had a freer hand to throw at a production whatever resources they felt it needed. And there were the hidden costs – all the various BBC overheads such as contracts, casting, studio, studio staff, offices in central London, telephone, electricity, insurance, production assistants . . .

NARRATOR: On location there must be particular budgetary considerations.

JOHN D: Oh yes, you've got to get everyone there, you've got to feed them. And it is much slower work: a location not being controllable as a studio is, you have interruptions and unplanned noises, and you have to embrace this to some extent and be prepared to use what you get. As you need more time, that has an impact on the budget, and the editing takes more time as well. And though you're not paying for a costly drama studio, you're usually paying for locations instead. Budgets for radio drama are standardised now – they're determined by airtime rather than how productions are made, at around £22,000 per hour – which makes it easier for the BBC but is a source of great frustration for me sometimes, as a two-handed studio-based drama would get the same budget as one of my overseas location-based shows, with its fifteen actors and weeks of editing.

So the way I've always worked is to design the production around the money I have. Always, it's a delicate balance – negotiating deals where we can, but also paying artists and crew fairly. It's a challenge to make it work, but doing it on location means that everything we spend goes into what ends up on air. There are no overheads being siphoned away to pay for fancy offices or administration.

And by the way it's hard to make a single drama work overseas – so we're usually talking about a series of two or three episodes such as my *Pandemic*, which we recorded in Thailand, *Severed Threads* (India and the US); now I'm off to the Philippines to record *A Kidnapping*, a story I developed with Andy Mulligan, who wrote *Trash*.

NARRATOR: Give us a clue . . .

JOHN D: It's about two British teachers at an international school in Manila who attempt to kidnap one of the children in their care.

NARRATOR: Don't miss your plane . . .

[JOHN DRYDEN VANISHES IN A PUFF OF SMOKE]

NARRATOR: Any pet hates, any of you?

JANE: Actors who sound as if they are speaking in inverted commas, as Gerard Murphy brilliantly put it, and also actors and directors who don't make sure that the speech is in period and use American intonations in Victorian plays. And I admit to having a general aversion to the 'airilies' such as TempoRARily. Or NecessARIly. Or MiliTARily. The different element in related words is almost always near the beginning; you should generally hit the first syllable. *Black*smith. *Silver*smith . . . Hearing 'bought' for 'brought'. Also, the new super-fine technology encourages mumbling; I believe eye contact with your colleague is very important. Now Rodway was not afraid to be big, he was never a mumbler. In a way it's more difficult now with stereo mikes because you both face that, not each other; with the old mono mike you looked across it at each other.

NARRATOR: Which would be better for a dinner *à deux* scene too, wouldn't it? Standing side by side at a stereo mike is an odd way to sit in a restaurant, beside your friend rather than oppo-site them.

TYDEY: I hate unnecessary sound effects. I use a bare minimum. After all, I started in TV and got tired of it because it's so literal, but in radio you don't have to hear the lift coming up or the car arriving as you might on TV . . . It's all a matter of what you leave out. I once did a play set in Africa. It was an hour long, but I used no sound effects at all: the language was so beautiful that I got letters from listeners saying they loved the sound effects. The only two that matter in classical drama are the screen going over in *The School for Scandal* and the final door slam in *A Doll's House*.

SASHA: Actors who don't prepare. The horror story is of the actor who arrives on the first day and opens his envelope with the script in it almost as if to show he hasn't read it. Although I've never seen this. Some actors cover their scripts with all kinds of markings and colours: Anna Massey had everything worked out like that, but when I asked her to go in a different direction with the part she could do it on a sixpence because the basic thinking had been done.

JANE: Brilliant.

TYDEY: I direct with a carrot not a stick. Actors are, in general, unnecessarily nervous: they're usually better than they think they are. I always think the truth of a performance lies on the actor's circumference – with some you have to push towards it, others give you too much so you pull them back (which I like better).

NARRATOR: John, your notes are always sharply to the point in a language I can understand. I once saw you confront an actress who'd done no homework at 10 a.m. on a Monday, and you had a broadcastable performance out of her by the time you started recording in the afternoon.

TYDEY: I also believe that the best director is often a good night's sleep.

[THEY ALL LAUGH AND EMBRACE. THE SOUND OF CLINKING PLASTIC CUPS]

~

So what do these highly individual directors have in common, and what do they, without exception, want of you as an actor? First of all, to dispose of an old myth about radio, this is more than a quick fill-in job for you: it's extremely demanding and nowadays as competitive as everything else. It's just that radio still has a slight air of cosiness: you may be in the bowels of a large and encircling building which seems to protect you from all slings and arrows – something uterine in fact – and of course you don't have to look your best, or even learn your lines. There was a time perhaps when lunches in the BBC could be a little liquid and a certain bluff (and mostly male) amateurism seemed to prevail, but actually this was always a mask for sharp judgements and seriousness, for acceptance and rejection. Now the wood panelling of the 1950s studios and the big black masonry microphone of mono days have been overtaken by the sleek silver of stereo and high-tech lifts and plastic passes worn like medallions round everybody's necks. Duck-egg blue seems to be the colour of all new hospitals and radio studios now.

Current working conditions sharpen what directors need, and all our witnesses agree that you must be prepared. It warms a radio director's heart to see the notes he's sent out on a project's historical background – the siege of Leningrad for instance – marked up as if an exam were about to be sat; or, as Sasha says, an actor's script with every stressed phrase marked like a musical score, even if it then changes. This kind of flexibility is essential on radio, because you hit the ground running and you may be committing something to posterity ten or fifteen minutes after doing the initial readthrough.

For which you absolutely have to be ready. A readthrough on radio is very different indeed from one in the theatre, which is only the prologue to as many as four weeks' preparation. A radio readthrough on the other hand occupies a good deal of the first morning, in other words a fair proportion of the overall time; once you've done it, the clock is beginning to run, on a one- or two-day job especially. So have a performance of some kind ready, just as an offering. Sasha especially admires Marcia Warren, who apart from being a brilliant adlibber is full of ideas. In the play they did together she thought her character should wear slippers, and brought them along on the first day so he could hear them slapping on the studio floor. Well, maybe, but perhaps it was a veteran's privilege: I'm not sure you should try this on your very first radio.

Always read the whole play even if you have a small part (John Tydeman says this is in case somebody doesn't turn up and you might get a better one, but I think he's teasing). And if there's no readthrough and you go straight to tape – that is, if time is really short and the play is technically complicated – then you have to be doubly prepared. The ideal is to have the readthrough on a separate, initial day, but this generally only happens on a long series, after which the schedule is also long and elaborate and involves availability.

In general you should understand your role as part of a story-telling machine, and pitch in and do your bit, which may involve doubling as a barman in the third act. Don't be prissy about this. And listen, all the time, both in your character and also to the other actors' techniques. When you're silent on mike, offer tiny reactions to what the other person in the scene's saying. Jane Morgan likes these very much – Norman Rodway used to call them Morgan Noises, when an actor would look across the old mono mike, catch their colleague's eye and do the audio equiva-lent of a raised eyebrow (probably a sort of 'hmmm?').

Sasha likes these more cautiously, and is inclined to edit them out, which isn't difficult. He thinks it sounds ugly to murmur in other people's speeches, and there's something to be said for dropping such verbal tics. Anyway don't change the script, unless you really sense it might be welcome: it's the result of many weeks of hard work.

Radio technique isn't rocket science: it's easy enough to learn. You talk louder the further you are away from the mike; you tend to exit by walking backwards. Use your visual imagination: the other actor may be only two feet away but you may have to throw your voice across several yards to her. These days you can actually kiss the person you're kissing: if you kiss your own hand at a stereo mike you sound like a person with huge lips. Always imagine what you're looking at, what the weather's like, how many people are around you, what time of day it is.

~

There is some difficulty in getting into radio in this country: it's one area where agents, with some exceptions, have little per-suasive power. Or don't exercise the power they might have if they befriended a handful of directors, which they could cer-tainly do. It's a pity – radio is better paid than it used to be, and such negligence is a hangover from the old days. And you may need an agent's pressure: BBC producers are increasingly celebrity-swayed – though they probably go to the theatre more often than TV directors, so might spot you in something. Two things you might do, one of which you may already have done – be one of the auditionees at your drama school for the four annual Carleton Hobbs bursaries, or the two from the Norman Beaton Fellowship if you haven't attended an accredited drama school. You'll do one classical piece for the audition, two other speeches, a three-minute duologue, an unseen piece of prose, and a team piece for your whole group; on the duologue and group piece you'll be directed – one of the main aspects of radio being that it's fast in the doing, so actors must be able to take notes and work quickly with a director. The bursary gives you five months in the Radio Drama Company in the second half of your graduation year. This used to be called the BBC Drama Rep. I once recorded on location with some of its members and it was hilarious: you walked down the street with any of them and they could imitate any voice that passed, not to mention the cars, the distant cries, the wind in the trees, the rushing river. They could also, brilliantly, create a rounded character from the briefest handful of lines.

Your contract with the RDC is relatively short (it used, impractically, to be thirty people for two years); you'll shuttle between a large number of different productions and sizes of part, and have continual practice in front of a microphone. This might seem to block you off from other work, but it might suit you if you have a particular ambition for radio; the prize has certainly done no harm to the careers of Richard Griffiths, Emma Fielding, Stephen Tompkinson or Joe Kloska, whom Mike Leigh once heard on the radio and then cast in a film. Agents may dislike the RDC, but that's shortsighted of them and actors love it. It also follows that if you haven't got one of those bursaries this is a time of year that's bad to be looking for radio work if you're the same age as the candidates.

If you've graduated already, you could get a voice-over agent who also handles radio; or prepare a voice reel – it's reasonably cheap, and any agent will recommend an engineer who will do one for you. Make sure it shows your range of accents, and put it up on your Spotlight page and invite the Radio Drama Company Co-ordinator to listen.

Drama schools vary a bit in the seriousness – and facilities

– they apply to radio technique: you can be in a fully equipped studio (RADA) or be making do somewhere with a broomstick instead of a mike. But the teaching will be from the front line, as the schools generally have guest directors in to teach rather than resident staff, so you're getting it from the horse's mouth.

~

In *Letters to Alice* Fay Weldon describes the effect of a radio broadcast of Jane Austen's *Emma*, at the moment that Emma decides to insult Miss Bates:

> All over the country, irons were held in suspension, and car exhaust bandages held motionless, and lady gardeners stayed their gardening gloves, and cars slowed, as Emma spoke, and that other world intruded into this . . . Hand in hand the human race abandons the shoddy, imperfect structures of reality, and surges over to the City of Invention . . .

With a drama, even if you turn off after five minutes, you've already used your imagination: you couldn't avoid it. Radio doesn't assault you or tell you what to feel, like all but the best of television and film; even the theatre distracts and beguiles your eyes, sometimes honourably and sometimes not. If the great strength of the theatre is that the human being you're watching suffer or rejoice is as real and present as you are and sharing the same air, you can't on the other hand be distracted on radio by what you think of the actors' looks or whether you've seen them before in something else. You invent what they look like. Radio liberates some actors who perhaps don't have the greatest presence on the stage, but are vocally well equipped, into their best work. The thin man can play Falstaff, the fat man Ebenezer Scrooge; Gwen Ffrangcon-Davies sounded pretty good in extracts of Juliet, Beatrice and Portia on radio when she was ninety-seven.

In radio, in other words, you do all the inventing; listening to a tape roll past its heads in some distant place you create the scene for yourself in any of Fay Weldon's locations. More than in any other form, except to a degree music, you see visions of your own making, everyone's being a little different: the medium makes you gifted. It's far more of a one-to-one activity than TV: as you listen you might look at the radio set, or at the ceiling or the wall, conjuring your own pictures; not fixedly, with three other people, at the same flickering screen. Even an audio book generally involves a narrator, introducing you to everyone; radio usually leaves you alone with the people, whom you then develop. This makes us feel very good. No wonder directors specialise in it, perhaps working in no other medium; no wonder as actors we tie ourselves in knots with the effort of doing it all vocally. It is a truly wonderful form and invariably fun to do; sociable too as you get older – I became so used to seeing friends in a radio studio after some years that I came to think there would be a great radio studio in the sky like a huge green room for everyone I'd ever worked with – a very cheery view of life after death. Its power is companionable, mysterious and familiar: John Tydeman says he once took a cab to go to a reception for Arthur Miller and wondered why the driver suddenly pulled into the side for a break. It was because an Arthur Miller play was being broadcast: John ended up late for the party but very cheerful as a radio producer.

Radio has survived against all the odds, and Britain's is probably still the best in the world. And iPlayer has had a huge impact on the popularity of radio drama – it is now downloadable, portable, personal in a way that it couldn't be just by being broadcast. How many times have you listened to a feature on Radio 4 and thought you couldn't possibly be interested, and five minutes later you were hooked, surprised and joyful? It's both old-fashioned, conjuring memories of *Mrs Dale's Diary* and *Journey Into*

Space and men with pipes, and also the most immediate and present: and it undoubtedly does things that the most advanced television can't do – is less and less able to do in fact. And it's certainly preferable to bad theatre. So yes, the scenery is definitely better.

11 Wrongs and Rights

It is often easier to become outraged by injustice half a world away
than by oppression and discrimination half a block from home.
CARL T. ROWAN, American author and journalist

When John Tydeman directed Paul Scofield as Othello on the
radio in 1972, nobody turned a hair. This was simply the next
stage in Scofield's royal progress, and, as so often with him, his
preparation for playing a great part on the stage; he went on
to do this one at the National Theatre in 1980. When Michael
Gambon played it in 1990, he got some very angry letters: within
a decade the idea of a white actor blacking up for Othello had
become extremely wrong. A black British actor finally took the
part on at the RSC another decade later – Ray Fearon in 1999.
These are landmarks in the modern history of Shakespeare's
tragedy. Now it is unthinkable for the part to be played by any
but a black actor, ideally perhaps with Northern African blood,
since Othello, famously, is a Moor.

Clearly this is not altogether to do with the offence of painting on a black face. I doubt if a white actor could play Othello
on the radio now, and it's not just a matter of the wrong vocal
quality. It's deeper than that: and the issue is intimately connected with the progress of race relations in Britain – its muddled, double-backing, often well-intentioned but still deeply
tense development.

~

I was recently in a production of *Antony and Cleopatra* at
Chichester. Out of the cast of twenty, there was a Pakistani Sikh,
a Mauritian, and four African actors. The remaining fourteen,

that is not quite three-quarters, were Caucasian. One night we had what is a standard ritual, a post-show question-and-answer with the audience. As the murmured queries came up about how we remembered the lines, doubts about modern dress and so on, one male questioner spoke out loudly and clearly. He said that he'd noticed – as he could hardly fail to do – that while Cleopatra was white in this production, there were 'a lot of brown and black faces around her': could we comment?

Terry Doe, a fine Ghanaian actor, replied with great courtesy and elegance that of course Cleopatra was a Macedonian, therefore Greek you might say, and therefore white, but as she ruled from Egypt, her servants would have been African. Thus the kind of effortless racism that allows itself a way out by implying that the questioner is only interested as a matter of cultural interest, honest, guv, was nicely kicked into touch; but in one way Terry was lucky to get away with it. Nobody seemed to be aware that in a previous version of the same production the part of Antony, one of the triple pillars of the Roman world, had been played by the excellent, Trinidadian, Jeffery Kissoon: Terry knew and I knew that this fact refuted our logic. Had the questioner then asked about that piece of casting, we might have had to switch to a different argument: it would no longer have been a case of casting black and Caucasian actors in their literal roles, but of colour-blind casting, in which you're not supposed to notice the difference. A black actor has as much right to be cast in a white part as a white actor, though the *zeitgeist* simultaneously requires that a white actor no longer has the right to be cast black. This last is positive discrimination with which no one is likely to disagree; but from the nature of his question such subtleties clearly hadn't occurred to the gentleman in Chichester. You could smell his subdued racism, but you couldn't prove it; our reply, concealing an alternative, had the slight air of a fudge.

I asked Terry later if he was feeling any fatigue as a result of all this adaptability, this negotiating of various positions about something that so deeply affects him. He was too diplomatic to say so, but I sensed the patience of a black man waiting for the white man to catch up. As we chatted I remembered that when I once produced *Henry V*, we briefly wondered – in alignment with Part One of his argument – whether the French should be black and the English white; and that in Trevor Nunn's National Theatre *Troilus and Cressida* the Trojans were predominantly black and the Greeks white, which will certainly have helped clarify that play's (to us) confusing nonchalance about explaining everyone's historic allegiances. In both cases you can detect a ghastly significance in the fact that the black side ends up beaten.

British society can be deeply, awkwardly, guiltily and confusedly racist – both institutionally and in an ingrained personal way. It is also, in very many respects, just, liberal and decent. It is not difficult to believe that the police may have tried to discredit Stephen Lawrence's family, while Baroness Patricia Scotland, who was born in Dominica, can sit in the House of Lords. Our prejudices are selective, but generally directed with the most hatefulness at the people to whom we have always been most hateful – the Africans we have conspired in enslaving, the Indians we have made servants of, or shot dead at Amritsar, the Chinese we addicted to opium. We've colluded in monstrous things and then, rather than enquiring into ourselves, despised and further punished – blamed, even – the people we abused. The generally harmless British tradition of John Bull nationalism shades into racism with great subtlety, but you can smell it for sure on the breath of UKIP, one of whose spokesmen recently farcically condemned an interviewer as racist because he had pointed out that UKIP had no black faces among them, underlining his point by bashing the interviewer on the head with a magazine. However this is also the land of Shakespeare and John Stuart Mill, of high intentions and unwitting mistakes. We rejoice in the diversity of contemporary Britain but may murmur to each other about its inconveniences. We like to hear four or five different languages being spoken on top of a bus, as long as they're not too loud, or too proprietary. No wonder if in show business the question of colour is contortedly controversial, as opposed, say, to in the US, where its tensions are part of the country's foundation, not forced into being as it has been here by mass post-war migration. And if a profession as liberal as the theatre can get into a tangle about race, then it's a serious business.

~

Achievement has no color.

ABRAHAM LINCOLN

David Harewood has been playing David Estes, Director of the CIA's Counterterrorism Center, in *Homeland* for Showtime and Channel 4. The possibility has occurred to many people – I don't know him so I don't know what he and his family think – that he is an example of a black English actor who had to move to the States to get the work he deserves. I think this underrates his reputation – he's hot here as well, and has played both Nelson Mandela and Martin Luther King. But in a recent interview he did tell a story of having to explain to his seven-year-old daughter why there weren't any brown people on the stage when they went to *Mamma Mia*. And another, of an audience member watching him in *His Dark Materials* in 2004 and commenting that though he was enjoying the show, he couldn't work out how a black man could have a white (he might have added Irish) daughter. On the other hand he didn't seem worried by the talking polar bear or the rest of Philip Pullman's fantastical array of witches, harpies and a boy with a knife so sharp it could cut the air.

Something tells me that this reaction, unlike our customer's feedback in Chichester, was relatively harmless, though of course disappointing; the speaker's bafflement has a kind of innocence within it. What it does say is that the paying customer is having something of a job keeping up with the current state of affairs. Audiences are becoming used to having to sort out in the early stages of an evening what they're dealing with this time: are you supposed to notice the different colours or not? Or come to that, the fact that Juliet is in a wheelchair? How literally should you take what you're seeing and what exactly is the deal?

In all this, most arguments are more passionate than logical, and wherever you turn among them you bump into a para-dox. What about a mixed-race company in which a black Iago, openly racist, attacks Othello for being a 'thicklips', or a black Titus Andronicus does the same to Aaron the Moor? What if a white actor turned up with his own face (or one painted black) in August Wilson's *Fences* or Kwame Kwei-Armah's *Elmina's Kitchen*, pretending to be a black man? The second idea seems only marginally more preposterous than the first.

Another paradox is that many examples in the debate are based on Shakespeare, usually the measure of all things but a somewhat unreliable friend when it comes to minorities: the idea of a black or Jewish character was fodder for his instincts as a showman and spurred him to a range of useful insults; you would need a computer scan to assess how often the fearfully fascinated able-bodied world describes Richard III as, for exam-ple, an 'abortive, rooting hog'. The argument will soon move on to *King Lear*. Where is the black actor for Lear? He (or even she) is not apparent in Britain, though common enough in the US, because there hasn't generally been time for an English black actor to have a fifty-year career that would get him to the right age for the part. Meanwhile, the more that black actors can appease the liberal conscience by playing either significant small parts or heroes and heroines, rather than agents of destruction like Iago, the more relieved the white British audience is. There is, I would say, nothing as challenging on racial themes in theatre writing here as the work of Bruce Norris (*Clybourne Park*), David Mamet (*Race*) or Neil LaBute (*This Is How It Is*) in the US.

It was inspiring to see the American Paul Robeson play Othello at Stratford as early as 1959, at the behest of Peter Hall; it is equally inspiring and still more inarguable to see British actors Chiwetel Ejiofor and Adrian Lester triumphing in the part more recently, Lester immediately after taking on the role of the great black American actor Ira Aldridge and presenting the audience with the shocking image of a whited-up face as Aldridge played out his days touring in a fit-up *King Lear*. No one could fail to rejoice that Lenny Henry has been triumphing in August Wilson's *Fences* in the West End under the direction of Paulette Randall, the first black British woman to direct on Shaftesbury Avenue. At the same time Greg Doran's tremendous all-black *Julius Caesar* for the RSC, like all great work, attracted a little malodorous whisper of criticism here and there. This was mainly among black actors (some admitting disappointment that they weren't cast) because the African accents came from all over Africa rather than a single place; and it was felt that the real colour-casting battle would not be won until Paterson Joseph's brilliant Brutus was playing opposite a white actor as Cassius.

Are we still failing to reflect a changed society, or are we just getting tied up in dialectical knots? Wherever you go as a white witness to these developments you come to a roadblock, and most routes round it leave you feeling bad. Frustration and thwarted ambition are synonymous with theatre – it's double if you're the wrong colour. There is some white guilt here too, but you can't make good art out of atonement. Harewood, however, is hopeful. He says there's no better place for younger actors to learn the ropes than here in the UK: though the situation isn't perfect it is getting better. Perhaps the playing field will only be even when all sides are as content to forget some of the past and see a white actor playing Othello and a black actor Iago as they already are a woman playing Hamlet and a man playing Rosalind. And what about a Chinese Othello in an otherwise white production?

~

We're generally only thought of as the Chinese takeaway man or the Japanese businessman.
Statement from Equity on behalf of East Asian actors in the UK

David K. S. Tse, to whom I introduced you early in this book, now comes to have dim sum with me. It's only a few weeks since the RSC put on a fourth-century play called the 'Chinese Hamlet' – *The Orphan of Zhao* – and ran into significant trouble by casting only three East Asian actors in a company of seventeen. There were immediate demands for an apology from the vice-chair of Equity's ethnic-minority committee. The RSC insisted they had auditioned a large number of East Asian actors who had then turned down their offers; also that they were at that time casting an ensemble which would be doing two other plays as well, and the casting had to work for everything. There were accusations of racism – or at least thoughtlessness; in reply the RSC may well have pointed to a number of events – their recent *Caesar*, an Indian *Much Ado* and an all-black production of Aphra Behn's *Oroonoko* – to rebut the argument.

The official statements on all sides had a certain nervous opaqueness: there was talk of meaningful dialogues, new discourses and forum processes to come. Meanwhile, most British Chinese and East Asian actors continued to feel they weren't getting enough work. The Open Door conference at the Young

Vic in London in February 2013 took it as a premise that the English theatre was institutionally racist; it was attended by directors of repertory and touring companies, casting directors and drama-school representatives; also by a hundred East Asian actors – in steep contrast to the 2001 Eclipse Conference, a similar event at Nottingham Playhouse, when David, who was speaking, found he was the only East Asian person present.

He feels that the casting of *The Orphan of Zhao* was a turning-point that brought his community together; also, in retrospect, that some of the accusations were perhaps misdirected, although the sentiments were right; and that the RSC is no more institutionally racist than any comparable organisation in this country. For instance, he himself directed an all-East Asian *King Lear* for them in 2006 – a Chinese co-production between Yellow Earth Theatre (YET) and the Shanghai Dramatic Arts Centre, which formed part of the RSC's international Complete Works season. The acting company was half British East Asians and half mainland Chinese; the play was adapted and set in the near future, when China is an economic superpower and the business languages are English and Mandarin; all the characters were bilingual. The Gloucester family spoke English as a first choice; Lear himself resembled Sir Li Ka-shing, the fabulously wealthy Hong Kong business magnate, the world's largest operator of container terminals and health and beauty retailer. In Lear's presence, the choice of language became crucial: in the opening scene his daughters Goneril and Regan flattered him by speaking flowery Mandarin, which played into his traditional Confucian expectations, but Cordelia literally couldn't – she'd been sent to an English boarding school as a child and lost a lot of her mother tongue. So she said, 'Nothing'. Lear was out of date in thinking this disrespectful; but in the society he represented, the giving of face (respect) is vital, and so is filial loyalty, piety and obedience. However, the world was moving faster than he was; and it was he, after all, who had sent Cordelia to England.

Remembering his own upbringing in the UK, David certainly related to her linguistic dilemma. He had founded YET in 1995 and ran it till 2008 as a platform for East Asian theatre-makers. From 2001 the company was revenue-funded by Arts Council England to stage one tour a year, but YET managed its finances prudently (among other things, David was paid part-time for a full-time job), so that it was able to set up co-training initiatives: a Writers' Scheme (called Yellow Ink) with Soho Theatre; a Directors' Scheme (Yellow Stages), with the Young Vic; and a play-reading festival, Typhoon, at Soho Theatre. David's successors then formed Yellow Academy with the drama school ALRA for new East Asian actors.

YET's story is certainly a matter for pride (or the necessity of it for shame): they remained the only revenue-funded East Asian national touring company, and they've advised new companies on grant applications and supported their marketing. Not long after David left, the co-artistic directors resigned and YET stumbled, losing its revenue funding during Arts Council cuts. There is hope that under the leadership of a new Artistic Director, Kumiko Mendl, confidence has been renewed.

To say British East Asian actors had limited opportunities before companies like YET and Mu-Lan would be putting it mildly, and David had grown up with this since graduating from Rose Bruford College in 1989. Auditioned by a BBC producer for the part of a Chinese waiter in the Midlands, he logically offered a Brummie accent. No, the producer wanted a strong 'Chinese' accent, really strong, as similar to Charlie Chan as possible; velly Chinese, velly inscrutable – a walking cliché in fact, with a cod voice. David turned down the offensive stereotype, a hard financial choice for a struggling young actor. Even now, when casting opportunities have slightly improved, they're generally still limited to Chinese criminality, such as trading in the opium for which the British were responsible. Chinese culture is usually represented by Triad gangs with whom the hero or heroine is grappling, as Jason Statham's character does in the movie *War*, or Katie Leung's does in the recent TV series *Run*. It's like having Romanians only playing drug dealers. David points out that even the recent BBC series, *Sherlock*, for all its *au courant* wit, did an episode in which ninja Chinese assassins were running a circus, which much displeased the British East Asian community, who must have felt they were back in unreconstructed Conan Doyle land.

Obviously enough, television, especially the Soaps, holds the key as an opinion-shaper. As usual, David wryly observes, the women are in the front line. At one time Chinese actresses generally played prostitutes: now you might see a nurse who happens to be Chinese – Jing Lusi played one wonderfully as a regular on *Holby City* – or even, in Channel 4's *Dates*, Gemma Chan as a Chinese lesbian resisting her brother's efforts to get her to date men. That's some progress. It is also helpful to make the English laugh, and Gok Wan in fashion and Benedict Wong (in his original comic persona) currently lead the field. Bringing up the rear are the unfunny men, with their threatening testosterone.

In fact the whole process of acceptance goes in little fits and blips. When David Yip did *The Chinese Detective* in 1981 and then *Brookside*, it looked as if change was on the way, but it didn't lead to TV opening its doors to integrated casting any more than the career of Bert Kwouk or Bruce Lee in cinema started a universal trend. When David K. S. Tse pitched the idea of adapting a Mo Yan novel after he won the Nobel Literature Prize in 2012, he seemed to get eager invitations to lunch with producers; but his subsequent attempts to confirm a time and place for them were met with silence. Now, after the Beijing Olympics and because of its booming economy, there's more genuine Western interest in China; but he fears that recent dramas – *Wild Swans, The Arrest of Ai Wei Wei* and *Chimerica* – while commendable in their scope, complexity and ambition, have been perceived as negative about Chinese politics because this is the default position of most of the China-bashing Western press. Ironically, only *The Orphan of Zhao*, despite its casting choices, celebrated Chinese culture rather than presenting it as a threat. In summary he points out that of the three main ethnic-minority groups – South Asian (from the Indian subcontinent, the largest), Afro-Caribbean (the second largest), and East Asian (China, Japan, Korea and the countries in the Association of Southeast Asian Nations), Afro-Caribbean actors broke through first. Perhaps this was because they were more vocal than their Asian counterparts (and had suffered more to be vocal about: their parents, if not they themselves, remember the signs outside bed-and-breakfasts warning 'No Blacks, No Irish'). Hugh Quarshie is now a long-time regular on *Holby*; there are black families on *Corrie* and *EastEnders*; they play leading parts at the RSC and NT. Then came the South Asians with *Goodness Gracious Me* and *The Kumars at No. 42*, and now he feels things are beginning to change for East Asians too. Finishing his dumplings, he points out that we all originally came out of Africa and that twenty-five per cent of the world is now Chinese-speaking.

This wryly indefatigable man is curious to explore whether America is more progressive in these matters, and is planning a trip to LA. I think I know what he'll find. The casting of Asians is as much a litmus for the emphases in American society as it is for British; once Asian women would have been prostitutes, then they were doctors, now they're care-givers, restaurant owners and lawyers. He'll also realise, if he doesn't already, that unlike here, there was an historical sweet spot, after the end of the Vietnam War in 1975 – and indeed, before it, in the liberalism of the

1960s, when a generation of theatre directors was coming of age. Outstanding Asian playwrights too, and scholarships awarded to Asian-American actors by American theatres; work in non-Asian parts in Brecht and Shakespeare. It helped if these actors were at heart more American than Asian, and so didn't quite conform to a stereotype. An earlier generation had a harder time because most of them were indeed more foreign, and it was also accepted that Asian roles could be played by white actors; a later one, from the 1980s and 90s, also suffered because the Establishment had become more conservative again.

~

Until the color of a man's skin is of no more significance than the color of his eyes, me say war.

BOB MARLEY, 'War'

Jatinder Verma's path to the creation of Tara Arts had very little to do with anything as conventional as becoming stage-struck or dressing up as a child, though he does cite memories of acting in *The Royal Hunt of the Sun* at school in London – a play about culture clashes if ever there was one. Perhaps it predisposed him to theatre as a site for public dialogues about the world he found himself in. So when (as mentioned in the Introduction) he quit the Youth Theatre and hired the Battersea Arts Centre to put on *Sacrifice*, he found, in a newly bigoted period of Britain's history, that the story resonated with young Asians: though Jatinder and his colleagues didn't live in Southall, in a sense they represented an educated Asian middle class looking for a language with which to become informed critics of society rather than soap-box protestors. Theirs was an English voice inflected with the outsider's experience, and they knew their subjects: immigration, schooling, generational conflict, colour of skin. Jatinder's Tara Arts went into junior schools and toured cities with big Asian communities, but, as he says, it was at least as important that they went to Spilsby in Lincolnshire, where there are no brown faces at all.

From the start their audience was very mixed; and as it was also quite middle class, the company was judged for aesthetic quality rather than passionate racial positioning. Looking at the established Asian repertoire, they found the only Indian classical play not about the epic past or religion, but revolution: *The Little Clay Cart* describes a shepherd overthrowing a tyrant and for the first time brought the working class into an Indian script. They put it on during the miners' strike. When they were then invited by the National Theatre to do *Tartuffe*, they remembered that the *commedia dell'arte* origins of Molière's play were very similar to a western Indian form of theatre called *Bhavai*; they remembered as well the writings of François Bernier, who was in touch with Molière while serving as the Moghul Emperor's doctor. Bernier observes the similarity between the Muslim Emperor's struggles with the Hindus and the Catholic–Protestant tensions of Louis XIV's reign; he also talks about the fakirs, travelling mendicants who, like Tartuffe, only really had eyes for the women. So Tara presented the play as a gift from the West to the Emperor of India in the style he would most easily recognise, on an open stage overhung with a canopy like a Moghul tent, accompanied by masks and music, quotations from Shakespeare and two narrators. One of these began the play with a ritual benediction in Urdu which the other then translated in a Peter Sellers Indian accent; this gave a National Theatre audience permission to laugh precisely because it was an Asian doing it.

Relocation of the English classics became a habit. Shortly before Shakespeare wrote *The Merchant of Venice* in 1596, there had been an anti-Jewish pogrom in England, and likewise one in Kerala, waged by the arriving Jesuits against Jews who had been there for centuries. Tara's 2004 production seemed to be being performed by a travelling troupe in Kerala, but not a word of the play was changed: Asian women in burkas watching it in Blackburn nevertheless said they felt they were hearing Urdu poetry. Verma saw Prospero in *The Tempest* – set in the Islamic Mediterranean world – as a fundamentalist committed to his own jihad, creating the opening storm as if it were a plane hitting a tower. He wasn't surprised by the character: Osama bin Laden's right-hand man, Ayman al-Zawahiri, was an intellectual and a surgeon, used to the leisurely life of the mind. In his vengeful and controlling phase, Verma's Prospero watches his daughter Miranda showing her face to Ferdinand and finds himself unable to control his 'son' Caliban's unruly initiatives; he begins to realise the limit and limitation of his jihad. Like 'Doctor Fadl', the leading Egyptian jihadist, who suddenly repudiated al-Qaeda and embraced peace, so, abruptly, does Prospero, in a mere two lines of text.

After nearly forty years running the same company, Jatinder must hold a record among artistic directors in Britain. What does he hope for now? To be in my head, he swiftly replies, as much as he has me in his; we're not quite there yet, not least because while he has Shakespeare in his, Kalidasa, the great Sanskrit poet and dramatist, hardly impinges on mine. When that happens, we'll be fully human. It's a simple point and a true one. And he's thinking about his legacy, knowing that even if his children reject it, their children may not.

A lifetime devising these versions of the classics could be seen as an acceptable formula for British audiences. I suspect there are those who criticise Tara for not being enough of the street fighters and too much the intellectuals, serving up palatable messages. I don't think that would be fair – Jatinder's work with Hanif Kureishi (on *The Black Album*) bespeaks his radical instincts and deep multiculturalism. But his intuitive taste is a huge asset: he regarded Peter Brook's *Mahabharata* as sublime, but was especially moved by a small point in all its gorgeous immensity: every character in Brook's multinational company in Paris performed the *namaste* (the Indian greeting traditionally done with hands clasped at the chest) in their own distinct way. Nothing could be more eloquent of the absorption by this eclectic group of actors of the Indian epic, or more moving to a man of Jatinder's temperament and history. Interestingly, he points out that the subsequent English version of the show reduced the text to an 'Indian' story because every character performed the *namaste* in the standard Indian fashion, becoming tourists of India rather than, as in the earlier version, finding the Indian within themselves.

~

When Amit Sharma, who was born in India, offered Iago as a drama-school audition in 2000, the Principal asked him what actors had inspired him. Oh, well, Robert De Niro, he said. No, but what others, said the Principal, what Asian actors? Oh, some, but mainly I watch Western films. No, but what Bollywood actors? his tormentor insisted. This was the moment when Amit realised that just as he was climbing out of an Asian box, the lid was closing on his head again. Why didn't the man ask instead in what exact way did he find De Niro so fantastic?

Attending a conference on acting training and race, he heard a young black actor speaking about being at Central and how he'd learned all these European accents – Irish, Scottish, French. Amit thought, But when will you use them? West Indian- or African-inflected English is all you're going to need for the stereotypical characters you're going to be asked to play. Another time he had to listen to a fellow actor at a workshop on Lorca remark that the Spanish master didn't write his plays 'for people like you'. But since Lorca is Spanish he didn't see why an English actor would be in any better position than an Asian.

He'd misunderstood: this time the problem was coming from another angle. Amit is not only Asian but has a mobility impairment called arthrogroposis: one leg is shorter than the other, and his arms don't fully straighten. So for the moment he was representing not alien Asia but a group which, if you imagine Afro-Caribbean at one end of a scale and East Asian at the other, is not even on it in terms of acceptance: disabled actors. In fact his condition, in the delicate terminology that allows for differences rather than degrees of disability, is an impairment and not strictly a disability – just as a deaf person is called just that and is seen as being distinct from a disabled one.

I wouldn't normally address disability in our theatre in the same chapter as African and Asian actors – as if it were no more than a category – except that the communities do often compare themselves to each other. Unlike in matters of colour, with disability you feel the clock swiftly turning some distance back and then laboriously inching forward again. A representative of one management recently told a colleague of Amit's, who had one foreshortened arm, that he'd never be on a stage of theirs with an arm like that, though whether the tone was categorical or melancholy isn't clear. What is clear is that the speaker could not have said an equivalent thing now, as opposed to thirty years ago, to a black, Indian or East Asian face.

Most non-disabled people are at some level afraid of disability: most have made nervous disability jokes, and physical 'perfection' is entwined in our response to the arts, otherwise dance theatres would be empty. The body making a decision to take an apparently unworkable form is an obscure, deep threat to many people's peace of mind; a measure of our civilisation lies in coming to terms with it. However, it would be as dishonest to deny this anxiety as to deny that disability often creates an unavoidable anger in the disabled person – at being helped too much, or too little, or in the wrong way.

Amit's parents, who brought him here from India in 1981 as a baby, were very keen to support the artistic aspirations suggested by his birth chart. What they may not have known was that they had arrived just a year after Nabil Shaban and Richard Tomlinson had formed the disabled-led theatre company Graeae, which hoped to dispel prejudice and popular myth through theatre, workshops and training.

Amit went to what was then called a Special Needs School. However there was a mainstream primary school next to it on one side, and a high school on the other, so he felt more integrated into the education system than he might have done. At that time most drama schools didn't seriously consider taking deaf or disabled students. So Amit was studying video production when the London Disability Arts Forum tipped him off about the actor-training course that Graeae were running called The Missing Piece; it offered a six-month training in voice, movement and Shakespeare. He signed up immediately, having this time auditioned as Puck (using a tennis ball); for the first time he felt the adrenalin rush of noticing people leaning forward attentively. (I'm not surprised – he is a charismatic and very engaging man.) He got in of course, and soon found himself touring in Büchner's *Woyzeck*; watching his guest director Philip Osment at work inspired him to direct himself one day.

And so he did. In 2012, five thousand people sat down in the gardens of Queen's House next to Greenwich Maritime Museum to watch the thirty-foot-high figure of Prometheus rising from the ground and defying the gods to bring fire to humanity – the act that made human civilisation possible. This enormous metal-constructed figure of gold against the blue night sky, lit eerily from within as by its own spirit, walked with a strange deliberate gentleness among us, as big, it seemed, as Queen's House behind him. He was operated by a small army of volunteer performers: others swung in wild formations in the air amid the smoke and fireworks, suspended high above the audience like an aerial ballet, backed by music, light and fire. This was not a narrative show, but the playing out of certain visions: of spring and winter, fire and ice. You didn't see Prometheus getting his liver pecked out as in the myth; at the happy ending, he appeared to be rescued not by Hercules but by humanity itself, in the form of a dancer. Significantly, it's a rich dream of free flight and untrammelled physicality, with, at its centre, a friendly Frankenstein whose every joint and bone and muscle – every physical function in fact – has been studied and rebuilt.

Prometheus Awakes was the opening show at the Greenwich and Docklands International Festival (GDIF) that year. Performed by a mixture of disabled and non-disabled people, it was the most ambitious outdoor show that Graeae have ever done. And Amit co-directed. What happened was that when Graeae's artistic director, Jenny Sealey, was invited to be co-artistic director of the London 2012 Paralympic Games Opening Ceremony, she invited Amit to back her up as Associate Director at Graeae. Then Bradley Hemming of GDIF introduced him to the radical Catalan company La Fura dels Baus to see if they could collaborate on a big outdoor show. In a way La Fura dels Baus seemed an unlikely partner with Graeae – not least because the former's practice in casting is to find likely actors in the street and playfully sign them up. I saw them in Barcelona in the 1980s and they frightened me to death with their apparently reckless, aggressive physicality – all of it ferociously disciplined of course. Nothing could seem more different from their panache than Graeae's necessarily meticulous construction of a model in which disabled artists can work. For six months, the companies auditioned volunteers: at each date on their proposed tour of outside venues they would need seventy or eighty. I should say performers: 'volunteers' is a word Amit doesn't like to use, because of its non-professional, goody-goody overtones. Together the two directors, Amit and Pera Tantiñá, with their creative teams, prepared the story, planned the projections, organised the schedule, hired interpreters and visualised the access. If Amit asked the extremely relaxed Catalan how long it might take to unclip the support lines from two cranes and re-hook them, the reply would gently come back – two minutes, or maybe four? Or maybe six? They rehearsed for just four days, and that not all the time: a day exploring the equipment and doing a briefing; a second day rehearsing and doing the technical; a dress rehearsal on the third which coincided with a major storm; and a final day with no rehearsal but a performance. And, amazingly, it worked. Amit proudly describes the project as bonkers, and then his face lights up with a one-man fusillade of explosive laughter, in which you can hear both joy and the strain of achieving it in his circumstances.

Like Jenny, he wishes Graeae didn't still have to exist after thirty years, and says you could measure the difference it's made in kilometres rather than miles, inches rather than metres. What he does know is that good storytelling makes you forget disabilities, in both the teller and the listener. But when you ask him who Graeae's allies might be in the mainstream, his face clouds over. He's thinking of the big institutions, whereas it's clear enough that the smaller and more compact the organisation, the more sensitive they are. Large outfits, or rather the various human cogs in their wheel that Graeae might deal with, are more likely to have a bureaucratic fear of thinking outside the box, most only feeling comfortable dealing with 'normal' (i.e. minor) disability. On the other hand Soho Theatre, the Royal Court, and, he hopes, the NT studio are listening with interest.

His face clears again when he talks of what he hopes to achieve in training and learning for disabled artists – especially circus training with trapeze, ropes and silks. Graeae are setting up workshops in Bangladesh, Brazil and India: there's nothing like the company in those countries. In that sense, he says, we're lucky with disability politics here. Even the semantics are better: the Americans still use the term 'handicapped'; India, exactly conversely to us, prefers 'special needs' to 'disability'.

Amit also hopes to collaborate with five disabled writers per year, although they tend to have very little confidence; he speaks of one girl who had been applying for writing courses, but had no replies because they didn't know how to deal with the fact that she had a heart condition that prevented her from standing up for long. So he organised a Graeae workshop and arranged to put a day-bed in a private corner of the room for her to lie down on; he organised taxis to and fro, using the government's Access to Work grant. His relish for such things takes you straight to the heart of the empowerment he, most movingly, feels.

He was, of course, like everyone else, amazed by the Paralympics. But he quotes Krishnamurti: if you see something beautiful, don't try to replicate it, it'll just spoil the memory. It's good advice in this case: like many disabled people looking for renewed facilities and access in London, he feels the national celebration hasn't left much in the way of legacy. He is angry of course, as he is that Daniel Radcliffe was asked to play the Cripple of Inishmaan, and that the next Richard III is again likely to be a non-disabled actor demonstrating his skill at impersonation. He feels this is the equivalent of a white actor blacking up for Othello. If you, the well-intentioned listener, feel yourself withdrawing a little in the face of this, he points out the illogic: no disabled person has the equivalent right to play a non-disabled part. Why shouldn't Juliet be played by a wheelchair user? It's a question that's been asked before, and Jenny Sealey, like Amit, declares herself speechless that the assumed answer is negative. She points out: 'Nobody would say casting a black actor makes a play become about that – so why is a wheelchair user any different?'

Now this is quite difficult, I say to him, there could be an uncertainty here. Looking around for examples, I remember being in a production of *Hamlet* when the Hamlet, as an experiment, played a dress rehearsal literally: he wore a dress. He was outvoted on it by the company afterwards because, in the play's infinity of descriptions of Hamlet, cross-dressing is an odd thing to overlook: no 'Look where sadly the poor wretch comes reading in women's clothes . . .'. So, is Juliet in the wheelchair because this director says Juliet should be, or because she is a disabled actor? Why does no one mention it? Do we overlook it, or respond to it? We seem to have been here before, and I think of Terry Doe.

Continuing to sound like an old theatre anecdotist, I decide it's time I mentioned Sarah Bernhardt, the most famous disabled actor ever. While performing in Brazil in 1905 in Sardou's *La Tosca* (which Puccini was to turn into *Tosca*), she injured her right knee jumping off the parapet. Gangrene set in and the leg was amputated, but eight months later she was back in Paris starring in *La Dame aux Camélias* (later adapted by Verdi as *La Traviata*) – in a wheelchair, which she greatly preferred to a wooden leg. In another world but likewise, the great singer-songwriter John Martyn spent the last six years of his career with an amputated leg, also playing in a wheelchair. Does this constitute acceptance for disability or the fact that enormous celebrity makes its own rules? Amit smiles: he knows I know the answer. But we're talking about a whole community looking for parity here, not superstars to whom anything is allowed. Well, would it not be better to do an all-disabled Hamlet, rather than try to cross over? He listens – patiently and good-humouredly. Then he points out that a level playing field is the priority, and that as far as integration with non-disabled people goes, the record is improving. The Lyric Hammersmith currently run an ensemble company called the Secret Theatre, which this year includes an ex-Graeae member: Amit reckons that by the time of the second show in their season they'll stop looking at her disability. He also notes that the Royal Court has employed Sophie Stone, the first deaf actor to graduate from RADA, and that the sophisticated public clearly has no problem with this, though institutions do. He just wants equality, and to achieve a bit of it he is prepared to make concessions: the lead actor in a previous show of his, an adaptation of Ted Hughes's *The Iron Man*, has a 'deaf voice' and Amit worked with him on articulation – not to hide the voice, but to give the actor confidence to compete. In what must feel like a snub, his colleague as yet gets no other work: the door stays closed.

As we talk, I realise I don't see how Daniel Day Lewis could have been improved on as Christy Brown. Or, perhaps, Ian Holm as Richard III, a Stratford performance that caused Peter Hall to be lauded by one audience member for his magnanimity in giving a disabled actor such an important part. When David Threlfall played Smike in the original RSC *Nicholas Nickleby*, there were similar stories. It's also possible that in the case of Daniel Radcliffe as the Cripple of Inishmaan, at some subliminal level the audience knows the actor isn't disabled – isn't that part of how it all works? Something prevents me from bringing this up, probably because I'm talking about ruthless commercial pre-eminence rather than sound principles, and an unruly market in which a capricious audience, our paymasters, vote as they please, with their pockets and feet; for the moment, for everyone I've talked to, principles are more urgent.

Certainly Graeae are reaching for the sky, with everything that implies. Clearly it's very difficult to get into the mainstream on the terms they want, and meanwhile they've formed their own mainstream, plus guest appearances: Cherylee Houston has made history as *Coronation Street*'s first disabled actress; Storme Toolis has played Nicholas Lyndhurst's daughter in *New Tricks*, complete with sex scene; but both are disabled players playing disabled people.

And then someone gets a particular break, as Nicola Wildin so spectacularly did at the Paralympic Opening Ceremony in 2012, and we can all rejoice, non-disabled and disabled alike. Asked in to audition for the opening ceremony only three weeks before the event, and assuming she wouldn't get the job because they'd need a circus performer rather than a wheelchair user with juvenile arthritis, she auditioned on a Monday, got cast on the Thursday, did her harness test and storyboarding the next Monday, and opened the ceremony two and a half weeks later with Ian McKellen, Stephen Daldry and Stephen Hawking in attendance. She then took part (as did McKellen) in the Graeae rendition of Ian Dury's great battle cry *Spasticus Autisticus*, written by Dury to show his disdain for the patronising tone of the 1981 International Year of Disabled Persons:

> I wibble when I piddle
> Cos my middle is a riddle . . .
> I dribble when I nibble
> And I quibble when I scribble . . .
> Hello to you out there in Normal Land
> You may not comprehend my tale or understand . . .
> So place your hard-earned peanuts in my tin
> And thank the Creator you're not in the state I'm in.
> 54 appliances in leather and elastic
> 100,000 thank yous from 27 spastics . . .

The song was banned by the BBC but was now reclaimed for the Paralympics. It certainly whacked the tiptoeing language that surrounds disability right out of the park, and how relieved we were to hear this aggression: it liberated us all and felt much better than arguing guiltily about quotas and percentages in a room somewhere. It was a great thing too to see Nicki break through the glass ceiling, with her apple and umbrella; best of all she did Shakespeare's Miranda – a perfectly judged choice, given Miranda's physical constraint and her rejection of it, her delight in a brave new world.

And now, while Nicki is waiting for more acting work, she is teaching Motivational Speaking in schools.

~

Perhaps a degree of honest exasperation is the price you pay for asking. One of the most infuriating conversations I've had recently was with a feminist playwright who declared that women should have first refusal on all roles of either gender because of the historic wrongs done to them by men; she was thinking of suing Edward Hall's Propeller company for following the original Shakespearian practice of using all-male casts on the same basis, declaring that the world had fortunately moved on since Shakespeare's day. But in respect to the plays of Shakespeare, I offered, Fiona Shaw has played Richard II, Kathryn Hunter King Lear and Maxine Peake Hamlet; and what about the all-female *Julius Caesar* and *Henry IV*? She repeated that women were owed for the wrongs of the past, so that was OK. With so little work for women, all-male productions are galling, of course they are; but still something was wrong with her argument, which had the odd effect of making me suddenly want to be living in the early seventeenth century.

Still, I got over it, as no doubt I have always got over any difficulties lying in the way of an able-bodied Caucasian who still has good health at seventy-one after a good career. It'll take longer for Amit Sharma to forget the film audition he did three or four years ago when the director realised he had an impairment, stopped talking to him like an adult, and became a carer with a rather slow-witted child, encouraging Amit to take his time before starting and then giving him a cheery thumbs-up at the end to congratulate him on his unlikely achievement. I marvel he didn't get a smack from an unstraightened arm. Or for Nicki Wildin to forget turning up for an audition for Comic Relief only to find that there seemed to be no lifts to get to their office. Or for Jenny Sealey to get over an email from Channel 4 after the Paralympics, asking her if she thought any of her disabled performers would like to be on their voyeuristic *Undateables*. So much for legacy.

PART FOUR – Summing Up

12 My A–Z

From Availability to Zhoozh

A is for Availability. I once had an agent who, if ever I groused about not having enough work, would say, from behind his great desk, that my availability was my greatest asset. We'd agree (again) that only the right project would do for me, and that when it came (as it would) I must be free to pick it up. When you have no work, he implied, no money, no prospects of any kind, you should nevertheless be glad, because you're at least there for the asking, whether by Steven Spielberg or *Holby City*. At such times I would skip down the stairs, light and insouciant, feeling, like Willy Loman, that a man is not a dime a dozen and that attention had been paid. It usually lasted until I got on the bus.

I'd been had, but not entirely: it's really hard to make a judgement about this. Sometimes you get a job you're so delighted with that you commit instantly, even though it doesn't start for another three months and then lasts a year; if, a bit improbably, you then get another something that will fit nicely within the next three months (your availability being your greatest asset) that's a bonus: you're committed for the next fifteen.

Caution about accepting a job that isn't quite at that level of delight in case something better comes up is one of the chronic neuroses of the actor. It's obviously not a dilemma you can discuss with the person making the offer, and possibly not with your agent either, who may be only too glad to have you booked and earning and unlikely to feel your plight as sharply as you do. Still, it sums up the life: sure enough, you've got to be free when the big sunshine comes out; on the other hand you've got to earn a living.

While I'm at it, A is for agent too, especially the one above; I left him in the end, as I was getting tired of my greatest asset. I wrote him a letter – generally the best, and certainly the most cowardly, way to take leave, so strangely reminiscent of breaking off a love affair. I (rather pompously, I now realise) said that as he had lots of thoroughbreds in his stable besides me, he wouldn't mind one of them bolting from time to time. I meant to post the letter and stuck on the stamp. Then I started to fret, in case, while it was still in transit, he rang up and I'd have to dissemble. So I dropped it into his office letter box one evening and half-ran away. Back in a few well-considered days came the reply. There was my stamp, cut out and stapled to the top right-hand corner. He advised me to be nice to my new agent if it was in me to be such a thing; pointed out of course his many selfless efforts on my behalf; as for the thoroughbred line, he said his thorough-breds never bolted, but sometimes the stable boys ran away.

I had to hand it to him. It was stylish in the great bitching trad-ition, and he must have worked hard at it. The only thing was, we were then obliged to have a feud. We would, in the way of things, bump into each other at first nights and such; the strain on him of cutting me dead clearly began to wear him down: what an effort it can be to remember that you're not supposed to be talking to a person who's coming down the street towards you. So after a couple of years I marched up to him at a premiere and asked him how he was and what did he think of the show. He melted like a snowman in the sun. Our implicit deal was then to Say Nothing Further About It; we had a most enjoyable drink together, and, to the amazement of my companion, who had had to listen to me moaning for a couple of years, made no reference whatever to the matter that lay between us.

B is for Being in the Moment. There's a very interesting little sequence at the beginning of Act Two of Chekhov's *Three Sisters*. The first Act has ended in high party spirits, and Andrei Prozorov has proposed to Natasha, a local girl; now the action cuts forward a year or so. Andrei sits reclusively in his study reading – it feels very much as if he does so every evening – while his now disliked wife and deaf servant come by. Natasha is on an economy drive – though she sees her own way round the house with a candle, she wants to make sure that no others are alight – a hard call as there's a Shrovetide party planned for that evening. She talks about her sisters-in-law, and especially her baby, but she gets little response from her husband.

Her place is shortly taken by the deaf servant, Ferapont, whereupon Andrei becomes more voluble, perhaps as a relief from his wife's rigmarole. Using the old man's deafness as an alibi for talking to himself, he reminisces about the pleasure of sitting in Moscow restaurants; Ferapont pops in semi-irrelevancies, such as the rumour that there's a single rope that stretches from one end of Moscow to the other. Eventually he leaves, but Andrei doesn't notice that he's gone:

> You can go now. Take care of yourself, old friend.
> (FERAPONT *goes*.)
> Yes, take care. Come back tomorrow and collect these papers.
> Yes, you can go.
> (*A pause*.)
> He's gone.

This authorised talking to himself, a courteous old employee keeping him oblivious company, is obviously a nightly ritual. Andrei is much out of love with his wife, but lacks the courage to stand up to her; no doubt this leads him to be particularly forthcoming to everyone else, while he plans morose mental revenges on her.

I have the most vivid memory of playing this scene in 1971, when I was twenty-eight. Andrei was the first really interesting part I had had, after standard-issue boyfriends and rebellious sons. Under the influence of Chekhov I felt for the first time ever that I wasn't Acting, but dealing with each new line as it came up in a state of mind which, though not fully expressed, had its particular rhythms, next to which what I actually said was almost coincidental. Chekhov is very modern in this way. It wasn't just a matter of going slowly or being vague – that would just be another form of Acting – but of allowing the thoughts to rise from whatever depths they were at and surface piecemeal, regardless of who heard them. It couldn't be rushed, any more than it could be delayed. I wasn't playing Andrei, but he me. And it didn't happen from the start but about halfway through the longish run; thereafter I never lost it as night succeeded night.

What is this, this feeling of doing your job well at last? In one way it felt like looking down at myself from the ceiling, while being fully absorbed in the matter in hand, just as musicians sometimes feel they're getting out of the way of the music and letting it sound through them. It's a good example of what the acting teacher Zeami Motokiyo describes as the ideal:

> What you are inside is what you look inwards at. But you must also become one with the audience and see yourself that way.

It also happens to be a cornerstone of Sanford Meisner's technique, this letting emotion and subtext build in their own good time; you may have studied him at drama school. But to find it out for yourself in performance is incredibly exhilarating. I suppose it comes from a sort of equilibrium, the confidence to sway out of and back into control; like someone who rides an unpredictable horse with an easy rein, or an orchestral conductor who on an impulse does nothing for a few bars, feeling it better for the orchestra to play freely. You're so sure of the state of mind and the emotions that it's safe to let things take their own course.

This beginning of being able to act properly thrilled me and I've never forgotten the night I first felt it. Later on I paid a little homage by putting in, at the end of Act One of my solo show about Chekhov, about a minute – sometimes longer, sometimes shorter – in which nothing happens. Chekhov has nothing to say for himself, so he idly fills the time in silence before giving up and going to have tea. As long as I was fully absorbed in whatever random things were scudding unexpressed through his brain, I noted that the audience always stayed with me. Chekhov lends himself to this (Shakespeare on the whole not). In Act One of *The Seagull* Dorn waits and waits likewise before commenting wryly that the angel of silence has passed over the company. The length of silence may well depend on the momentum of the show and its audience each evening.

Now, if I see an Andrei in *Three Sisters* miss the opportunity above, I don't make a judgement – of course not, he will be pursuing other things – but I do feel a certain self-satisfaction. Nor do I go around talking about it much: but this is my chance to tell you, in the hope that you know, or soon will, what I mean. It was certainly the moment I thought I might have a future.

C is for Corpsing. Etymology uncertain but we all know what it is. Also known as Going Up, Breaking Up or Cracking Up; the shaming but strangely persistent phenomenon of interrupting the show, even bringing it to a halt, because of a private joke that bursts its bounds, demolishing all attempts at keeping up the professional illusion and reducing the actor(s) to helpless, probably silent but still incapacitating gasping and heaving.

Etymology not all that uncertain, actually: corpsing probably originates in an ignoble effort to make an actor playing a dead body shake with laughter. Very good for the Forum Scene in *Julius Caesar*, where you might justify it as a way of keeping Caesar's corpse from dropping off and snoring – during the ninetieth performance, say – while Brutus and Antony at great length persuade the citizens of his virtues and vices. So it could be defined as an attempt to make a colleague disgrace themselves rather than disgracing yourself – leaving the instigator able to carry on with the audience's approval and no sign of complicity. In this respect the verb becomes transitive – to corpse someone.

It's the one thing an audience has no interest in or tolerance of, despite reedy avowals from offenders along the lines of 'it shows them we're human'. Bollocks. Audiences understand if the set falls down or some other mishap occurs – they sympathise and enjoy your efforts to regain the initiative – but not if they see you laughing at something impenetrably private. They've paid their money and feel utterly excluded, their belief lost, much of the point of an expensive evening gone. Corpsing has of course no justification at all.

I once organised, for a matinee of *Love's Labour's Lost* at Stratford on Boxing Day – small, soporific audience – a change of costume for the four young Lords and the Page who come disguised as Muscovites to woo the ladies of France. In the play it's a daft idea which is immediately seen through, and it recommended itself to me for further daftness. Duly, after much negotiation with Bermans the Costumiers in London, five Father Christmas costumes appeared at the Stage Door (the one for the diminutive Page being particularly fetching). Giggling like idiots, Ian Charleson, Richard Griffiths, Paul Whitworth and I climbed into them for our Muscovite entrance (the women – this being the key to it – were already onstage). Instead of the usual merry Russian gypsy tune on Moth's balalaika, we arrived to the strains of 'Jingle Bells'. The audience were be- rather than a-mused; it was a sort of vacuum; the Princess of France and her ladies slid gently off their formal side-by-side position on a leafy bench like a pack of cards collapsing sideways; an odd air of tolerance exuded from the auditorium.

When the bill came in for me, it was intercepted by a wag in the Finance Department who put it through the books, so the RSC paid for the whole thing in the end. Whether that constitutes forgiveness I'm not sure. I'm also not sure, thirty-five solemn years later, that I approve. I was clapped on the back by all sorts of people for several days as a good sport – who would have thought Michael would do a thing like that? – but the silence emanating from John Barton, the show's director, was in high contrast to the jollity. The next time he directed me would be as Hamlet, so at least he didn't sack me.

This is an example of Transitive Corpsing: the intention was to make the girls incapable. However, despite their sideways list, I think they maintained themselves rather better than we did. Which, come to think of it, is rather the point of the play: the women's maturity set against the men's exuberant childishness. So really it was all in the interests of narrative clarity . . .

Fifteen years before, I had walked on in Ian Holm's *Richard III* at Stratford. There's a scene when the citizens of London are coerced into accepting him as King while he pretends to be a man of God reluctant to take on worldly office. Dressed for his devotions, he comes down from the walls of Baynard's Castle to mingle with the crowd. There came a night when, for a joke, many of Richard's victims in the story so far – Clarence, Lady Anne, King Edward – all dressed up as citizens, hempen homespuns in hoods, and joined us, looking upstage at Richard and pulling faces at him. So Ian Holm knelt to the ex-King Edward and kissed his hand; then he spotted Clarence and Lady Anne. 'Cousin of Buckingham,' he declared, slapping his ghostly brother Clarence on the shoulder, and then – 'and you sage, grave men' – he slipped Lady Anne's hood off and revealed her to all – possibly in her curlers, I don't recall.

At no point did Ian Holm waver, let alone corpse. Instead, everybody else did: it was a magnificent turning of the tables. And who knows: there may be some people around who remember that inspired piece of staging in the RSC's 1964 *Richard III* when Richard's victims (one of them – a contemporary touch – in Carmen rollers) appear to haunt him in the midst of a very jovial crowd of citizens, prefiguring the famous moment towards the end of the play when their ghosts visit him in his tent and denounce him.

Intransitive Corpsing meanwhile – when you make yourself laugh – happens to the most surprising people. I could name a number of persistent corpsers, some of them very famous indeed, knights and dames included. In some it is a state of mind more or less managed: the actor is on the edge of breaking up all the time, perhaps at the absurdity inherent in the very business of acting, but generally finds ways of concealing it, though a familiar colleague will always be able to tell. You probably know who I'm talking about. Without quite knowing why, the audience becomes infected with the same glee and anticipation of fun. The ranks of such corpsers is of course swollen every time the doorknob comes off in your hand, or the letter isn't there when you go to pick it up, or it's the wrong letter when you read it, or a stage hand appears crossing the stage as the lights come up (as he did in a production of *Hamlet* I was in, at the moment just before Claudius said, 'How dangerous is it that this man goes loose'); or, best of all, if someone makes a funny mistake – a spoonerism for instance, especially a rude one. Then the audience will take their cue from the self-control or otherwise of the victim.

But of course all corpsing is disgraceful, absolutely indefensible. So why have I told you these stories? To make you laugh, of course.

D is for Drying. I suppose actors are asked if they forget their lines as often as surgeons are asked if they ever make mistakes, and if so, what happens. Well, what do you think? Would you ask a bridge-builder what was the consequence of a bridge falling down? It happens, doesn't it – perhaps it did to you at your end-of-year showing. You suddenly have no idea what's next. It's as if you'd driven up a side road that's come to a sudden end. There's nothing to do but go back and try again. So you pick up at the beginning of the sentence. No, still no good, tumbleweed rolls down the road. You jump forward to something you're sure of. You know you have to keep on, and above all not think about it or try to work out what happened till you're offstage.

It happens because you're not concentrating; it happens when you are concentrating but not on the important thing; it happens because something distracts you; it happens because you have a moment of self-criticism about the bit just gone by; it happens if you're pissed off with your colleague – but to you, and not, unfairly, to him. As you get older it happens for no apparent reason at all, like an intimation of professional mortality, and that's no fun. But long before you're old, it happens: it's God's mean little joke, warning you not to get above yourself. In every case a good recovery and new energy make up for it.

And it doesn't happen nearly as often as it almost happens – when you just find the missing word with a nanosecond to spare. It's like being about to apologise for forgetting someone's name as you introduce them, and suddenly the name comes back to you, arriving on the very tip of your tongue. A friend of mine still introduces his second wife of some thirty years by his first wife's name; they're still together, and you will work again after drying. Drying has reason and no reason. It's also not the end of the world.

Rupert Everett tells a story of drying twice in a row in front of a studio audience in Hollywood; his manager instantly ran onto the stage to fuss round him and hiss one piece of advice: 'It's OK, just don't let them *see* you *crash*.' True enough: the audience will believe almost anything is intended; so, confidently and in his character, he called the script girl and make-up to attend to him as if this stoppage was somehow all part of the show. The audience wasn't given the chance to believe the unthinkable was happening. Sometimes in the theatre, as a last resort, an actor will stop, go and get the script, bring it back on and continue. If so, make believe, madly, that your journeying was in some bizarre way part of the play. Paul Scofield used to laugh openly when he made a mistake, chiding the audience with one of his little confiding chuckles, as if they'd tricked him into it.

Any of these is better than jumping into the next act – *apropos* of which (for in the absence of a solution, we must descend into anecdote): Judi Dench, apart from being the greatest of actresses, is such a superb colleague that she has unhesitatingly allowed me to tell this story about the first night of our production of *Filumena*.

It had been a joyous thing to set up, rehearse and (eventually) to play. Comically audacious, Eduardo de Filippo starts his play *fortissimo*: the husband Domenico bursts onto the stage beating his head with self-disgust, closely followed by a triumphant Filumena in her nightgown. It emerges – and you have to listen carefully – that Filumena is a retired prostitute, Domenico her lifelong and faithless lover: he's escaped all her attempts to get him to marry her, and she has now feigned a mortal illness, called in the doctor and the priest and talked Domenico into a deathbed wedding ceremony. Having secured him, she leaps from the bed – fooled you. As the row between them spills onto the stage, you gather a further outlandish fact, that she's had three sons in her life, only one of which is Domenico's, but she'll never tell him which for fear he'll make him his favourite and neglect the others. For the moment, all that's clear is that she's stolen money from him to bring the three of them up.

She also knows that the girl Domenico's brought in at her deathbed as an occasional nurse, Diana, is his new squeeze; while they're rowing, two waiters arrive to lay the table and deliver the celebratory dinner Domenico has promised Diana, confident that by then Filumena will be dead. Diana arrives to find Filumena in full and furious sail and, for all Domenico's protestations ('I have to eat, don't I?'), is routed by her.

All this is a fair amount to take in, especially when everyone is acting in the style of grand opera. When, on the Press Night, no less, Judi cut from page three to fourteen, neatly excising all the supporting information and backstory and indeed the entire part of Diana, we suddenly entered a land beyond hope, a Bermuda Triangle where you forever circle pointlessly. She looked at me and I at her. I started patching text together like a demented tailor – sentences that started 'You mentioned the other day that you had three sons' and so on – and we got back into some kind of shape. The greatest danger was that Diana, having from the wings heard herself removed from the action, might have given up and gone back to her dressing room, rendering our efforts fruitless. Fortunately, she was made of sterner stuff.

We were on track again, but the aftershock nearly laid my marvellous colleague out. This turned out to be the night that Filumena would describe her life as having been led, not, as de Filippo had it, in the slums of San Giovanni, Vergine, Forcella, Tribunale and Pallunnetto, but in a rich new amalgam of San Carbonara, San Bolognese and San Milanese, with a little Valpolicella on the side. Perhaps this was because Judi had just come back from a couple of months in Italy – but certainly not Naples – filming *Tea with Mussolini* with Franco Zeffirelli.

We went out to dinner, she and I and Peter Hall, licked our wounds and drank to the god of deep disappointment. Not only do you Lose Some, Win Some, but You Specially Lose the

One You Were Sure You'd Win. In the morning, the notoriously waspish Nicholas de Jongh took the whole of page three of the *Evening Standard*, headed it 'A Night of Pure Joy', and went to heaven over the production. That afternoon we sold £40,000 worth of tickets, and within a very few days had sold out the three-month run. I promised myself never again to worry about such things, and have completely failed to keep my promise.

And that's probably enough said about this bloody business of . . . er . . . oh yes. Drying.

E is for Equity, which represents actors, cabaret artists, models, voice-over specialists, stage managers, fight directors, circus performers, choreographers, dancers, singers, variety and stunt performers, designers, TV and radio presenters, walk-on and supporting artists, and many besides. Laurence Olivier was a member and so was Jean From Birmingham (as she was billed), who was stripping in a nightclub in Barcelona when I met her in 1985, trying to chalk up her forty weeks to achieve full Equity membership, as you had to in those days. My own forty weeks as a walk-on at Stratford was done for much the same purpose (and I probably changed my costumes as often). All you had to do was get the first job; as a provisional member you were immediately protected by working-hour agreements and minimum wages for Repertory, Touring and Subsidised Theatres; if Equity were to call a strike you would have downed tools too. After forty weeks, you got the rest of the package: the right to work in the West End, TV and movies.

At eighty-plus years, Equity UK is quite a young organisation; the Variety Artists Federation (now amalgamated with us), is over a hundred, as is American Equity, which was whimsically started up by Edwin Booth as a sort of Green Room club in Gramercy Park in New York, but in short order was bloodying itself on defaulting producers and dressing rooms like coal cellars, even going on strike in 1920. Our union was likewise started informally in 1931 by a group of high-minded actors of enough repute to matter who declared that they would work in future only – and this was the point – with other performers who had joined the new organisation. This precious idea of the closed shop for a hard-pressed profession survived until Margaret Thatcher blitzed it in the 1980s as part of her general assault on the unions. While to some minds the idea of a closed shop smacks a little of vested interests, cronyism even, it certainly gives a union bargaining power; however, in terms of Thatcher's offensive, the idea that a group of actors could threaten to bring the government down as effectively as the National Union of Miners does have its genial side. In any event, to the shame of the European Court of Human Rights, who had condemned it in 1981, the closed shop became illegal in the UK in 1988, and Equity had no choice but to fall in. For us it was a disaster: it meant that skills were no longer essential for employment so the unskilled were able to undercut hard-won basic wage agreements in an industry that is already precarious, since what it offers is infinitely valuable without being strictly essential. Next time you hear the Halifax using one of their staff rather than an actor for a voice-over, blame Margaret Thatcher. It's taken twenty-five years for Equity to recover its confidence.

The history of both British and American Equity is studded with triumphs, extraordinarily so given the inherent weakness of any entertainment union. There is, as you might expect, a circularity about the issues: American Equity also established a closed shop, only to see it brought down in 1947 by the Taft–Hartley Act – a piece of Congress legislation passed in defiance of President Truman's veto. They stood firm against segregation in the 1940s and against the McCarthyism of the 1950s: unlike the Screen Actors' Guild they refused to co-operate with the Hollywood blacklist. Both British and American Equity have always fought the destruction of historic theatres and helped establish public funding for the arts; at the outbreak of the Second World War British Equity got a number of theatres reopened (and provided ENSA with a list of artists available for work), so live theatre survived the conflict in some style. By the 1960s members were refusing to perform in apartheid South Africa except to multiracial audiences; in 1976, Equity blocked the sale of programmes to the South African Broadcasting Corporation, and the result was a virtual blackout of British TV there. Similar bans were enforced here on working in UK clubs which operated a colour bar, and one in Coventry was picketed. In a parallel with McCarthyism, we stopped the scandalous BBC decision in the 1940s to withhold work from certain artists because of their political views. Virtually none of this would have been possible without the solidarity and confidence of being a closed shop.

In Britain, the number of unqualified actors working is in the event proving to be less of a problem than the number of trained ones who see joining Equity as a questionable choice rather than an obligation. However, the scale of fees reasonably allows for low earnings (rather better than does the US system), so the strongest argument for not joining is removed. Membership is going up at the rate of a thousand a year: you should be among them. Look at what you gain.

First-time West End producers have to put down a deposit so that you still get paid if things go wrong; you have Accident Benefit and Backstage Insurance; advice on commission rates that agents can take, on National Insurance, tax, Jobseekers' Allowance, welfare benefits and pensions. Free medical advice too (including a consultation and some treatment) through the British Association for Performing Arts Medicine. An Equity Trust provides support during recuperation from illness; the Benevolent Fund makes grants to members facing financial hardship. Discounts are available on many goods and services.

So join.

Employers contribute to Equity's pension scheme; lawyers help not only with the obvious stuff but with wills, probate and conveyancing; there's job information and a digs list for whatever town you're going to. An insurance scheme to cover you for those bad moments when HMRC – baffled as they always have been by our peculiar status as sometimes employed and sometimes self-employed – open your books at great cost to yourself; the inspired activities of BECS (the British Equity Collecting Society), who look under every stone for residuals the agents have missed; recently Equity have even made some progress with TV companies in slowing down the barbarous speed with which they roll credits at the end of a drama. Five years ago the minimum wage in the larger West End theatres was hoisted by forty per cent to £550 and now it's £633. Minimum pay and conditions have been established just about everywhere you work – for film, TV, ballet, opera, theatre both large and small and for dancers in floor shows; and you're entitled to go to the Magicians' Convention in Blackpool and the Clowns' Convention in Bognor Regis. What more could you want?

And on the broad public stage? Well-organised rallies against low pay in provincial theatre (they led to a three-year settlement), and against VAT increases. Successful campaigns to save jobs and conditions for singers and stage managers at the ENO and ROH when they closed for refurbishment. Recently, Equity have been arguing with David Cameron about funding cuts and challenging Westminster City Council's threat of a complete removal of their support of arts and culture. You could have joined the TUC's rally opposite the Houses of Parliament to protest against the squeeze on ordinary families, cuts to public services and benefit changes. The Lesbian, Gay, Bisexual and Transgender (LGBT) History Month takes place every year in February with active Equity support. Soon the Creating Without Conflict conference will discuss bullying in the arts. One or two of these enterprises may make you smile for one reason or another of your own, and sometimes the jargon gets you down, but Equity's alignment with the Labour movement is exemplary. And all for one per cent of your previous year's income; or if you're earning really poorly, the special minimum is a couple of quid every week.

So what's your excuse?

Now I know that in some ways unionism and show business make uneasy partners. It took me a long time to come to terms with Equity: when I was younger and more intolerant, I used to refuse to have anything to do with it, though of course I was a member. A system that determined that you finished rehearsals at 5.30 p.m. even if the actor or director was in mid-sentence because that was the official working day done, or a demand for a coffee break when nobody really felt like coffee, seemed to me stupid and unartistic. The zealotry of some Equity deputies within companies (every company has to have one to keep an eye on management's behaviour) pissed me off, as it seemed a substitute for getting on with the creative job. Also at that time there was quite a hefty Marxist presence in the union, which in theory I approved of but which verged on the bullying. I felt it from the other side too, when I had the experience of running a touring company as well as being an acting member of it. Michael Bogdanov and I had raised all the money for our English Shakespeare Company ourselves in 1986, but the budgets were perilously tight: if we lost a week's booking anywhere and therefore its income, we had huge unstoppable bills to pay such as the actors' (including my) wages. Unbelievably, the Equity deputy made it his business to convince the company that we were a couple of shysters creaming high salaries for ourselves off the project. This kind of class-enemy rhetoric is very persuasive to people whose Marxism had never found a proper outlet, particularly young men. It was a murderously instructive time.

Now of course I see how important a responsible union is. Equity has survived in style, and the cut of its jib is a lot more convincing than sometimes in the past. Christine Payne is the first woman to hold the post of General Secretary. A new President, Malcolm Sinclair, has the authority of a prominent and popular working actor. It has the youngest Council in living memory, the first to contain a majority of women.

So go on, join. A young actor who's serious about making a career – serious enough to read this book, in fact – but who decides not to is setting himself or herself apart from the rest of the community, and without that community we're done for. We must believe that we stand together and achieve far more as a group than as individuals; I would call joining a moral obligation.

And by the way, from the day you do, your professional name is protected. This meant that as soon as another actor with the same name as me joined, he had to change it – which he did, to Johnny Vegas. Need I say more?

F is for Fear, which is not the same as nerves. It's the catastrophe lying beyond them, an animal terror of the very thing you've trained for and longed to do. In extreme cases, Stage Fright is a mysterious event that afflicts not so much the habitually anxious but the most confident actors in their middle years, maybe as a payback for their good luck. The dark archive is full of legendary collapses; the night the star could not be raised from his dressing-room floor to start the show and didn't appear on the stage again for ten years; the actor who on a Press Night could remember not a single word. Laurence Olivier used to say that nerves were a luxury you can't afford. Easily said – but when he played Shylock he had such a bad attack of stage fright that he asked his colleagues not to look him in the eye onstage and then he'd be all right. Yes, Laurence Olivier. I didn't understand the bit about not being looked in the eye until I came to do a David Mamet play – the one on which I kept throwing *True and False* out of the window, so it serves me right. *The Shawl* is a brilliant adjustment of writing style to the matter in hand – and also presents, as it happens, some difficulty in the learning: it has Mamet's usual orchestrations, broken rhythms, stops and starts, but also a very plain, uncolourful style. Instead of this sort of thing from *Glengarry Glen Ross* (very easy to learn):

> What you're hired for is to *help* us – does that seem clear to you? To *help* us. *Not* to fuck us up . . . to help *men* who are going *out* there to try to earn a *living*. You *fairy*. You company man . . . You fuckin' *child* . . .

I was looking at:

> MISS A (*softly*): Yes.
> JOHN: Please . . . ?
> MISS A: Yes.
> JOHN: Recently.
> MISS A: Yes, the loss of my . . .
> JOHN: Of your mother. Yes. (*Pause*)
> MISS A: You see that . . . ?
> JOHN: Wait a moment now . . .
> MISS A: I . . . you *see* that?
> JOHN: Please. Try to . . . just . . . try to relax your . . .
> MISS A (*Simultaneously with 'your'*): My mother.

A solid hour of it.

I lived like an anchorite trying to get this nailed down, just as it was written – triple dot pauses, compulsory emphases and runs of simultaneous speech for two characters starting on a specific word and ending on another. I shall always remember the horrible brown flock sofa in my rented flat into which, script on lap opposite it, I beamed my frustration and increasing panic. By the time we got to the first runthrough – the one you must always forgive yourself for – my grip on the text was still so insecure that I wondered if I might be in serious trouble. As I stumbled along, in a nice variant on Olivier's predicament, I myself couldn't look anyone else in the eye, for fear that I would see incredulity and shock in the other, mostly younger, ones. Here I was, the leading man, out to lunch and likely to bring the whole edifice crumbling down and them with it. It was a bit like the lifelong dream of being on the stage unaccountably naked, or for some reason festooned with spinach.

Anyway, I now knew what Olivier meant. A weird brew of affronted vanity, genuine fear, dogged belief and scepticism plays around the edges of most actors' minds; now it seemed to be gathering into a boiling mass ready to engulf the germ of confidence without which I couldn't step onto a stage at all. What, it seemed to be saying, could be more doomed and unlikely than to stand up and talk for an hour more or less without stopping? The fear was, for a significant time, utterly disabling. The relief of asking around and finding that many people have this trouble with learning Mamet was enormous – and this particular text was known, to the few who'd done it, to be almost wilfully tough to hold down. And so the bad dream began to evaporate – but only in its own good time. I had to watch those slithering half-sentences, broken phrasings and momentary interruptions like a hawk every night.

Self-consciousness tightens the jaw and fixes the stare. Multiply it several times over, and you're getting close to stage fright. Unmoored, your mind wanders pointlessly about. This is a thing that hovers, waiting for you to notice it; it's over there in the corner of the room, like Philip Larkin's bedroom wardrobe that comes to mean death as he lies awake in 'Aubade'. It's plainer as you get older of course, when you're worrying about your memory in any case. You tell a story in a rehearsal break and suddenly can't remember its protagonist's name. Ah, there you go: you're losing your grip and soon you'll lose your nerve. Someone, probably younger, kindly prompts you. You have a brief word about such things, perhaps cracking a joke about thinking you've got that disease – erm, it starts with 'A', what's it called? Anyway, I have a theory about forgetting names – they're the first things to go, because, as Juliet says, a name isn't a real signifier; 'cupboard' carriers an image of a cupboard within it, and so does 'onion', but what does Johnson mean? Or Williams? I bet Trevor Nunn and Michael Hamburger don't have their names forgotten.

The solution to stage fright? There are probably specialists earning a semi-honest buck treating it. The truth is you just have to calm down and work even harder. Go over the lines twice before you go to sleep instead of once, and in the morning too, over and over again. You may wobble a bit during previews, but then there are so many distractions to blame it on; once you're in fifth gear and moving through the run you should be fine. I have no other answers; it's a battle to the death (or rather the retirement) between willpower and natural decay. Behind it of course is the fear of becoming unemployable – because, believe me, directors talk to each other: 'Oh, she's very good, but isn't she having trouble with her lines now? I couldn't risk it.' They may have got the wrong name (having forgotten the right one), but someone ends up out of a job.

G is for Going It Alone. Do, when you can and if you can, according to your capacities and good luck. I sometimes get asked about the English Shakespeare Company that I ran with Michael Bogdanov – the last independent large-scale classical group to have been blessed with the money to offer a serious challenge to the RSC and the National. It's a very good story, and the reason some now middle-aged actors went into the profession. The question asked is: How is such a thing done? Could I do it as well? It's very difficult to answer and the lesson is indirect: it entirely depends on what you've the temperament to do and the breaks you get.

Mine and Michael's was a happy conjunction of judgement, hunch and the right political moment, which might not be repeated. But at least get hold of a play and some friends and put it on above a pub if they've a room to rent or lend. Think all the time about what you might be able to do, and what's stopping you. Develop a solo show about a subject that interests you, as long as it'll interest other people and its method is idiosyncratic – try not to start it with 'I was born such and such a date, went to school and wrote my first novel . . .', which is a very uninteresting way of getting an audience's attention. How you then get it up is another matter, but ask around – there are ways and also lucky breaks. Soon enough you'll find yourself at a sports centre on a Monday evening, unable to get in because they've forgotten you're coming; but you might end up in a four-star hotel in Hong Kong the following week. The one constant is the British Sunday-evening gig, the one I dread the most (at least until I get started): 6 p.m. and an hour and a half to kill in an empty town, the Costa and Pizza Express shut and a few kids hanging about the Market Cross looking for something vaguely disruptive to do but probably not doing it.

Take heart from the extraordinary career of Ken Campbell, perhaps the most self-defining and subversive theatre artist of the last quarter of the last century, his own masterpiece, improviser and iconoclast. He owed nothing to anyone except the goodwill of the venue. A nine-hour adaptation of the science-fiction trilogy *Illuminatus!* at the National Theatre, a twenty-two-hour staging at the ICA of Neil Oram's play cycle *The Warp*; the first stage version of *The Hitchhiker's Guide to the Galaxy*;

and the hysterical *Shall We Shog?*, in which he introduced the Nub, a nonsense Shakespeare vocabulary an actor might use to give himself a breathing space when he dries: Ken would signal a riff of it with the warning word 'Nub' and always end with 'Milford Haven', the town that very incongruously appears in *Cymbeline*. Consider also the phenomenal Steven Berkoff, who's always created his own work. Or your favourite progressive companies: Kneehigh, known as the National Theatre of Cornwall, Punchdrunk, Propeller . . . or any number of younger ones soon to become Arts Council clients and wondering if that compromises their individuality. Somebody had to start them, somebody had to have the idea.

In 1996 Phelim McDermott did *A Midsummer Night's Dream* for us at the ESC, with his working partner Julian Crouch: its opening sound wasn't Mendelssohn but Sellotape being unrolled, around a mile of it over the evening: Sellotape to create the forest and bower, Sellotape insects and a glittering Sellotape web in which Titania was literally stuck to Bottom. In the end Puck rolled up the set and walked off. But then Phelim had just done *70 Hill Lane*, about the haunting by a poltergeist of his family home, and the house was constructed entirely from Sellotape: all its bric-a-brac was stuck to a taut length of the stuff. How could we resist?

Twenty years later Phelim is still wonderful; impish, penetrating and voluble, like a Shakespearian clown but much less tiresome. Describing the guests at his fiftieth birthday party as 'mainly family and improvisers' and wondering if fifty is the halfway mark in a life, he has a lot to do. For, sure enough, he's an improviser in his life as well. That's Impro, by the way, not Improv: Improv's American, associated with Chicago's Second City company of the 1960s, whose members, he slyly notes, tended to move on swiftly to movie and TV stardom. But Impro is real, funky English improvisation, ruthlessly based on ensemble: it's not even Mike Leigh, which is often infinite research to a scripted end, but an evening when you start with nothing at all, ask the audience for a situation to develop, and do so. It's when you do his *Life Game* at the NT, in which he invites famous people to tell their life stories and a team of Improvisers to play it out. Sounds simple, but it can be very funny and moving to see an actor play such a person's granddad or favourite teacher as they're being described. Asked as part of this how he wanted to die, Barry Cryer said, In bed with my wife, eating a prawn sandwich without dropping a single one of the prawns. Imagine the Impro that developed from that.

Phelim's never been in the mainstream much, though he's sometimes dipped into it: for *The Addams Family* in Chicago, for the Old Vic, *Così fan tutti* and Philip Glass's *Satyagraha* (about Gandhi) at the ENO and the New York Met. And his *Shock-headed Peter*, which grew through Impro games and toured the world. At no point has he sat by a phone and waited: if he didn't have work as an actor, he made it up. Nothing he does is predictable. He sidestepped drama school; he believes the way to do it is to do it, whatever way you can, not wait to be given permission.

But he did, with Julian Crouch, Lee Simpson and Nick Sweeting, form a company, Improbable, which now, after twenty years, is an NPO (National Portfolio Organisation in Arts Council terminology). The only thing Phelim seems to feel uneasy about is becoming another acronym, a CEO, writing five-year plans to maintain their funding. This week Improbable have their first board meeting, three board members to an artistic directorate of four. Sounds about right to me.

Phelim continues to bubble like a series of pots at different stages of the boil. His *Beauty and the Beast*, at the Young Vic in 2013, tells the old story from the point of view of the real life *coup de foudre* between its two extraordinary performers – Mat Fraser, who was damaged enough by thalidomide as a baby to seem, he says, like a beast in the world's eyes, and Julie Atlas Muz, the astonishing New York burlesque artist who was once Miss Coney Island. Now he's exploring the work of Arny Mindell, an American psychologist who's traced a route through Taoism, quantum physics and Jungian psychology and now investigates body problems in which physical symptoms are mirrored in your dreams – as they were for a woman whose severe body rash led her to dream continually of tigers. Also near-death experiences with people giving out minimal signals, such as when someone, stuck in a coma and being treated like a vegetable, might burst out and yell their visions like a shaman. He reckons an edgy Impro show on all this might develop in about ten years. But then, what do we do about the artistic health of our elders, he asks, looking directly at me, perhaps thinking he shouldn't leave that one for ten years.

It's not that Phelim's completely happy, but his sour grapes about the Establishment have turned into sweetish ones of his own devising. Oh yes, and the Comedy Store. Every week or so – to keep himself in trim – he still guests, doing stand-up with Jeremy Hardy, Paul Merton and Josie Lawrence. I know of no one more independent than Phelim. He says he still wants to join the RSC to show his parents he's got a proper job, but he doesn't mean it.

H is for Home and Heart. One of the most painful relationship break-ups in my life coincided with the late stages of rehearsal for Hugh Whitemore's *The Best of Friends,* a play which could equally have been entitled *The Best of Friendship*, since that was entirely and unabashedly what it was about. Its working model was the triangular relationship, mostly conducted in letter form and in no way sexual, between three over-sixties who hardly ever met: George Bernard Shaw, Sydney Cockerell (the one-time director of the Fitzwilliam Museum in Cambridge), and Dame

Laurentia McLachlan, a Scottish Benedictine nun and Abbess of
Stanbrook Abbey:

> COCKERELL: I declare friendship to be the most precious thing
> in life. But it is like a plant that withers if it is not heedfully
> fostered and tended. It is only by constant thoughts . . . and
> by abounding sympathy at all times, that friends can be
> kept. I implore my children to remember this, so that the
> blessings that have been mine may be theirs also.

As you can imagine, this advice helped a great deal; while
matters were at their worst and I was sleeping hardly at all, I
slept even less because of wondering how I would fare the next
day at rehearsals – only to find I could do two runthroughs a day
of this uplifting play with no difficulty. It was as if another set
of muscles came into play in the working day, older and more
doughty, refusing to be affected. Meanwhile, if home's where
the heart is, I went out each morning carrying it on my back
like a snail. Or perhaps home became the rehearsal room itself
and the breathing entrails of the play, no longer anything to do
with bricks and mortar at all. Eventually we opened, and when
the party concerned came to the show, I thought she compared
rather unfavourably with the characters on the stage. This wasn't
fair, of course, but it showed that, with a little help from my fictional friends, I was surviving.

In any case, if you're an actor, where, physically and spirit-
ually, do you live? Where does the oxygen come from to move
your blood around? Is it an address at all, or somewhere in the
little patch of land between audience and performer, between
one performer and another, in the rooms and platforms and studios where you have the good fortune to be a sounding board
for words and visions beyond your own ability to devise?

In the workaday world, the possibilities are various. As you
start out, you might be living with your parents, or in a flat-

share, not necessarily with other actors; or a flat or room of your own – or, like Gavin Fowler, at the bottom of someone's garden. At other times, you might, whatever your orientation, have a lover or lovers who stay part of the time with you and you part of the time with them, or perhaps two of you are together all the time. You may at some point have children. You may or may not be the sole earner. If so, you have a bargain to strike, easy for some, not so easy for others. I have friends, my contemporaries, who've been together, apparently without difficulty, since they were at drama school; on the other hand one of the actors I interviewed for this book told me anonymously that he was upset at not being able to hold down a relationship because at this stage in his life his work always – very obviously – came first by several miles. It's the sort of comment at which you nod in understanding, as if it were an axiom, and then wonder what the problem really is – can it really be impossible to learn your lines and take care of someone else at the same time?

The theatre specialises in an utterly beguiling kind of love; infatuation, certainly, sometimes, but also a deep and candid affection between people who work together towards a desired end; a kind of sibling love, both boisterous and careful, which sometimes shades into something erotic but more often not. You certainly get used to seeing each other at your most hesitant and fragile, as well as in your glory – a glory which in everyone is different, according to the uniqueness of their talent.

And sooner or later, you go on tour together. Or very far away. You may spend most of your time phoning home or you may behave as if you were single. Look at a company on the road, touring by the week. Some rush home on a Saturday night, out of the stage door almost sooner than the audience, in great convoys along the motorways of the land. These are the truly homesick: they want to be home by midnight. They have only until Monday afternoon before being in another part of the country, when the homesickness will begin again. If they do wait till the Sunday morning to leave, this may not be a reflection on the relationship, more a concern for safe driving. The less fortunate might go directly to the next date, rather than go home and do their solitary housework or have a slightly disorientating drink with friends.

The pattern repeats itself if you're all in the same city, perhaps having come into London with your show. Those who rushed home on tour are now out of the stage door and onto the Tube, like rats up a drainpipe: others have limitless time for a drink. This is odd in the former as they may only have been away from home for three or four hours: it's as if the show was a raid on another kind of world and they're glad to have got away with it. Backstage visitors are less welcome for this first group and essential for the second, as company. When I toured full-time I noted an increasing tension among nuclear families. Loyal partners fear their counterparts going on tour, and not only for romantic reasons. For the tourer to arrive home at one in the morning, be tired on Sunday when they're supposed to be so happy, and leave on Monday, is tough on everyone; on them, on the partner – who perhaps is currently living a less interesting life, and has only limited curiosity about what funny thing happened during the Saturday show; and on the children who were almost getting used to being without one of their parents, and now start getting used to having them both around again. The experience may be in some unacknowledged way a disappointment, and everyone starts the following week off-kilter. And still more so the week after. There are times when a company reconvening at the theatre on a Monday seem to breathe a faint sigh of relief, as if the road and each other were gradually becoming their real base; and yet here you are in a city with unknown digs and all manner of alienation, and the tour will soon come to an end anyway. It can make you feel guiltily confused.

But not as guilty as if there's someone in your company that you've been positively looking forward to seeing, whose image kept floating up while you played with your children on Sunday. If that happens, God help you and yours. Some relationships do start at work, in the headiness of playing together, especially on tour. It happens, though not perhaps as often as civilians imagine, and probably no more than in any other profession – but with an extra barmy muskiness, as in the lovers' delusions of *A Midsummer Night's Dream*. Theatre is a sexy thing: you say and are told more gorgeous things than in life, and imaginations get inflamed. Some lifelong partnerships are formed, even at the expense of others that had seemed for life; others deflate on the last night. Do be careful, and try not to confuse one thing with the other. The bottom may fall out of your infatuation when you finish touring, and you may have done some damage.

I've no witty conclusions to draw on this delicate subject. I see many glamorous public relationships between powerful individuals; civil partnerships still defining their terms; the need for certainty and also for adventure in men and women, and men and men, and women and women – and of course, for women, the great difficulty of balancing children and career even when supported by the most brilliant partners. Similarly I have gay friends who are exercised by the question of at what point in their careers it would be right to have children. Many actors marry other actors, many would rather cut off their own heads. No names, no pack drill, but I know of heavyweight figures in the theatre who have alternated between passive and proactive partners all their lives. Or stayed with the passive, as is often found in other métiers: the less dominant partners of very successful musicians are often called on in company to confirm where the performer is due to be on a certain night eighteen months hence, while those of writers are generally charged with keeping the sandwiches coming. But then there are Alfred Lunt and Lynn Fontanne, fifty-five years married till death did them part (often playing stage adulterers, so secure were they): they adorned a US postage stamp and had a Broadway theatre named after them. There were, until Michael's death, Michael Williams and Judi Dench; and many others. What people choose, change their mind about, are blown off-course by, make amends with, hope for and sometimes get – where they put themselves in fact – is as fascinating in our industry as it is in life itself. The difference being that we are also earning a living by enacting what people choose, change their minds about, are blown off-course by, make amends with . . .

Which is where Laurence Olivier comes on, one more time. I met him only once, and among many precious things he said that afternoon, he told me that when he sometimes had domestic rows with his adored Joan Plowright, he never quite knew whether he was really angry with her or was improvising a juicy scene of an angry man having a domestic row with his beloved wife.

I is for Imitation and Impersonation. What is the difference between Rory Bremner, who was good enough at impersonating Gordon Brown to get through to Margaret Beckett on the phone, and Michael Sheen, who makes you believe he really is Brian Clough even though he doesn't look like him? And do you enjoy that better than Mike Yarwood doing Clough for laughs?

Well, Bremner and Yarwood are impressionists. With great skill they remind you of their subject for a short while; they brilliantly do a voice and a look that we all know, the audience laughs and there an end. For Sheen, as for Daniel Day Lewis or Anthony Hopkins, say, that's really just the start: they aim to conjure up the person both for the next couple of hours and also beyond that, so that you can imagine them stepping into real life and existing in all manner of situations. Meanwhile, to blur the distinction there's Tina Fey, a brilliant actress who did Sarah Palin both as an acting study, to the point you'd have accepted her on TV as the real thing, but at the same time to create the laughter of revenge.

If you play a real-life character, historical or alive, you have the chance to enjoy the company of someone you wouldn't have cared to spend an evening with in real life. First you measure the script and take a view as to whether it's just a matter of physical suggestion or profound transformation. If your subject's long enough dead there are only photos to go on, or before that, paintings and drawings. Sometimes there are crackly old recordings of their voices and equally jerky film sequences, all hairs in the gate and rips in the negative. There's a clip of Queen Victoria but it sounds like a train rushing through a tunnel, and a rather better one of Florence Nightingale. There's Christabel Pankhurst but not her mother Emmeline. Frustratingly, Charles Dickens and Oscar Wilde are out of reach, unrecorded and unfilmed (there's what is almost certainly a fake recording of the latter's voice, at first endorsed and then denied by his son); perhaps that's a good thing, in that the performance of Oscar can more fruitfully become the actor's (there have been notable successes in the part), but disappointing in that it would be fascinating to reproduce what was described as brown velvet played like a cello, its Irish rhythms perfectly inflecting his aphorisms. Well, assume that's true, and try it. In the case of Dickens, it would be good to work out how much the hysteria that greeted his public readings owed to the shortage of oxygen in the packed gas-lit halls and how much to his talent.

You try the British Library Sound Archive; you try YouTube maybe. From time to time you wonder why the public so often wants to see familiar characters rather than something created by an author – but that's not your business at the moment. You work out what the structure of the jaw might be that would produce such a voice. You get the hunch of the shoulders, the walk, the imperious look. You hope to be creepily taken over; it also occurs to you that you're not so much imitating a person, but making up your own version of them to imitate: you might call that Impersonation.

You open the play (quite a tough first night, with everyone watching with double scepticism) or spend six weeks filming it. And then someone says, 'Nah, that's just an imitation, not a performance.' Or at best, that it's just an 'impersonation'. The latter is a small step forward: it indicates that within you, at some point, like rain seeping through to the water-table, meaning has dripped down. You've come to know what the person feels about something outside the script; you could project him or her into an I for Imaginary situation and then I for Improvise. You're entering the land of Sheen, who is so possessed by Frost, Blair and Clough that the shape of his face seems to change by force of suggestion alone. This is very satisfactory, and it's no disrespect to say that the audience has done some of the work. Maybe it started with a small tilt of the head, and then the audience returned the compliment and took over, with occasional boosts of confirmation from the actor.

I is also for me: for thirty years on and off I've played Anton Chekhov in my solo show, dogging his footsteps, crossing Siberia, but in more comfort and better health. I wanted to know how he might have looked at me and whether his laugh was sudden or slow – also, what Tolstoy meant when he declared with delight that he walked like a girl. This best loved of writers is reported as being congenial and excluding, hilarious and morbid by turns. Stanislavsky found him haughty, while the serf in Chekhov disliked Stanislavsky's wealth and pretension. His chair in his dining room was next to the door to his study, so he could be gone in a second. I concluded Chekhov was the perfect subject for a solo show, because, confronted by a live audience, he would surely oscillate between accessibility and *froideur.*

I tried to look as like him as I could, using many tricks out of my box. In fact all anybody imagines about Chekhov is a pair of pince-nez and a goatee beard and darkish hair. That's enough with any well-known face – a shorthand that conversely makes it possible not to notice if someone you know well has bought new glasses or changed their hair colour a little. The great cartoonist Al Hirschfeld captured Buster Keaton and Jack Benny with single penstrokes that look as if they took all of five seconds to execute. But I knew Chekhov had a particular, broad Russian brow, regular eyebrows, a certain hairline. Through the 1980s, I convinced myself that I knew exactly what he sounded like and how he walked – with a little help from Tolstoy, with whom description was generally in safe hands. Still that wasn't enough – I felt I had to get the exact tonality of my own invention. When I came back to it ten years later I not only changed the script but unhooked the obsession. He now became me, my voice, but informed by the qualities we know he had – humour, charm, of course, but I think also an unexpected irascibility or censoriousness, perhaps due to illness. I played Chekhov less through stretching out to him, more through myself, and was much happier with the result: I like to think it caught the whole scale, not just the quarter-tones. It was also less effort for the audience, who at some level is always aware of what the actor is up to. They knew it was me pulling a trick, tongue partly in my cheek, and also believed they were in Chekhov's company. It was, I suppose, a collusion.

In these things, Meryl Streep is always a benchmark. She doesn't seem to accept limitation, especially in the spectacular case of *The Iron Lady.* She looks exactly like Margaret Thatcher and has also, in the way of genius, become her: her performance goes beyond most of the definitions. For a few minutes at the beginning of the film, as she buys her pint of milk, you don't really recognise one of the most familiar faces in the movies, any more than did the innocent bystanders unaware they were taking part in a film with hidden cameras. The only mild critical murmurings about this superb piece of work I've heard have expressed a kind of resentment at having been fooled – oh, it's only a laborious impersonation, all externals. Not so. It's the product of sustained work over many months before shooting, and also of a kind of dauntless instinct. The performance she gave in *A Prairie Home Companion* as the garrulous Yolanda is in the same class and that was an imaginary person. Now, in her hands, Thatcher too has become an imaginary person, all too like the real one.

J is for Jealousy. An old chestnut. Actors are regarded as dissemblers, with their 'darlings' and their always giving their love (or luv) to each other, their generalised kissing and all the rest of it. The truth, don't you know, is that they're consumed with resentment and rivalry. They have hissy fits if they don't get the part: they've always got their knife into somebody, usually the person they're kissing. They upstage each other. They put pins in each other's make-up sticks. And so on and so on.

Who could be worse? Well, the general run of academics for one. An agent of mine came with me to an event hosted by a distinguished Shakespeare specialist. During the amiable dinner she needed to call her father, who was a professor specialising in nineteenth-century melodrama at a distant university. During their conversation she mentioned our host's name in passing, and back fizzed the question, sharp and anxious: 'Is he publishing?'

There might not seem much conflict of interest between specialists in Shakespeare and nineteenth-century melodrama. But one difficulty in being an academic writer – or even a novelist with a good idea – is the length of time it's going to take to get your work out to an expectant public, and therefore a clear and present danger that somebody else may do it first. Secretiveness becomes a necessary defence: if you ask a writer what he's writing you won't get much of an answer. To some extent this happens with actors, particularly if they've got an eye on a classical part – that is, one in a play that gets done regularly. If you haven't actually got the contract signed and sealed, it seems like bad luck to discuss it. It sounds grand – 'I can't talk about it yet' – but is actually fearful, a compound of superstition (like quoting *Macbeth*) and well-based caution: what if the word got out and someone – your interlocutor even – rang their agent and got the part away from you and into their own hands? I did once know an actress who tried to do this to a friend, but it's preposterously unlikely, and by and large belongs to the mythical past of pins in the make-up. On the other hand, even with your contract and with rehearsals under way, someone else is going to open in the same play a week before you do: they'll get the first-string critics, you the second. Calamity – though the truth is that, eccentrically or not, the part of the public that's interested is quite likely to want to see both productions.

One day you meet a 'rival' in the street. You throw your arms around them, greet, laugh and – up to a point – exchange notes. Charity, good humour and affection fill the air. This is to the amazement of your friend, if you have one with you, who knows all your insecurities and small jealousies, and is now struck by your apparently unfeigned pleasure at meeting one of their objects. The point about this is that both are true. You must be friendly, even if your heart is breaking. You may by the same token think you'd be a much better Juliet than someone, but if she's good, you sure as hell have to admit it. Enthuse over exceptional work, wherever it comes from. You'll feel much better about yourself.

A few years ago I was queuing to fill my car at a petrol station and flipped through a newspaper as I waited my turn. The New

Year Honours List had been published and an old colleague-going-on-friend had got one. I was truly glad: he'd always seemed to me an undersung hero. At last some sense had sunk into the system and he'd been rewarded. I was and remain relatively unmoved by honours, but I thought how pleased he would be. Imagining his reaction, I looked up from my paper with a thoughtful attitude. Gusts and clouds of steam, as if under huge pressure, were billowing out from under the bonnet of my car. There I was, a still-life at a garage, thinking a generous thought about a colleague, while my car engine expressed the turbulence. Better still, as I rolled along, I imagined the same image being repeated in petrol stations, bus stops, breakfast tables and churches all over the land.

Which leads to:

K is for Knowing Who Your Friends Are. Most actors are affectionate beings: why not? Friendship is as precious to us as anyone else, though it can have a slight overheatedness, as if we were all going through a war together. What sometimes distorts tender feelings is professional overcrowding, financial insecurity and high unemployment, all of which can produce suspicion and jealousy – and most destructively, public bickering, which confirms the impression that we're a loose confederation of show-offs.

The health of our profession depends on community as a means of survival. We go to St Paul's Church in Covent Garden for the memorial service if a colleague dies, and might have a gossip about her, with just a touch of vinegar, at the party afterwards. If the tribe is threatened it forms an alert circle, looking outwards at the Government, the Philistines, the Press. If you work with someone again after several years, you immediately pick up the conversation, soon asking candidly after their health, unless it's obviously bad. Meanwhile they will be checking out your waistline, apparent blood pressure and motor reactions. If you work with someone new you praise them for something they've done and ask them what they've been doing lately, often accompanying it with the phrase 'I should know.' (We should drop this one: how can anyone remember everything?) You bond any way you can. If you're a man among men you're as likely to be discussing the best way to roast potatoes as to be discussing sex; if you're a woman among women you're as likely to be discussing sex as the best way to roast potatoes. You always slightly distrust management on principle, as Archie Rice in *The Entertainer* does the 'little man with the hook' who's standing just out of sight in the wings.

Much of the time, the taking up of professional causes is done without strain across different areas of interest, as if Cubists were passionately standing up for landscape artists. A director of the National Theatre who didn't beat the drum for regional and fringe theatre or actors' rights to a pension – every element in the profession, in fact – would be seen as a bad choice. The response to the recent Arts Council cuts, particularly in 2008, was extraordinary and effective – not only because of the passion, but for the reasoning and advocacy skills on show from practitioners, which much surprised the Minister. These guild loyalties are so intense that they can be mistaken for disinterested friendship. Actually they're very interested, a Darwinian means of survival. Underneath them lies the complication that we're all intensely aware of each other; that there's only so much money in the pot, and only so much work, especially if we're in the same generation and conceivably in competition. We support each other in public if not always enthusiastically in private. But if you hear someone say that *x* and *y* were once close, perhaps trained together, but their ways separated because they were rivals, you're listening to a large admission of failure.

Especially since there are few communities that I know that

are better at friendship and companionship in general. Firemen perhaps, or mountaineers (I'm guessing). In a life in the theatre you might have fewer intense personal friendships, but you're carried along by a quite extraordinary tide of goodwill, welcome, shared endeavour, tolerance and humour. This is why we take each other's phone numbers on a last night, even if it proves to be impracticable to stay in touch once the glue of the play has dissolved. I'm often struck in talking to drama students just graduated about the one or two in their year who have quickly become stars. I hear genuine pleasure tinged with ruefulness: it's as if they were speaking of a more successful brother or sister; I wonder if it isn't part of the training. Like most friendships formed in school, these seem to weaken with the years; but the need to have heroes in their own generation is important.

I recently had a seventieth birthday party, and was much exercised by the invitation list: was so-and-so a real friend, or just a close colleague, or a pal, a cheerily passing ship in the night? Why would anyone come anyway? It turned out to be one of the happiest days of my life: the realisation that I was actually loved rather than liked by people who in some cases came from foreign countries for the event will keep me going for the rest of it.

As always, a friend is someone you don't keep up a brave face for. Confusing as some of it is, in truth you'll have just the same percentage of loves as anyone else, perhaps with members of the same profession and perhaps not. What you get with the theatre is a bonus. In many jobs the distinction between professionalism and intimacy is clear enough. You work with these people, but you socialise with those: these people are your friends, those your colleagues. This is a lot more fun than that; and at least you don't often have to plan the perfect dinner party for your husband's new boss.

Which also leads to:

L is for Luvvies and Other Insults. e.g. Thesps, Aktorrrrs and Turns. Let's be cheerful about all this, and keep a sense of humour when a journalist (as one recently did) describes the stage as a place where 'luvvies strike their poses'.

I suppose the 'luv' in 'luvvies' means we make real love into something as cheap as chips and just scatter it loosely around. But when I started out, theatre people often signed off a letter with 'luv', not 'love', because it was a matter of being precise about it. It was so that you, the recipient, didn't get any ideas, and a rather puritanical definition of how you stood with the writer: this close and no more, friendly but no challenge to your real lover for instance. 'Luv' was really a term of respect, and 'love' a true admission. Nowadays men from all walks of life are always kissing in the street, and emails all end with at least one x: it makes the theatre seem almost restrained.

Aktorrrrs: I can't really account for the fact that some people can't pronounce the actual word, as if it were somehow embarrassing. Is this some kind of English dismay? A compliment to your legendary diction, rolling rs as they should be rolled? Or because it would somehow be insulting to suggest that acting were a serious job with a proper name?

'Turns' is at least accurate and brings us fraternally close to circus performers – and that's fine by me.

It's odd, isn't it? Lawyers also wear silly wigs and do their best with hopeless scripts they don't believe in, using a technique they often seem to have learned off TV rather than the other way round. They too schmooze the judge and attack the other counsel before having a drink with him in the evening; but the public doesn't seem to have trouble with them. And as for the doctors, I knew an eye surgeon who said, chillingly, that he liked going to the theatre because it reminded him of work in *his* theatre: you never quite know what's going to happen. But we don't call doctors *doctorrrrs* or lawyers *barrristas*.

The truth is the public only really likes actors if they're national treasures. Then a whole different, and deferential, vocabulary comes in. Even then, the thing to remember is they're probably never going to love you, not really. Tonight I've been watching *The Review Show* on TV: an American academic professed herself 'put off' by all the praise for Daniel Day Lewis's portrayal of Abraham Lincoln before she saw it. She said she was afraid it had been oversold and she was in for something 'thespy', something 'scenery-chewing' – and was pleasantly surprised. Why would she be surprised? She then purred with an unmistakable kind of fervour that she now thinks Day Lewis is a complete genius: 'It's the best screen performance of our lifetimes . . .'

But why would she have expected anything else?

So to Thesps. Few people know the origin of the word, but it sounds suitably dismissive, like wasps. However let me tell you (and the TV academic) who Thespis was: he was the first actor. In about 534 BC, he stepped out of the Greek Chorus line, speaking and walking as if he was an individual character, arguing with his companions: thus dramatic argument was born. That's one version: Aristotle, with two centuries' hindsight, thinks he was more likely a singer who played several characters as he delivered his song, perhaps slipping on different masks to do so. If so, he was definitely a Turn – or an Impersonator. Or he may have been the first to work without a mask at all, painting his face with white lead and wine. Or perhaps he was a sort of travelling balladeer. At any rate, a soloist of some kind. He may have written his own plays, including one about the ill-starred Pentheus, torn apart in his female clothes after spying on the Bacchant women – the story also covered by Euripides. He may have invented touring, hitting the road after his successes in the Athenian tragedy competitions: he would load his costumes, masks and other props in a horse-drawn wagon and go from city to city, like some Victorian actor-manager. I like this last version as it rings a bell for me; anyway, you can take your pick – he seems to be an endless resource for what we'd most want the first actor to have been like.

My favourite story of Thespis is that he came from Icaria – now a residential suburb of Athens, but once the first Greek town with the good taste to give a welcome to the god Dionysos, who brought its citizens theatre and taught them how to make wine. Thespis of Icaria was so delighted with this wonderful potion, which somehow brought him happiness and drowned his sorrows, that he took to travelling around the countryside near Athens sharing the new-found secret with the locals: unfortunately, they drank too much if it, concluded that Thespis must have poisoned them, and in their drunken state, killed him. When they awoke the next day, the fumes had cleared and there he was, dead; they realised their terrible mistake, fearfully (and liverishly) buried his body under a pine tree, and ran away. The only witness was a little dog belonging to Thespis's daughter Erigone, which ran home howling, pulled her to the spot where her father had been buried, and scratched at the soil. Despairing, Erigone hanged herself from the branch of the pine tree, first rather unreasonably praying that all young Greek women should suffer the same fate as she had. The Athenians were horrified when they began to find their daughters hanging from trees and, not knowing the cause, appealed to the Delphic Oracle to explain the deaths. The Oracle directed them to sacrifice the first grapes of the annual harvest to Thespis's memory and make a festival in honour of Erigone, at which the young girls would safely play on swings suspended from the trees, singing festive songs. Thus was established the earliest Dionysiac ceremony that involved drinking and feasting, singing and dancing and the sacrifice of goats, and ultimately dramatic festivals. Whichever of these stories of Thespis you favour, I think we Thesps should hold our heads high.

M is for Make-up. King Lear soaps his eyebrows till they're flat. He covers them with white Leichner No. 20, or perhaps sticks false ones on. The base colour for the rest of his face is a mixture of No. 5 and No. 9, the two vital sticks in his box: No. 5 a sort of amber and No. 9 brick-red. He doesn't apply them where he's about to stick his beard and moustache, which wouldn't then hold because of the grease; not too high on the forehead either, because of the wig. He applies deep lines on his brow with lake liner (a thin crimson wand like a pencil – the numbered, as opposed to named, sticks are more like stubby candles). A broad straight line of No. 20 again comes down his nose (for prominence); the cheeks are sunk with brown shader beneath white highlights on the bone. A little dot of carmine red between the eye and the nose – it really does make the eyes seem brighter. A gash of red lipstick, especially for the large theatres and 'character' portrayals. A brown pencil to define the lips.

Then the King powders thickly with Brown and Polson's cornflour, but not so much that it hides his earlier artistry. He flicks the considerable excess off with a brush made of a rabbit's foot – a venerable object of a kind possibly used by Edmund Kean and Charles Macready; the Victoria and Albert Museum still has one in a case. He brushes his hands off on a towel, looks appraisingly in the mirror, and stands, while a figure like Norman in *The Dresser* approaches with his kingly cloak and coronet. He is Donald Wolfit in 1944, getting ready to play Lear at the Scala Theatre while the bombs dropped on the West End – and already out of date.

Because once upon a time not long before there had been a five-foot Polish Jew called Max Faktor, who'd died just before the hostilities. Motherless from an early age and with a father barely there, Max easily fell into make-believe; at seven he was selling candy in his local fleapit and at nine he was knotting hairs as an apprentice to Lodz's leading wigmaker. By fourteen he'd found his way into the Imperial Grand Opera in Moscow. As he turned twenty-one, he opened his own shop in Ryazan, supplying patent cosmetics. A touring theatre company picked him up on their way through and took him to the Court, and soon Max was Tsar Nicholas II's favourite, beautifying the Romanov dandies and *femmes fatales*, an honour that led to him being closely monitored by the security police.

In 1904, acutely feeling Russia's anti-Semitism, he decided to emigrate to America. But he was imprisoned by his own success: how could he get released from royal service? Easy – he went to a doctor wearing a thick patina of yellow make-up to look especially sick, got permission to take a rest cure, then slipped away through Bohemia with his wife and away to New York. When he arrived at Ellis Island the immigration officer misspelt his name as 'Factor', and it stuck.

He set up his stall at the World's Fair, but things went badly: a business partner stole his stock and profits, and his wife died from a brain haemorrhage. Max's reaction to disaster seems always to have been prompt, and he rapidly remarried, refathered and redivorced: then he married for a third time and went West, setting up in Los Angeles as 'Max Factor's Antiseptic [don't ask me!] Hair Store'. The new movie industry meanwhile was following him West: the railroad had reached California's spectacular locations, and in 1908, the year Max arrived, D. W. Griffith started directing for Biograph. Here was an opportunity. The old theatrical stick greasepaints made by Ludwig Leichner (which Max also sold on commission) were too crude for the screen – unsurprisingly, for Leichner was a Wagnerian baritone. So film actors were devising their own concoctions out of paprika and cold cream, brickdust, Vaseline and flour: trouble was, they developed cracks as soon as their expressions changed. So Max invented a cream base in tubes, in twelve nuanced shades. Greta Garbo and Fatty Arbuckle were entranced by his 'flexible greasepaint'; Johnny Mercer writes in the song 'Hooray for Hollywood':

> To be an actor,
> See Mr Factor,
> He'd make a monkey look good!

Max was a made man. Imagine it. There were no make-up artists at the studios, so the stars would come at the crack of dawn to his salon off Hollywood Boulevard to be made up en route to the set; Chaplin and Keaton would arrive anonymously, emerging into the street an hour later as the little man and the poker face. Gloria Swanson, Mary Pickford and Jean Harlow might drop in for confidential consultations with Max, bumping into Bette Davis, Joan Crawford and Judy Garland; someone should make a movie of it all, crunching the dates a bit to make the encounters possible. A special yellow product devised by Max reduced Rudolf Valentino's swarthiness and launched his career as a heart-throb; a new body make-up concealed Douglas Fairbanks's tendency to perspire all over the set. Max cut Swanson's hair short, devised Joan Crawford's smear effect and Clara Bow's bee-stung lips – which he hit upon by using two dabs of his thumb on the upper lip and one on the lower.

Then Technicolor arrived, and with it an interesting problem: Max's old formulations picked up the colour of whatever was nearest to the actors on the set, so they became as red as the curtain they were being shot against. The answer turned out to be a solid cake, more porous, to be applied with a moist sponge. Now things begin to feel familiar: when I started work I used the round little Max Factor pancakes myself, and very flat and lifeless they were. But still, victory over the Wagnerian tenor favoured by Donald Wolfit was complete.

By 1964, Max Factor for the theatre seemed very advanced –

even though Panstik, a non-greasy cream extremely swift in the application and supposedly idiot-proof, had been invented back in 1948. I didn't like Panstik – Lana Turner and Rosalind Russell enthusiastically endorsed it, but I thought it too crude even for the theatre. The Leichner tradition just about survived in the few sticks I still had left over from school plays; tradition also dictated that they be kept in a cigar box rather than the fancy new tin make-up boxes. To this day I have some nose putty too, in a stick like the numbered Leichners. Unconvincing and tough to use it was too: you'd get a ball of it from the tube, dampen your fingers so it wouldn't stick to them, knead it till it was soft, park it on the bridge of your nose and start modelling it as you wanted: like a tough dough it never rubbed quite thin enough. Later we discovered mortician's wax for the noses – a grim thought, like the (probably untrue) idea that wig hair was seized from corpses. Then we found the very caustic Collodion (a friendly word for cellulose nitrate) for scars, and plastic prosthetics – you made a wrinkle in your skin and the Collodion held the wrinkle in place all evening. Then further chemicals were discovered – acetone, latex and PVC. Nowadays a false nose is made with tissue so thin you can't see it in the next make-up chair.

Stage make-up has always seemed a very poor relation to its counterpart in film; and nowadays it is almost aggressively offhand, especially for men. Though the gallant tradition whereby women are allowed to wear pretty much what they like continues, a man might throw into his cigar box (or even plastic bag) no more than a mascara brush, probably by Max and bought from Boots, and maybe a stick of Erace and an eyebrow pencil, and some tissues and cream to get it all off. If you do need caked colour, by the way, PAM (Precious About Make-Up) is good and not too flaky. In translucent powder Mac is probably the best brand for evenness. Once in a while you might need the full, cunning character make-up and you go shopping before spending hours in front of the mirror – though it's unlikely to be like Laurence Olivier's three-hour session for Othello in 1964, all buffing with silk scarves until it became too dry to come off on Maggie Smith's white nightie (which he insisted on for the strangling, perhaps to advertise the miracle of the make-up). It was an astonishing creation in itself, but now, like the fact that the performance happened, very racially incorrect. Finally, try to use a film make-up palette rather than Max's pancake or Pan-stik; but even as you abandon him the man from Lodz is there with you in Boots in any town on the morning of your Dress Rehearsal. The very sign above your head is a word he invented: Make-Up. And to cap it all, he's now rhyming slang for the likes of you and me, because nowadays – better than Luvvies, Turns or even Thesps – we're all Maxes.

N is for Notices. They're not out yet, just forming on the horizon, so you can dream or dread as you like, or simply decide not to read them. When judgement is delivered, over the next few days, you'll sense it in the air anyway, even if somebody doesn't drop a malevolent brick, as in 'I didn't agree with what the *Guardian* said about you, I must say.' (Has anyone actually done this or is it theatre lore?) If you do read them you'll quickly forget the good ones; if they contain even a single reservation about your performance you'll remember it for ever; the bad ones will make you want to give up altogether. There's not much to be said for this experience, but it seems to be part of the game and most people who say they don't read reviews aren't telling the whole truth. I used to claim to be able to detect a bad notice inside a paper by looking at the cover like a water-diviner, feeling some hidden vibration and putting it aside. Each time you'll say, I'd forgotten how stupid critics are – and with one or two honour-able exceptions the standard of theatre criticism in Britain is at a low ebb, fast capitulating to fashion and the catching of the eye. Some reviewers have no hesitation in inventing things to discredit you: I was described in *Antony and Cleopatra* as wandering around disconsolately in a blanket when I was in fact wearing an unmistakably handsome military uniform: so, a flat lie. There are always some critics who will creatively mis-remember something to damn a performance, e.g. say the set was blue when it was white. Times are changing, and the idea of expert theatre critics is losing ground. And in these days of blog reviews anyone can let rip at a production while remaining anonymous behind a user's ID such as Knucklebuck or Grumpyman: it's like a coconut-shy. It sounds elitist to say it but public reviewing is a responsible job that should be done with care and an open mind. I've had good correspondences with reviewers; I also know that they work under terrific pressure. The best have robust opinions but are also concerned that they may not have 'got it right'. Meanwhile the study of reviews is a lonely and miserable business, its occasional pleasures rarely enough to satisfy you.

On the other hand, consider politicians: they have bad notices every day, with public mockery or attack and vile caricatures to accompany them, making their heads look like contraceptives, and so on. And, unlike a play, everybody – everybody – sees these on the Tube and laughs.

It's also true that actors can get a bit dog-in-the-manger about critics, and may even threaten them in the street. Well, you might as well quarrel with the weather. Do put up with them: the best might even give you something to think about. In any case, whatever personal bravado you summon to deal with them, they may matter quite a lot to the show. In a commercial setting, you need, nine times out of ten, good notices to get an audience and have a run; if your season is of a predetermined length, their importance is more a matter of reputation. Either way your job is much the same: keep it up and get it better.

Some reviews are so bad you're proud of them: your performance has stung the critic to unusual artistry. Here's a corker to finish with. Michael Billington (of whom I've become very fond) wrote of my Angelo in *Measure for Measure* that I played him less like a puritan whose 'blood is very snow broth' (Shakespeare) but rather, like a soiled Prince Charming hotfoot from the Actors' Studio. His remarks have become immortal, in that they found their way into an anthology of bad reviews that Diana Rigg once published under the inspired title *No Turn Unstoned*. I'm rather proud of it, and certainly didn't answer back to Michael Billington. I preferred in the end to take the advice of Ralph Richardson on replying to critics:

> I would not dream of writing to a critic, first out of common humanity, for a critic like the rest of us must have some value on his time, and secondly for the reason that I keep my head out of lions' mouths. If the critic says I give a bad performance and I write to him, he can always reply, 'Dear Sir, I did not like your letter either.'

O is for Out of Work. You never quite get used to this strange, deep silence. Nothing happens for days, weeks or months, though you seem to be reminded every half an hour that good things are happening for other people. If you're just starting out, apart from the probable poverty, it feels ominous, suggesting you've made a great miscalculation in your life; is it too late to do something else?

It's no comfort, but in fact there's sometimes no work, not of any kind, not even for someone who's just played Saint Joan. Her back catalogue isn't much comfort then; she begins to suspect that some confidential blacklist with just one name on it has been circulated through every theatre and casting office in the land, headed, 'Don't Touch Her'. Wherever you're at, the feeling is the same: you're both defiant and sorry for yourself, and quite unable to settle down to learning Italian, as you always promised yourself you would.

To state the obvious: to be an actor is to be accompanied most of the time by a sickening sense of dependency. Waiting for this call or that, hoping for the best, second-guessing what someone else wants of you, horribly frustrated. Everyone tells you casting decisions aren't personal; they are of course, though they're also not, in the sense that every director knows he is generally spoilt for choice and your rejection is not usually accompanied by mocking laughter and behind-the-hand sniggering at the very idea of you.

The worst long-term damage is temperamental: what it does to you and your behaviour. It brings out the lackey in you if you're talking to someone who could be helpful, and, to compensate, the misanthrope in private – neither of them a very good reflection of what you are. You try to keep up a social life, though you'd rather hibernate like a wounded animal. You have to be ready for certain questions from members of the public you meet socially; if you don't have your story prepared, the person, cudgelling their brains to remember what to say to an actor, may embarrassedly ask if you're 'resting', which somehow implies that you're not much good. If on the other hand they get the impression that you might be famous, though unknown to them, they may suppose sagely that you're considering your options, attributing to you a range of choice you don't really have, almost genuflecting. In each case they're trying to get a cue from you they can work with.

Then one day the agent calls – the agent themselves, not one of their office assistants who does all the nuts and bolts stuff. Something's come in that could be good – provisionally, of course: it's suddenly urgent that you make up a brand-new showreel to give the producer, as the casting decisions are imminent. Then, as you call up a showreel specialist or a friend with a webcam, one of the best Fringe venues calls you direct to offer you a new play – no money but it's cutting-edge, and you must immediately start researching Hungarian dances or brain surgery. The very next day – it always seems to happen – your agent rings again with another meeting for you, for a very small part in a TV serial. You jot down the dates while wondering what to do about the new play and the showreel. Needless to say, the dates for all three jobs clash.

You go to the two meetings, for the movie and the TV serial, full of pseudo-confidence and a belief in the law of averages. You play oleaginous, sharklike, seductive, unassuming, whatever's wanted, then kick yourself all the way home. You wait all next day for the phone to ring: it doesn't. Is no news good news or has the offer been made to someone else? You've only not yet been stood down because the first choice might fall through, and there you'll be, ready, willing and waiting. You sit in a cafe and stare at your phone, as you can at a mobile, getting progressively more miserable – not only because you haven't got a job but because you're conforming to the image of a desperate actor staring at a phone in a cafe. You can't even do that in an interesting way, it seems.

The phone rings – no news, but an audition for a commercial the next day. Very rich pickings if you get it. You mentally demote the other three jobs and go for the commercial. You're surprised to be asked for your passport number – huh? They photograph your left profile, right profile, holding up your hands, your palms and your back – it's like a police ID or applying for a visa. You brightly announce your name as if you were enjoying yourself at an impassive camera, wagging your tail. Then you go home and wait again.

You don't get the commercial or the movie, and the Fringe play drops away because you didn't respond quickly enough. You're left with your twelve lines for TV, and you immediately want to call and accept them before they evaporate. One way or another, you can finish this story yourself . . . Still, as they say in *Godot*, it passed the time. But how are you supposed to get used to it all? Well, with a sense of humour, the benefit being some good stories . . .

The actor's been out of work for nearly a year. He gets a job – not a big part but OK. He has to be restrained from learning it all before the first rehearsal – and talking about it all day too. He goes to work on the first day, humming, acutely interested in everybody around him, hyper-aware, preternaturally sensitive. Six hours later he's home, rhapsodising as he comes through the door to whomever he comes home to: the director is a sweetheart, the leading actress lovely, not at all like her image on the telly; the writer is solicitous. After such a readthrough he can hardly wait to feel the impact on the public – and the Olivier Award committee. There's a fellow he worked with a couple of years ago; he hasn't changed a bit. The rehearsal room is perfect.

And you know the very best news of all? Shall he tell you? He's got the day off tomorrow.

Do you know a better story about being an actor?

P is for Prizes. There's nothing to say about winning an Award: it's very nice. You come over all gracious and make a nice speech and go to bed happy. But you're the only happy person in the room. Everyone else is either indifferent (other categories) or enraged (yours).

As far as the process of choosing a winner goes, you might as well compare someone who specialises in meringue glacé with one who's good at gutting a fish on the basis that they're both preparing something to eat. Comparing a performance as Oedipus Rex with one as Francis Henshall (*One Man, Two Guv'nors*) or a Shirley Valentine with a Medea is about as stupid an activity as you can get involved with. Yet the annual hoopla of Awards goes on, as it does in most countries and in most media, and we're supposed to be pleased as it 'advertises the industry'. The winner takes all, and the runner-up can't help feeling bad, even if he's won ten awards before. It's a mean trick to play on us. Richard Griffiths and I got going together at the RSC in the early 1970s. One year we were both up for prizes, in different categories, for what were then the SWET Awards, now the Oliviers. We went to the party and it was full of friends and good fellowship and a really nice preparatory dinner with only a small streak of anxiety running through it: all those provisional acceptance speeches were being prepared under the breath – mine was slightly distracting me from every conversation I was having. It was all supposed to be good sport, and up to a point it was. Then chairs were pushed gently out from tables, glasses refilled, eyes modestly trained on the tablecloths. Neither Richard nor I won. I felt I was dropping down a lift shaft. I hated the winner, whom in fact I dearly loved. Richard clearly felt the same. On the way out he clasped me and asked me – very much as if I were to be responsible for him for the rest of his life – never to let him be tempted to go to such an event again.

For of course in the moment of the opening of the envelope – slowly, so slowly and sadistically – we'd both realised, suddenly, devastatingly, dementedly, how much we wanted to win. All our talk of 'What does it matter? It's a great bunfight and no hard feelings' was revealed as the sham it was, curdled in the sour taste of defeat – you were, according to the all-seeing panel, only the second best. You might as well have been the eighteenth.

It was worse for one Very Famous Person (he doesn't want to be reminded of it): he'd been tipped off he'd won, and was, rather incautiously, halfway out of his seat to collect when the winner's name was uttered and he had to sit down in it again.

How could it be otherwise? I suppose some people may rise above this, but, you know, I doubt it. Much the best Award ceremonies are those when the winner is known: nine tenths of the spectators can relax for a start, and the winner can polish his speech as the wine goes down.

Our trade is bedevilled by Who's Best. It's slightly implied in the curtain call; it's invariably reported by the critics; it's reflected in the honours system; it's a nightmare: the job is hard enough as it is. Prizes play on the essential greed and competitiveness that we can't do without as actors, but which we spend most of our working lives trying to temper. Most award ceremonies are implicitly or explicitly corrupt, all the more because of the pretence that they're decided by the public. (Yes, they're involved, but at what stage are they superseded perhaps by a final panel of professional judges, so how much weight do their votes actually have?) I won't name names or I'll get involved in some petty lawsuit; but there are invariably vested interests in the panel, or vested interests in the subsequent progress of the panel's recommendations to the final announcements (was this the VFP's downfall?): new contenders never previously discussed sometimes arrive at that late point.

Have as little to do with it as possible. Think of the permanent posture of the Very Famous Person frozen halfway out of his chair.

Q is for Quite Good. Angelo, struck dumb by desire for Isabella in *Measure for Measure*, declares, 'This virtuous maid / Subdues me quite . . .' Think of what you could do with that final, absolute monosyllable. It's not just adverbial information; you can load it with all Angelo's pent-up feeling. It's a cutting, open vowel waiting to be filled up with desolate passion.

You can't always do this in Shakespeare. Animal noises for instance. When Puck at the end of the *Dream* says that 'the

hungry lion roars', I wouldn't suggest doing a roar with the word
'roar', but for some reason Angelo's 'quite' seems to sit up and
ask for onomatopoeia – perhaps because it expresses the speaker's own feelings, not his observation of another animal, which
would come under I for Imitation.

How odd then that the word now has two nearly opposite
meanings. Angelo means that Isabella has completely, one hundred per cent, without reservation knocked him for six. In other
contexts 'quite' is a modifier, as in 'rather': 'I rather enjoyed it.'
This virtuous maid subdues me rather.

But as far as I can recall Shakespeare always uses 'quite' as an
absolute, as when Ophelia says Hamlet is 'down, quite down'.
Now, sooner or later some member of the public, some friend of
a friend or even a friend, will tell you that you were 'quite good'
in a play. If it's an Englishman you're probably being patronised;
if an American it's high praise, suggesting you were definitive,
unsurpassable. In other words the American use is closer to
Shakespeare – of course: his language has been as secure there
as it is here, ever since the Settlers arrived in Virginia while he
was writing *Antony and Cleopatra*.

That's not all: Hamlet talks about drinking 'liquor', a word for
alcohol we don't use in Europe but which is normal in the US;
he also tells the audience he'll 'have' the players play something
like the murder of his father before his uncle. Deeply as we're
indebted to American influences, 'I'll have him call you' is a
usage not much heard in Europe – yet.

Likewise: Jaques says in the Seven Ages of Man that all the
men and women are 'merely players'. In *Troilus and Cressida*
Ulysses claims that in the absence of degree, 'each thing meets in
mere oppugnancy.' But Jaques is not diminishing the calling of
being an actor: he is saying they are entirely players, the absolute
embodiment of the idea. And Ulysses is not talking about a little
bit of oppugnancy. I don't think Shakespeare ever saw 'mere' as

a small thing. I had the idea to call this book *Merely Players* but it would have taken too much explaining: it probably would have been OK in America, where they'd have got the Shakespearian meaning.

R is for Representation

O world! world! world! Thus is the poor agent despised . . .
                    SHAKESPEARE, *Troilus and Cressida*

Agents get only a slightly better press than critics. Jokes spring up around them like mushrooms, bitter retaliatory jests to comfort you in your almost biological frustration with them. Like bespectacled Continuity Girls and cigar-chomping Producers, the Press think they too know what agents are and assume they're good for a laugh, useful only for a respectful statement when a client dies. The anecdotes have even crept into the edges of this book. But I'm drawing a halt and standing up for agents for a moment, if only because I'm tired of the old jokes.

Most agents are serious and intelligent, reasonably loyal and quite imaginative. Empathise a bit: they work exceptionally hard if they're any good, spending many nights at the theatre and travelling round the country to see the clients at the end of an office day. Some are conventional in their wisdom, their career models a little outdated, while some think outside the box; some are relaxed about your decisions, others highly assertive. Their advice is usually sound enough – with the important proviso that you must always be allowed to back a hunch if you have one, even if it's to do a job that pays less well. It's true that I'd never have gone to the RSC (for nearly a decade) if I'd followed my agent's initial advice: it was an audition for a small part but I knew the director a bit and reckoned I might be able to impress enough for the lead, and did. But I don't blame the agent for not having the same hunch: you'd have to be having hunches all day, on behalf of everyone, all at the same time.

Most agents used to be male: they worked on their own or maybe with one partner, rarely two, believed in a theatre career for their young clients, leading confidently on, at a suitably prominent moment, to TV and film. They did have longish lunches sometimes; but the industry was less pressured then, and they could have a social life as well. Nowadays the big ones have grown still bigger and merged with other giants; small ones with any influence are rarer; belt-tightening is everywhere and you can't plan or predict very much. The American system is different and interesting, by the way: you might have a Manager who discusses career trajectory with you, and an agent who just does the deals. I'm not so sure this is good; your financial advantage and your artistic progress can surely coexist within the same brain.

When an agent approaches you after your showing, first of all be pleased – most only take two or three drama students a year as they're so labour-intensive. Even so, ask whatever contacts you've managed to get what their reputation is. Spotlight used to run an advisory service about this – check if they or Equity still do. If your contact hasn't heard of the agent, be careful; it suggests they're second-league – but on the other hand they may be brilliant but just starting out and you could be one of their great acquisitions. It's a risk. For them the risk is knowing they may lose you to a bigger agent if you really do well. If you join a big international agency from the start, you could get lost, but conversely scripts are coming across the desk in greater numbers. There's rather a brutal division between the Class One Agent and the Class Two. Ask around.

However, there's been one important development I need to tell you about. At one time an agent would never sack a client: they'd just let them wither on the vine until they got fed up and left. It would have been ungentlemanly for the agent to instigate a parting. Now agents will dump clients if they're not doing well – especially young actors with whom they haven't achieved a quick return on their initial investment, which can, in services at least, be quite large. It's easy to do – there's hardly ever a binding contract for them, as there isn't for you. A very good and indeed nice agent I know says, about taking on a young actor, that you have to throw them at the wall and see if they stick – an unsavoury metaphor but a true one.

Annie Hemingway had an unpleasant experience with hers on *The Syndicate*: if he came to see the show she didn't know it, since he didn't come round and never referred to it afterwards; then, having got her no further work for eighteen months, he dropped her. Now she has new representation and stage work for a year – a tour of *The Spanish Golden Age* – but she became so discouraged after *The Syndicate* that she told me she might even quit. This would be a real waste, and part of the injustice done to women by the system.

Certainly if an agent doesn't come and see you work you should start looking around before you get the boot. At such moments the bell tolls dismally for all of us. Whatever stage your career is at, if you get your marching orders, it may be difficult to find a good replacement. The business is now very hard-nosed and practical, and for most agents the main motive is money – it has to be, at least up to a point. When an agent says they would take you on as they respect you so much but they have someone else similar to you, it may be an excuse: they think you're not a juicy enough prospect.

Try not to ring too often when you're out of work – they haven't forgotten you (though the good ones will give you a call anyway every couple of weeks just to keep you going). Never ring an agent when they're on holiday unless it's a true crisis: they do deserve a break. You can expect many things from an agent – tough bargaining, loyalty and a certain amount of hand-holding; but don't monopolise them.

You'd think with all this agent paean that I was looking for a new one, but no, I'm happy where I am. On the other hand she is my seventh.

S is for Shakespeare. I have only one more thing to say about Shakespeare (for the time being), and it has to do with a young friend of mine. He's a good actor but he's never done a Shakespeare play. So he came over one day to get some help with a couple of soliloquies – he had an audition coming up. We chatted until the moment couldn't be put off any longer. He told me what piece he was going to do, I enthused at his choice. He then settled himself into a sort of lotus position, equally balanced on each lower cheek, and started retracting his chin toward his Adam's apple, as if he wanted to swallow something a bit too big for his mouth – or perhaps to stifle a yawn, or perhaps he was trying not to puke. I realised afterwards he'd been hoping to open up the cavity at the back of his throat for what was to follow. Then he started.

A voice quite unlike his own came out, tipping his lines into a sort of seesaw action – surge and relapse, surge and relapse: the surge generally ended about halfway through each verse line, whereupon the steam went out of the rest of it like a rapid puncture and a new surge started on line two. It sounded like some incantatory foreign language in rather a predictable rhythm, or some mooing cry. It was hypnotic in a way, but I had, I must say, no idea what he was talking about – even though I knew the speech, having played the part myself. He seemed to be in agony – and this was a soliloquy delivered by a very self-confident character, on his own terms and in his own time.

I suggested to him that if you talk to the audience, as you do in a soliloquy, they're not only listeners but possible participants. So in this instance he should talk to me: I'm intrigued by your character's behaviour in the play and am looking forward to your explanation of it. So before I can speak (because I'm not allowed to of course), you're going to answer my unasked questions. It's a bit like a comedian breaking off to say to his audience, 'Here, I know what you're thinking, yes I do . . .' But if he did that, what about the verse? my friend asked. Never mind the bloody verse, I said. That'll follow you, and anyway we can have a word about it later. The main thing is you're having a conversation, not unlike the one we're having now, the two of us, in this session, with the difference that I'm sworn to silence. He had another go, his eyes increasingly lighting up with the pleasure of acting well – taking his time, even quite amused by my interest as his audience, his misery evaporating.

This is not a story about him being hopeless and me a good teacher – it's rather an extreme example and most actors I can think of would have said the same thing. But really it's time someone pointed out that speaking Shakespeare is not as hard as all that; those who tell you otherwise are trying to hold on to their own territory. I know very well that the more you do Shakespeare the better and more familiar you become with his characteristic little tricks, and so the more surefooted. But the main thing is to get started, and to see that you have rights of ownership not only over some of the most extraordinary combinations of words ever committed to paper, but also over some of the most ordinary. For Shakespeare added something absolutely unique to verse theatre – the beguiling naturalness to life, the everyday turn of phrase such as has given this book its title. The trick is to see where the changes come, to spot them craftily lying within or on either side of some great rhapsody.

That's more likely learned with time, trial and error, than in training, rather as you only really start driving after you've passed your test. But in another sense Shakespeare is so close at hand that you can reach out and touch him. Some of the words have to be looked up, but the rest is a cinch, in the first instance at least. It could have been written for you.

The problem for my friend was that he viewed Shakespeare as being as remote from him and his life as the Japanese Noh theatre (some of whose strangulated voices his rather resembled). What he had picked up was a bit of doctrine – that he wasn't allowed to breathe at any time except at the end of a blank verse line, and whatever happened, he had to keep the metre going. He'd also been told, perhaps by the same someone, that as a result he couldn't really change the subject and have a new idea in the middle of a line, since he was only allowed to breathe at the end. Allowed? I raged amicably at him. Who says? You make sense of the lines, commit yourself to them, and we'll allow you anything.

So I say, don't let the verse police get you. They get in everywhere, and you have to distinguish them from the really useful people, whom you'll know by their relaxed approach and lack of dogma. Shakespeare wrote for a mixed audience who, in the same split second, had to get what he was saying, whether they couldn't read or write or had been to Oxford and spoke Latin – was he going to make it difficult?

The only real problem is the breathing. We're simply unused to sustaining our thoughts or letting them grow to a point with the sustained vigour, passion and volubility of a Shakespearian hero. The more soundbites and slogans take over in our lives, the less puff we're going to have to roll several lines of blank verse over each other to reach a conclusive point. Even when we do, in very general terms, it's typical of middle-class English speech to start a thought, then monitor and censor it as it goes along, qualifying and perhaps neutralising it before the end – it's a form of apology for having an opinion. Again very generally, this is where Americans have an advantage, not only because, having inherited Jacobean language so quickly they are in some ways closer to it, but because there's a characteristic in American speech to start strong and stay strong to the end, even if a certain amount of local colour is lost on the way. I would have said this was a wild simplification, but I have a recording of President Bush and Prime Minister Blair saying virtually identical things one after the other, but in quite different music. First Bush, building steadily to a climax at the end:

> It gives all sides a chance to reinvigorate progress on the roadmap – we are committed to the vision of two states, Israel and Palestine, living side by side in peace and security.

This was immediately followed by Blair, building to a climax on 'roadmap' and dying away gradually afterwards:

> This is part of a process to get us back into the roadmap which we continue to believe offers the only realistic route to the two states, Israel and Palestine, living side by side in peace.

They're both using an aspect of what used to be called Rhetoric, in which Shakespeare was a master. And it is possible (I suppose) to be inspired by Bush's sustained confidence, while unnerved by Tony's dying fall. Just don't tell anyone that you heard me compare the disgraced President of the United States to a Shakespearian actor.

T is for Turning It Down. Refusing an offer makes you feel grand but also nervous. What if the thing you've passed on turns out a huge success? How sure are you of your own judgement? Are you mad?

When you've sent your message saying no, a deafening silence follows. As you don't want to be badly thought of, you wonder if you should make amends to the director, like a young person in need of reassurance that they're still loved. But directors know this. The plain fact is that if you turn them down, most won't ask you again, at least not for a while. Directors have a high degree of *amour-propre*, and, yes, they take it personally. Still, you might think of writing them an appeasing letter or email, directly rather than through the agent who does the turning down. Probably better not to – stand by your decision, and it's better done professionally. If you do write, don't apologise and ask to be thought of again – the director, having to lick his wounds for a bit, will curl the lip and won't be forgiving you quite yet. Don't say you turned it down because you didn't like the script – well, obviously, you didn't like the script *enough*. Just wish them well and walk away. At the most say – with an air of mystery – that it wasn't 'for you': this invokes an actor's inviolable instinct for what gets his juices flowing, and is unlikely to be questioned. In any event your letter will shortly go into the bin. The director desired you and has been snubbed, and so doesn't want to be reminded of you. The exception might be if you know them personally, once had a talk at a party, or maybe have worked with their partner. Then you could write in a companionable way, and they might – *might* – appreciate it; and if they don't reply, well, to hell with it, you've shown willing. Better let it go.

There are good and bad reasons for turning something down, and of course it all depends how you're situated, financially and professionally, the latter a thing very difficult to know. I wouldn't on the whole turn down a job because the money's not much good; the money is invariably not much good, and really isn't the reason you came into this. (Conversely – and illogically – I wouldn't blame anyone for dong a crappy job for the money.) You never know what might come out of a not particularly attractive offer – for one thing it's a new director.

But there's also a new Reason to Turn It Down floating around, linked to the insanity of Political Correctness. I heard of a drama-school production of *Jerry Springer – The Opera* which was difficult to cast. A handful of the students refused to participate, because of the show's (tongue-in-cheek) blasphemy. To put it simply, they're heading for the wrong profession. You're going to have to empathise with many things you don't agree with, and you obviously wouldn't refuse to play Richard III or Medea because you disapprove of mass murder and infanticide. If there was ever a profession in which you have to get over yourself, this is the one.

U is for Understudying. Well, it's changed a bit: these days at least you get listed in the programme. And the RSC has a dedicated public performance for its understudies now, as definitive a showcase as you could ask for; they also require that everybody in the cast – everybody – is available to understudy if needed. I mischievously like to wonder what kept them so long: in my own company of twenty-five years ago, there were likewise no exceptions, and John Woodvine covered a Messenger as well as playing Falstaff.

At one time understudies didn't get a rehearsal, let alone a performance; they were simply expected to be ready for the sudden call, come what may, through their own diligence. Now, even outside the subsidised theatres, there will be some serious attempt to rehearse them before the show opens: their contractual obligation to keep the curtain up is a lot easier to discharge after a little practice, albeit with the undermining paradox that the rehearsals are generally only with the other understudies, a situation that will never be encountered again.

If you're in a big theatre with a big cast you'll already be playing something in the show, so you'll have got used to listening to and watching the play in rehearsal. And at least it's a proper director, albeit the assistant, who's likely to rehearse you, with a qualified eye on how you can duplicate your principal's perform-ance but at the same time bring something of your own. This is obviously better than the old understudy rehearsals under-taken by a Stage Manager holding the prompt copy and dictat-ing the moves, feeling able only to deal with the practicalities, not the art. And with luck your conscientious principal director will find the time, perhaps before leaving, to have a look at your work, thus giving you a chance to show what you can do.

The most unlikely star directors are very solicitous about their understudies. Peter Stein is a great maestro, former director of the legendary Schaubühne in Berlin, who would seem to con-form to the European autocratic model of the job. Certainly his note sessions are not for the faint-hearted, if you define 'faint-hearted' as taking criticism personally rather than seeing that it's only based on determination to get the show better. (When I did *The Seagull* with Stein, his belief that I was probably the most qualified Chekhovian in the cast led to some of the most scathing criticisms I've ever had.)

But he's not what he seems: the Schaubühne, which he ran though the 1970s and early 80s, was that rarity, a true co-opera-tive, in which, he insisted, the director could be frustrated in his choice of play and any aspect of policy by the vote of the lowliest actors in his company. I was amazed and moved when some very nervous walking understudies (that is, understudies who had no part of their own in the production itself) arrived for duty in the last week of *Seagull* rehearsals to report to this awesome figure, only to find that he gave over a whole precious day's work to them – explaining his interpretation of the play, his view of the char-acters, attending carefully to them all, while the principals took the day off. It was the same concern, by the way, that led him, when we were rehearsing in Italy, to let two young actors in the cast go briefly back to London to audition for films, on the basis that they needed such commercial work as much as they needed his artistry – it was a matter of earning a living. Thus began the movie careers of Elliot Cowan and Cillian Murphy.

As a walking understudy you mainly sit. The job each night is to be in a dressing room and on call from half an hour before the show in case someone doesn't show up or collapses during the evening. You're released at the Company Manager's discretion at some point close to the end of the performance – traditionally as your principal makes their final entrance. Walking understudies, in other words, get through a lot of books, but getting to that relaxed point is hard; the management may have saved themselves a few bob by bringing you in late on in rehearsals and have probably given you more than one part to cover. This is very tough indeed, coming close to the role of a 'swing' in musicals, who covers many chorus and ensemble parts and, musicals being what they are, goes on quite a lot. (They generally do this with remarkable effortlessness.) Most studio, fringe and small theatres are too poor to carry understudies, preferring to hold their breath, cancel in the case of illness or dragoon somebody in to read the part from a script. So the job combines a sense of uselessness with latent high anxiety. Incongruously it reminds me of my father, who was in the Territorials, sitting in a barn in Suffolk for months with his gun looking out to sea in case the enemy decided to attack Aldeburgh.

Nobody could pretend understudying is a brilliant job, but yes, somebody's got to do it. And it can be a mild means to an end, as it might be worth learning Macbeth or Cleopatra for future use. There can be further jolts to your possibly depleted ego: if your principal is off during previews for any length of time you'll find yourself saving the day on a nightly basis, but only until the management finds a starrier long-term replacement. This is tough. You'll get dutiful thanks but not much else, except your performance fee. At the time of writing, in addition to your minimum salary, the Equity obligation for understudying in the West End (it varies from sector to sector) is fifteen (supporting role) to twenty-three pounds (leading role) per week, and the performance fee the same again for each night you go on. But you'll have done a great service.

Sometimes actors are replaced for the most wretched of reasons. In the later stages of the recent West End revival of Peter Nichols's *Privates on Parade*, the programmes were slipped with the announcement that Sophiya Haque would not be playing Sylvia Morgan that night. She had died with tragic suddenness, but the replacement slip stayed in the programme, as did Sophiya's CV, for reasons I hope of respect rather than economy. Christopher Hampton's psychoanalytic drama *The Talking Cure* (2002) was thrown into deep shadow at the National Theatre because the gifted and much-loved James Hazeldine, who was playing Sigmund Freud, died in late rehearsals. The Cottesloe doesn't carry understudies. Two actors in turn were hired to take over the part but swiftly withdrew after a day or two of rehearsals, unable, I imagine, to bear the miserable implications. The Press Night was postponed while Dominic Rowan, who was already playing his own part in the show, learned Freud and took over. He wasn't an understudy of course, but he certainly saved the day, and a tragic event resulted in luxury replacement casting. Arnold Wesker has written a book – *The Birth of Shylock and the Death of Zero Mostel* – that describes how his 1976 play *Shylock* was prevented from becoming the Broadway hit it was predicted to be by the sudden death, just ahead of opening, of its star.

These are the ghosts haunting all understudy or replacement events. If you go on in happier circumstances, the adrenalin rush will get you through the first performance. Understudies rarely do badly on their first night. Everyone is behind you, management and colleagues and audience, you may get a bottle of champagne and a solo curtain call. But by the commonplace second or third, if it happens, you need to be watchful: your grasp on the part may not be very tight, through lack of practice, and things can revert to uncertainty. You haven't had the opportunity to develop a proper relationship with the person you're playing opposite, with whom, of course, you've never rehearsed. Your principal, meanwhile, if worthy of the name, will be helpful, open, supportive. Note it well: it'll be you one day.

Meanwhile, whether you're sitting upstairs, absolutely ready but with time to think, or doing your time as a mute footsoldier and watching your principal on the stage, warm yourself on the showbiz legends. Kerry Ellis went on for Martine McCutcheon in *My Fair Lady*, then moved easily on into *We Will Rock You*, *Miss Saigon* and *Les Misérables*; the young Albert Finney, playing the First Citizen in *Coriolanus*, got a huge boost when Laurence Olivier injured himself; so did Anthony Hopkins from going on for Olivier in *The Dance of Death*. (Olivier did allow himself to comment in his memoirs that Hopkins 'walked away with the part of Edgar like a cat with a mouse between its teeth'.) Edward Bennett played Hamlet in London for David Tennant. And so on. In my second year of work I went on for two months at the RSC as Berowne in *Love's Labour's Lost*, after being whipped into shape by John Barton, who clearly didn't think I was much good. Still, the adventure made me quite full of myself, until I later found out that the RSC had gone to many lengths to find someone more famous before – defeated – declaring that 'as was right and proper in a company like ours', I would be doing the job. My spirits rose again when I got a letter at the end of it and an *ex gratia* payment of sixteen guineas (nearly a week's pay) together with a warm letter from Peter Hall which made me feel I was a made man – until one day I came across its exact text in his office, drafted for his signature by his PA to remind him that the event had happened. I was obscurely incensed by this fudge, in a newcomer's muddled way: now I think his letter, not to men-

tion the sixteen guineas, was rather a fine gesture, an honourable half-truth.

So being an understudy is to be accompanied by a sea of trou-
bles of one kind or another, an exercise in doing your best in
adversity. Do the job well – all joking apart, it's essential – and
I hope you don't have to do it for too long.

V is for Voice-Overs

> *Here at Sheppard and Morgan we do what it says on the tin. We
> ride the razor blade. Because of blue-sky thinking. Because of
> who we Are . . .*

That's what it says here. And this is Take Nineteen: the reason
being that the director's now asked me for an 'internally facing'
version that will be 'inclusive for all audiences'.

A good game with commercial voice-overs is guessing what's
being advertised:

> *Anything is possible. We're going viral. Tomorrow is now. Yester-
> day is here. The bottom line is where we're going and where we
> come from . . .*

So that's – a revivalist group? Fitted kitchens? The Mormons?

> *Welcome to Now. Be iconic. Win hearts and minds. In the next
> eleven seconds 228,000 perspectives will be uploaded . . . Now is
> going nuclear. Tick the box before it becomes Then.*

Adventure holidays? Boris Johnson on the Olympics? A Party
Political Broadcast? No, it's an airline.

> *In a no-win situation? Need some joined-up thinking? We are
> the bridge to tomorrow. Invite people and places to get on mes-
> sage today.*

No, I've no idea either.

> *Think outside the box. We've got the Wow Factor. What is it? Bottom-line effectiveness. Go cherry-picking on a level playing field.*

Take Twenty:

> *Hard Creativity is seven times more likely to work than Soft Creativity. Keep your powder dry and go the extra mile. Now you're cooking with gas. It's a win-win situation.*

Talking of win-wins: it's only a session fee for an hour at the moment but if they want Take Twenty-One we'll be into a second hour or part thereof, so the fee doubles. Then if they pick up the option, that's the start of the fabled voice-over money. I once got it – just once.

> *What do we need most? Low-hanging fruit.*

You bet.

> *Stretch the envelope. Massage the numbers, hit the ground running at the end of the day. Unleash your 360-degree focus.*

In this verb-free, full-stop- and question-mark-rich zone, I must remember to focus in a circle.

And finally the brainy stuff – the director's no longer talking about paragraphs but stanzas:

> *It's a state of being. Unrestrained creativity. Ever-present Innovation.*

For Take Twenty-One he's suggesting I read it 'with a smile on your face'. Sorry, it got wiped off. 'Michael, are you ready to go again?' 'Yes, ratchet it up.' 'So that's a yes, is it?' (Meaning: don't take the piss.)

> Create. Rack it up. Win hearts and minds. Go the extra mile. Creativity sells up to seventeen times more than non-creativity.

Take Twenty-Two. Got it.

~

Spending a day in a voice-over sound booth may not be innovation-awarded but it's certainly an opportunity to stock up on pencils. Now I doodle as I listen by long-distance phone to the client in New York, where it's breakfast time, or Amsterdam. They're having trouble hearing my delivery, but they think it's all right. The director has suddenly become aggressively on my side.

The only tricky bit about writing this piece is I can't quote the real thing. Writers of commercials are as touchy as *Holby City* and *Star Wars* about plagiarism, and you're supposed to dump the scripts when you're done. You'd be better off trying to plagiarise J. K. Rowling. So I've made them up, and believe me, the originals are weirder.

Of course I'd rather be doing a documentary this morning: the clichés are classier. I wish I was reading some tasty narration on a subject I'd like to learn about. There's more money in it: whereas a commercial voice-over is like a sort of audition which might or might not lead to wealth, the fee for a narration is guaranteed and probably OK for three hours' work. If I'm to be cooped up in a high-tech broom cupboard like this, I might as well have interesting company:

> Nicolae Ceaușescu little knew what lay ahead of him as he took his bath this particular morning . . .

Or maybe a nice historical one:

> *Now, with the help of papers that have recently come to light, the BBC are able for the first time to say exactly what happened that afternoon at Runnymede between King John and his nobles . . .*

With an audio book the money's also guaranteed:

> *Happy families are all alike; every unhappy family is unhappy in its own way.*

Ahead of me lie forty Tolstoyan characters who all need their own voices, so that my script looks like a kid's kaleidoscope of merging and sculpted colours. I know that with the best will in the world my lips and tongue will seize up at about 3 p.m. each day, but at least I don't have to do what Stephen Thorne told me in a coffee break he was recording the other day, all on his own; eleven Norwegian nuns, all their voices to be distinguished from each other.

Voice-overs are a corruption of radio but they do take skill; and in fact the directors are usually good sorts, as are the clients, despite the cosmic enormity of the jargon. It's not a waste of time or your technical talent to learn to shave half a second off your previous timing, or emphasise words four, five and seven rather than six and eight.

So get yourself a showreel. Accept that you'll do banks and insurance companies (if you can face it) if your voice sounds middle-class, and washing machines if you're Essex and have a good High Rising Terminal (look it up). Get yourself a voice-over agent. Because this doesn't involve their coming to visit you in the theatre, you might not recognise them in the street, but they're on the case and giving you a heads-up night and day with mobiles, because indeed you might be called at an hour's notice in the middle of the evening. Mine knows me as Micky

P and sends round-robin emails that start 'Hi Luvvies' or 'Hi Guys'. There was a time no one would touch commercials. Now we all do.

And always remember, the creative multiplier is profound.

W is for Wigs. If you visit the huge Wong Kei Chinese restaurant at 41 Wardour Street in Soho you may be interested by a commemorative clock and two plaques on the wall outside announcing that its foundation and coping stones were laid by Sarah Bernhardt and Henry Irving respectively. For in 1904 this was to be the new home and workshop of Willy Clarkson, Costumier and Perruquier. Willy would be Wig King of the West End almost until the Second World War, with a private clientele that included Nellie Melba, Sarah Bernhardt and Benoît-Constant Coquelin (the Cyrano de Bergerac of the age); and also the London Constabulary, who sometimes required their officers to be cunningly disguised. (Sherlock Holmes can be imagined being on good terms with Willy.) Clarkson is reported to have regularly said after emerging from first nights: 'Quite wonderful, my dear. Not a wig join in sight!' – from the pictures I've seen, he must have been quite short-sighted. He also supplied Clarkson's Lillie Face Powder (endorsed by Lillie Langtry) to Adelina Patti and Marie Tempest. He had something of the same relationship with these actresses as Max Factor, arriving the same year in New York, was to have with his Hollywood stars.

Max had speculated that human hair, about 135,000 strands, would be better for a wig than straw and mattress stuffing, and persuaded Cecil B. de Mille, then a novice producer, of it. What a sweatshop he must have presided over. Likewise Willy Clarkson, who was once fined a shilling for making fifteen female employees work on a Sunday; on any day, they must have had a hell of a time. Even nowadays, when crowns for teeth can be made from a computer scan, wigs may be the last of the by-hand trades that the computer can't reach. The technique is called ventilating; a small needle which looks like a little fishing hook takes one to three hairs at a time, and weaves them into the net foundation. It takes ten hours for one person to knot a wig (which may then have to be changed) and I shouldn't think they can work more than a couple of hours at a stretch. It takes more than a week to complete a fuller wig. Can you imagine a trade so self-sacrificial, and so bad for the eyes?

Even so, a wig is always the source of some worry, though it's unlikely to fall off. However fine the lace, it may give itself away by crinkling with your laugh lines; the parting of the hair is notoriously difficult to do, for some impenetrable reason. If the hair is too coarse and too set it will offer inadequate movement as you exert yourself. You can feel very self-conscious the first time you put it on, which is usually at a technical rehearsal: if you're lucky and have a good relationship with whomever is supervising (the maker will probably have delivered the wig and moved on) you can work miracles together in the next few days before you open.

Nowadays, if you fix it with spirit gum, be sparing – just a dot at the sides and the brow should be enough, with perhaps a bit of pinning at the back to anchor it. We used to wear stocking caps – literally a circle of nylon wide enough to be tied in a topknot – to hold the hair steady under the wig, but they're a bit out of fashion now. Whatever you do, don't mix spirit gum with moisture, for instance by dabbing it with a damp cotton wool or gauze, as we used for some reason to be advised; it'll turn cakey white in a moment and you'll have to start all over again.

The trickiest part is at the back where – especially if you're wearing a collar – the wig can kick. Short of using toupee tape there and even spirit gum, a drastic solution, you may be able to get a new kind of elasticated wig that applies a little tension to the neck and holds itself in place. You're never going to get realistic grading into your own fluffy neck hair with a wig – for most theatres this doesn't matter, but if you're close up, and if the wig is to be of your own hair colour, best to have a half-wig: either a piece that starts at the front and joins with your own hair at the crown, or the opposite, so that you use your own at the front (avoiding some of the problems of wig lace) and the wig picks up the work at the crown – which leaves you with the problem of the neck again.

Nowadays, because of the standards set by film and expected by a theatre audience too, a wig will be fronted with very fine lace, between 20 and 40 denier. On the other hand the wig with which Donald Wolfit topped it all off in 'M is for Make-Up' had a front that looked like coarse sheeting and in fact was made of cotton. It was stuck down with a hard white varnish mixed with a little surgical spirit, and then had to be coated in Leichner 5 and 9 to cover the join. His wartime touring company were always sent to Willy Clarkson's natural heir, Madame Gustave's in Long Acre: a smelly, Dickensian shop whose proprietor, surprisingly, was Italian. There they were allotted one of three wig types: 'Barbaric', 'Half Flow', and – Madame Gustave's pronunciation – 'Elizabeth-ian'. So count your lucky stars.

X is for Exit (yes, it is). Once upon a time there was an actor called Robert Atkins. He was what my generation called an actor laddie, an out-of-date old fellow. He spoke as if everything he said was of significance, with a rolling rhythm, rotundity and musicality and grandeur. He especially recommended himself to me by saying that a great hero of mine playing Hamlet would, with a bit more sex appeal, have made a very passable Laertes.

When he played Polonius, it's said that Atkins closed his scene with Ophelia like this:

> I would not, in plain terms, from this time forth
> Have you so slander any moment's leisure
> As to give words or talk with the Lord Hamlet.
> Look to't, I charge you. Come your ways, exit.

That's to say, as Hamlet advises later in the play, he suited the word to the action; but he spoke the final action as well. Since Ophelia goes off with him – and in fact his line is not even the end of the scene: she has one to come – you may see that Robert Atkins wasn't quite an ensemble player.

Nowadays an Exit sign in a theatre is a little man in green running at a staircase. Once it would be the illuminated word EXIT, which in idle moments on stage you could mentally turn into TIXE, TEXI, XITE, XETI, ITEX and ETIX, with increasing desperation, before turning in relief to another illuminated sign and reconfiguring that as an imaginary shady impresario – Nosmo King. By the time you'd done all that you'd probably have missed your cue, or D for Dried.

Y is for You're On a Shortlist. Well, there's something to be said for it: someone has nodded in recognition at you and not marched straight past, oblivious. It'll usually be your agent who first uses the phrase to you, probably quoting the casting director or producer or director, as if this were some great sport about to be enjoyed by all, rather than a matter of life and death. You of course get tense immediately and start doing the maths; or perhaps take those bets with yourself, like: if the light goes from green to red before the bus reaches it I won't get the part, but if it doesn't and we get through, I will . . .

The history of Shortlists is the history of winners; people generally don't talk much about being the runners-up. Every time someone nabs some sensational role and it's in the press, you can be sure there's someone in despair; and there will at least have been the pretence of a Shortlist.

There's a Shortlist in casting, a Shortlist for prizes, and every other part of the industry that compares someone with someone else and finds them, relatively, lacking. What's worst? A shortlist of ten? That makes the odds too long to take seriously. Of five? You're still unlikely to get the job. Two? It's like the flip of a coin, and somehow as random. You become insanely interested in knowing who the other person is, and when you find out, you despair: yes of course, she/he is perfect – why do they hesitate?

One day in 2011 Gina Bramhill got a call from her LA agent saying she'd been 'pinned'. She thought of butterflies on a board, and of voodoo. No, she was on a shortlist of four, for a major part in an American TV pilot about life on the Oregon Trail during the Gold Rush of the 1850s. All being well, she would go on to a 'three-wing' and then, with luck, to a 'double-banger' before the crucial decision was taken. This was happening because she'd spent ten minutes the previous week in a London casting director's office doing a routine filmed audition which was then beamed across to the producers in California. She hadn't thought twice about it, as she has a well-developed sense of how to handle such things: pitch for the job and then forget about it, throw the script away, don't even check the dates. It was going to be directed by someone who'd worked on *The West Wing*, one of the big successes, like *Mad Men* and *The Wire*, *Treme* and *Homeland*, that have hoisted American TV out of the relative contempt it was once held in in movie circles.

This interested me because it was rather different from what had happened to me in a similar situation just twenty-five years before, when I was on the first night of a holiday in St Paul de Vence in the South of France. They seem now like innocent times, in that I wouldn't have known what a double-banger was and certainly hadn't done any preliminary audition: you couldn't do such a thing in London then and have it in LA at the press of a button. But my agent was calling me to say that out of the blue I was down to the last two for the part of Sherlock Holmes in a pilot to be made by CBS; it sounded a lively tale in which (and it was a fresh idea then) Sherlock had been cryogenically preserved and relaunched in the 1980s into the baffling world of jet travel and cumbersome computers. I'd heard nothing about it, but the crucial test had to be the day after tomorrow, and it was between me and John Wood, a highly recommendable Sherlock who'd already played the part in Tom Stoppard's *Travesties*. Whoever was chosen would likely be on the plane to LA within a week.

I can't say I was too sorry about my change of plan; in fact it had the air of a reprieve. My companion and I had, as we'd say now, Issues to sort out on Cézanne's rocky hillside, which had seemed preferable to Kilburn; but I wasn't looking forward to it much as I'd already noticed how beautiful neutral ground can in these circumstances swiftly develop the look of post-nuclear devastation. At the same time I didn't really see myself getting the job. It was expensive to come back for the test, and expensive again to fly back to St Paul to continue arguing with my friend. Also, I'd been busy setting up a company and we'd just had our money confirmed; but by doing the test I was committing myself to three years of six months per year in Los Angeles should the pilot go to series. What would be the effect of this on my project? The agent disposed of it in nothing flat: cancel all plans. Cancel the company, this is Hollywood. Yes, but Hollywood television, I said, not Hollywood movies. Yes, but HOLLYWOOD, he repeated.

Gina on the other hand definitely knew about the project, now that she remembered it. And now that she was 'pinned', the director wanted to speak to her urgently, as did the writer, without prejudice, about the cyber-test she'd done. Her sassy agent advised her to ask them if they'd like her to re-tape, doing a version with a different quality. No, no, they said, it ain't broke, don't fix it; she'd caught just what they had in mind in her test. Gina now saw how lucky she'd been – sometimes you self-tape, but this time she'd had a good casting director with her to guide her away from the ideas she'd had on reading the script, to something else more likely to play well with these two gentlemen.

Amazingly this pinning of four was their signing-off moment from the process: they had no further influence on the decision. Choosing the Three-Winger was the work of the studio. Another actress then having been dropped, two names would go forward to the network, and they would have the final decision. The director and writer were quite used to that. In the meantime both actresses' agents (and this had been the same for me) were to negotiate every detail of the hypothetical deal – money, car, cellphone – all of it binding for the next three years should the pilot be one of the tiny handful that goes to a series. At this point both artists are committed; the network then makes it definite for one of them and abandons the other as if she had never been.

Gina got the part, and so did I – but not before I'd flown back to St Paul for another week of sun-soaked recriminations. I had an immediate costume fitting on my return to London. The money, as it was in those days, was good (my mother commented, 'No more buses for you' – wrongly, I'm afraid). The only thing was this matter of being committed for the next three years before even shooting the pilot. I didn't fancy that, but figured by now I was bound upon a wheel of fire, and the odds are very long against going to series – about sixty-five to one against in most years. Thank God it didn't make it. Better still, this was a Backdoor Pilot, the kind that can still be released as a one-off (it's still out there on retail, just to prove we had the idea first).

I flew out with my costume in my suitcase – Harris Tweed suit, deerstalker and all the rest of it – to shoot in one of the hottest

377

places in America, Needles Point in Arizona. Gina was advised to go out and celebrate when the happy call came through, only to be pestered all night with phone calls from California requiring a copy of her passport to be scanned and sent before daybreak. Like me, she did it, had a good time, and we're both still living in London, neither of us taken up by Hollywood.

The pilot season seems to bring out these dramatic rituals. So does the commercial audition, which takes you no further than Wardour Street. Having announced your name as cheerfully as you can, you might be asked to improvise being a barman. You might, and I speak from experience, recall Jim Downey's Bar on 44th and 8th in New York, a favourite watering hole of mine. My friend there was Frank, the chief barman, who could pour a whiskey sour to the rim without spilling a drop while looking in the other direction. Though I say it myself, my off-the-cuff account of him at the audition was an inspired riff of which Phelim McDermott would have approved. The poor fellow also had throat cancer and one of those air-gulping implants, so that was, I'm sorry to say, all to the good for the audition. The casting director said she could listen to me all night (or I suppose it might have been all day).

Now, what you must always, always remember is that the subsequent decision has nothing to do with her or anyone like her: it's up to some teenager in the back room on the other side of the world. He's called a Producer, though not as I understand the term. In due course, your agent calls to see if there's a decision; there's a riffling of papers, the agent might be asked to spell your name, and the jubilant announcement comes: No, he's not here, he's not even on the Shortlist. The strange thing is that this is done in the same kind of triumphal tone of congratulation as if you'd got the job.

Z is for Zhoozh and Polari

Give 'em the old hocus pocus
Bead and feather 'em
How can they see with sequins in their eyes?

KANDER AND EBB, Chicago

The rep director I quoted in the section about Theatre as seeing Week Three of rehearsals as time to 'Zhoozh It Up' was using the word in its strictest meaning – to make something more interesting or attractive. By the time he was done, the production would look zhoozhy: it would have risen to the occasion, have glitter and dazzle as well as worthiness, be a good night out. It would be, in a word, fantabulosa. Liberace would approve.

Just as camp isn't adequately defined as effeminate, the meaning of Zhoozh is hard to pin down. Zhoozhy is easier: it means something or someone is attractive anyway, male or female, omi or palone – perhaps by nature rather than as a result of being Zhoozhed. And is this the right spelling anyway? Or should it be Zhush? Or even Jooj? The word is rarely written down: that's the point of it, as of the rest of the pungent unofficial language it comes from, Polari. Or is it Parlare? Or Parlyari? Parlary, Palarie, or Palari?

Though there is some American Yiddish in Polari, like the magnificent word *meshugenah*, meaning crazy, its small vocabulary is not as rich as Yiddish in general. Still it's quite a brew, not unlike it in wit and vitality, having also absorbed a little Romany and some rhyming slang. It's understood in East End fish markets and West End theatres. Some of it has entered the mainstream – cod, naff (probably from the Italian), barney, bijou, cottaging, cove, drag, hoofer, mince. (When Princess Anne fell from her horse at the Badminton Horse Trials, the Press, to avoid reporting the word she really used, said that she'd told photographers to 'naff off'. Unfortunately 'naff' has a far coarser acronymic meaning, but I'll not tell you what as it would really wipe the smile off your eek.)

Cant language – that is, an argot used by a group to exclude other groups or the world at large – has many roots and is of many kinds. Some go way back to Jacobean times – the pamphleteer and dramatist Thomas Dekker talks of coney-catching, canting morts (insincere women) and bene coves (good men) in his splendid account of the metropolitan underworld, *The Bellman of London*, written in 1608, when he describes cant as being used 'to the end that their cozenings, knaveries and villainies might not be so easily perceived and known'. Such languages are designed to keep the users' activity secret: thieves, gypsies, sailors, circus and fairground people, whores, puppeteers, Punch and Judy people – and, crucially, until the legislation of 1967, British gays.

The evening that I'm writing, the House of Commons has resoundingly voted for gay marriage. I celebrated this remarkable event, coming forty-five years after gay legalisation, by going to see a revival of Peter Nichols's *Privates on Parade*. The play was written in 1977 and I re-encountered in it something that had delighted me when I first started out – a world in which George was rechristened Georgina, Terry Teresa, where one queen would call another 'Daughter' – rather as gay men now sometimes use 'Girlfriend' as a tone of mild rebuke (to anyone). That initiation, being 1964, was during the RSC's noble assault on the eight very butch History plays of Shakespeare; a time when the fine and much-missed actor John Normington was universally known as Norah; when at show time you had to get your lallies into your tights, put your slap on and start trading. Such talk was not current among the directors – oh Lord, not at all, they were a determinedly heterosexual lot – but among some very butch, though gay actors. I loved it and joined in it because this was a generous clan who welcomed outsiders. I think the community's view was that though firmly married, I was reasonably zhoozhy myself: I had also just come from university, where gays were still strictly in the closet. It all came easily to the staunchest of us: Vada the Bona Palone with the Zhoozhed-up Riah and the Bijou Willetts ('Look at the girl with the fancy hair and the little breasts'). And the culture it expressed would, astonishingly, remain illegal for another three years; if you were gay, you had to watch out for a charpering omi or a sharpy-palone (policeman or policewoman) and scarper as soon as you saw them.

I would guess that Julian and Sandy, the heroines of BBC Radio's *Round the Horne* from 1965 to 1968, may have got a more enthusiastic reception from a newly liberated hetero than gay audience. Certainly by the end of this decade of rapid change, Polari had become public property, and the gay (Good As You) liberationists of the 1970s gave it up as inward-looking and frivolous, no longer necessary. Perhaps they sensed that there were to be more serious twists in the road ahead, such as the infamous Clause 28, forbidding local authorities to 'promote the teaching in any maintained school of the acceptability of homosexuality as a pretended family relationship', which eventually got onto the Statute Book between 1988 and 2003 (2000 in Scotland).

Since Clause 28 was removed, Polari has undergone a slightly nostalgic revival, oddly enough along the cutting edge of stand-up comedy (occasional use by the much-missed Rik Mayall and by David Walliams) and rock 'n' roll – Morrissey's compilation album *Bona Drag* contains the track 'Piccadilly Palare', which celebrates how bona it is to vada a lovely eek. You can even read books on it, such as Paul Baker's *Polari: The Lost Language of Gay Men*. Maybe it'll be on an A-level course soon. That would really set your riah on end.

13 Family Secrets

The Japanese – The Greeks – Edmund Kean and His Dagger –
Trelawny of the Wells – You and Me – Let Me Play the Lion Too

> In our profession there are circularities within circularities, unlikely
> congruences, examples set and then contradicted; for all that the tribe
> is diverse and scattered, there are rarely as many as six degrees of
> separation between any two of us.
>
> MICHAEL PENNINGTON, *Let Me Play the Lion Too*, Introduction

I could also have said that there are, buried deep in its earth,
hidden lines of succession, secret logics, kinships across time
and place. We smile at the fact that the veteran actor Donald
Sinden owned Henry Irving's dagger, which might have been
Edmund Kean's before him. It exposed him to some teasing,
but I know why he treasured it: as he said, he believed in the
touching of hands.

So do I, and in my A–Z, Z could also have been for Zeami: that
is, Zeami Motokiyo, not a well-known name but a great teacher
of acting, who's already cropped up a little in this book. Like
the best of Stanislavsky, his insights seem to be coming from an
exceptionally wise friend standing right there beside you as you
work:

> When you play anger, don't forget to have a tender heart . . . it
> creates a sense of novelty.

This is one of the great secrets, after all, to imply the opposites
in your character without inconsistency – the tenderness in a
fighter, the courage in a coward. Here's another:

382

Sometimes an actor seems to be at his best when he is doing nothing.

So long, that is, as you can hear his thoughts on the move before he speaks again. Zeami's manner sometimes veers off into an extreme lyricism, which may or not strike a chord. Here is how he accounts for the simultaneous strength and delicacy of a good performance:

The metal hammer moves, the precious sword glints coldly.

But he invariably bumps you back to earth with canny advice:

The unskilful performance of a bad player is an example for a good player: the mere sight of it makes you correct your own defects.

He has wise counsel on how to manipulate your audience:

When there is a large crowd and a noisy atmosphere, wait as long as possible till they are quiet. Concentrate their attention and just at that moment, begin: success will be yours!

This especially applies when there is royalty in attendance, as anyone who's played at Clarence House will confirm:

When someone important attends, the play only begins when he arrives; some of the audience comes late, others stand or sit in disorder, not ready to appreciate . . . So when the player appears he should perform more gaily than usual, use a louder voice, and carry himself briskly so as to attract attention.

Unusually for a teacher, Zeami was the son of a great actor and became one himself. His writing is laced with a profound regard for the man who taught him everything and whom he

deeply misses, one who had 'the true flower, a subtle and profound mystery'. His father was clearly an actor for all seasons,
who played the big commercial dates but also did the toughest
kind of touring:

> No matter how small or out of the way the town or village
> might be, my father carefully respected the customs and sen-
> sitivities of his audience.

Zeami's tenderness intensifies as he watches the older man's
powers begin to wane:

> He was like an old tree which had fewer branches and leaves
> but still bore some flowers . . . by his last performance he had
> turned over all his parts to younger players and now only per-
> formed some easy role in a charming way . . . But he had truly
> mastered the secrets, and the flower remained to him.

Watching this leads Zeami to understand how age works in the
playing:

> This is how it is with an old person: he wants to look young
> in everything. Perform very gaily. Bring down your foot,
> stretch your arm forward and put it back by your side just
> a little after the beat . . . However youthfully an old per-
> son behaves, he does things late – it cannot be helped, his
> strength is declining.

Related to this is his understanding of an actor's vitality:

> The best praise for a young player is that he plays like a vet-
> eran; for an old player that he has youthful vigour . . .

In this wise and tender work you often hear a familiar call to
arms:

Practise daily to gain deeper understanding of your art, but not in order to be successful . . . Sometimes you will succeed and sometimes fail – that is the law of cause and effect, beyond human power.

There is a central tension throughout: should Zeami be passing on his father's mysteries, loosening the stranglehold exerted by an older generation? Can acting be taught at all? Is something always lost when its trade secrets are out for all to see? Zeami sometimes speaks as if the whole job is indeed a sleight of hand: once it is over and the trick is revealed, the audience will not be so easily deceived. Apart from this, his conviction and modernity, his odd pragmatism and his lyricism, stop me in my tracks. And you know what? He was writing, give or take a couple of years, in 1400.

For Zeami Motokiyo was a Noh actor – in fact he and Kan'ami Kiyotsugu, to give his father his proper name, more or less invented the form; and he was writing in feudal Japan about the remote, fascinating but, for a Westerner, almost incomprehensible world of Noh theatre. With the actor's typical mix of realism and dogged belief, Zeami was convinced by turns that his refined art would die with him and that 'life will end but the Noh never will'. Sadly, in his own time he watched it decline, and he ended his life in exile.

~

Today, at eleven in the morning, in a plain wooden single-storeyed house rather than a theatre in Tokyo, singularly unatmospheric and not much bigger than the sum of the stage and auditorium within it, four musicians – on flute and three drums (for shoulder, hip and stick) of varying sonorousness – take their places in front of a cypress tree painted on the back wall. The varnished stage, a pillar at each corner, is in fact made of cypress wood, highly polished so that the actors can seem to glide across it. Giant resonators lie beneath it to enhance the sound when, as they often will, the actors stomp heavily on the floor.

The sound of a single drum is followed by a distant, melancholy flute. Along a long runway, the *hashigakari*, with infinite slowness, something like an exquisite pantomime dame (at this stage you're still inclined to make cheap comparisons with the West), wearing brocaded wrappings and white socks, moves towards the stage; he has a topknot and a mask made of painted cypress. The mask suggests a demon or a ghost, and is so three-dimensional that it looks different at different angles. The actor's slowness is trancelike, infinitely suggestible: when he arrives and begins, you have acres of time to imagine any number of things as he turns his head by slow degrees towards and away from you – this actor's stillness was described by Zeami as 'snow piled in a silver bowl'.

The plaintive music becomes suddenly emphatic – making a counterpoint, as it were, between a congratulatory and a pathetic tone. The actor performs a series of sudden gestures accompanied by that mockable but haunting guttural Noh cry, very specialised by virtue of being produced – dangerously if you don't know how – by the resonators in the throat rather than those of the head. This may be greeted by applause. The figure turns out to be the ghost of some ancient warrior come for vengeance, or some lover unable to find peace beyond the grave. Later these dead people will enact the moments of their death. Or it may be some god or goddess.

How odd is this? Even the word Noh is uncommunicative – it simply means talent, and isn't generally used by the Japanese. In some ways this doesn't feel like theatre at all: it is certainly hard to think of a stage manager at her desk and a tannoy and the calls to the actors and the cues and the reassuring backstage detritus. And it is performed entirely by men. The atmosphere is hushed, and refined almost beyond reach even of the Japanese. What can it have to do with us? It could hardly seem more impenetrable, more hermetic. Kabuki, the modified popular version of the Noh, is hard enough, even though it started as a wake-up call to this older style (in 1603, the year that the Elizabethan age gave way to the Jacobean in England).

Noh has had moments of fashion among twentieth-century practitioners, the best of whom have, briefly at least, been fascinated by its purity and suggestiveness. But the sheer hypnotic oddity of it has always ushered it back into its own shadow: there are only a couple of thousand Noh performers in Japan now. With the public, it fell seriously out of fashion after the Second World War, its conservatism too reminiscent of the old Japan which, with American coercion, was being expelled by Western democratisation. By now, and at a generous estimate, the audience at a performance is a couple of hundred enthusiasts. On the other hand the Kabuki, with its remarkable female impersonators, the *onnagata,* opens a window not only to Japanese cross-dressers such as the notorious Takarazuka – whose tradition of male impersonation links them somewhat voyeuristically to the androgynous female dancers who historically entertained the Japanese Imperial Court – but even to Shakespeare and the *travesti* tradition.

And yet, and yet. The Noh rivetingly depends on the reduction of objects to suggestive shapes: a fan stands in for the moon rising; an object too big for the stage, such as a boat, is represented by a semi-improvised model; a gesture in empty space tells the story. No wonder Peter Brook has been influenced by it. In fact, what could be more contemporary, more of our own time?

However, the historical channel through which the Noh has flowed is as narrow as the *hashigakari* itself: it's a wonder it's still with us at all. Just as there are five categories of Noh plays, so their traditional accoutrements were greedily policed by five families, the most valuable masks and costumes held in their private collections, shown only to a select few and only on the rarest occasions. With a flame so masonically guarded, indeed there was a question for Zeami to settle about what we would call legacy. After all, there's always been a sense that there's something barely communicable about all performing, what Shakespeare called a 'mystery'. If so, should it be protected or exposed? In the end Zeami feels that yes, his particular knowledge should be available to his successors: the great secrets should be handed on, even if only to one actor in each generation. He decides to come out. He writes it all down. And so the mystery he and his father inherited, wherever it had come from, remains intact.

~

Obscure and locked away as it might seem, Noh, like many ancient forms of theatre, has its origins in folk rituals, in the songs celebrating springtime rice planting and the harvest festivals in Japanese villages. Many of the successive dance forms of ancient Japan, mixing metaphysics and eroticism, were designed to appease the gods – and in the earliest myth to provoke their curiosity as well, as when the sun goddess Ametarasu hid in a cave and made the world dark and so had to be tempted to look outside it by an exhibition of wild, Bacchic dancing by the other gods – whereupon the earth's light came on again.

Sometimes you begin to sense a connection with the West. Like fragments of film suddenly vivid in deep surrounding darkness, we can glimpse blind Japanese minstrels going from town to town and Homeric bards doing the same thing in Greece; or harvest festivals in Japan and Thespis on the road out of Icaria with his wagon. Meanwhile the lightness and dark of the Ametarasu story reminds you of Prometheus saving fire for mankind. The difference is that the miracle of Greek theatre was tied closely into the public definition of Athens as a modern city state, whereas the later, inwardly looking Orient, with its young shoguns and their favourite dancers and its perverse delicacy, fed only on itself; so its favourite theatrical form, the Noh, was never a democratic affair, not for a moment.

~

Around the agora in Aphrodisias in western Turkey there is an astonishing set of friezes: stone heads of actors, off-duty and out of their masks and looking exactly like friends of mine. I can spot the camp one, the saturnine one, the life and soul of the party, every one of these actors – laughing uproariously, almost winking at you, somehow off-limits, open-mannered, pleasantly in-your-face. As classic images they're completely unique, something between friendly gargoyles and the mischievous sketches (or 'babooneries') of satyrs, green men and huntsmen, farmers, workmen and wrestlers in the margins of illuminated sacred books and psalters of the Middle Ages, or carved into the recesses of some English cathedrals. Their theatre precedes the Noh by many centuries and is likewise Men Only, but the sense of fellowship and energy is tangible, utterly unexpected in what we think of as the hieratical world of Greek tragedy. The odd thing is that, familiar as they seem, their looks didn't matter at all from a professional point of view, as they disappeared behind masks.

And now they go to work. Compared to the cypress masks of the Noh, Greek tragedy masks were makeshift affairs of cork or cloth, with a rudimentary wig attached which left the actors' ears free so that they could hear their colleagues. They have the odd effect, perhaps because of their intense look, of making the wearer more visible from a distance. Maybe a bit louder as well: on the stage visibility and audibility depend on each other. Now the actors get into high-soled buskins like platform boots, *cothurni*, to make them look taller to fourteen thousand people, some of whom are sixty metres away. One of them straps a wooden projection onto his chest and stomach to imitate female breasts and belly.

It may have been commonplace for these men to step onto the *omphalos* (the 'navel'), the precise centre point of the acoustic miracle of the theatre at Epidaurus, but now it gives you the strangest feeling of something numinous, more than natural. For one thing, you suddenly become louder, as if the volume had been dramatically turned up: an already perfect acoustic has become simply unbelievable. Once it was thought that this perfection was due to the direction of the wind or the slope of the auditorium – or even (which would be disappointing to learn) proto-megaphones in the masks. However a persuasive new theory from the Georgia Institute of Technology suggests that just as you can affect the acoustic of a room with ridged padding, the corrugations in the fifty-five rows of limestone seats at Epidaurus acted like traps, filtering out the natural lower frequencies such as the noise of the trees and the murmuring of the spectators. This ought to take out the lower tones in the actors' voices too, but there is a phenomenon called virtual pitch whereby the listener's brain – the memory, really – steps in to replace the missing frequencies.

In practice, as long as your diction is precise and you don't go too fast, every one of the fourteen thousand will hear you. This is a piece of magic we've forgotten in theatre design. Even the Greeks don't seem to have realised what they'd done at Epidaurus: wooden benches soon appeared to replace the uncomfortable limestone, and the knack was lost. Still, it remains evidence of the general theatrical sophistication of the time: sliding trucks of scenery, sound effects for sea battles; bronze tubes you rolled stones inside to make a storm. The tall structures (*periaktoi*) that swivelled on their bases to present a new face and therefore a new scene, are still favoured by designers today. There were trap doors to lift actors onto the stage, and above all, a crane device to hoist one of them on high to suggest the arrival of a god to settle things – the original *deus ex machina*. But the words were always more important.

The actor with the female equipment appears on a raised platform, the *skene*. He confronts a Chorus on the lower stage before him. He is now Clytemnestra, Queen of Argos, presiding over a tableau of her dead husband Agamemnon and his mistress Cassandra: she has murdered them both in their bath. Music is playing in eastern quarter-tones, on a flute as in the Noh, and a *kithara*, a lyre. Clytemnestra states her case:

> Like a fisherman casting a net, I spread this deadly robe around him . . . like a dry cornfield I gloried in the blood he sprayed me with . . . he has drunk down the evil cup he filled.

The Chorus, who represent the citizens of Argos (but also in a sense those of Athens, the watching audience), are horrified. They threaten her with homelessness, but she makes her best point, that what she has done is just revenge for Agamemnon having sacrificed their daughter Iphigeneia to the gods to secure a following wind for his warships to Troy:

> This man slaughtered our daughter as if he were killing an animal. Should you not have driven him out?

This is not quite fair to the Chorus: with calculated even-handedness, they had warned Agamemnon against pride (*hubris*): they told him that his expedition to Troy to avenge the elopement with Paris of Helen (Clytemnestra's sister) was ridiculous; they warned him of the resentment building up in the city. Agamemenon then destroyed his country's resources as surely as he destroyed Troy and his own daughter. On top of which he arrived home with a Trojan mistress, under Clytemnestra's nose.

But Clytemnestra warns the Chorus that her lover Aegisthus is on his way to protect her and save the city; as she sleeps with him Agamemnon's cries for mercy will strangely excite her. In the face of such female lasciviousness the Chorus retreats into neutrality:

> There is bitterness against bitterness here. So who shall be the judge?

And so *agon*, dramatic argument, begins. The story winds through two further plays, *The Choephoroi* and *The Eumenides*, and another generation of characters, mainly Orestes and Electra, to a point so morally insoluble that the goddess Athena has to step in, cancel the cycle of revenge and establish the democracy of Athens – where the play itself is taking place. In Greek tragedy the mythic past coexists with the present; the story begins with Agamemnon's return to Argos and ends on the afternoon of the show. The audience have already marched in a procession, accompanied by much drinking and dancing, and had a great meeting in the market place: the more wine you drink and the more you dance, the closer you get to Dionysos (Bacchus) the god of wine and theatre – a twin portfolio that amuses us, but was very significant to the Greeks. Now they take their seats in the theatre: rather than falling asleep they have become one entity, ready for a challenging show, in a state of ecstasy (which literally means being 'outside', or as we would say, 'beside yourself').

In the late fifth century BC, going to the theatre was an integral part of being a citizen, intimately linked to the democratic project: it was a civic responsibility to bear witness to the dilemmas and tough moral decisions in mythology that were also facing Athens now. The phrase 'What shall I do?' recurs over and over again in the plays, and there is always a decision to be taken by the audience. If a man is seen as a traitor should he still have a decent burial (*Antigone*)? Is there such a thing as justifiable homicide (*Agamemnon*)? What is the responsibility of the victors towards the conquered (*The Trojan Women,* written only a year after Athens had brutally suppressed a rebel city state)? Can a man be held responsible for killing his father and sleeping with his mother when he didn't know who they were (*Oedipus*)? A writer could also overstep the mark: one Phrynichus produced his *Fall of Miletus* in 492, a year or so after the town of that name was conquered by the Persians, and so upset the audience (Herodotus reports that the whole theatre fell to weeping) that rather than winning an award he was fined a thousand drachmas and his play was banned. (Athens may have been the cradle of democracy but for a moment it was as if Phrynichus were living in the Soviet Union.) And if these dilemmas became too vexing, there would be a comedy to follow in the programme (as there would later be in the Noh), which would wickedly satirise contemporary politicians to their faces for their venality and foolishness, before the audience settled down for a third play, another tragedy. And so on for five days.

They had always been storytellers, but now actors imitated women or slaves or gods – almost a blasphemy, except that the anonymous mask protected them from the presumption of it. Rather as in the medieval mystery plays, the audience might have known some of these actors. They were as much citizens as they were: they too had fought against the Persians and survived. At Aphrodisias their faces grinned and gurned out at you all round the agora as you did your shopping; they were not celebrities, exactly, but certainly local heroes, perhaps neighbours and friends with a particular gift – or a secret, lightly carried. In one sense they were respected as healers, witnesses to the truth, but after the show, don't tell me these attractive individuals didn't sit around and have a smoke and a bottle of retsina and a good laugh over whatever had gone wrong in the performance that night.

A century later Greek actors became quite professionalised: they even had a union, the '*technitai* of Dionysos', and some of them made a lot of money. But at this earlier time I imagine they were paid in creature comforts and were more like the citizens who now participate in the Passion Play at Oberammergau. Either way, what they and the later Noh actors were doing must lead to the same state of mind, the same anthropology as ours now. These ancient predecessors will have talked easily and unembarrassedly about almost anything; after all, they faced the strangest things in their line of work. They too would be delicate about a colleague's *amour-propre* and inclined to praise and reassure him: they would try not to laud his rivals, but not denigrate them too ingratiatingly either. And they would always feel very slightly outside the general run – not better than, just outside. We share with them a gallows humour, based on the expectation of nightly humiliation. Like them, we're sometimes not quite sure where being a colleague shades into being a friend: we certainly feel sympathy when one of us disgraces themselves, even if we can't approve. This is and always has been a tribe, a community, a fraternity (and now a sorority), one for all and all for one. The grit in the oyster is that for all this, you are absolutely, committedly and for dear life, in it for yourself.

~

The nineteenth-century actor Edmund Kean was certainly in it for himself, and if you get sentimental over the profession it's worth remembering him, both his genius and his egomania. Kean is the greatest Shakespearian outside living memory, but you couldn't have called him a colleague; it would never have occurred to him to be anything but a soloist, and nobody would have expected it. He was, emphatically, where the money was. At a certain time in his life he refused point blank to rehearse with other actors since they disturbed his concentration; he preferred to buy his costumes and learn and practise his part at home until the opening night. On one occasion he refused to play with such and such an actor because he was 'a bloody thundering bugger' – well, all leading men feel things like that but they'd hardly say them out loud. In his prime he earned ten thousand pounds a year and his nightly rate was forty times that of his colleagues.

All stars attract opprobrium: Walter Scott called Kean 'a tup-penny tearmouth'; Leigh Hunt said his voice was 'something between an apoplexy and a cold'. He was, certainly, the opposite of what a Shakespearian actor of the time was supposed to be, all lofty declamation and elegant diction. His insight into Shakespeare was radical. In his first major success at Drury Lane he played Shylock as dark, twisted and psychotic, with black beard and butcher's knife, rather than in the traditional comic red beard and wig of the Jewish moneylender; no one had seen anything like it before, and though neither version would recommend itself to audiences now, it suggests a new kind of sensibility at work. Imagine his Macbeth, described by William Hazlitt in 1825, stumbling out of King Duncan's bedchamber after committing the murder:

> It was a scene which no one who saw it can ever efface from his memory. The hesitation, the bewildered look, the coming to himself when he sees his hands bloody, the manner in which his voice clung to his throat and choked the utterance, his agony and tears . . .

This is a nineteenth-century barnstormer behaving as if he'd trained with Stanislavsky – especially if you consider the hesitation and bewilderment. The only thing wrong with your

395

evening, if you'd been there, would have been that you'd had to wait so long for it to start; it might have taken an hour to cajole Kean to the theatre out of an upstairs room at the Shakespeare's Head on Russell Street – much the worse for wear, leaving behind him a couple of ladies of the street, or rather one of them, as he might bring the other along to the theatre. Even then, the performance might have to be delayed while Kean, on his first entrance, took the time to bow and make a speech, sometimes defending himself against the latest scandalous accusations in the press.

You might go back the next night to see him play Richard III:

> He fought like one drunk with wounds: and the attitude in
> which he stands with his hands stretched out, after his sword
> is taken from him, had a preternatural and terrific grandeur, as
> if . . . the very phantom of his despair had a withering power.

What you didn't know was that at half past five the management had been running round town trying to find another actor who knew the part, as Kean, either offended or especially drunk, had gone AWOL. Maybe Macready could be persuaded to stand in . . . maybe they should change the play . . . The next night – for this is a true repertoire company, except that Kean always played the lead – here is Hamlet in the Nunnery Scene with Ophelia: 'As he exited he suddenly returned impulsively to kiss Ophelia's hand and then hurried off the stage.' I recognise this one too: it's the inspiration of a modern Hamlet running back to embrace her – or hit her – to achieve closure on their affair.

The next night it's Richard III again: 'In the tent scene he stood for a while as if in a reverie, drawing lines on the ground with the point of his sword, before suddenly recovering himself with a "good-night" to his lords.' This is the best of all – modern, almost Method acting, precisely tracing the emotional changes

second by second, unafraid of silence, finding unresolved para-
doxes between the lines.

Coleridge described watching Kean as being like reading
Shakespeare by flashes of lightning. He had no advantages of
birth or amiability, not much in the way of looks, very skinny
legs, and little musicality; but he had eyes like fire. He kept a
pet lion who might share his sitting room with him, and whom
he was said to have tamed with these eyes. He was short – like
another great Richard III, Ian Holm – with gypsy looks (Ireland has always claimed him but actually he was brought up by
an aunt in London); he was obsessively, jealously, passionately
committed to his job at the cost of his own health – Hazlitt (an
unusually considerate sort of critic) tried to persuade him not
to play Hamlet and Richard III in the same day. He was often
hoarse, so he must have misused the voice a bit, not to mention the drinking, for he was often 'wide', including on stage. For
someone so disorderly his acting was fanatically precise – nothing improvised, even the sudden transitions. Difficult, competitive and jealous though he was, through the hellraiser's mask
you get recognisable glimpses of anxiety; his experience of stage
fright later in life – when he stood there on a first night unable
to start, not knowing what play or place he was in – makes my
blood run cold; and he was capable of an odd tenderness and
sudden, extravagant generosity. With his peers (if he didn't feel
threatened) he could be a lamb: Macready found him 'unassuming . . . partaking in some degree of shyness' and also spoke of
the 'touching grace' of his singing. At the same time Macready
acknowledged his barbaric splendour: when Kean delivered the
three words 'I answer – No!' in the part of Sir Edward Mortimer
in *The Iron Chest*, his rival felt it was time to take early retirement. We owe Kean the credit for restoring Shakespeare's original ending to *King Lear* at a time when Nahum Tate's ridiculous
happy finale was the norm – but only because, as he told his

wife, the London audience 'have no notion of what I can do till they see me over the dead body of Cordelia'.

He did good behaviour a bit, writing humble letters and making apologetic speeches to the audience, but you probably wouldn't have him to dinner; he was a man who once said he 'had to shag' before going on the stage. At his most scandalous periods the public might hurl orange peel at him, shouting him down for his morals while admiring his acting; a Boston audience organised something like a lynching party on behalf of American womanhood (whom by the way he never tampered with) that made him flee for his life. On another visit to Boston he peeped through the curtain at the beginning to see a pitifully small house and immediately cancelled the performance and subsequent tour. Canada was more tolerant: a group of Huron Indians saw him in Quebec and were so taken with him that they made him an honorary Chief. In his last London performance as Othello, which also starred his son Charles as Iago, he collapsed on stage: 'I am dying . . . speak to them, Charles' . . . and expired six weeks later.

What first drew me to Kean, though, were his quarrels with producers: his wonderfully snippy letters to the Drury Lane management are like the ones you might write to the National Theatre and then not post. Kean did, and so we have them:

> I suppose ye think that Richards and Hamlets grow on every hedge. God grant you may have a good crop of them . . .
> Yr humble servant E. Kean.

Every age chooses its favourite actor. Kean ruled London and, *in absentia*, its dinner parties, until his early death at forty-four, in 1833. A good age to die: the same age not only as good old Chekhov but also Billie Holiday, Jackson Pollock and F. Scott Fitzgerald.

Nowadays we have our infrastructure of good practice, personal behaviour, minimum salaries, collaborativeness, public generosity to each other. The theatre of Kean's time seems like a scrum – unhinged managers, desperate dressers, drunken actors challenging each other to duels, fighting over money and billing and status. Around the star was not the modern well-trained ensemble – the splendid Duke of Exeter, the promising Messenger – but a random and extremely motley crew. Most contemporary Shakespearians are appreciated because of the implicit sense that they're not only stars but good eggs: Judi Dench is loved both for her gifts and for her legendary modesty. But Shakespeare needs outrageous show-offs too: the main parts are so extremely, blatantly dominant and they're what you came into the business in the hope of playing. And if there was only one actor, now out of reach and unrecorded, that I would like to have seen, it is Kean, side by side of course with Eleonora Duse. His theatre was ours with the gloves off, and I'm not sure where we'd be without him.

~

Kean turns up – most unexpectedly – in Arthur Wing Pinero's 1898 play *Trelawny of the Wells*, which tells the story of Rose Trelawny, the star of a thinly disguised Sadler's Wells Company in London. Rose's mother once worked with Edmund Kean, and it turns out that as a young man her future grandfather-in-law, Sir William Gower, who seems to like the theatre about as much as rat poison, nevertheless vastly admired him ('Ah, he was a splendid gypsy!'). Smoothly taking this surprising cue, Rose shows him the order, chain and dagger Kean wore as Richard III and then gave to her father. Sir William is overcome:

(*Handling it tenderly*) Kean! God bless me!

She then dresses him in them, and he is wonderfully inspired to emulate his hero:

> Lord bless us! How he stirred me! Kean! [*To her, in a whisper*] I'll tell ye! I'll tell ye! When I saw him as Richard – I was young and a fool – I'll tell ye – he almost fired me with an ambition to – to . . . [*He paces the stage, growling and muttering, walking with a limp and one shoulder hunched. She watches him, seriously.*] Ah! He was a little man too! I remember him! As if it were last night! I remember . . .

This moment is the beginning of a happy outcome for the play, but perhaps the loveliest thing about it is that in life Edmund Kean was everything Sir William despised. Still, the crusty old right-winger has a stage-struck kid inside him, and feels that being an actor is all right, even magnificent, as long as you're very successful indeed and not a mere 'troubadour'. This is well observed: the public's enthusiasm for leading actors is in inverse proportion to their scorn for failures – they love not the practice itself but the exceptions that prove the rule. Nowadays their choices, if unanimous enough, may well end up as national treasures, though it's hard to imagine Kean as quite that.

In fact he stands in exactly the opposite camp to the good companions Pinero celebrates in the play, which enchantingly captures the smell of gas and oranges in Victorian backstage life. There comes a moment in Act Three when Ferdy Gadd, the vain romantic lead who is married (a wonderful touch) to the company soubrette Avonia Bunn (who respectfully calls him Ferdinand), storms onto the stage. He is outraged; he, 'the Romeo, the Orlando, the Clifford', has now, humiliatingly, been offered a part in the pantomime. It's a thing that hasn't happened to him, he says, since he shook the dust of the Theatre Royal Stockton-on-Tees from his feet. At first he declines to supply the name of the offending role, but it turns out to be, to everyone's muffled mirth, the Demon of Discontent. Sounding very much like Edmund Kean rebuking the management of Drury Lane, Ferdy sends a message to the Manager:

> Acquaint Mr Burroughs with my decision, and add that I hope his pantomime will prove an utterly mirthless one. May Boxing Night, to those unfortunate enough to find themselves in the theatre, long remain a dismal memory; and may succeeding audiences be scanty and dissatisfied . . .

It takes the devoted Avonia to read a few of the Demon's lines, tentatively and perhaps with intentional inadequacy, to make him realise that after all

> There's something to lay hold of here! I'll think this over. *[Rising]* . . . I have thought this over. I play it.

And they all go off for a drink.

Besides suggesting a kinship with Vincent Crummles's troupe in Dickens's *Nicholas Nickleby* and many subsequent theatrical narratives, Pinero plants some suggestive ideas in his story. Rose leaves the theatre to marry a posh young admirer; she is rescued from her upper-class bondage one night by her old colleagues and whisked back into the theatre, only to find that her experience of what she rather surprisingly calls 'real people' (her potential in-laws are insufferable) has killed her talent – at least for the kind of melodramas that once made her a star. Fortunately her old friend Tom Wrench has written a new kind of naturalistic play (of the kind exemplified at the time by the work of the quietly revolutionary T. W. Robertson), and she turns out to be well suited to the soberer challenge. Meanwhile her beloved Arthur, unable to forget her, has crossed over in the other direction: though not an especially good actor, he has run away and joined the Bristol Old Vic in order to be a part of her world.

In ways small and large, Pinero's play is an unapologetic act of solidarity with a certain kind of theatre; actors love doing it and the public only a degree less watching it – there is something that slightly excludes them, the very thing that does so in life. It was already a gesture of nostalgia, since Sadler's Wells was by now in decline, having narrowly escaped a fate as a bath-house to become a skating rink and then a prize-fighting arena before being finally condemned as unsafe twenty years before Pinero was writing.

Ferdy's crisis is not even my favourite moment in the play. At one point, James Telfer, once the company's actor-manager and much given to licensed reminiscence ('One of the best Macduffs I ever fought with was bow-legged'), finds that his style fails to fit with the new wave of realism. After the first rehearsal of a new production he is found sitting disconsolate and alone in the Green Room by his wife:

TELFER: My part is confined to the latter 'alf of the second act.
MRS TELFER: It affords you no opportunity, James?
TELFER: [*Shaking his head*] A mere fragment.
MRS TELFER: [*Rising*] Well, but a few good speeches to a man of your stamp . . .
TELFER: Yes, but this is so line-y, Violet; so very line-y. And what d'ye think the character is described as?
MRS TELFER: What?
TELFER: 'An old, stagey, out-of-date actor.'
[*They stand looking at each other for a moment, silently.*]
MRS TELFER: [*Falteringly*] Will you – be able – to get near it, James?
TELFER: [*Looking away from her*] I dare say. [. . .]
MRS TELFER: Hush! Let us both go home.

～

When I look at the colleagues I've brought into this book and then at Rose Trelawny's troupe, I see we wouldn't make a bad company either. Janie Dee could be the leading lady and Charlotte Wakefield the ingénue and they could have a sensational duet in the second act – such as Sarah's and Adelaide's in *Guys and Dolls*, which would also give David K. S. Tse the chance to play Nicely-Nicely Johnson and thus sing 'Sit Down You're Rockin' the Boat'. Amit Sharma could play anything he wants and not just Richard III; we could get Gwilym Lee back from *Midsomer Murders* to be the *jeune premier*, Gavin Fowler either from his garden shed or from the Moscow Film Festival (he's been getting into movies) to be the threat to the *jeune premier* because of the appeal of his devilish gypsy looks to other people's fiancées; Annie Hemingway (with her new agent's approval) would be the comedienne, but not only the comedienne; and in the second production we could mix it all up and have everyone play parts for which they're not the obvious casting. Rather like the Actors' Company in the 1970s, we would choose our directors in turn: Phelim McDermott or Jatinder Verma could direct the first project, John Dryden could come and make a sizzling docudrama for radio, Mike Newell would hear it (as Mike Leigh once heard Joseph Kloska) and make a movie of it.

Stephen Boxer and I would be the heavyweights, I guess. Boxer has just been emphatically stage centre again, chopping his own hand off every night as a brilliant Titus Andronicus at Stratford (can this really be that fellow from *Doctors*?). And we could have the company launch right away now that I'm back from my King Lear in New York and celebrating a birthday within a birthday – my seventy-first and, during the same weekend, the fiftieth anniversary of my turning professional. At our launch, I suppose someone will call me, with a bit of luck, an old lion; I'm still roaring to order, and getting a cold as a substitute for nerves on first nights.

This same idea would have occurred to me whomever I'd quoted in the book: it takes moments to make a good theatre company. Our profession is like an amoeba continually about to take definite shape: there are so many talented people out there, all of them ready for the off even if they don't know each other. They'll be willing to give each other moral support when one of them is offered a part in the pantomime, or equally become like those merry Greeks with their talent for – their understanding of the necessity of – having a laugh the moment even the most tragic curtain comes down.

~

You should never lose the heart of a beginner, even in old age.
ZEAMI MOTOKIYO

I doubt if Edmund Kean would have been much good as Bottom in *A Midsummer Night's Dream*, though Ferdy and his friends – and perhaps my group too – would have made a good team of Mechanicals around him, as long as Ferdy wasn't too offended at having to play Flute the bellows-mender. The major difference between Edmund Kean and Nick Bottom the Weaver is that the latter, egotist as he is, is also, in Shakespeare's brilliant hands, a team player: he manages the difficult trick of promoting himself and the interests of his company at the same time. When he and his colleagues set about casting their production of the tragedy *Pyramus and Thisbe* – 'A very good piece of work, I assure you, and a merry'– he is given the main male part, Pyramus, but doesn't seem, for all his enthusiasm, to have read the story: 'What is Pyramus? A lover, or a tyrant?' In other words it was more important, as for Ferdy Gadd, to have the main part than to know what it was. However he immediately offers to give it up: he doesn't really like playing lovers, as his 'chief humour is for a tyrant'. There is no such part in this play, so he has to content himself with Pyramus, to whom he promises to bring such a 'condoling' tone that the audience will have to 'look to their eyes'.

There is some difficulty as the other offers go out. Flute is reluctant to be Thisbe as it involves playing a girl – a therapist would say he is not at ease with his sexuality. Bottom leaps into the breach again, and suggests playing that part as well as Pyramus, covering his face with a mask when he does Thisbe's lines. Imagine it. Starveling and Snout then behave like good ensemble artists, accepting their parts without question; Snug is offered the lion but is worried he won't be able to learn the words, or rather, the right kind of roar. But Bottom has a lion performance up his sleeve as well:

> Let me play the lion too. I will roar, that I will do any man's heart good to hear me: I will roar, that I will make the Duke say 'Let him roar again; let him roar again.'

The problem here is that the ladies, always the most vocal part of a theatre audience, might become frightened and then the actors will all get hanged. But Bottom has the solution:

> I will aggravate my voice so that I will roar you as gently as any sucking dove. I will roar you an 'twere any nightingale . . .

The beauty of his desire to play the lion as well lies, as often with Shakespeare, in the setting-up and then in the wake of the obviously funny line. It wouldn't be as good if he hadn't already accepted Pyramus and claimed Thisbe as well: as the third part of the magic three of comedy, the lion is the punch li(o)ne. Bottom knows he can terrify in the part; but like Zeami, he also knows that 'being strong and dreadful is quite different from being interesting'. So to play a lion's voice filtered through that of a dove will have the virtue of surprise, and, as Zeami might say, create a sense of novelty. (Zeami, by the way, made his professional debut as a lion, at the age of eleven: he so impressed the young shogun that he was immediately claimed as the great lord's catamite – that's what comes of playing such a part.) Bottom also understands the power of theatre as a means of wooing the women – like most heterosexual male actors, he is at heart a ladies' man who has gone into acting to show off to the girls. He will impress them first and then soothe them with his gentle, chivalrous ways.

Is Bottom any good? Some good, I would say, though perhaps in a rather old-fashioned, James Telfer-ish style. What he certainly is is an enthusiast; his desire to control everyone comes from over-eagerness and is mitigated by a certain bonniness of disposition. Self-confidence has rarely been so attractive. He has excessive zeal for the cause and is quite free from self-doubt. In fact, he exemplifies the boisterous good faith without which the theatre falls apart.

So let him play the lion too, I say, and the sucking dove.

And you too: I wish you a good lifetime of terrifying and wooing, of roaring like a nightingale and cooing like a dove, of conquering, condoling and sparing. And of being asked – many, many times – to roar again. One day you'll be called an old lion too. And don't let anyone tell you otherwise – this is the world's best job. Good luck.

Acknowledgements

My thanks to Timothy West for permission to include the first scene from his play, *The Gun in My Left Hand is Loaded*; to Fay Weldon for an extract from *Letters to Alice* (Sceptre, 1993). To William Russell and the Critics' Circle Archives for Ralph Richardson's letter about the critics; to Amber Lane Press for the quote from *The Best of Friends* by Hugh Whitemore (Amber Lane Press © 1988); to David Mamet for letting me quote from *The Shawl* and *Glengarry Glen Ross*; to Alan Brodie and the Estate of Eduardo De Filippo for permission to quote from the Italian text of *Filumena Marturano*.

'War' is performed by Bob Marley; Words by Carleton Barrett / Allen Cole, Published by Fifty-Six Hope Road Music Ltd. / Blackwell Fuller Music Publishing LLC Administered by Blue Mountain Music Ltd

The excerpt from Samuel Beckett's *Worstward Ho*, copyright © 1983, Estate of Samuel Beckett is used by permission of Grove/Atlantic, Inc and Faber & Faber Ltd.

'Razzle Dazzle' by Fred Ebb and John Kander. Unichappell Music INC (BMI) and Kander & Ebb, INC (BMI). All rights administered by Warner Chappell Music LTD

'Spasticus Autisticus' by Ian Robins Dury and Chaz Jankel © Templemill Music Ltd (Prs) and Heathwave Music Ltd (Prs). All rights on behalf of Templemill Music Ltd administered by Warner/Chappell Music Ltd. All rights reserved.

'Hooray for Hollywood', words by Johnny Mercer, music by Richard Whiting, © 1937 (renewed) WB Music Corp. (ASCAP). All rights administered by Warner/Chappell North America Ltd.

The translations from Eduardo de Filippo's *Filumena Marturano*, from Aeschylus' *Agamemnon* and from Chekhov's *Seagull* and *Three Sisters* are my own.

For the quotes from Motokiyu Zeami, I've adapted, combined and edited freely passages from privately published books I owned in the 1970s.

All reasonable efforts have been made to trace the origin of Carl T. Rowan's quote.

As for Further Reading, if you'd like to know more about Max Factor, the book to get is by Fred E. Basten, published by Arcade, from which you'll hear about Max Factor Jr's Kissing Machine, which measured the pressure at which a new line of lipstick started smudging. Relatively little has been written about Eduardo de Filippo, but the world on which he drew can be vividly sensed from *Midnight in Sicily* by Peter Robb, and from Norman Lewis's *Naples '44*. Here you will learn the consequences not only of defying the Camorra but of putting sugar into your espresso at the wrong moment.

My thanks to Dinah Wood, Editorial Director, Drama, at Faber, for her extraordinary patience and editorial skill; to Kate Ward my project editor, to Michael Downes my copyeditor, and to Emma Cheshire for her work on the Permissions. Also to Jodi Myers for astute suggestions backed up with email addresses, and to all my fellow travellers quoted along the way.

In the end, the book is for Mark, Prue, Louis and Eve, for all of whom I daily thank my lucky stars.

Index